MW01616406

Late Ancient Knowing

The publisher gratefully acknowledges the generous support of the Classical Literature Endowment Fund of the University of California Press Foundation, which was established by a major gift from Joan Palevsky.

Late Ancient Knowing

Explorations in Intellectual History

———

Edited by

Catherine M. Chin and Moulie Vidas

UNIVERSITY OF CALIFORNIA PRESS

University of California Press, one of the most distinguished university presses in the United States, enriches lives around the world by advancing scholarship in the humanities, social sciences, and natural sciences. Its activities are supported by the UC Press Foundation and by philanthropic contributions from individuals and institutions. For more information, visit www.ucpress.edu.

University of California Press
Oakland, California

Library of Congress Cataloging-in-Publication Data

Late ancient knowing : explorations in intellectual history / edited by Catherine M. Chin and Moulie Vidas.
    p.   cm.
  Includes bibliographical references and index.
    ISBN 978-0-520-27717-5 (cloth, alk. paper) — ISBN 978-0-520-96092-3 (electronic)
    1. Civilization, Ancient.   2. Intellectual life—History—To 1500.
3. Chin, Catherine M., editor.   4. Vidas, Moulie, editor.   I. Title.
CB311.L29   2015
930—dc23   2014034644

Manufactured in the United States of America

24   23   22   21   20   19   18   17   16   15
10   9   8   7   6   5   4   3   2   1

In keeping with a commitment to support environmentally responsible and sustainable printing practices, UC Press has printed this book on Natures Natural, a fiber that contains 30% post-consumer waste and meets the minimum requirements of ansi/niso z39.48-1992 (R 1997) (*Permanence of Paper*).

CONTENTS

Introduction

Knowing

Catherine M. Chin and Moulie Vidas

This is a book about knowing as a historical practice. It is not strictly about the content of late ancient knowledge, in the sense of answering questions like *What did late ancient people know about geography or astronomy?* or *What did people living in fourth-century Rome know about India?* Instead, it is about how the process of knowing shaped a variety of historical actions in late antiquity, and in turn how a variety of historical actions and circumstances produced what became the content and practice of knowing. In this book, we consider late ancient knowing to be both the intellectual grasping of knowledge, as late ancient epistemology suggests, but also, and more important, the very practical process of negotiating the late ancient world as it was known, or as it came to be knowable. In much modern scholarship, late ancient knowledge—knowledge about the human, knowledge about the world and the cosmos—is relegated to specialized fields in either the history of science or the history of theology and philosophy. Yet such knowledge was not marginal or arcane to its knowers; it was fundamental to the way they understood themselves to act and exist, how they defined themselves as material and immaterial beings amidst other material and immaterial beings. This book examines a few key ideas in the imaginative world of late antiquity and considers how these ideas shaped, and were shaped by, the ways that late ancient people lived within their imagined worlds.

Our desire to look at knowing as a historical activity grows out of two scholarly trends. The first trend has arisen in a variety of the natural and social sciences in the last few decades, in which human activity has increasingly been analyzed not as separable from its physical environments but in relation to them, and especially in relation to nonhuman elements or actors within those environments. For example, studies of relations between human beings and other animals, or the effects of urban environments on human behavior, or the impact of environmental change on human history have created new ways of understanding human action as relational to its surrounding conditions. In studies of knowledge practices within this broad contextualizing trend, researchers have often focused on what is called "situated" or "embodied" cognition.[1] Research on situated cognition construes at least some human thought as inextricable from the physical environment, including the body, in which the human being is able to think. Thus, we may persistently count or compute on our fingers, or use material objects as mnemonic devices, or more elaborately, we may use different models of visualization to structure and analyze large quantities of information. Whereas the study of such activities has had a significant impact on fields like educational psychology, information systems, and cognitive science, the fundamental question raised—how individual people practice the activity of knowing—has become central to the study of premodern history only in recent works.[2] Clifford Ando's *The Matter of the Gods,* for example, has argued that instead of "faith," we should think of an active, empiricist model of knowledge as an engine of Roman religion.[3] Daryn Lehoux's *What Did the Romans Know?* has emphasized the active nature of knowing and the multiple contexts—physical, legal, political—in which it occurs, and which it informs; and it takes seriously those elements in the ancient worldview that seem most alien to moderns as a way to explain how ancient worldmaking worked.[4]

During the same decades that saw the rise of the field of situated cognition, the practice of writing premodern history was also shaped by structuralist and post-structuralist theories of the discursive construction of knowledge.[5] These theoretical approaches, more literary and historical than the social-scientific approaches to situated cognition, have tended to analyze structures of discursive organization as the means by which the material that we call "knowledge" can be recognized as such, particularly in cases of large-scale intellectual history or the history of ideas—for example, in Thomas Kuhn's famous analysis of the shift from a Ptolemaic to a Copernican worldview in *The Structure of Scientific Revolutions* or in Foucault's question in *The Archaeology of Knowledge:* "What in fact are *medicine, grammar* or *political economy?*"[6] These approaches thus see the activity of knowing as thoroughly conditioned, indeed created, by larger patterns of discourse and embedded in systems of social and cultural power. This historiographical trend has given scholars of the ancient world a useful hermeneutical lens through which to examine how knowledge was created and ordered in antiquity, as for example in Trevor Murphy's study *Pliny the Elder's Natural History: The Empire in the Encyclopedia*[7] or in the collection by Jason König and Tim Whitmarsh, *Ordering Knowledge in the Roman Empire.*[8] Such studies allow us to understand the social, cultural, and ideological forces that shaped the structures of ancient knowledge on a broad scale.

The basic question that this volume asks is how to integrate the idea of smaller-scale individual and embodied human knowing, as an active process physically situated in daily life, into an analysis of how particular ideas arose and worked within larger discursive fields in the late ancient world. In other words: How can we understand the relationship between the large-scale structures of knowledge available to late ancient knowers, the activity of knowing particular things, and the practical range of possibilities that late ancient knowers considered themselves to have for action in the world?

In order to address this broad methodological question, we have asked the contributors to this book to identify a particular late antique concept or construct and try to answer two questions about it: first, What did late ancient people know about this concept or construct? And second, How did they go about, or how did they theorize going about, the practical activity of knowing it in their lives? We have not tried here to create a comprehensive list of important late ancient concepts, nor have we tried to impose a uniform set of answers to our methodological question; this book is intended to be suggestive and varied rather than definitive. By using these two questions as a framework for each essay, however, our contributors have been able to consider late ancient knowing not as a simple question of the content of knowledge, nor exclusively as a way of understanding how objects of knowledge come into being, but as a diverse and complex set of strategies for living in the known world.

Approaching knowledge as a set of strategies for living both in the world and with the world allows us to center on and distinguish two interrelated aspects of this project of knowing: finding and establishing a working order and integrating human activity into it. The first involves knowing not in the sense of accumulation or even discovery of the mass that is to be known; rather, taking that mass as given, this activity subjects that mass to a fundamentally taxonomic work, dividing, as it were, darkness from light, heaven from earth, sea from dry land, and placing these elements in proper relationships with one another. The second involves the application of that order to make one's way through the world. The combined process is the activity of knowing both in a theoretical and in a practical sense.

Following this division, the parts of this book describe knowing in two complementary but different modes. The chapters in Part One, "Finding Order," center on the inner workings of knowledge itself, interrogating their subject matter on the nature of cognition and making a contribution to a broad history of epistemology in our period. The chapters in Part Two, "Putting Things in Order," take on a different task, addressing central topics in the political and social history of late antiquity as problems of knowledge. How does our view of late ancient emperors, or the countryside, or Christianization, change when we center our investigation on what and how the people of that period knew about these topics? These essays contribute to our understanding of the late ancient world as it was experienced, imagined, and reflected upon at the time. This division is one of emphasis—not a sharp division of labor. As we will show later in this introduction, the chapters in Part Two also address the general mechanics of embodied knowing—tracing, for example, how invisible concepts were made tangible in late ancient lives. Both parts aim to know not just about people in late antiquity but also, and necessarily in a speculative mode, to know the late ancient world along with people in late antiquity. This book is therefore an experiment in the sympathetic imagination of the imaginations of other people.[9]

The remainder of this chapter introduces the book's approach to "knowing," first by considering one paradigmatic late ancient writer's remarks on it and then by exploring what we see as the most important patterns emerging from the essays included in this volume. Boethius (ca. 480–524) is one of the most prominent exemplars of late ancient knowing, a polymath and politician whose writings both adapted and transmitted classical Greek and Neoplatonic philosophy to the Latin West.[10] At the beginning of the sixth century, relatively early in his writing career, Boethius coined the term *quadrivium* to describe the four mathematical disciplines of arithmetic, music, geometry, and astronomy. The adoption of *quadrivium* in subsequent centuries to stand for the content of these disciplines has somewhat blunted the force of the original image of the fourfold path,[11] presented at the outset of his treatise on arithmetic. *De Institutione Arithmetica* is a very loose translation of a work by the second-century Pythagorean Nicomachus of Gerasa, and after a dedication to Boethius's father-in-law, Symmachus, it opens as follows: "Among all those men of ancient authority who, following Pythagoras, have excelled in the purer reasoning of the mind, it is clear that almost no one has made his way through to the height of the disciplines of philosophy without searching out such nobility of wisdom as if by a fourfold path, which will not be hidden from those who correctly attend to skillfulness."[12] The image of knowledge, in this case mathematical knowledge, as a multiform and sometimes hidden path leading to a summit of perfection is not unique in late antiquity, particularly in writers engaging with the Neoplatonic tradition. Augustine, for example, famously uses the language of paths both negatively, to describe his own education as "miserable roads that we were forced to travel" in *Confessions* 1, and as well to describe his search for a "path" to the enjoyment of God through Platonism in *Confessions* 7.[13] In the remarks on the *quadrivium* dedicated to the sixth-century Symmachus, we may even have an echo of his great-grandfather the fourth-century Symmachus, and his characterization of religious knowledge in his third *Relatio*: "It is not possible to reach so great a mystery by one path alone."[14] The practice of knowing, in this image, is the practice of recognizing and following manifold paths that may at first seem hidden in a trackless world.

It is worth emphasizing that this practice of knowing is not a matter of accumulating information. Boethius knows neither a lot nor a little but rightly or wrongly.

As the personified Lady Philosophy tells Boethius at the unhappy end of his career, in *The Consolation of Philosophy*: "As everyone knows, the nature of the mind is such that, for just as many truths as it rejects, it takes in false ideas, from which arises a fog of confusion that prevents the perception of truth."[15] Boethius, in this text, does not need more information in order to understand the world; he needs to see the world more clearly. The paradigm of knowing as right recognition, as opposed to accumulation, is clear in the content of *De Institutione Arithmetica* itself, which is not about calculation but about rightly discerning the inherent properties of number and ratio. For example, one of Boethius's definitions of an even number is as follows: "An even number is what can be divided into two equal or two unequal parts, but in neither division is there an even number mixed with an odd number or an odd mixed with an even number, excepting alone the principal even binary number, which cannot be divided into two unequal parts because it consists only of two unities [i.e., 2, which is made up of 1 and 1]."[16] Understanding even numbers is a matter of discerning how they can be sorted into their constituent parts. This method of knowing, of finding the appropriate path through a mass of given material with which one is presented, is the basic approach of a large number of late ancient educational texts. For example, grammatical textbooks typically present grammatical knowledge as an understanding of the proper division of a given language and use syllables, the constituent parts of words, as an organizing principle for understanding language.[17] Similarly, the paradigm of knowing as correct pathfinding in astronomy is very literal: Boethius describes his earlier astronomical training in *The Consolation of Philosophy* as the mathematical study of solar, lunar, and stellar paths.[18] Knowledge of the universe is an understanding of how to recognize the patterns according to which all the universe's parts relate to one another. The persistent idea of knowing in these texts is that knowing is the ability to see the correct order that structures and underlies the objects of study. Such order constitutes the paths that knowers follow.

This knowing is also understood to have quite practical implications. Knowing is not merely recognition of the structure of abstract fields of study but recognition of the reality that structures human experience. Boethius claims that correct understanding of astronomy, for example, guides his own behavior: "You [Philosophy] showed me the paths of the stars with your rod . . . and shaped my behavior and the entire course of my life following the heavenly order."[19] Whether such celestial patterns can be recognized in the paths of human affairs more generally is the initial question of the *Consolation*: in one of the poems of book 1, Boethius laments that God, the "founder of the starry cosmos, . . . steers all things to their correct end" except human action.[20] Philosophy's task in the remainder of the work is to persuade Boethius that this is not the case, that Boethius is simply failing to recognize the patterns of human and divine activity in the world, just as he failed to recognize Philosophy herself in the opening of the *Consolation*.[21] The connection between right recognition of the underlying structures of the world and daily human action appears at a variety of points in Boethius's career, not just in the *Consolation*. The *Variae* of Boethius's contemporary and successor Cassiodorus contain requests from the Ostrogothic ruler Theodoric for Boethius to design both a sundial and a water clock for the Burgundian king Gundobad and to select a harpist for the Frankish king Clovis to tame "the savage hearts of the barbarians."[22] *Variae* 1.45, on the clocks, contains a long description of Boethius's astronomical and mathematical knowledge as his qualification for undertaking this task, as well as a nod toward his work on the "four gates of learning." *Variae* 2.40, on the gift of the harpist, echoes Boethius's arguments in *De Institutione Musica* on the ethical nature of the proportions of sound in music. Later, when Boethius fell from Theodoric's favor, in the mid-520s, he claimed that he was accused not only of treasonable behavior but of sacrilege: that is, the practice of prohibited magic or astrology in the aid of his political treachery.[23] Boethius claimed at the end of his career that his condemnation was connected to the vilification of certain paths of knowing.[24] In all these cases, what may at first seem to be a merely academic knowing is construed not only as an intellectual response to what exists in the world but also as an opportunity to act in and modify the world through the conscious application of the world's own patterns. This knowing is a practical, political, and indeed physical engagement.

The chapters in this book follow the people of late antiquity as they walk the many paths of knowledge, as they recognize order in the bewildering details of natural, human, and divine affairs. We study this work of recognition as an action in its own right, as well as the connection between this action and other actions— how the process of recognition was conditioned by other elements of the cosmos and how it facilitated, and often directed, interaction with these elements.

The labor of perceiving and maintaining order in the complexity of daily life— even in its most mundane aspects—is at the heart of several of the essays collected here. In Part One of this book, we will see late ancient knowing as an act that transforms separate and even conflicting elements into coherent wholes; it manufactures order not only from the discrete details of the world around us but sometimes even from different types of inquiry and modes of cognition. In the chapter on medicine, for example, Heidi Marx-Wolf documents the transdisciplinary nature of late ancient medical inquiry; she concludes that Porphyry's tractate on the fetus "participates in a very broad, flexible, universal, even totalizing understanding of *scientia*" that renders philosophical and medical knowledge indistinguishable. Mira Balberg writes that through their treatment of artifacts in the Mishnah, "the rabbis make the point that their greater normative enterprise in fact encompasses everything there is in the world," creating a rabbinic system of knowledge that is "tantamount to the knowledge of the world as such." Catherine Chin's essay on cosmos examines the implications of the ideas that everything in the late ancient cosmos was enchained and that the purpose of cosmological knowledge was the uncovering of the singular rationality that governed the connections and resemblances between the different agents and elements of the universe.

Transdisciplinarity, the production of comprehensive systems of knowledge, and the idea of a single cosmic order are not uniquely late ancient phenomena, but these chapters show how they were inflected in ways particular to our period. In "Cosmos," we see Priscillian ridiculing the misguided and "crassly material" view of planetary powers that results from not recognizing the single power of a single, Christian God. The increased importance of monotheistic rhetoric in the self-understanding and presentation of late ancient individuals and groups thus offered an important context in which such agents could assert the singularity of the cosmos and the corresponding unity of a system for knowing it. In "Artifacts," Balberg writes that the comprehensive nature of the rabbinic system of knowledge was used by the rabbis as part of their comprehensive claim to total authority, raising the possibility that such systems worked similarly in the many other new claims to authority made in the rapidly changing religious landscape of the period. And although Marx-Wolf acknowledges that the strong connection between medicine and philosophy is a point of continuity between ancient and late ancient knowing, she also notes that the latter presents "a more intense and global theologizing of medicine." Even where the totalizing feature of knowing was not intensified in late antiquity, its implication was that developments that were unique to the period in one field—say, theological discourse—impacted the configuration of intellectual life altogether.

From our perspective, conditioned by a modern association of rationality with a human subjectivity that observes the world and is in some way detached from it, what is striking about this drive to totalize is how it places our subjectivity in relationship with what we usually see as its objects. The late ancient world was both intelligent and intelligible, as Jeremy Schott makes clear in "Language": it was not only spoken about—it also spoke. In Chin's words, the cosmos was both the subject and the object of knowing; it was itself a rational organism. The specificity and pervasiveness of this logic of cosmic intelligibility teach us that by knowing about the world, late ancient knowers also came to know themselves, because human beings and nonhuman elements participated in the same rational discourse and therefore also transformed each other.

Although this rationalization of the cosmos is certainly related to legacies of classical philosophy, we find erosions of the line between subject and object in chapters dealing with nonphilosophical traditions. A fascinating aspect of the rabbinic treatment of artifacts, as Balberg explains it, is the place given to the way these artifacts are used or even to the way a specific user thinks about a specific item. These are seen not as attributes incidental to the artifacts but as themselves defining features of them. The distinctiveness of these features is best observed in processes of change: if a user changes his or her mind about the artifact, that change in thought actually effects a change in the essence of the artifact.

This transformative, reality-constituting nature of knowing is evident in the practical applications of order that are described in Part Two of this book. On the one hand, the actions of thinking or knowing, whether by God or the cosmos or human beings, establish reality; but physical action necessarily attends the recognition of that reality and is sometimes summoned simply to bring the physical world into accordance with the real order of things. Michael Kulikowski's "*Ordo*," Kristina Sessa's "Cleric," and Matthew Canepa's "Emperor" show this process at work in the determination of social and political structure. In these chapters we see how social position, ecclesiastical office, and the sovereign were imagined to be part of well-ordered if not rigid systems that aimed at harmony with the omnipresent cosmic or divine order. This pervasive but invisible cosmic harmony was maintained by very tangible means: the ordering of greetings between social actors, the design of urban and rural landscapes, the identity of priests, the sounds of soldiers' chants; removal from priestly office and punitive measures felt on the body or observed in public announced the system by marking details that fell out of their correct place. To be sure, the correlation between political and cosmic order worked to justify those who had political power. But this system cannot be simply read as a strategy of political legitimation. As Sessa and Kulikowski show, this order was often not aligned with actual social realities and the interests of those in power, and as Canepa argues, it was recognized even by the emperor's enemies. More important, the similarity between how this enchainment worked in clearly political spheres and in less obviously political spheres, such as in relation to artifacts or meteorological phenomena, shows us the political implications of the latter but also the insufficiency of a political explanation for the former.

It is important to look at the way knowing imposed practical order not only when the result was successful and enduring social structures but also when, from our perspective, the actions seem mistaken or irrational. That is the case with the actions explored by Edward Watts in "Christianization" and Dayna Kalleres in "Demon." Watts argues that the conversion of the Roman Empire had to be imagined before it could be implemented but that Christian thinkers imagined it wrongly, relying on mistaken knowledge by using as a model the ancient Israelites' experience in Canaan. Kalleres argues that examining counterdemonic apotropaic measures as products of knowledge (although they themselves were also producers of knowledge, making demons present in daily life) allows us to appreciate their users as sophisticated, intuitive agents rather than victims of superstition or fear. In both cases, we can see how the access that knowledge provided to invisible realities and archnarratives empowered informed agency—even in cases wherein we may be tempted to see particular historical actions as inevitable, materialistic, or primitive.

The absorbing and expansive nature of knowing did not, however, produce a uniform and homogeneous experience of knowing; on the contrary, it often resulted in epistemological heterogeneity. This heterogeneity is a theme through both parts of this volume, as epistemological differences arose both from practices of recognition and from practices of ordering. The inclusion of different bodies of knowledge—traditions of the past, systems of competing groups, different disciplines, and even different species—in a singular discourse effected a preoccupation with and an awareness of epistemological difference. It meant that late ancient knowers were always aware of different perspectives and that even if these perspectives were perhaps seen as inferior or superior to their own, they were at the same time overlapping and constitutive of their own knowledge. In that sense, it is not only from our modern perspective that the merging involved in late ancient knowing seems surprising; late ancient knowers themselves often felt that they were uniting conflicting elements and crossing or at least testing the boundaries of knowing.

One form of heterogeneity stems from a familiar aspect of late antiquity. Late ancient knowers sought knowledge in texts or traditions that they took care to transmit from the past, and although they did not always see or acknowledge the otherness of such knowledge, they also worked hard to adapt and reinterpret it to make it their own. In "*Ordo*," we see how an ideological and rhetorical system of ordering society that originated in the Roman Republic was modulated to come into accord with profound changes in social structure in the late empire; and we also see the same system informing Christian discourse, which, having elements hostile to social structure dating from its apocalyptic origins, needed itself to be brought into accord with this system. We have already noted how Watts's "Christianization" shows us Christians relying on a biblical model only to understand very late that this model simply did not work in the late Roman world. Canepa's chapter documents how sovereigns of both the Sassanian and the Roman Empire incorporated and reinterpreted earlier imperial presentations in their own.

The knowledge that late ancient knowers inherited from the past or acquired from their surroundings could be problematic, because it was associated with their contemporary rivals. Chin shows us that Priscillian does not write off Greco-Roman cosmology; he reinterprets it. To use the distinction that we made with respect to Boethius earlier, it is not that Priscillian thought his opponents did not know enough about cosmology; it is that what they knew they did not know rightly. Schott's reconstruction of the different interpretations of Apollo's answer to Julian in his oracle at Daphne expresses beautifully this combination of overlapping knowledge and radically divergent interpretations of this knowledge. "Everyone who heard Apollo's oracle," Schott writes, "heard the same oracle. They agreed, too, about its ostensible meaning." But they differed in its interpretation: Julian understood it through the prism of the classical tradition, reading it in light of the historical accounts of Peisistratus's purification of Delos; John Chrysostom saw in Apollo's answer an admission of defeat by a Christian martyr.

The more striking kind of heterogeneity, however, emerged not from differences among human beings but from differences between human beings and others—from efforts to see human subjectivity as not unique but in fact akin to an activity of knowing in which all beings participated. Beth Berkowitz's "Animals" examines late ancient debates on animal rationality, documenting how far certain authors went in attributing to animals what we would call a humanlike intelligence. But Berkowitz's analysis also shows that this assimilation was not a naive projection of humanity into other species; it was done with full awareness that it went against both common intuition and considerable philosophical argument and that its adoption could cause serious ethical problems. In such cases we cannot characterize the totalization and expansion of a single rationality in passive terms, as an almost unconscious premise for knowing, but must rather see it in active terms, as a contested intellectual practice pursued on many levels. More important, this expansion resulted not in any smooth, undifferentiated way of knowing but in a system that thrived on multiplicity and tensions.

This tension between the disposition toward a pervasive and accessible singular rationality in the world on the one hand and the recognition of the limits of human subjectivity on the other is most apparent in late ancient constructions of divine knowing. God is the source of intelligence and yet, as Ellen Muehlberger writes in her chapter on angels, late ancient knowers "pushed the highest god out of the realm of incomprehensibility toward the truly alien." We will return to the strangeness of the divinity itself momentarily. For now, we can find a similar dynamic between epistemological difference and similarity in what Muehlberger proposes was the solution to this divine strangeness: the communication with angels. As her analysis shows, late ancient representations of communication between angels and human beings imply a psychological similarity between the subjectivities of both species. But it is also essential for such representations that the angels are different from human beings, participating more fully—according to a passage by Gregory of Nyssa to which Muehlberger alludes—in divine rationality. Angels become familiar and part of the everyday, but they are "normal . . . in their abnormality." A striking expression of this dual nature of angels is the transformative capacity that they represent: they are similar enough to human beings for the latter to strive to be like them, but if human beings succeed, they will exceed the limitations of humanity, becoming something quite different.

Here is where the strangeness of God becomes both the root of the problem of late ancient knowing and, at least for some Christians, its solution: as Lewis Ayres explains, Augustine's narrative of knowing God construes this knowing as a persistent striving to push beyond the limits of the created order by simultaneously looking within creation and recognizing creation as ordered toward the redemptive yet transcendent Word. The simultaneity of this human intellectual action, located within and beyond the world in the process of striving, can be glossed as faith; the simultaneous activity of the divine within and beyond the world becomes grace. For Augustine, moreover, this faith was particularly Nicene, and this grace particularly Trinitarian; thus what may appear to the modern social historian of Christianity to be merely a dominant faction in a range of Christian theological factions in late antiquity becomes, in Augustine's homiletic retelling, the immediate instantiation, or even the incarnation, of the universal divine order in the concrete particulars of Nicene Christianity. As illuminated by the limit case of divine knowing, late ancient knowing is an activity that takes place in multiple cognitive spaces, some of which, disconcertingly, are both utterly foreign to and wholly continuous with our quotidian and fragmented human experience.

These essays show us a late ancient knowing that is a habit of systematization built on epistemological heterogeneity, an inquiry after a singular, universal rationality that is nonetheless experienced from multiple, incomplete perspectives. The sense of limited perspective is in part a consequence of the systematic ambition itself: comprehensive knowledge may give us a sense of control, but it may also remind us how much we do not really know, how much knowledge is in fact removed from our daily experience. A globe gives us a sense that we know the entire world, but it also reminds us of places that we will never visit and that we cannot even imagine. Kulikowski observes that knowing the social stratification of the empire as a whole reminded local elites in the smaller and more remote cities of those higher up in the social order. Sessa shows the concern with objective criteria for the priesthood that were designed to surpass subjective perspective but often clashed with pervasive intuitions about and realities of ecclesiastical leadership. Cam Grey's "Countryside" reflects on the countryside itself but also on how imagining the countryside probes the perspectival boundaries of an urban author.

This principle of bringing order to heterogeneity is even more applicable to how late ancient knowers tied daily life to intricate knowledge of invisible elements and the invisible connections between those elements. In almost all the chapters of this book, we see late ancient knowers insisting that the most quotidian details of life, the most closely experienced facts—the agrarian cycle, social position, using a pot—are essentially misunderstood if they are not placed in the context of pervasive systems that require a tremendous intellectual effort, a great deal of knowing. But even as this embedding endowed daily life with cosmic significance, it also meant that the actions and bodies most intimately known were in fact part of a system known only from very particular perspectives. Late ancient knowing was premised on a great deal of common knowledge, but it also filtered that common knowledge through very specific and very contested lenses, such as the intricacies of rabbinic *halakhah* or Trinitarian theology. It was extremely ambitious, seeing itself as a part of a pervasive knowing that existed in the minds of things, animals, and gods, or that was even identical with the universe itself; yet in examining their participation in this broader knowing, late ancient knowers also shaped the limits of particular knowledge. The navigation between these tensions was not simple. It required a certain art, even if this art was habitual rather than deliberate. It is this art, the everyday activity of late ancient knowing, that we trace here.

NOTES

1. For an excellent overview of the range of ideas that fall under these rubrics, see *The Cambridge Handbook of Situated Cognition,* ed. Philip Robbins and Murat Aydede (Cambridge: Cambridge University Press, 2008); cf. also Margaret Wilson, "Six Views of Embodied Cognition," *Psychonomic Bulletin and Review* 9 (2002): 625–36.

2. One important and by now well-established strand of scholarship concerned the work of memory in the ancient and medieval periods. See Frances Yates, *The Art of Memory* (Chicago: University of Chicago Press, 1966), or, influenced by Yates, Mary Carruthers, *The Book of Memory: A Study of Memory in Medieval Culture* (Cambridge: Cambridge University Press, 1990) and *The Craft of Thought: Meditation, Rhetoric, and the Making of Images* (Cambridge: Cambridge University Press, 1998).

3. Clifford Ando, *The Matter of the Gods: Religion and the Roman Empire* (Berkeley and Los Angeles: University of California Press, 2008).

4. Daryn Lehoux, *What Did the Romans Know? An Inquiry into Science and Worldmaking* (Chicago: Chicago University Press, 2012). Note, though, that whereas Lehoux restricts his inquiry to knowledge about the natural world among members of the Roman elite, the present collection addresses a broader set of objects and knowers.

5. The classic application of this problem to the writing of history is Hayden White, *The Content of the Form: Narrative Discourse and Historical Representation* (Baltimore: The Johns Hopkins University Press, 1987); for a history of the issues behind this historiographical turn, see Elizabeth A. Clark, *History, Theory, Text: Historians and the Linguistic Turn* (Cambridge, Mass.: Harvard University Press, 2004).

6. Thomas Kuhn, *The Structure of Scientific Revolutions* (Chicago: University of Chicago Press, 1962); Michel Foucault, *The Archaeology of Knowledge,* trans. A. M. Sheridan (New York: Pantheon, 1972), quotation from p. 31.

7. Oxford: Oxford University Press, 2004.

8. Cambridge: Cambridge University Press, 2007.

9. Cf. Elaine Scarry, "The Difficulty of Imagining Other Persons," in *The Handbook of Interethnic Coexistence,* ed. Eugene Weiner (New York: Continuum, 1998), 40–62.

10. The best overview in English of Boethius's life and work remains Henry Chadwick, *Boethius: The Consolations of Music, Logic, Theology, and Philosophy* (Oxford: Clarendon Press, 1981).

11. On the reception of Boethius, see Alison White, "Boethius in the Medieval Quadrivium," in *Boethius: His Life, Thought, and Influence,* ed. Margaret Gibson (Oxford: Blackwell, 1981), 162–205; and John Marenbon, *Boethius* (Oxford: Oxford University Press, 2003), chapter 9, "Boethius's Influence in the Middle Ages," 164–82.

12. *Anicii Manlii Torquati Severini Boetii De Institutione Arithmetica Libri Duo, De Institutione Musica Libri Quinque; Accedit Geometria Quae Fertur Boetii,* ed. G. Friedlein, vol. 1.1 (Leipzig: Teubner, 1867); see also the translation of Michael Masi, *Boethian Number Theory: A Translation of the "De Institutione Arithmetica"* (Amsterdam: Rodopi, 1983).

13. *Confessions* 1.9.14, 7.18.24; on Boethius and Augustine, see Anna Crabbe, "Literary Design in the *De Consolatione Philosophiae*," in Gibson, ed., *Boethius* (above, n. 11), especially 251–63; and Edmund T. Silk, "Boethius's *Consolatio Philosophiae* as a Sequel to Augustine's *Dialogues* and *Soliloquiae*," *Harvard Theological Review* 32 (1939): 19–39.

14. *Relationes* 3.10; on the reception of the *Relationes* in late antiquity, see Domenico Vera, "Sulle edizioni antiche delle *Relationes* di Simmaco," *Latomus* 36 (1977): 1003–36. We are grateful to Michele Salzman for this reference.

15. *Consolatio Philosophiae* 1.P6.21. We use the Latin text edited by W. Weinberger, *Boethii Philosophiae Consolationis Libri Quinque,* Corpus Scriptorum Ecclesiasticorum Latinorum, vol. 67 (Vienna: Hoelder, Pichler, and Tempsky, 1934); we have also consulted the translation of P. G. Walsh, *Boethius: The Consolation of Philosophy* (Oxford: Clarendon Press, 1999).

16. *De Institutione Arithmetica* 1.5, trans. Masi, *Boethian Number Theory* (above, n. 12).

17. See discussion in C. Chin, *Grammar and Christianity in the Late Roman World* (Philadelphia: University of Pennsylvania Press, 2008), chapter 2, "Imagining Classics," 12–14.

18. E.g., at *Consolatio Philosophiae* 1.M2.6–12.

19. Ibid. 1.P4.4.

20. Ibid. 1.M5.

21. Ibid. 1.P1.13–14.

22. We use the translation of S. J. B. Barnish, *Cassiodorus: Variae* (Liverpool: Liverpool University Press, 1992).

23. *Consolatio Philosophiae* 1.P4.37.

24. Ibid. 1.P4.40–41.

PART ONE

Finding Order

1

Artifact

Mira Balberg

In the book of Leviticus we find a lengthy description of the procedure for inspecting an afflicted house—that is, a house in which mildew was seen in one of the walls. Once a house has been rendered impure on account of such affliction, the Pentateuch stresses, everything that is in it is immediately rendered impure as well. Thus, in order to protect one's property from impurity, prior to official inspection by a priest the house should be cleared of all its contents—namely, furniture and utensils, clothes and bedding, cushions and boxes, and everything else a person may own.[1] The creators of the Mishnah, a formative Jewish rabbinic codex that was compiled around the turn of the third century C.E., took note of the biblical text's attention to what may seem like an entirely trivial matter: everyday household objects. A mishnaic tradition attributed to Rabbi Meir (a mid-second-century sage) presents the care for such articles as a heartening indication of the Torah's compassion for human beings:[2]

> Said Rabbi Meir: What is it that might be rendered impure for him?
> If you will say his wooden articles and his clothes and his metal articles—he
>   immerses them, and they are then rendered pure!
> Rather, what is it that the Torah spares?
> His clay articles, his pitcher and his ewer.
> If this is how the Torah spares his negligible property, all the more so his precious
>   property;
> If so for his property, all the more so for the lives of his sons and daughters;
> If so for that of the wicked,[3] all the more so for that of the righteous.

According to Rabbi Meir, in regard to most articles there is no real reason to be concerned that they may contract impurity, since they can be purified by a simple act of ritual immersion. The only articles that will actually become unusable if they contract impurity are clay articles, which cannot be immersed and must be broken down if they have become impure. However, since clay was a cheap and ubiquitous material in the rabbinic period, clay objects (such as pitchers and ewers used for oil) were of relatively little importance and were easily replaceable. If God spares even such lowly and disposable articles, says Rabbi Meir, then all the more so he spares the lives of human beings.

This passage powerfully makes the point that household objects, even of the most mundane kind, are an inseparable part of human life. Clearly, utensils and furniture are not as important to persons as the lives of their children; but nonetheless persons have some sort of personal investment in them—which, according to Rabbi Meir, scripture remarkably acknowledges and respects. To understand the human habitat, to be attentive to human needs and concerns, is also to be conscious of the array of things that inhabit the world in which human beings work, sleep, cook, eat, sew, plow, dress, paint, write, and perform various other activities—which all involve, at least in most cases, some artifact. This applies to the affluent modern world as much as it applies to the world of second-century Palestine: although we rarely take heed of the fact that there is hardly any facet of our daily life in which we do not make use of various artifacts, the most banal and mundane objects are what allow us to perform the most basic tasks as well as the most elevated and highly esteemed activities. As the French sociologist Bruno Latour put it, if you are convinced that inanimate objects make no difference in human lives, try "hitting a nail with and without a hammer, boiling water with and without a kettle, fetching provisions with or without a basket, walking in the street with or without clothes, zapping a TV with or without a remote," and so forth.[4] The realm of everyday life, then, is laden with and defined by artifacts.

The Mishnah, from which the passage I quoted above is taken, is perhaps best described as a treatise on the everyday—an everyday that is designed, shaped, lived, and reflected upon in accordance with Jewish law as the rabbis who created the Mishnah understood it. It is a lengthy and systematic attempt to encompass every single aspect of the human world—from the manufacture of wine and oil to the upkeep of one's henhouse, from building a staircase to hiring workers—insofar as all these aspects are in some way mandated by *halakhah*. With this tremendous attention to the details of which daily life consists, it is not surprising that we find in the Mishnah recurring references to artifacts—both to specific items and to artifacts as a general category. I am using the word "artifacts" as a less-than-perfect translation for the Hebrew term *kēlim* (sg. *kĕli*), which serves in rabbinic literature to denote usable objects of all kinds—furniture, clothes, utensils, and so on. I choose the word "artifacts" (rather than "articles" or "vessels," sometimes proposed as translations for *kēlim*) to emphasize both the inclusive nature of this category and the most critical quality of a *kĕli* as the rabbis understood it—namely that it is an object made by and for human beings. Objects that have not been in any way given form or processed by human beings, such as rocks or logs of wood, do not fall under the category of kēlim, and the rabbinic science of artifacts, which will stand at the center of this chapter, does not apply to them.

It is easily understood why the Mishnah, as a text that applies norms to every aspect of daily life, closely engages with various artifacts and their functions: the attempt to legislate what people should or should not do in specific circumstances closely involves the question what they should or should not do with specific artifacts. When discussing the Sabbath, for instance, as a day on which no labor may be performed, the question which artifacts may or may not be used is crucial; likewise, when setting down detailed rules regarding the retrieval of lost objects, this entails a consideration of different kinds of artifacts that people may lose; and other similar examples are abundant. In this respect, artifacts are of concern to the rabbis of the Mishnah insofar as they play a part in the various actions and behaviors that the Mishnah is trying to regulate. However, the rabbis did more than occasionally refer to artifacts in the course of developing other halakhic topics; they also dedicated an entire tractate in the Mishnah, and a very sizable one, solely to the topic of artifacts.

Tractate Kēlim,[5] which is the second largest in the entire Mishnah, introduces a remarkably meticulous, systematic, and extensive categorization and classification of hundreds of artifacts that are commonly and uncommonly found in the human lived world—from pots and pans to needles and pipes, from weaving looms and shovels to toilet seats and shoe racks, from baskets and mantles to flutes and helmets, and many, many more. For each and every one of these artifacts, the tractate's purpose is to determine its susceptibility to impurity—namely to decide whether a particular artifact may contract impurity or not, in case it had contact with a source of impurity (such a leprous person, a menstruating woman, a dead body, an afflicted house as we have seen above, and several other sources).[6] The normative function of this tractate, then, is to give the readers or listeners guidelines as to how they should manage their belongings in case these belongings have had contact with a source of impurity (that is, what they should take the trouble to purify and what does not require purification); but in order to do so, the rabbis develop an extremely elaborate body of knowledge, which I will refer to here as a "science of artifacts." This knowledge entails not only inventorylike information about all the artifacts that conceivably inhabit the human world, but also—much more important—fundamental principles for inquiring what an artifact is and how it functions. In other words, the halakhic system of purity and impurity serves for the rabbis as a template through which they map the material world as they know it—to the extent that the material world is processed by human beings.

The questions of what motivated the rabbis of the Mishnah to take on such a taxing enterprise, and why they considered such exhaustive knowledge of artifacts an important part of the education of their real or imagined audience, drive one to the much broader and complicated questions of the rabbis' intentions in creating the Mishnah as a whole and of the nature of this compilation as such, with which I cannot engage here.[7] My purpose in this chapter is not to determine why this knowledge was created and developed but rather to explore what this knowledge consists of and how it is structured. Taking as a given the fact that the rabbis thought that a comprehensive knowledge of the world of artifacts is necessary for the halakhically erudite Jew, I examine, first, what the rabbis considered worth knowing about artifacts and, second, what the rabbis conceived to be the ways of knowing artifacts. What were the conceptual tools with which the rabbis categorized and classified what seems like an endless assortment of objects? More important, what does this system of knowledge tell us about how the rabbis made sense of the world that surrounded them—and of the human beings that inhabited it?

As I will show in the following pages, an examination of the rabbinic science of artifacts reveals a distinct way of knowing—of mentally approaching the material world, reflecting on it, and classifying it. This way of knowing, I suggest, is guided by the underlying view that humans are not wholly separate and detachable from the material objects that surround them, but rather that they experience and perceive their material belongings as extensions of their own bodies. Correspondingly, one knows artifacts not only by taking inventory of their objective qualities (size, shape, matter, etc.) but also by knowing their subjective qualities—that is, what they mean to the individual who owns them or uses them. In other words, for the rabbis knowing artifacts is inextricable from knowing oneself.

CLASSIFYING ARTIFACTS: BIBLICAL ORIGINS AND RABBINIC DEVELOPMENTS

As is the case with almost every area of rabbinic expertise, the mishnaic science of artifacts rests on biblical foundations. Several verses in the book of Leviticus provide some basic rules and distinctions regarding the impurity of artifacts, rules and distinctions that the rabbis develop and expand according to their own interpretation of the text and, as I shall argue later on, according to their fundamental perceptions regarding the relation between human beings and the material world. At the core of the knowledge of artifacts, then, seems to stand a hermeneutical enterprise—that is, an attempt to apply the edicts of the Pentateuch in a consistent and methodical manner to the rabbis' own lived world.[8] However, the mishnaic knowledge of artifacts is informed by certain ideas and principles that far exceed the biblical text, and it is these principles that will stand at the center of my inquiry here.

The key text for the classification of artifacts appears in Leviticus 11:31–33, in a passage that discusses the impurity conveyed by creeping and crawling creatures:[9]

Those are for you the impure among all swarming things; whoever touches them when they are dead shall be impure until evening. And anything on which one of them falls when dead shall be impure: be it *any article of wood, or a cloth, or a skin, or a sack—any such article that is put to use* shall be dipped in water, and it shall remain impure until evening; then it shall be pure. And if any of those falls into a clay vessel, everything inside it shall be impure, and it itself you shall break.

Whereas several biblical texts make the point that various artifacts are susceptible to impurity if they have contact with one of the sources of impurity,[10] the verses above are of particular importance in that they (presumably) make the points that not all artifacts contract impurity and that not all artifacts contract impurity in the same way. In other words, these verses open up a space for the construction of knowledge, insofar as knowledge is based on a set of distinctions and categorizations. I shall begin, then, with an exposition of the rabbinic knowledge of artifacts as based on the categories laid out in the biblical text and then continue on to explore the unique rabbinic take on knowing artifacts, namely on the subjective processes of conceptualization and reflection applied to them.

The first distinction, obviously, is a distinction of material. The passage above mentions only five kinds of material that may contract impurity: wood, cloth, skin (i.e., leather), sackcloth, and clay. This presumably indicates that all other materials are not susceptible to impurity at all. However, another biblical text, which discusses the need to purify all the loot from the Israelites' war with Midyan, mentions other kinds of materials as well, thus indicating that those are also susceptible to impurity: "You shall also cleanse every cloth, every article of skin, and all the work of goats, and every object of wood. . . . Gold and silver, copper, iron, tin, and lead—any article that can withstand fire—these you shall pass through fire, and they shall be pure" (Numbers 31:20–23). Taking these verses into consideration, the rabbis also included metal articles ("gold and silver, copper, iron, tin, and lead") among the artifacts that are susceptible to impurity. Finally, the rabbis added two more kinds of material to the list: bone, which they derived from the mention of "the work of goats" in Numbers 31:20, taking it to refer to anything that comes from goats (including the horns), and glass, for which they admitted not having any biblical proof text.[11] What is excluded from the rabbinic list, then, are articles made of stone, earth, and dung, which the rabbis considered insusceptible to impurity—not only because they were not mentioned in the Bible but also, as I will argue later on, because they were seen as too close to nature, as not sufficiently man-made.

Leviticus 11:33 also puts forth an important distinction concerning how different articles contract impurity: it maintains that whereas most articles contract impurity from the outside (when a source of impurity has contact with their external surface), clay articles contract impurity from the inside (when a source of impurity falls into them). This curious ruling generated a whole array of rabbinic discussions regarding how impurity is contracted by different artifacts, which we will not get into here; but it also brought forth another criterion that was central to the rabbis' classification of artifacts, which pertains to the ability of the artifact to serve as a receptacle. Since the verse seems to assume that clay artifacts need to have an inside to become susceptible to impurity, the rabbis concluded that at least clay articles must be able to function as receptacles in order to contract impurity. They also attempted to apply this requirement to articles made of other materials (except for metal), for which it is often much more difficult to determine what constitutes a receptacle and what does not. (For example, is a cushion stuffed with feathers, or a hollow pipe, to be seen as a receptacle?) Accordingly the rabbis often stretch and tweak the definition of "receptacle" in different directions. Thus, immediately following the determination of material—which is the organizing principle of the tractate as a whole—the determination whether a particular object is a receptacle or not is the first step that the rabbis take in its classification.

The most important criterion that guides the mishnaic science of artifacts, to which essentially almost all the rabbinic discussions in the tractate are dedicated, and on which I will focus hereafter, lies in one biblical clause that easily goes unnoticed: *any . . . article that is put to use.* In its context in the Leviticus passage, this clause seems to offer merely an explanatory definition to the general term "article" (kĕli), namely: What is a kĕli? It is something that is put to use. The rabbis, however, interpreted this clause as restrictive: only those articles that can be put to use are susceptible to impurity. Thus, the most critical thing one ought to know about an artifact (besides the material of which it is made and its shape) is whether it is usable or not; and it is through the definition of usability that the rabbis develop a new conceptual framework and a new way of knowing that leave the biblical texts far behind.

When classifying and categorizing objects according to their usability, the rabbis exclude not only objects that are man-made but nothing conceivable can be done with them (for example, a piece of woven fabric of a size of less than three fingers on three fingers)[12] but also artifacts that are not yet usable and objects that are no longer usable. For example, a pot that is still on the potter's wheel or a sandal whose straps are torn are both insusceptible to impurity, even though pots and sandals as such are by all means usable objects. Accordingly, in order to determine the susceptibility of different artifacts to impurity one must know exactly, first, if and how they are used; second, at which point during their manufacture they become usable; and finally, what defects terminate their usability and thereby their susceptibility to impurity. The determination of susceptibility to impurity thus requires an extremely detailed knowledge of the exact form and function of every artifact under the sun, and it is mainly this knowledge that the Mishnah attempts to construct and lay out. To illustrate briefly the form in which this excruciatingly detailed knowledge is presented, I will quote here a sample of two randomly chosen mishnaic passages. The first attempts to determine at which point various wooden artifacts can be considered usable:[13]

> Beds and cots [become usable—i.e., susceptible to impurity] after they are rubbed over with fish skin. . . . Wooden baskets—after their rims are bound round and the rough end is smoothed off. . . . A wicker case for flagons or for cups, even if the rough ends are not smoothed off inside.

And the list goes on and on. (There are similar lists for artifacts made of other materials.)

The second passage discusses the point at which different metal artifacts can no longer be considered usable and thus become insusceptible to impurity:[14]

> If a shovel has lost its blade, it still remains susceptible to impurity, because it is like a hammer. . . . If a saw has lost one tooth in every two, it becomes insusceptible; but if there is a length of one *sit* of teeth left at any place,[15] it remains susceptible. If an adze, scalpel, chisel, or drill has been damaged, it remains susceptible to impurity; but if it has lost its sharp edge it becomes insusceptible.

In addition to their concern with determining the beginning and end of usability for each object, the rabbis were conscious of the fact that many artifacts can be used for more than one purpose: for instance, a chest is primarily used for storage, but one can also sit on it; a bedsheet is primarily used as bedding, but one can also use it as a curtain; and so forth. The elaborate mishnaic science of artifacts thus assesses the usability of specific artifacts not only vis-à-vis their original or more common functions but also vis-à-vis possible secondary functions.

In its extremely elaborate lists of artifacts, which encompass a dizzying array of household, agricultural, military, artistic, and even musical objects, tractate *Kēlim* serves as a particularly extended example of one of the most prominent genres in the Mishnah—namely the genre of inventorylike lists. Lists appear in the Mishnah as part of the exposition of almost every halakhic topic and provide detailed answers to questions such as what plants can be sown together, what jewelry one can or cannot wear on the Sabbath, what writs can and cannot be written during festival times, and so on, and so forth. The prominence of such lists is curious, since the overarching principles that govern the classification of objects into those lists are usually fleshed out explicitly in the Mishnah itself, in a way that seems to make the lists somewhat redundant. It is plausible that the primary purpose of these lists is didactic, as in the case of other practices of list making in late antiquity, most notably Polemius Silvius's *Laterculus*.[16] Whether these lists reflect the effort of rabbinic disciples to apply the principles that they have learned to real-life examples or the lists were provided by the masters in order to allow the disciples to deduce the principles on their own, they seem to attest a certain pedagogical setting.[17] Nevertheless, I believe that these lists serve not only a didactic but also a rhetorical purpose, which is especially pronounced in the case of tractate *Kēlim:* by classifying every conceivable object under a halakhic rubric, the rabbis make the point that their greater normative enterprise in fact encompasses everything there is in the world. There is no zone, not even the most negligible, that is beyond the scope of *halakhah* or is insignificant for the rabbis' legislative endeavor: every minute aspect of the individual's life is underwritten by rabbinic law in such a way that in order to decipher the halakhic script of the everyday, one must approach the rabbis. These lists thus construct the rabbinic system of knowledge as utterly comprehensive and as tantamount to the knowledge of the world as such, thereby establishing the authority of the rabbis themselves as the only competent bearers of this knowledge.

THE FORCE OF LABOR AND THE FORCE OF THOUGHT

So far I have shown that the question of usability stands at the center of the mishnaic endeavor of classifying artifacts and that the primary purpose of the elaborate lists provided in tractate *Kēlim* is essentially to determine how and at what point different artifacts go into and out of usability. However, the rabbis go beyond the question whether a particular artifact can be put to a particular use or not in a given condition; they also suggest a unique perspective on what usability means. First, they make the point that only what is designated for human beings may become susceptible to impurity:[18] for example, only rings meant to be used by human beings are susceptible to impurity, whereas rings made for animals and inanimate objects are not.[19] Second, and more important, the rabbis maintain that some forms of use are actually not use at all, and thus artifacts made for certain purposes are not susceptible to impurity. A prominent example for this principle is the ruling that items made only for decorative purposes are not susceptible to impurity.[20] How are we to understand these additional requirements, which exceed the basic notion of usability and integrate the question of what one uses the artifact for into the science of artifacts?

A helpful direction for answering this question can be found in one of Karl Marx's most fundamental observations, according to which artifacts are in essence extensions of the human body. Human beings, Marx noted, make artifacts as ways of prolonging their bodies and allowing themselves to act in ways desirable to them: they thus put labor into natural resources and process them in such a way that nature becomes "man's inorganic body."[21] When we fill a cup with water from a fountain, the cup functions as an extension of our mouth; the clothes we wear are an extension of our skin; the plow we use is an extension of our hands and feet; and so on. We thus see whatever we do with artifacts as if it were done by us, and we say not "my gun shot him" or "my pencil drew the picture" but rather "I shot him" or "I drew the picture." A similar understanding of artifacts, I suggest, stands at the basis of the rabbinic science of artifacts. The susceptibility of an artifact to impurity is determined not merely by its usability but also by the question whether this artifact plays an active part in the lives of human beings, in such a way that it can be considered an important and consequential part of the human habitat, part of one's "inorganic body." The fact that something is produced by human beings is not enough; it also has to function as a supplement to the human body—something that defective and incomplete artifacts, artifacts not made for immediate human use,[22] and even decorative artifacts, cannot be said to do.

I propose, then, that the main criterion that the rabbis set for assessing the impurity of artifacts is not quite usability but rather a sense of continuity between the owner or user of the artifact and the artifact itself. This continuity, as we shall immediately see, is determined not only by what people do with an object but also—and perhaps especially—by what they think about an object. Continuity between person and artifact, which is the prerequisite for the susceptibility of the artifact to impurity, is seen by the rabbis as attained through a twofold process: first by investment of labor in the artifact and second, and more critical, by the investment of thought and deliberation in it. Thus, in the Mishnah susceptibility to impurity is ultimately determined by the questions whether an artifact matters to people or not and whether they conceive of it as part of themselves or not.[23] In other words, a highly significant part of the rabbinic knowledge of artifacts is the knowledge of how people relate to particular artifacts—which is, in essence, a knowledge of human subjectivity.

Artifacts are essentially products of human manipulation of natural elements. Human beings invest labor in wood, metal, sand, vegetation, or any other naturally found material, and through their labor they transform this element into part of the human arena, or—to use a somewhat dated expression—transform it from nature to culture.[24] In the rabbinic view, it is this transformation that inscribes the material element into the world of impurity. For as long as a material entity is in its unprocessed state, it is beyond the reach of impurity and is not affected by it in any way: for instance, natural water reservoirs, trees, and animals are not susceptible to impurity, and even if a corpse (the ultimate source of impurity) falls directly on or into them, they do not become impure.[25] However, once the water has been drawn, the tree has been made into a chair, and the animal has been slaughtered, it becomes susceptible to impurity. It is of interest here that artifacts made of stone, earth, and dung—materials that are closely associated with the natural environment and that go through very minimal processing in order to be adapted for human use—are considered by the rabbis to be part of nature and can never be susceptible to impurity.[26]

The manipulation of natural elements is, in a sense, a process of humanizing the material world. Impurity, I contend, is perceived by the rabbis as a phenomenon that primarily affects people, and it can affect nonhuman entities only insofar as they are seen as part of people's "inorganic body." The ability to become impure is thus constructed in the rabbinic discourse as a manifestation of the "humanness" of the artifact, which is tantamount to continuity between person and object, as I argued above.

As in the Marxist paradigm, in the Mishnah the transition of a material object from the natural to the human realm and from inconsequentiality to consequentiality takes effect through labor. The decisive moment in which an object is transformed into an artifact is known as "completion of labor," *gemar melakhah*, a phrase referring to the very last action required in order to consider an artifact fully manufactured and ready for use—for instance, hitting a metal object with a hammer one last time in order to give it its final shape or baking newly made clay objects in a kiln. Part of the rabbinic science of artifacts is determining what constitutes this final action in the process of manufacture for different artifacts. However, for the rabbis the completion of labor in and of itself is a necessary but insufficient condition for the "humanization" of material elements such that they become exposed to impurity in the same way that human beings are. The critical process that allows for the transformation from nature to artifact, and from insusceptibility to impurity to susceptibility, is thought. Put differently: in order for an artifact to become susceptible to impurity, the conclusive physical action applied to it, which signals the artifact's readiness to be used, must be followed by a mental action.

"Thought" (*mahshavah*) is a term used in the Mishnah to denote a person's intention to make use of a particular artifact. The moment at which an object is rendered consequential enough to be impure—that is, inscribed into the human realm—is the moment in which someone deliberates using this article and begins to see it as her own. To be sure, thought alone is entirely ineffective unless the artifact's manufacturing process is complete (or at least unless it has reached a stage at which the artifact can be used as is); but once it is complete, the artifact does not become susceptible to impurity until one in fact plans to make use of it.[27] Furthermore, artifacts made by an artisan for sale and not for personal use are not susceptible to impurity prior to their selling, since no thought can subject an artifact to impurity except the thought of the one who owns it.[28] Thought is thus tantamount to the consideration of something as one's own, or in Marxist terms, to the consideration of something as part of one's extended body. There is indeed a close correspondence between the decisive role of thought in the determination of susceptibility to impurity and its decisive role in the determination of ownership: a central principle in the rabbinic laws of ownership is that if an article is lost or stolen, the finder or thief legally becomes the new owner of the artifact once the original owner has "despaired" of getting the article back—that is, has severed her previous mental ties to the article in question.[29] A critical component of ownership is actively thinking of an article as one's own, and it is only when an article is actively considered to be one's own that it is susceptible to impurity.

The process that inscribes artifacts into the human realm, then, is ultimately a mental process: it is the investment of an artifact with the subjectivity of its owner through the act of deliberation and the establishment of a personal relation between the one who uses something and the thing used. Furthermore, the rabbis point out that susceptibility to impurity is contingent upon thought not only when first establishing relations with an artifact but also when reestablishing such relations after the artifact has become unusable. For instance, we find a ruling that "a [three-legged] table one of the legs of which has been removed is not susceptible to impurity. If a second one is removed, it is not susceptible to impurity. If a third is removed, it becomes susceptible to impurity once he thinks about it."[30] Whereas a two-legged or a one-legged table is considered an inconsequential artifact, since it cannot be used for any purpose (unless it is repaired), the tabletop itself can potentially be put to various uses. However, in order for the tabletop to be transformed into an object that matters–in this case, not from nature to artifact but from junk back to artifact—one has to want to make use of it.

This unique aspect of the rabbinic understanding of the workings of impurity allows us to gain a new perspective on the rabbinic knowledge of artifacts that we have examined thus far and to see it as geared, at least in part, toward the mapping and systematizing of human subjectivity. If artifacts are classified according to their ability to become impure, and this ability is closely dependent upon the extent to which humans invest thought and deliberation in those artifacts, then the knowledge of artifacts is ultimately the knowledge of how people relate to artifacts. The human habitat is constructed not only through labor but also, and perhaps especially, through mental processes of appropriation and attachment, and thus those processes themselves are an underlying object of knowledge. In order to know artifacts, the Mishnah suggests, one is required to know oneself: to decipher the susceptibility of artifacts to impurity is to reflect actively on one's own mental and physical connections to the material world that surrounds her.

Tractate *Kēlim,* then, is an attempt to set basic observations regarding how human beings relate to artifacts and to determine at what point each artifact is likely to be seen as consequential or inconsequential to human beings and what kinds of thought processes can be seen as transforming what kinds of artifacts. The rabbis do leave some room in this system for the personal relation of the individual to his or her possessions (that is, sometimes the only way to determine whether an artifact has become susceptible to impurity is to ask the owner whether she has made a conscious decision to use it), but for the most part they are attempting to construct a standardized subjectivity—a set of general assumptions on how human beings operate vis-à-vis artifacts that is independent of the peculiarities of each individual.[31]

A powerful illustration of this attempt to standardize subjectivity can be found in the rabbinic ruling that the process of making an artifact matter (and thus of rendering it susceptible to impurity) through thought works only in one direction. Whereas artifacts can be thought into impurity, they cannot be thought out of it: that is, they can stop being part of one's extended body not through mere thought but rather only through actual, physical change. In the words of the Mishnah: "All artifacts descend into their impurity by thought and do not ascend from their impurity except by a change of deed."[32] For example, when one makes a pair of shoes, she has to take a conscious decision to use these shoes in order for them to become susceptible to impurity; but the shoes do not simply cease to be susceptible to impurity once the owner makes a new pair and decides to stop using the old ones: rather, the first pair of shoes remains susceptible to impurity until the shoes are physically harmed in a way that makes them unusable. This ruling can be understood in strictly pragmatic terms, as stemming from the fact that from a legislator's point of view it is impossible to keep track of the fluctuating relations of individuals with their possessions in order to determine those possessions' susceptibility to impurity. Whereas it is quite easy to pinpoint the initial decision of a person to use an artifact, the moment in which one decides to stop using something is much harder to locate. Thus, choosing the point at which the artifact is physically unusable as the marker of loss of susceptibility to impurity is the most feasible solution. However, I propose that behind this pragmatic solution lies a particular view of how subjective attachment to artifacts actually works, a view guided by the premise that the average person does not break her mental attachment to her possessions so long as they are still usable. This assumption may seem strange to those living in the affluent world of the twenty-first century, who daily throw away perfectly usable artifacts, but it was taken for granted in the world of antiquity, in which most people owned very few things, on which they were highly dependent.[33] In this setting, even if a particular individual does happen to make a decision to stop using an artifact, this choice does not influence the status of this artifact, since the rabbis apply to this case the general rule that they have devised for a standard consciousness.

These assumptions about how people think of and treat artifacts, which guided the rabbis in creating the mishnaic tractate, bring us to the question of the relation between this body of knowledge and the lived reality of the rabbis and their contemporaries. Unfortunately, here we are essentially in the dark. It is safe to say that the Mishnah faithfully reflects the material culture of its time, not only in that it provides an elaborate inventory of the artifacts that were in use in the first centuries C.E. and describes their various functions, and modes of production, but also in that it gives its reader a genuine sense of how greatly people were invested in their personal possessions and the significance that they attributed to them. It is very difficult to know, however, whether the rabbinic mapping of artifacts and the guidelines for the determination of susceptibility to impurity had any impact beyond the realm of the rabbinic study house. First, we do not know how familiar the teachings of the rabbis were among the wider public;[34] and second, we do not know to what extent, if at all, teachings related to purity and impurity were of any practical applicability at the time when the Mishnah was compiled. The impurity of household objects is a matter of concern only for those who are careful to maintain a bodily state of purity (and thus refrain from touching artifacts that have become impure or eating food that has been handled with or kept in impure artifacts), and the question how many people in Palestine of the first few centuries C.E. were in fact concerned with ritual purity was and still is a topic of ongoing debate.[35] Even scholars who hold that purity in everyday life was a matter of concern for a substantial number of people during the Second Temple period often assume that after the destruction of the Jerusalem Temple in 70 C.E. the practices of purity became more and more marginal, in such a way that by the time of the compilation of the Mishnah this topic had become mainly theoretical.[36] The question remains, however, whether to see the mishnaic descriptions and prescriptions of purity practices as evidence for the lived reality of previous generations (or of small pious groups that still attempted to maintain those waning practices at the end of the second century) or as scholastic edifices that did not have any real impact on the lived reality of Jews in Palestine of that period.

Although this question cannot be answered with certainty in an almost complete absence of extrarabbinic sources from this period, in a recent article Joshua Schwartz argued that tractate *Kēlim* reflects a prevalent practice of intentionally sabotaging household furniture in a way that makes it officially unusable (and thus insusceptible to impurity) but still allows it to be somehow used in its compromised state.[37] In this way people were able to prevent their essential household objects (of which furniture is but one example) from being rendered impure, by utilizing to their benefit the rabbinic principle that defective artifacts are insusceptible to impurity. As Schwartz writes, the utilization of this principle is an indication of extensive acquaintance not necessarily with the rabbinic science of artifacts but only with its basic guidelines:[38]

> It is hard to imagine that the average householder (or probably even rabbi for that matter) could keep track or follow the minutiae of the decisions pertaining to the numerous utensils mentioned in *Kelim*.... The average householder probably related to the general principle that a "broken" implement was not susceptible to ritual uncleanness.

Although Schwartz cannot show conclusively that this intentional damaging of artifacts to which the Mishnah alludes was indeed practiced in Palestine of the first centuries, I find persuasive his argument that the mishnaic knowledge of artifacts is a combination of scholastic study-house discussions and basic, widely familiar principles. It is quite possible, then, that the general ideas that the rabbis devised on the impurity of artifacts were applied, in a technical and simplified manner, in the everyday lives of owners of artifacts and shaped how artifacts were thought of and handled. It is regrettable that the paucity of evidence does not allow us to go beyond the realm of conjecture here.

RETHINKING THE HUMAN

Although the practical implications of the mishnaic science of artifacts may have been limited or even nonexistent, the very enterprise of creating and developing this incredibly elaborate body of knowledge and the principles by which this knowledge is guided speak to fundamental aspects of the rabbinic understanding of the human as such. We have seen that for the rabbis artifacts were classified according to their owners' relations to them: that is, according to how mentally and physically invested in them their owners could be seen to be. This investment of human subjectivity in an inanimate material object, I proposed, was seen as transforming the nature of the object in such a way that it acquired a quality that the rabbis identified as quintessential to human bodies: the ability to contract impurity.

Here it is important to add one further dimension to the mishnaic picture, which will allow us to see its notion of the relations between human beings and their material environment in a fuller light. The same essential principle for the determination of susceptibility to impurity in artifacts—namely the question of continuity with the owner—also applies to human bodies. In various passages in the mishnaic discussions of purity and impurity we find the notion that body parts and areas that one does not strongly identify with oneself, or bodily components about which one does not care, cannot contract impurity.[39] Thus, for instance, any source of impurity that resides inside the body (like impure digested food or a dead fetus)[40] does not render one impure, since it is not accessible to and controllable by the person; invisible parts of the skin cannot be rendered impure by skin afflictions;[41] and invisible bodily areas need not have contact with the purifying water during purification.[42] In addition, whatever dirt or obstruction that one has on one's skin does not constitute a barrier between this person and the purifying water during ritual immersion so long as the person is not bothered by its presence.[43] Although I cannot discuss these fascinating aspects of the mishnaic purity laws here, it is important to note that the rabbis ultimately viewed the impurity of the human body as governed by the same principle as that by which the impurity of artifacts is governed: its various components have to matter to the individual and to be identified with the self in order to be susceptible to impurity.

This conceptual framework, in which artifacts and human bodies are both assessed vis-à-vis their subjective relations to their owners, provokes us to rethink the basic distinction between "person" and "world." Ingrained in modern consciousness is the view of the human body as a sealed envelope in which the self is contained, and which is wholly distinct from the material world—organic and nonorganic alike—that surrounds it. The Mishnah, in contrast, presents a view according to which the human body, which is in essence a material entity, is part of the greater material environment that surrounds the person, and both the body and the artifacts that were made or purchased by the person as extensions of the body must be invested with human subjectivity in order to be seen as part of the self. In other words, the Mishnah suggests that the human being should be seen through a broader lens, one that includes not only the individual bodily monad but also the material elements that the person has made part of himself or herself.[44]

The call to integrate the material environment and the world of inanimate objects into studies of society and culture has become increasingly prevalent in the past decade, especially owing to the work of scholars active in the field of ANT (actor-network theory). Thus one of the most influential shapers of this field, Bruno Latour, writes: "No science of the social can even begin if the question of who and what participates in the action is not first of all thoroughly explored, even if it might mean letting elements in which, for lack of better term, we could call *non-humans*."[45] Similarly, the political theorist Jane Bennett writes: "Humans are never *outside* of a set of relations with other modes [of existence]. . . . A material body always resides within some assemblage or other."[46] However, whereas Latour, Bennett, and other scholars of similar persuasion (who are often referred to as "post-humanists") are trying to introduce a perspective that is not unequivocally centered on human beings but sees them as but one component in a larger system, I am suggesting that the Mishnah (which is without question a text whose only point of concern is human beings) presents a picture in which a consideration of the nonhuman is a vital part of understanding the human. The Mishnah's science of artifacts reminds us that the ancient world was a world in which "things" mattered; it was a world in which most people owned few articles and in which what they owned was tremendously important to them—as the passage with which I began, regarding the Torah's sparing of household objects, poignantly illustrates. One's garments, utensils, furniture, working implements, and so forth, were one's dignity, one's livelihood, one's comfort, and one's well-being. As such, they constituted not only part of one's habitat but also part of one's self-perception and part of one's making as a person. This realization, I believe, urges us to think the concepts of selfhood and personhood in antiquity, which have been a topic of much recent interest, through the perspective of subjective relations with the material world.

Finally, I would like to suggest that the mishnaic science of artifacts, like the decisive roles of subjectivity and consciousness in the mapping of the material world, also challenges some of the ways in which we tend to think of knowing. For the rabbis, as we have seen, artifacts do constitute objects of knowledge; but this knowledge is primarily attained not through cerebral contemplation of artifacts from an external point of view but rather through the physical and mental connectedness of human bodies with the artifacts that surround them, and through reflection on this connectedness. In the Mishnah, artifacts are knowable and decipherable in terms of impurity only insofar as they are seen as extensions of the human body and as entities in which one has invested one's own subjectivity; in other words, knowing in the Mishnah is seen as contingent upon appropriation. The material world is accessible for conceptualization and for the application of human categories because it is itself humanized, and it is humanized because it is seen as fundamentally part of the one who perceives it. This brings to mind Maurice Merleau-Ponty's powerful words on the dual nature of the body as both subject and object:[47]

> My body is a thing among things; it is caught in a fabric of the world, and its cohesion is that of thing. But because it moves itself and sees, it holds things in a circle around itself. Things are an annex or prolongation of itself; they are incrusted into its flesh, they are part of its full definition; the world is made of the same stuff as the body.

For Merleau-Ponty, perception, and thereby knowledge, is possible not simply because we are part of the world as objects but also because we turn the world into a part of us as subjects. To be in the world, to relate to the world, is to turn the world into me, in such a way that the body and what is external to the body are seen as "made of the same stuff."

The Mishnah, I propose, structures and develops in a unique and incisive way the mode of knowing through appropriation to which Merleau-Ponty points. The rabbinic science of artifacts is not a body of knowledge constructed by going beyond the self but a body of knowledge of the world through the self—and ultimately about the self. As such, the Mishnah's treatise on artifacts invites further explorations not only on what is worth knowing but also on what it means to know.

NOTES

1. Leviticus 14:24–36.

2. Mishnah *Nega'im* 12:5; see also Sifra *Metzora* 5:10 (ed. Isaac Weiss, *Sifra de-bei rav* [New York: Om Publishing, 1946], 73a).

3. Although neither the Bible nor the Mishnah says this explicitly, there is a tradition according to which afflictions come about as punishments for sin. Therefore the one whose house is afflicted is identified here and in several other places as "wicked."

4. Bruno Latour, *Reassembling the Social: Introduction to Actor-Network Theory* (New York: Oxford University Press, 2005), 71.

5. The title *Kēlim* was apparently given to the tractate rather early in the course of its textual development, since at its very end we find a statement attributed to Rabbi Yose that refers to the fact that the tractate begins with rulings regarding impure objects and ends with a ruling regarding pure objects: "Happy are you, *Kēlim*, that you have entered in impurity and departed in purity." This statement suggests that the tractate was already known by this title before the final redaction of the Mishnah.

6. The sources of impurity are listed in Leviticus 11–15 and in Numbers 19. They include primarily persons with genital discharges, persons with skin afflictions, and dead creatures.

7. For a helpful survey of the problematics of defining the Mishnah's genre and purposes, see Yaakov Elman, "Order, Sequence, and Selection: The Mishnah's Anthological Choices," in *The Anthology in Jewish Literature,* ed. David Stern (New York: Oxford University Press, 2004), 53–80.

8. This is to say not that the rabbis actually derived all their teachings and rulings strictly through a process of biblical interpretation and extrapolation but simply that the Pentateuch functions as the framework of law that they attempt to develop and apply, whatever their exact method of doing so may be.

9. Jewish Publication Society translation (emphasis added), with slight modifications.

10. In Leviticus 15 we find recurring statements according to which every article on which a person with impure genital discharge sits, lies, or rides becomes impure, and in Numbers 19:15 it is mentioned that every open vessel that resides in the same tent as the dead is made impure.

11. As mentioned explicitly in Tosefta *Kēlim Bava Batra* 7:7.

12. Mishnah *Kēlim* 27:8.

13. Ibid. 16:1–2.

14. Ibid. 13:4.

15. According to the commentators, *sit* is the distance between the tips of the outstretched thumb and forefinger.

16. On the didactic setting and principles of Polemius Silvius's *Laterculus,* see Elizabeth Dulabahn, "The *Laterculus* of Polemius Silvius," PhD dissertation; Bryn Mawr College, 1986.

17. On the pedagogical dimension of the Mishnah and its use for the training of rabbinic disciples, see Elizabeth Shanks Alexander, *Transmitting Mishnah: The Shaping Influence of Oral Tradition* (New York: Cambridge University Press, 2006).

18. This principle, it should be noted, applies also to food: only food that human beings regularly consume or that is designated for consumption by human beings is susceptible to impurity, as the Mishnah makes clear in *Tohorot* 8:6 and *Uqtsin* 3:1–3. For an elaborate discussion of the impurity of foodstuffs in the Mishnah in comparison with the impurity of artifacts, see Mira Balberg, *Purity, Body, and Self in Early Rabbinic Literature* (Oakland: University of California Press, 2014), 74–95.

19. Mishnah *Kēlim* 12:1.

20. Ibid. 24:13.

21. Karl Marx, *Early Writings,* trans. Rodney Livingstone and Gregor Benton (London: Penguin Classics, 1992), 329.

22. One of the Mishnah's principles is that artifacts made as supplements for other artifacts that are not directly used by human beings (e.g., covers for utensils or instruments) are not susceptible to impurity. Similarly, several articles that are designated for sacred use only are not susceptible to impurity, since they are not meant for human beings.

23. In this view I differ somewhat from Howard Eilberg-Schwartz, who dealt extensively with the topic of the subjective component in susceptibility to impurity; see Howard Eilberg-Schwartz, *The Human Will in Judaism: The Mishnah's Philosophy of Intention*

(Atlanta: Scholars Press, 1986), 95–130. Eilberg-Schwartz centered his discussion on naming and argued that the susceptibility of an object to impurity depends on whether or not human beings title it as artifact (and likewise with food, which human beings do or do not title as such). Naming is an important component in the Mishnah but hardly accounts for its conceptual system in its entirety. See my discussion in Balberg, *Purity, Body, and Self* (above, n. 18), 88–90.

24. The view that susceptibility to impurity is a manifestation of pertinence to the realm of culture as opposed to that of nature was presented by Vered Noam, *From Qumran to the Rabbinic Revolution: Conceptions of Impurity* (Jerusalem: Yad Ben Zvi Press, 2010), 288 (in Hebrew).

25. The biblical origin of the notion that natural elements are not susceptible to impurity is Leviticus 11:36–37, according to which natural reservoirs of water and plants that are still connected to the ground cannot become impure even if a dead creeping creature falls directly on them.

26. The large number of stone vessels from the Second Temple and mishnaic periods that were found in various areas in Palestine suggests that, since stone vessels were considered impurity-proof, this was a material of choice for communities and individuals concerned with the observance of purity. See Roland Deines, *Jüdische Steingefäße und pharisäische Frömmigkeit* (Tübingen: Mohr Siebeck, 1993), 228–33; see also Eyal Regev, "Pure Individualism: The Idea of Non-Priestly Purity in Ancient Judaism," *Journal for the Study of Judaism* 31 (2000): 176–200.

27. Mishnah *Kēlim* 26:7.

28. Ibid. 26:8.

29. See Mishnah *Bava Qamma* 10:2, *Bava Mezi'a* 2:1–2, *Kēlim* 26:8.

30. Ibid. 22:2.

31. See also Eilberg-Schwarz, *The Human Will* (above, n. 23), 123–29.

32. Mishnah *Kēlim* 25:9.

33. On the reluctance to throw away potentially usable articles in antiquity, see Kathryn Kamp, "From Village to Tell: Household Ethnoarcheology in Syria," *Near Eastern Archeology* 63 (2000): 84–93.

34. The traditional view, according to which the rabbis were the uncontested leaders of the Jewish society in Palestine after the destruction of the Jerusalem Temple in 70 C.E., was significantly undermined by the influential work of Seth Schwartz, who argued that the rabbis' impact was extremely limited and that most of the Jewish population in Palestine at the said period was detached from halakhic Judaism. See Seth Schwartz, *Imperialism and Jewish Society, 200 B.C.E. to 640 C.E.* (Princeton: Princeton University Press, 2001), 101–76.

35. See E. P. Sanders, "Did the Pharisees Eat Ordinary Food in Purity?" in *Jewish Law from Jesus to the Mishnah: Five Studies* (London: SCM Press, 1990), 131–254; Roland Deines and Martin Hengel, "E. P. Sanders' 'Common Judaism,' Jesus, and the Pharisees," *Journal of Theological Studies* 46 (1995): 1–70; Hannah Harrington, "Did the Pharisees Eat Ordinary Food in a State of Ritual Purity?" *Journal for the Study of Judaism* 26 (1995): 42–54; John Poirier, "Purity beyond the Temple in the Second Temple Era," *Journal of Biblical Literature* 122 (2003): 247–65; Hanan Birenboim, "Observance of the Laws of Bodily Purity in Jewish

Society in the Land of Israel during the Second Temple Period," PhD dissertation, The Hebrew University of Jerusalem, 2006 (in Hebrew).

36. This view was first presented by Jacob Neusner, *The Idea of Purity in Ancient Judaism* (Leiden: Brill, 1973), 72–107; for a more refined view, which sees the diminishing ubiquity of purity observance throughout the tannaitic period as a gradual process, see Yair Furstenberg, "Eating in a State of Purity during the Tannaitic Period: Tractate *Teharot* and Its Historical and Cultural Contexts," PhD dissertation, The Hebrew University of Jerusalem, 2010 (in Hebrew), especially 254–62.

37. Joshua Schwartz, "Reduce, Reuse, and Recycle: Prolegomena on Breakage and Repair in Ancient Jewish Society," *Jewish Studies Internet Journal* 5 (2006): 147–80.

38. Schwartz, "Reduce, Reuse, and Recycle" (above, n. 37), 179.

39. For a detailed discussion of the rabbinic mapping of the human body, see Balberg, *Purity, Body, and Self* (above, n. 18), 48–73.

40. Mishnah *Miqva'ot* 10:8 and Mishnah *Hullin* 4:3. See also Noam, *From Qumran to the Rabbinic Revolution* (above, n. 24), 296–300.

41. Mishnah *Nega'im* 6:8.

42. Mishnah *Miqva'ot* 8:5.

43. Ibid. 9:2–3.

44. The view that in certain social contexts personal possessions are actually viewed as part of their owner's body was influentially suggested by the anthropologist McKim Marriott in his studies of Indian society; see McKim Marriott, "Hindu Transactions: Diversity without Dualism," in *Transaction and Meaning: Directions in the Anthropology of Exchange and Symbolic Behavior*, ed. Bruce Kapferer (Philadelphia: Institute for the Study of Human Issues, 1976), 109–37. Several anthropologists have continued to develop this theme in their studies: see Cecilia Busby, "Permeable and Partible Persons: A Comparative Analysis of Gender and Body in South India and Melanesia," *Journal of the Royal Anthropological Institute* 3 (1997): 261–78; Edward LiPuma, "Modernity and Forms of Personhood in Melanesia," in *Bodies and Persons: Comparative Views from Africa to Melanesia*, ed. Michael Lambeck and Andrew Strathern (Cambridge: Cambridge University Press, 1998), 53–79; Marilyn Strathern, *Property, Substance, and Effect: Anthropological Essays on Persons and Things* (London: Athlone, 1999). For a useful survey of this topic, see Chris Fowler, *The Archeology of Personhood: An Anthropological Approach* (New York: Routledge, 2004), 53–78.

45. Latour, *Reassembling the Social* (above, n. 4), 72 (emphasis original).

46. Jane Bennett, "The Force of Things: Steps towards an Ecology of Matter," *Political Theory* 32 (2004): 347–72 (quotation from pp. 353–54; emphasis original).

47. Maurice Merleau-Ponty, "Eye and Mind," trans. Carleton Dallery in *The Primacy of Perception and Other Essays on Phenomenological Psychology, the Philosophy of Art, History and Politics*, ed. James Edie (Evanston: Northwestern University Press, 1964), 159–91, quotation from p. 163.

2

Animal

Beth Berkowitz

ANIMALS AT THE EDGE

According to one early rabbinic law, a person who makes an oath about the ridiculous is punished with flogging:[1]

> A vain oath: one incurs flogging for [taking] it intentionally but is exempt for [taking] it accidentally. What is a vain oath?
> . . . He swore regarding a matter that is impossible to him:
> He said, "If I have not seen a camel flying in the air," or "If I have not seen a snake like the beam of an olive press."

Given that there are almost infinitely many ways to imagine the impossible, it is interesting to see what is conjured up by the Mishnah, a second-century-C.E. rabbinic Hebrew-language collection of laws from Palestine: a flying camel and a gargantuan snake.[2] Later rabbinic commentators wondered: Why not a flying mouse? Isn't that just as ridiculous? And, conversely, they challenged: Is a gargantuan snake really so impossible?[3] The Talmuds ponder these questions, but I start with this mishnah to suggest that animals serve frequently in antiquity to define the limits of reality. Animals sit at the edge of personhood, like a variety of human characters—women, children, slaves, foreigners.

The problem of knowability is unique for animals, however, and goes back in biblical texts to the goring ox. Could the owner of the goring ox have predicted his animal's behavior? If yes, then he becomes accountable for the damage that his animal caused. Colin Dayan, in her *The Law Is a White Dog*, puts it this way with respect to common-law torts:[4]

Harm is . . . determined by the "nature" or "propensities" of an animal, whether lux-
ury or useful, tame or wild. Crucial also to this judgment is what can be known by a
human about an animal, or what can never be known or understood or foreseen.

Animals press the boundaries of what we know, and that is why, I tender, the rabbinic legal passage above uses animals to imagine the unimaginable.

This chapter deals with what late ancient authors knew about animals, with a
focus on rabbinic literature and on real animals rather than ones used in metaphors or allegories.[5] My interest here is in knowledge on a number of levels: knowledge possessed by animals, knowledge possessed about animals, and knowledge
possessed about knowledge. To put all this together, my question is: What did late
ancients think they knew about what animals know, and how did they think they
knew it? It is a question about animal intelligence and human intelligence and how
the relationship between them is variously configured in antiquity. As scientists,
historians, culture critics, and activists today rethink the intelligence of other species in relation to our own, it is useful to consider how our predecessors formulated and debated some of the same questions.[6]

For philosophical writers in the Greek tradition, the question was cast in terms
of animal reason (*logos*). Do other species possess reason, and if they do, is their
reason comparable to that of human beings? The stakes of this debate for animals
were high: a creature without reason had no share in human justice. Early Christian writers confronted these questions as they integrated Greek philosophy with
biblical traditions. For rabbinic authors, however, it was the prosaic framework of
torts liability, not the discourse of reason, that afforded them opportunity to reflect
on animal intelligence. Knowledge about animals, for the rabbinic legal texts, continually circles back to the question of who pays for what when. If we read those
texts creatively, however, we may see emerging from them a veritable theory of
animal intelligence.

In this essay, I will first give a brief overview of the animal in the larger landscape of late antiquity, and I will then examine a series of rabbinic texts about an
ox who sets fire to a stack of grain on the Sabbath. This "clever ox," as one Talmud
commentator describes him,[7] serves as the focal point for my exploration of
human knowledge about animal knowledge in late antiquity. What we find in all
these texts—by classical philosophers, by church writers, by rabbinic jurists—is
not a turn away from animality, as is sometimes thought to have transpired in late
antiquity, a rejection of things corporeal or carnal—but rather an outpouring of
interest in the animal and its relationship to the human.

A word about "the animal": in his lecture "The Animal That Therefore I Am,"
Jacques Derrida problematizes the term:[8]

Among nonhumans and separate from nonhumans there is an immense multiplicity
of other living things that cannot in any way be homogenized, except by means of

violence and willful ignorance, within the category of what is called the animal or animality in general.

"The animal," Derrida observes, is a homogenizing term that reduces an infinitely complex reality and reflects a deep-seated anthropocentrism. In this chapter I will explore the vocabulary for other species that was devised by ancient writers and consider how their words dictate the terms of discussion—as ours do for us—and serve either to legitimize or to problematize animal-related practices.

CLASSICAL DEBATES ABOUT ANIMAL REASON

Across the span of his writings, Aristotle denies to animals reason (*logos*), reasoning (*logismos*), thought (*dianoia*), intellect (*nous*), and belief (*doxa*).[9] The crisis Aristotle generated was this, according to Richard Sorabji: If animals have no reason or intellect or belief, then how do they do all the things that we see them do? If on the basis of something other than reason, such as perception (*aisthēsis*), then reason itself must be redefined to exclude capacities that animals display, and perception correspondingly expanded to include those same capacities. Aristotle took exactly this tack, argues Sorabji, restricting reason to the development of beliefs, and beliefs about beliefs, that he considered unique to human beings, and expanding the category of perception, which he attributed to all living beings.[10] Stoic writers shifted the balance back, reincorporating a good deal of perception, memory, intention, and emotion into the category of reason but, following Aristotle, still denying it to animals. Thus the Stoics ended up attributing to animals—whom they called *aloga*, creatures without reason, rather than the more inclusive *zōia* (living beings) or the conventional *thēria* (beasts)—very little capacity beyond the most superficial apprehension of appearances.[11] The Stoics, then, along with Epicureans and Peripatetics, became responsible for an emerging view of animals that took them to be extremely limited in cognitive ability. The Pythagorean, Cynic, and Platonist traditions of late antiquity challenged this philosophical turn, pointing to animal speech and skills, and virtues and vices, as indicators of animal reason.[12]

The late ancient writers who inherited this welter of traditions consequently presented animal reason as a question to debate, for and against, with their own ancient texts lining up on one side or the other. A case in point is the first-century-C.E. Jewish philosopher Philo in his essay *On Animals,* which he stages as a debate between his nephew Alexander and an interlocutor, Lysimachus, joined by Philo himself, on whether animals possess reason.[13] Lysimachus and Philo adopt the Stoic and Epicurean dismissal of animal reason after entertaining Alexander's Pythagorean and Cynic sympathies. Plutarch, writing a generation after Philo and using many of the same sources, structures his essay *Whether Land or Sea Animals*

Are Cleverer as a competition between land and sea animals. It is really a unified argument for the cleverness of all animals, however, scattered with colorful evidence like the elephant who employs surgery to remove javelins from his beloved master (970.14), or the snake who eats fennel to restore his fading sight (974.20).[14] Another essay of Plutarch's, *Beasts Are Rational,* turns to book 10 of the Odyssey and shifts the spotlight away from the main characters, Circe and Odysseus, and toward the nameless men whom Circe turns into pigs.[15] In Plutarch's imagining, Circe gives the men the chance to be turned back into humans. The essay's punch line is that the men actually prefer to remain pigs! One of these pig-men, a character named Gryllus ("Grunter"), enumerates all the ways that being an animal is better than being human. The third-century Neoplatonic philosopher Porphyry, in his essay *On Abstinence from Killing Animals,* likewise disposes of Stoic arguments and advocates the Pythagorean position that animals are rational and as such deserve justice.[16] Porphyry goes so far as to claim Aristotle, along with Pythagoras, Empedocles, Democritus, and Plato, for the side that favors the notion of animal reason, even though Aristotle was more typically and persuasively marshaled for arguments against that position. The implications for moral philosophy and practical ethics were never far behind in these discussions.[17] Animal sacrifice loomed particularly large as an enduring Greek and later Roman practice at stake in the debates: If animals have reason, how can one justify killing them and offering them to the gods?[18] The widespread belief in the transmigration of souls between human beings and other species posed the reverse problem: If animals do not have reason, how are they able to be reincarnated as human beings, who do?[19]

These positions repeat over and over in an intertextual trail typical of ancient writings: Porphyry borrows heavily from Plutarch, who draws on the same traditional Neoplatonic sources as Philo. It is therefore not surprising to see the same themes cropping up in other genres of Roman writing—in Justinian's *Digest* when it declares animals devoid of reason—as well as in early Christian texts.[20] The Christian author who addresses these themes most directly is Origen in his *Against Celsus,* where he draws on conventional Stoic arguments to argue that among all His creations God cares most for human beings.[21] At stake in Origen's argument about the inferiority of animals is the superiority of Christians, Ingvild Gilhus argues: Christians are to pagans as human beings are to animals, according to Origen's logic.[22] The first half of each binary (the Christian, the human) has a unique claim on the ability to discern truth and on the restraint necessary to act virtuously.[23] Augustine also echoes the Stoic line of thinking when in *The City of God* he restricts the scope of the Sixth Commandment, "You shall not kill," to humans and polemicizes against the Manichaeans' vegetarian practices and ideas.[24]

Alongside these philosophical speculations arose a genre of natural history, also originating with Aristotle, that dealt in more concrete ways with animal intelligence.[25] Natural histories by Pliny, Aelian, and Oppian reproduce the full spectrum of positions from Stoic to Platonist, sometimes presuming an ontological divide between (reasoning) humans and (nonreasoning) animals, at other times formulating what Gilhus calls "a web of correspondences between them that criss-cross the natural world."[26] The natural historians frequently attribute a menu of high-level cognitive attributes—wisdom, intelligence, cooperation, and justice—to horses, elephants, dogs, bees, and other species, and they tell stories about intimate human-animal interactions, always to support some broader view of the natural world and the divine, usually with some moral for (the Roman) man.[27] This animal lore was domesticated by Christian writers and associated with both the Old Testament and the New in order to illustrate the wonders of God's creation and the many lessons it held for (the Christian) man, such as in the widely circulated *Physiologus*.[28] The scope of animal cognition is far from resolved within and across these works, which take a variety of approaches to just what kind of thinking and feeling animals can do.

ANIMAL REASON IN THE MISHNAH

The same may be said of the Mishnah, whose authors frequently grant a good deal of sophistication to animal powers of discernment, habits of behavior, and emotional range, yet at other times conceptualize animals as a form of animate property and, as we will see in the next section, presume a stark ontological divide between human and animal.[29] Passages that attribute to animals relatively complex cognition include Mishnah *Bava Qamma* 4:2, which imagines an ox who habitually gores others of his own species but not animals of other species, an ox who gores people but not animals, an ox who gores only young animals but not mature ones, and an ox who gores only on Sabbaths but not on weekdays.[30] The presumption is that the ox is able to differentiate in all these ways—by species, by age, by size, and by calendar—and to show preferences based on these distinctions. Mishnah *Bava Qamma* 4:6 speaks of an ox who intends to kill another animal but by accident kills a person, who intends to kill a gentile but instead kills a Jew, or who intends to kill an insufficiently developed infant rather than a fully developed one. The presumption throughout, once again, is that an ox is fully capable of differentiating by species, here also by individual, and possibly even by religion![31] The given in all these scenarios is that an ox is capable of purposeful behavior.[32] Mishnah *Bava Qamma* 5:6 deals with the other end of the intelligence spectrum, what we may call the "disabled" ox: if a deaf, mentally unsound, or immature ox falls into a pit, the owner of the pit is declared liable, presumably because such an ox could not be expected to watch his step. The categories that appear in this mishnah—deaf, mentally unsound, and immature—are typically applied by rabbinic law to people and almost never to animals, befuddling the commentators on this passage, for whom the concept of a deaf or mentally unsound ox likely seemed strange.[33] Disability implies ability and is generally understood within the Mishnah to be a distinctively human problem.[34]

These are torts highlights, but animal intelligence is implicitly raised in other rabbinic legal areas as well. Of chief interest among these is Mishnah *Sanhedrin* 1:4, which requires the administration of a full criminal trial for an animal suspected of a capital crime.[35] (The two animal capital crimes are murder of a human being and sexual intercourse with one.) Criminal trials for animals seems to imply both cognitive ability and moral culpability on their part, but a later mishnah requiring judicial execution for convicted animals explicitly rules out that possibility, challenging: "If the person sinned, did the animal [too] sin?"[36] Other mishnahs present between human beings and animals a parallelism whose underlying assumptions about animals are similarly difficult to unearth or to find coherence among. Mishnah *Shabbat* 5 and 6 deal successively with the question of what an animal, a woman, and a man may go out wearing on the Sabbath, and Mishnah *Bekhorot* 5 and 6 compare the blemishes that disqualify an animal from the altar with the blemishes that disqualify a priest from performing Temple worship. Do these parallels between people and animals reflect a presumption of fundamental similarity or continuity? Elsewhere the Mishnah couples animals not with human beings but with other kinds of property: Mishnah *Sukkah* 2:3 permits building a sukkah on top of a camel the way one may on top of a ship or on top of a tree. We need not be too bothered by the possibility that the Mishnah features complicated, shifting, contradictory conceptualizations of animals, however, since the Mishnah does the same for women, slaves, children, gentiles, Samaritans, and other human beings, and perhaps adult Jewish males and even rabbis themselves if we look hard enough, and the lesson we may learn is to seek not coherent conceptualizations—"the attitude toward"—but rather sets of problems and interests associated with each category.

The early rabbis' vocabulary for animals points to the same variety of conceptualizations that their laws do. They draw from the Bible their generic word for animal, *behemah*, which literally means "mute" or "dumb," but they further subdivide the term along several axes: they distinguish between domesticated animals (*behemah* used in a stricter sense) and undomesticated ones (*hayah*), and within domesticated animals between small and large species (*behemah daqah* vs. *behemah gasah*) and between cattle and birds (*behemah* vs. *of*). At times the early rabbis refer to animals as "possessors of life" (*ba'ale hayim*) and "what has in it the breath of life" (*davar she-yesh bo ru'ah hayim*); and the question of exactly when and why they use these more expansive and even poetic terms deserves further study.[37] Often the early rabbis speak simply of particular species: they mention many common domesticated species, such as dogs, cats, goats, sheep, pigs, chickens, and pigeons, and they develop a standardized list of dangerous species, comprising the lion, wolf, bear, tiger, leopard, and snake.[38]

The Mishnah nevertheless gives pride of place to Exodus's ox and is in fact entirely self-conscious about its biblicizing preferences,[39] as we see in Mishnah *Bava Qamma* 5:7:[40]

> It is the same for the ox and for any domesticated animal regarding: falling into the pit; and for separating from Mount Sinai; and for double compensation; and for returning a lost object; for unloading; for muzzling; for mixed species; and for the Sabbath. And thus [it is also for] undomesticated animals and fowl [and] the like. If so, why was it said "ox or donkey"? Rather since the biblical verse spoke in the present.

This mishnah anthologizes animal-related rulings from the Torah and declares that the rulings apply not only to the ox and donkey—the animals usually speci-fied by the Torah—but to all animal species. According to the Mishnah's herme-neutical principle, when the Torah mentions the ox or donkey, it does so not to exclude other animal species but simply to address "the present": that is, the most common scenario.[41] Animal legislation, we see here, affords the Mishnah's authors an opportunity to reflect on their hermeneutical practices.[42] Evoking the creative and often self-conscious intertextuality of the Roman philosophers and natural historians who adapted Plato's and Aristotle's views of animals, the Mishnah anchors its discourse on animals in the language and law of the Torah even while it establishes hermeneutical principles that give the rabbis relatively free rein in that discourse's development.

MISHNAH *BAVA QAMMA* 3:10: SHAME, SLAVERY, SABBATH OBSERVANCE AND OTHER THINGS UNIQUELY HUMAN

In at least one case, as we shall now see, the Mishnah posits a stark ontological break between human beings and animals, echoing the Stoic traditions.[43] We will go on to see this rather extreme mishnah, perhaps the most binary in the corpus in its thinking about people and animals, become the launching point for the later talmudic commentaries to probe the scope of animal knowing. Mishnah *Bava Qamma* 3:10 presents cases wherein the owner of an ox should not be held respon-sible for damages caused by his animal:[43]

> There are [cases wherein a person] is liable for the act of his ox but exempt for his own act; [and there are cases wherein a person] is liable for his own act but exempt for the act of his ox:[44]
> His ox who shamed [a person], he (the ox's owner) is exempt [from paying com-pensation for shame], but he who shamed, he is liable.
> His ox who blinded the eye of his slave or knocked out his tooth, he is exempt, but he who blinded the eye of his slave or knocked out his tooth, he is liable.

His ox who injured his father or his mother, he is liable, but he who injured his father or his mother, he is exempt.

His ox who set fire to a stack of grain on the Sabbath, he is liable, but he who set fire to a stack of grain on the Sabbath, he is exempt because he is judged with his life.

For the first two cases—shaming a person and blinding or knocking out the tooth of one's slave—the mishnah dissociates the ox from his owner: if one's ox should inflict these damages, one is free from liability.[44] The second two cases—injury of parents and setting a fire on the Sabbath—presume no such dissociation, and the owner is held liable for his ox's acts. Nevertheless, the degree of liability is marked as different depending on whether one's ox or the owner himself is the agent of the injury. If the person himself commits either of these two acts, he is criminally liable; if his ox commits them, he is only civilly liable. The principle underlying these latter legislations appears to be that a person cannot receive capital punishment for an act his animal commits, even if that act is a capital crime.[45] The owner is still, on some level, identified with his animal, since he is held civilly liable, but not to the extent that he can be executed because of something his animal did. For the first two cases, by contrast, the owner is not identified with his animal to any extent whatsoever.

This mishnah is more complicated than it looks—the term "exempt" shifts meaning, and logical principles morph as we move through it—but I think we can read it as setting forth basic principles by which human beings can be differentiated from animals.[46] This mishnah anthologizes disparate cases, despite some ambiguity that it creates regarding liability structures—as well as repetition with other mishnahs, something that disturbed talmudic commentators—in order that we may see parallels among the cases and draw out from them a paradigm of human difference.[47] Within these four legal areas—shame, slave ownership, honoring parents, and honoring the Sabbath—the human being is declared to hold a greater degree of liability than if his ox were to behave in the same way. Unlike animals, this mishnah seems to suggest, human beings can experience and inflict shame, own members of the same species, and sacralize (and profane) family and time. The implication of this mishnah is that it cannot be considered equivalent when an animal engages in such relationships, even when that animal is one's own and one is in most other cases responsible for the animal's behavior.[48] This mishnah thus articulates through its liability discourse, and through the biblical prism of the goring ox, a conception of the uniquely human. That conception is itself rooted in biblical themes like Sabbath observance (which, perhaps ironically, animals are indeed directed by the Pentateuch to observe!) but also in contemporaneous Roman ones like shame and social status. Whereas in many of the other passages I discussed above the Mishnah presumes a fairly high level of animal intelligence, in this passage the Mishnah lets its audience know the animal's limits.

PALESTINIAN TALMUD *BAVA QAMMA* 3:10:
THE NEEDY OX

This passage of mishnah provides a forum for later rabbis to further probe and to extend the bounds of animal intelligence beyond what the Mishnah itself grants in many other cases. The Palestinian Talmud, comprising commentary on the Mishnah from the generations of rabbis (i.e., amoraim) who lived in the two centuries after the Mishnah's codification, sets the terms of inquiry, whereas the Babylonian Talmud, whose commentary extends one or two centuries after its Palestinian counterpart, more fully explores the epistemological challenges that face human beings in their quest to know what animals know. Echoing the natural histories of Pliny and Aelian as well as the arguments for animal intelligence found in Plutarch and Porphyry, the Palestinian Talmud in the course of its commentary proposes an ox capable of humanlike, multistep strategic action. In imagining and inquiring about "the needy ox," as I will call him, the Palestinian Talmud creates the kind of dialogical debate about animal reason found in texts like Plutarch's and Porphyry's.

The Palestinian Talmud brings Mishnah *Bava Qamma* 3:10 to bear on a dispute regarding the prohibition of Sabbath labor. The background for the discussion is Mishnah *Shabbat* 13:3's ruling that destructive acts be excluded from the category of prohibited Sabbath labor. If an act is done purely for the purpose of destruction—what the Mishnah calls *meqalqel*—it does not fulfill the definition of labor. The dispute featured in the Palestinian Talmud regards two acts, injuring a person or setting something on fire. The rather complicated question is this: Are these two acts exceptions to the general principle (that the category of Sabbath labor includes only productive labor) that they, despite being destructive, still incur liability? Or are they included in that principle such that one is liable for them, just as for all other labors, only if there is some productive component associated with them? A statement by Ben Pedaya cited within the Palestinian Talmud claims the former, that injuring a person or setting something afire do indeed constitute prohibited Sabbath labor even though these are not considered productive acts. The early Palestinian amora Rabbi Yohanan disagrees, reinterpreting Ben Pedaya's claim so as to undermine its legal import:[49]

> Ben Pedaya said: All those who destroy are exempt except for the one who sets fire and the one who makes a wound.
> Rabbi Yohanan said: With respect to the one who sets fire, he is not liable until he needs to for the ash, and for the one who makes a wound, he is not liable until he needs to for the blood.[50]

In Rabbi Yohanan's rereading of Ben Pedaya, liability for Sabbath violation is incurred only when one ignites for the purpose of using the ashes or injures for the purpose of using the injured's blood. Rabbi Yohanan claims, in effect, that even igniting and injuring must have some constructive component in order for a person to become liable for them on the Sabbath. They are not exceptions to the general exemption for destructive labors.

So far we have a dispute with no relationship to animal torts, and one would have good reason to wonder why the Talmud speaks of it here in *Bava Qamma* at all. The meeting ground, a close reader may anticipate, is the case of the ox or person who sets fire to a stack of grain on the Sabbath, the last of the four cases in *Bava Qamma* 3:10. In a brief back-and-forth, the Palestinian Talmud imports our mishnah about animal liability into this discussion about Sabbath liability in order to challenge Rabbi Yohanan: "But we teach 'his ox'!" (Mishnah *BQ* 3:10). A number of assumptions are packed into this very brief but logically complex challenge, assumptions that we may see as mirroring the dichotomous thinking of the Mishnah (assumptions that the parallel pericope in the Babylonian Talmud will make explicit). The first assumption is that the ox of our mishnah, who sets fire to a stack of grain on the Sabbath, cannot possibly be doing so because he needs some by-product of the fire. Second, the person of our mishnah must be acting in a fashion paralleling the ox, with whom he is being compared. Therefore, the person in Mishnah *Bava Qamma* 3:10 must be igniting a fire not out of some need or productive purpose but simply in order to destroy. All this being the case, the person of our mishnah would appear to incur capital punishment for setting a fire on the Sabbath for which he has no need—in other words, for purely destructive Sabbath labor. This runs against Rabbi Yohanan's position that setting a fire on the Sabbath does not fall under the general exemption for purely destructive Sabbath labor. In other words, our mishnah poses a problem to Rabbi Yohanan's claim that even setting a fire on the Sabbath must have some constructive dimension in order for it to fall within the scope of the prohibition of Sabbath labor.

The Talmud goes on to rescue Rabbi Yohanan by simply overturning the initial assumption: "'His ox'—he needs the ash." The Talmud rereads Mishnah *Bava Qamma* 3:10 along the same lines as Rabbi Yohanan rereads Ben Pedaya, repeating the same words. The ox who sets a fire on the Sabbath featured in Mishnah *Bava Qamma* 3:10, just like the person who sets a fire on the Sabbath in Ben Pedaya's legislation, does so because "he needs the ash." That means setting a fire on the Sabbath, like any other Sabbath labor, must have some constructive dimension in order for it to constitute forbidden labor.[50]

The talmudic exchange at first presumes—in a "we all know" gesture—that an ox is simply incapable of strategic action. The ox would have to sense that he has some need for ash and understand that lighting a fire would produce it. The editor goes on to simply reject these limitations on animal cognition. One can chalk up the editor's approach to his desire to shore up the legal stance of Rabbi Yohanan regarding Sabbath labor, but the editor could conceivably have found other means of doing so, and he considered this solution, one claiming expansive animal cognition, to be persuasive to his audience. At the same time, the given of the pericope is otherwise. The instinctive starting point, which likely takes its cue from the relevant mishnah, is that an animal could not possibly build a multiphase plan of action based on his perception of his needs.

BABYLONIAN TALMUD *BAVA QAMMA* 34A–35B: THE CLEVER OX

The pericope in the Babylonian Talmud builds on these core materials in the Palestinian Talmud to explore much broader themes regarding animal intelligence and intentionality and the epistemological channels by which human beings—specifically, rabbinic scholars—make claims about them.[51] The Babylonian Talmud also produces a new representational schema that exists neither in this mishnah, which features a stark divide between human being and animal, nor in the Palestinian Talmud pericope, which offers an intriguing parallelism between human beings and animals regarding their respective needs and abilities to pursue them. What the Babylonian Talmud newly introduces is the suffering animal.

The Babylonian Talmud pericope begins with the same dispute about destructive lighting on the Sabbath, though in the Babylonian Talmud the dialogue is cast between Rabbi Yohanan and Rabbi Abahu:[52]

> Rabbi Abahu teaches before Rabbi Yohanan: All those who perform a destructive act are exempt except for the one who injures and the one who sets a fire.
> He said to him: Go out and teach it outside![53] The one who injures and the one who sets fire is not a mishnah.
> And if you want to say it is a mishnah—one who injures refers to one who needs to for his dog; one who sets a fire refers to one who needs to for its ash.

Rabbi Yohanan takes the same position here as in the Palestinian Talmud, though offering not one but two strategies for challenging the exceptionality of igniting and injuring: first, the words in the text that describe these acts as exceptions are an inauthentic part of the text; second, these words should be reinterpreted so that the acts do have some constructive component. Rabbi Yohanan's reinterpretation in the Babylonian Talmud is slightly different from the one cited in the Palestinian Talmud: the injurer here is one who "needs to for his dog" rather than "needs the blood."[53] The one who sets fire stays the same from one Talmud to the other, as a person who "needs its ash." The case of the ashes will become the inspiration for the pericope's reflections on animal resourcefulness.

As in the Palestinian Talmud, our mishnah comparing human and animal liabilities—especially with respect to igniting a stack of grain on the Sabbath—is then brought to bear on Rabbi Abahu and Rabbi Yohanan's dispute. The basic structure of the back-and-forth, we will see, is the same. Our mishnah is at first said to challenge Rabbi Yohanan, since it appears to be describing a purely destructive act but nevertheless assumes full liability for Sabbath labor. Then the pericope reverses the initial assumption about animal behavior to claim instead that the ox (like the person) described by the mishnah is acting constructively or strategically, setting a fire in order to produce ashes:[54]

> We teach [in a mishnah]: His ox who sets fire to a stack of grain on the Sabbath, he is liable; but he who sets fire to a stack of grain on the Sabbath, he is exempt.
> And he teaches—"he" is comparable to "his ox": just as his ox does not need it, so too he does not need it, and it teaches "exempt because he is judged with his life."
> No! "His ox" is comparable to him: just as he needs it, so too his ox needs it.

The pericope creates an analogy from the ox to the person ("'he' is comparable to his ox,'" *hu dumya de-shoro*): what we know about the person must come from what we know about the ox. Since we know that an ox cannot act strategically—in the pericope's language, "his ox does not need it" (*lo qava'e leh*)—neither must the person be acting strategically ("so too he does not need it"). As in the Palestinian Talmud, the pericope proceeds to simply reverse the claim, arguing instead that it is perfectly plausible for the animal to be acting out of need ("so too his ox needs it," *qava'e leh*). Where the Babylonian Talmud differs from the Palestinian, besides in making the thinking explicit, is that it highlights not only the conceptual processes that an animal is capable of—yes, an animal can plan out behaviors in order to address his or her needs—but also the conceptual processes by which "we," rabbinic scholars, the Talmud's human authors and audiences, define such capacities. The Babylonian Talmud's initial proposal instructs us to extrapolate from animal behavior to human behavior, but the rebuttal asks us to move in the reverse direction, to extrapolate from human behavior to animal. We are, in effect, invited into an imaginative exercise in anthropomorphism. If we move in epistemological terms from people to animals instead of from animals to people, as the pericope asks us to do, we get a different set of assumptions about what is or is not possible for animals to accomplish.[55]

The pericope goes on to probe these claims:[56]

> How do you find it?
> Rav Ivya said to him: What are we dealing with here? With a clever ox who has received a bite on its back, and he needs to burn it in order to roll himself in the ash.
> And how do we know?
> Since after he burned it, he rolls in the ash.
> And is there such a case?
> Yes, for there was an ox in Rav Pappa's household whose teeth were hurting him; he went and burst open the cask and drank the beer and was healed.

Apparently expecting some resistance to its claims, the pericope asks for a concrete example of animal behavior of this sophisticated type. Rav Ivya, an obscure fourth-generation Babylonian rabbi, provides it: the animal has been bitten on its back and seeks the ashes as a remedy for the bite.[57] Rav Ivya describes this ox as a *shor piqe'ah,* which the Babylonian Talmud's major medieval commentator, Rashi, interprets to mean a particularly clever ox, a *shor hakham.*[58] Once again, the pericope questions the evidence for high-level animal behavior, now asking how we can know that the animal's purpose is indeed what we have described. The sequence of events, replies the pericope, is sufficient evidence for the causal link between them: if the animal is seen first to light a fire and then to roll in the ashes, we can safely presume that it did the first *in order* to do the second. The pericope proceeds to seek additional evidence for the foregoing claims about purposive animal behavior, which is supplied by an anecdote about an ox once owned by Rav Pappa. Rav Pappa's ox, it is told, was driven to drink by his toothache; he broke open the lid of a vat of a beer and helped himself as he sought relief for his pain.

The ox owned by Rav Pappa may be intended to reflect the extraordinariness of Rav Pappa himself—who but a great rabbi would own an animal capable of knowing that a swig of beer would make him feel better?[59] The pericope does not explicitly deny such perspicacity to the normal run of oxen, but neither are we left with the impression that these capacities are entirely typical. The remaining pericope, however, clearly defines the limits of animal consciousness. An ox, it is argued, cannot intend to cause shame:

> Our rabbis said before Rav Pappa: Can you say that his ox is comparable to him? Behold he teaches: His ox who embarrasses [a person], he (the ox's owner) is exempt [from paying compensation for shame], but he who embarrasses, he is liable. His ox is comparable to him! He (the ox) intended to embarrass—how do you find it?!
>
> For example, he intended to injure, as the master said [in a baraita]: He intended to injure even if he did not intend to embarrass.

Rav Pappa's students push back on the pericope's claims about purposive animal behavior as well as the epistemological pathway by which those claims are derived. Surely the imaginative exercise in anthropomorphism has its limits, they point out. That limit is shame. The students refer to another part of our mishnah, that part differentiating the shame payment for the ox and for its owner. In another "we all know" gesture, the pericope asserts that an ox cannot intend to cause shame.[60] If so, the interpretive strategy that has so far been adopted for this mishnah, wherein the behavior of animals is derived from that of humans, is upset, since a person's desire to humiliate another cannot possibly be replicated in the ox. But whereas earlier the pericope simply backtracked from its initial "we all know" about animals and permitted some far-reaching claims about animal capacities, here the pericope adheres to the limitations on animals that it initially presumes. The pericope goes on to reconsider its assumptions not about animal intelligence but about the legal stakes of the mishnah. The shame spoken of here, claims the pericope, basing itself on a prior tannaitic teaching, is shame caused by the intention simply to injure, not the intention specifically to shame. As such, intention to shame is off the table, and a minimal parallel between human being and animal—both of whom can intend to injure, it is presumed—is left to stand. This pericope defines the scope of animal thinking and feeling with the outer limits marked by shame, perhaps because shame is so fundamentally shaped by consciousness of the Other (unlike the self-soothing of the animal anecdotes) and because it is the trait understood to be quintessentially human, going back to the account of human origins in Genesis.

The Babylonian editors follow the Palestinian Talmud's lead here and link these materials with the Sabbath labor dispute, but they have injected a new interest in epistemology: How do we know what we know about animals?[61] The stam's persistent skepticism here—"How do you find it?" "How do we know?"—is entirely typical of talmudic discourse, but distinctive to this pericope is that the subject itself is knowledge, and so the epistemological terms are doubled or dual: How do we ourselves know what animals themselves know? The amoraim and stammaim of this Babylonian Talmud passage also together contribute a new portrait of the animal in pain. In the case of the ox with a bite on his back or an ache in his teeth, cognitive abilities are set into motion by suffering. While the mishnah at hand highlights difference and limitation, the Babylonian Talmud leans more toward identification and empathy, not least in its nearly comic characterization of the animal who appreciates alcoholic beverages. At the same time, the Talmud may be assuming that it is only something like pain, an experience of the body and of the senses, that could spur an animal to great cognitive heights. So even while the pericope encourages a certain empathy with and admiration for the clever ox, it may also be invoking some of the same binary thinking that anchors this mishnah. Moreover, the talmudic pericope explicitly puts some emotional experiences beyond the animal's ken.

CONCLUSIONS: ANIMAL LESSONS

As I write this essay about what late ancient thinkers knew about animals, I ignore what my computer's grammar check "knows" about animals in its efforts to change "who" to "that" and "he" to "it" when I use the personal pronouns in reference to animals. Somehow the spellchecker "knows" that animals should be grouped with objects rather than with living beings when it comes to grammatical taxonomies.[62] Like the talmudic pericopes that start with what we all know animals cannot do, think, or feel, our grammar helps to instill within us our sense of differences between animals and human beings.

Rabbis, like others in antiquity, called attention to this difference in order to bring into relief what makes a human being a human being and, more specifically, a rabbi a rabbi. Rabbinic knowledge of the animal's knowledge became a way for rabbis to know rabbis, Jews, and other human beings. According to that knowledge, nonrabbis, non-Jews, and nonmen frequently recede to the margins of the human, just as barbarians do in relation to Rome, and pagans, Jews, and sectarians do in relation to the church. Along these lines, the Babylonian Talmud at one point imagines a nonrabbinic Jew as a fish that may be ripped apart and as a donkey seeking to bite the rabbinic disciple (*Pesahim* 49b). In another talmudic passage, the gentile is said to prefer sexual intercourse with a Jew's animal to that with his own wife (*Avodah Zarah* 22b).

But the discussion of the clever ox harnesses notions of the differences between human beings and animals not only in order to reinforce certain differences— between human beings and other species and among human beings—but also in order to upend other kinds of difference. Drawing a line that may strike modern readers as arbitrary, our passage argues that complex intelligence and emotion are not unique to human beings—but shame is. The Talmud insists that anthropomorphic extrapolation about animals has its limits, but it shows us how this extrapolation can work to increase our knowledge, to allow us to perceive animal capacities that otherwise we may not.[63]

Late ancient inquiries into the animal mind allow us to observe the function of similarity and difference, and of center and limits, in late ancient knowing. Animals provided the tantalizing possibility of different, only partly penetrable knowing subjects. Knowledge about animals thus served extraordinarily well to help distinguish between self and Other among human beings and to serve as a metaphor and parallel for the tensions, fears, mysteries, and attractions in that relationship. Knowledge about animals, like knowledge about various human Others, combined what was taken for granted with imaginative challenges to it. Thus did the project of knowing animals—especially trying to know what they knew—populate the margins of late ancient reality with its fantastic Others, creatures unusual or impossible, like the flying camels and massive snakes of the Mishnah, or the Talmud's clever ox.

NOTES

1. Mishnah *Shevuot* 3:8 (Kaufmann manuscript: available at http://jnul.huji.ac.il/dl /talmud/mishna/selectmi.asp), and see parallel Mishnah *Nedarim* 3:2. The famous Mishnah *Hagigah* 1:8 declares that the legal practice of annulling vows, like this camel, "flies in the air." According to Mishnah *Avot* 5:9 (and parallel Sifra *Qedoshim* Parshata 2:7), attacks by wild animals (*hayah ra'ah*) are God's punishment for vain oaths.

2. For information on rabbinic works, see Hermann Leberecht Strack and Günter Stemberger, *Introduction to the Talmud and Midrash*, trans. Markus Bockmuehl (Minneapolis: Fortress Press, 1992), and relevant articles within *The Cambridge History of Judaism*, vol. 4, *The Late Roman–Rabbinic Period*, ed. Steven T. Katz (New York: Cambridge University Press, 2006).

3. Palestinian Talmud (hereafter PT) *Nedarim* 3:2 (37d); PT *Shevuot* 3:8 (34d); Babylonian Talmud (hereafter BT) *Nedarim* 25a; BT *Shevuot* 29a–b. BT *Shevuot* 29a also asks: What if the oath taker in fact saw a large bird but described it as a camel (in which case the subject of the oath would no longer be ridiculous)?

4. *The Law Is a White Dog: How Legal Rituals Make and Unmake Persons* (Princeton: Princeton University Press, 2011), 207.

5. What Patricia Cox Miller calls the "bestial imagination"—e.g., the "lamb of God", the "beast within." (See *Poetry of Thought in Late Antiquity: Essays in Imagination and Religion*, [Burlington: Ashgate, 2001], 15–102.) Late ancient texts feature a wide variety of fantastical and mythical beasts, including part-human, part-animal creatures and talking animals. My subject here is largely restricted to the mundane domesticated animal. For a vast bibliography (stopping with 2006) that includes the metaphorical, mythical, and mundane, see "Animals in Graeco-Roman Antiquity and Beyond," at http://www.telemachos.hu-berlin.de /esterni/Tierbibliographie_Foegen.pdf. See also the well-organized but now somewhat dated bibliography at the end of Richard Sorabji, *Animal Minds and Human Morals: The Origins of the Western Debate* (Ithaca: Cornell University Press, 1993), 220–32.

6. See the many works written by Frans de Waal and Marc Bekoff, two scientists who have produced widely accessible writing on intelligence, morality, and culture among non-human animal species.

7. See Rashi's commentary on *Bava Qamma* 35a, s.v. *be-shor piqe'ah*.

8. Jacques Derrida, "The Animal That Therefore I Am (More to Follow)," trans. David Wills, *Critical Inquiry* 28 (2002): 369–418; quotation from p. 416.

9. See Sorabji, *Animal Minds* (above, n. 5), 12.

10. Ibid. 67–71.

11. Ibid. 20–29, 40–44, 71–72. On use of the term *aloga*, see ibid. 46.

12. Ibid. 78–89.

13. The text is preserved only in Armenian and is translated by Abraham Terian, *Philonis Alexandrini "De Animalibus"* (Chico: Scholars Press, 1981). See discussion in Ingvild Sælid Gilhus, *Animals, Gods and Humans: Changing Attitudes to Animals in Greek, Roman and Early Christian Ideas* (New York: Routledge, 2006), 42–44.

14. Plutarch, *Moralia,* trans. Harold Cherniss and William C. Helmbold, vol. 12, Loeb Classical Library, vol. 406 (Cambridge, Mass.: Harvard University Press, 2001), 309–486. For discussion of Plutarch on animals, see Roger French, *Ancient Natural History: Histories of Nature* (New York: Routledge, 1994), 178–84.

15. Plutarch, *Moralia* (above, n. 14), 487–533. For discussion of both these essays, see Gilhus, *Animals, Gods and Humans* (above, n. 13), 44–52.

16. See Gillian Clark, *On Abstinence from Killing Animals* (Ithaca: Cornell University Press, 2000).

17. The ancient touchstone on the subject is the much-cited Stoic Chrysippus, who is reported to have declared that no relation of justice can exist between man and irrational animals because of their essential unlikeness (*Stoicorum Veterum Fragmenta,* ed. H. von Arnim (Stuttgart: Teubner, 1978), 3.367:89 and 3.371:90).

18. See Gilhus, *Animals, Gods and Humans* (above, n. 13), 114–60.

19. See ibid. 78–92.

20. *Digest* 9.1.3: "Nec enim potest animal iniuria fecisse, quod sensu caret" ("An animal is incapable of committing a legal wrong, because it is devoid of reasoning": trans. Alan Watson, *The Digest of Justinian*, vol. 1 [Philadelphia: University of Pennsylvania Press, 2009], 278).

21. The relevant section is book 4: 74–99; Origène, *Contre Celse*, trans. Marcel Borret, vol. 4, Sources Chrétiennes, Textes Grecs, vol. 150 (Paris: Éditions du Cerf, 1969); for English translation, see Henry Chadwick, *Contra Celsum* (Cambridge: Cambridge University Press, 1980), 242–63.

22. Gilhus, *Animals, Gods and Humans* (above, n. 13), 57–61.

23. But see Miller, *Poetry of Thought* (above, n. 5), 35–59, who argues that while corporeal beasts are mute and morally neutral for Origen, Scripture's beasts are pregnant with meaning, an "amazing play of the soul," "vessels for the presence of God" (p. 42).

24. Augustine, *City of God* 1.20; *On the Morals of the Manichaeans* 2.17.54–59. See Sorabji's discussion (above, n. 5), pp. 195–98; Gillian Clark, "The Fathers and the Animals: The Rule of Reason?" in *Animals on the Agenda: Questions about Animals for Theology and Ethics,* ed. Andrew Linzey and Dorothy Yamamoto (Urbana: University of Illinois Press, 1998), 67–79; Gilhus, *Animals, Gods and Humans* (above, n. 13), 267–68. For further discussion of relevant Christian writings see Sorabji, *Animal Minds* (above, n. 5), 198–205.

25. See French, *Ancient Natural History* (above, n. 14), chapters 3–6, for the Roman period.

26. Gilhus, *Animals, Gods and Humans* (above, n. 13), 71.

27. On moralizing in the natural-history genre, as well as the construction of Roman identity and ideology, see French, *Ancient Natural History* (above, n. 14), focusing on Pliny, especially 196, 207–18, 230, 248; on Aelian and Oppian, 260–76.

28. On the *Physiologus,* see French, *Ancient Natural History* (above, n. 14), 276–86; Miller, *Poetry of Thought* (above, n. 5), 61–73. For an anthologizing of patristic texts on animals, see D.S. Wallace-Hadrill, *The Greek Patristic View of Nature* (New York: Barnes and Noble, 1968), 31–39.

29. For a parallel "moral schizophrenia" regarding animals that Gary Francione identifies in the contemporary United States, see his articulation in "Animals as Property," *Animal Law* 2 (1996): 1–6.

30. And see parallel Tosefta *Bava Qamma* 4:5.

31. See parallel ibid. 4:6.

32. This is explicit in Tosefta *Bava Qamma* 4:6: "'When it gores'—[the owner is liable for damages only] until it intends to gore." The rabbinic tort category called *qeren,* the word for an ox's goring horn, symbolizes every variety of torts case in which intention to harm is present, so that the ox in fact becomes the paradigmatic case of intentional harm.

33. The wording and logic of the text are ambiguous, and the BT pericope (*Bava Qamma* 54a–b) offers a variety of interpretive possibilities. See also the parallel Tosefta *Bava Qamma* 6:13.

34. There is much new writing in disability studies, which has many interesting overlaps with animal studies. For the Hebrew Bible, see *This Abled Body: Rethinking Disabilities in Biblical Studies,* ed. Hector Avalos, Sarah Melcher, and Jeremy Schipper (Atlanta: Society for Biblical Literature, 2007); and for late antiquity, see Robert Garland, *The Eye of the Beholder: Deformity and Disability in the Greco-Roman World* (London: Duckworth, 1995); Nicole

Kelley of Florida State University is working on a monograph dealing with disability in early Christianity. In *Whether Land or Sea Animals Are Cleverer* 963 (above, n. 14: pp. 344–47), Plutarch argues that the application of mental-disability language to animals (e.g., a "mad" dog) implies that normally they possess mental ability. On our changing perception of animals with disabilities and the growing sophistication of devices used to assist disabled animals, see Neil Genzlinger, "The Lives of Animals, Disabled and Otherwise," *New York Times,* April 9, 2014, C1 of the New York edition.

35. See the intriguing parallel Tosefta *Sanhedrin* 3:1, which expands the trials to other species and also systematically compares trial procedures for animals and humans. For discussion of animal trials in rabbinic literature, see Avigdor Aptowitzer, "The Rewarding and Punishing of Animals and Inanimate Objects: On the Aggadic View of the World," *Hebrew Union College Annual* 2 (1927): 117–55. There is much scholarship now on animal trials in medieval and modern Western Europe and the United States; the touchstone is E. P. Evans, *The Criminal Prosecution and Capital Punishment of Animals* (New York: Dutton, 1906).

36. Mishnah *Sanhedrin* 7:4.

37. My impression is that *davar she yesh-bo ru'ah hayim* comes into play when animals are being explicitly contrasted with or, alternatively, being exploited to an extreme degree as though they were inanimate objects; sources include Mishnah *Eruvin* 1:7; Mishnah *Gittin* 2:3; Mishnah *Bava Qamma* 1:1, 7:1; Mishnah *Menahot* 9:9; Mishnah *Ohalot* 6:1, 15:9; Tosefta *Gittin* 2:4; Tosefta *Zavim* 5:4. *Ba'ale hayim* is used largely in the BT and forms part of an expression that appears only in the BT, *tza'ar ba'ale hayim* ("the suffering of living creatures"), that became the major rabbinic resource for animal rights.

38. For synthetic discussion of and references for classical rabbinic texts featuring animals, see Elijah J. Shochet, *Animal Life in Jewish Traditions: Attitudes and Relationships* (New York: Ktav, 1984), 83–194; Abraham Shemesh, "Biology in Rabbinic Literature: Fact and Folklore," in *The Literature of the Sages, Second Part: Midrash and Targum,* ed. Shmuel Safrai, Zeev Safrai, Joshua Schwartz, and Peter Tomson (Minneapolis and Assen: Fortress Press and Van Gorcum, 2006), 509–20. See also Joshua Schwartz, "Dogs and Cats in Jewish Society in the Second Temple, Mishnah and Talmud Periods," in *Proceedings of the Twelfth World Congress of Jewish Studies (Jerusalem, July 29–August 5, 1997), Division B: History of the Jewish People* (Jerusalem: World Union of Jewish Studies, 2000), 25–34; "Cats in Ancient Jewish Society," *Journal of Jewish Studies* 52 (2001): 211–34; "Dogs in Jewish Society in the Second Temple Period and in the Time of the Mishnah and Talmud," *Journal of Jewish Studies* 55 (2004): 246–77.

39. Exodus in turn owes its ox to the Code of Hammurabi and other ancient Near Eastern legal traditions; the most complete study remains J. J. Finkelstein, *The Ox That Gored* (Philadelphia: American Philosophical Society, 1981).

40. The biblical cases of which this mishnah speaks are: Exodus 21:33–34 (the pit; ox and donkey are specified); Exodus 19:12–13 (separation at Sinai; this case uses the broader language of *behemah*); Exodus 22:3 (double payment for theft; ox, donkey, and sheep are specified); Deuteronomy 22:1 (returning a lost animal; ox, sheep, and goat are specified); unloading (Exodus 23:5; donkey is specified); muzzling (Deuteronomy 25:4; ox is specified); mixed species (Leviticus 19:19 on cross-breeding, where *behemah* is used; Deuteronomy 22:10 on cross-yoking, where ox and donkey are specified); Sabbath (Exodus 20:10, which uses *behemah;* Deuteronomy 5:14; ox and donkey are specified, and *behemah* is added).

"Ox or donkey": "donkey" (*hamor*) is written in smaller letters in the Kaufmann manuscript (above, n. 1).

For parallels to this Mishnah passage in the Mekhilta, where the Mekhilta extends the Bible's rulings to other species of animals, see Mekhilta de-Rabbi Yishma'el Mishaptim 10 s.v. *ve-khi yigah shor* (p. 280); Mishpatim 16 s.v. *hamor 'o shor 'o seh* (pp. 302–3), in *Mechilta d'Rabbi Ismael*, ed. H. S. Horovitz and I. A. Rabin (Jerusalem: Shalem, 1997). Tosefta *Bava Qamma* 6:18 and Tosefta *Sanhedrin* 3:1 also give sustained and explicit attention to the question of extrapolating from the Bible's specified species to other animal species.

41. The Mishnah does apply the *exclusio* method to one case of biblical animal legislation, that of fourfold or fivefold compensation, where it is contrasted with the inclusive hermeneutic employed for the double-compensation case; see Mishnah *Bava Qamma* 7:1.

42. This is the only place in the Mishnah (and Tosefta) where the expression "the biblical verse spoke in the present" appears (it does appear several times in midrash *halakhah*). A similar principle is furnished for interpreting the words of earlier sages; see Mishnah *Shabbat* 6:6, 6:9; Mishnah *Eruvin* 1:9; Mishnah *Nedarim* 5:5; Mishnah *Eduyot* 1:12; Tosefta *Gittin* 3:12; Tosefta *Kēlim* (*Bava Mezi'a*) 7:6; Tosefta *Niddah* 6:18.

43. Scholarship in the past fifty years has shown rabbinic literature's multiple lines of familiarity with Greek and Roman culture and argues that it is effectively approached as Roman provincial literature. (See, for example, Hayim Lapin, *Rabbis as Romans: The Rabbinic Movement in Palestine, 100–400 C.E.* [New York: Oxford University Press, 2012].) It tends to be difficult to show, however, that particular rabbinic teachings are familiar with particular Greek or Roman ones.

44. Translation based on the Kaufmann manuscript (above, n. 1). The first line is in reverse order in the standard printed edition. The last line in the printed edition is somewhat different, ending "he is held liable with his life" (*mit'hayev be-nafsho* rather than *nidon be-nafsho*).

45. Mishnah *Bava Qamma* 8:1 suggests that the exemption here regarding shame has to do with the fact that the person did not intend the harm: "If he fell from the roof, and he injured and he shamed [a person below], he is liable for the injury but exempt for the shame [*boshet*], as it is said, 'and she puts out her hand and seizes him by his genitals [*mevushav*]' [Deut. 25:11]—he is not liable until he intends [it]." Mishnah *Bava Qamma* 8:3–5's material on slave torts suggests that the exemption here regarding the slave is based on an approach to Exodus 21:26–27 (which requires a master who blinds or knocks out the tooth of his slave to free him) that sees it as an exception rather than as a broad paradigm. Our mishnah exempts the ox owner likely because the mishnah considers the liberation of a slave to be an irregular and unusually severe penalty, which it does not wish to extend beyond the owner himself to the same damages when caused by his ox.

46. The last two cases may have a motivating logic similar to that of the slave case: striking a parent and lighting a fire on the Sabbath are explicit prohibitions in the Torah whose uniquely severe penalties should not be extended to the case wherein one's animal commits these offenses.

47. The mishnah appears initially to claim that there are cases wherein one is more liable for an act if one's ox does it and cases where one is less liable if one's ox does it, but in fact one is more liable in all four cases if one does the act oneself. The second two cases do not

in fact reverse the liability structure, as the mishnah implies, but rather up the ante from civil to criminal liability. "Exempt" shifts from the first case to referring to a pure exemption from all penalties, to referring in the last two cases to an exemption from monetary penalties but liability for criminal ones. In the second case, the word "exempt" has yet another referent, which is liberation of the slave. "Liable" may shift meanings too, since commentators understand the liability for the ox who lights the stack of grain to be a case of half rather than full liability.

48. Mishnah *Bava Qamma* 8:2 repeats the same legislation about shame and expands the exemption to all other categories of personal injury compensation besides direct damages. See Tosafot on *Bava Qamma* 34b s.v. *shoro she-biyesh patur.*

49. The Tosefta (*Bava Qamma* 3:4), by contrast, adumbrates all the cases wherein the owner is liable both for himself and for his animal, and exempt both for himself and for his animal:

> There are [cases wherein a person] is liable for the damages [caused] by himself and for the damages by his ox or his donkey, and [there are cases wherein a person] is exempt for the damages by himself and for the damages by his ox.
>
> In what manner is he liable for the damages by himself and for the damages by his ox and his donkey?
>
> He damaged on private property, he is liable; his ox and his donkey, they are liable.
>
> He damaged intentionally, he is liable; his ox and his donkey, they are liable.
>
> He set fire to the stack of grain of his friend on the Day of Atonement, he is liable; his ox and his donkey, they are liable.
>
> In what manner is he exempt from paying for the damages by himself and for the damages by his ox and his donkey?
>
> He damaged on public property while he is walking, he is exempt; his ox and his donkey, they are exempt.
>
> He killed unintentionally, he is exempt; his ox and his donkey, they are exempt.
>
> He injured the sanctified [animal], the convert, or the liberated slave, he is exempt; his ox and his donkey, they are exempt.
>
> And he is exempt for the damages by his male slave and his female slave.

The Tosefta is the mirror image to the Mishnah, mapping out all the instances—and they cover a good deal of torts ground—when a person is equally liable or equally exempt whether it was he or his ox who committed the tort. Does the Tosefta consider the animal to be more like a person than the Mishnah does because it features the cases wherein the liabilities are the same? I think not. Both the Mishnah and the Tosefta presume that for the large majority of tort cases, an animal's acts are considered equivalent to those of the owner himself. In other words, animals owned by people are not considered to have independent agency. The Mishnah goes on from there to pinpoint cases wherein this is not so—though not because the animal has independent agency in these cases but rather because the animal cannot participate in the owner's *nomos* for certain uniquely human interactions. Neither the Mishnah nor the Tosefta, at least in these passages, seems to entertain the possibility that an animal can create his or her own discrete culpability based on independent volition and distinct agency.

50. PT *Sanhedrin* 3:10 (3d); translation based on the Leiden manuscript, available at maagarim.hebrew-academy.org.il.

51. My explanation of the pericope conforms to that of the *Pne Moshe* commentary by Moshe Margoliot, though I do not import the Bavli's language as he does.

52. The manuscripts and early printing for this pericope found in the transcriptions of the Sol and Evelyn Henkind Talmud text databank (available at lieberman-institute.com/) feature very little variation. I will mention any significant variants and for convenience use the Vilna standard printed edition as the basis for translation. A parallel pericope is found in BT *Shabbat* 106a.

53. Besides the parallel pericope in *Shabbat,* the expression "Go and teach it outside!" appears also in a number of other pericopes (*Betzah* 12b; *Yevamot* 77b; *Sanhedrin* 62a). According to Rashi's commentary on the expression in *Betzah,* the speaker is claiming that the teaching at hand "was never taught in the study house."

54. The medieval Talmud commentator Meiri explains: "he needs the blood that flows out of the wound for his dog or for some other purpose" (*Bet ha-Behirah* s.v. *le-inyan isur*).

55. The literature on the relationship between the PT and the BT is vast; see reference works above in note 2.

56. The pericope presumes that purposive behavior is of a higher order, though one could argue that it is of a lower order than purely destructive behavior, which Maimonides and his commentators interpret as in some cases an attempt to assuage one's anger (*Hilkhot Shabbat* 12:1).

57. "An ox in Rav Pappa's household": according to Rashi, *hinkheh* refers to his teeth; according to Rabbenu Hananel, his gums, which is followed by the medieval Talmud dictionary, the *Arukh,* s.v. *h-n-kh.* Further, the Munich manuscript (available at http://daten .digitale-sammlungen.de/~db/bsb00003409/images/) has *pasqeh* instead of *patqeh,* which can have the same meaning, "divide" or "split open," and the Florence manuscript (accessible through http://jnul.huji.ac.il/dl/talmud/bavly/selectbavly.asp) has *nediata* instead of *neziata,* which is the word for a cask of wine or beer.

58. BT *Gittin* 69a uses similar language to describe rolling various substances in ash and inserting into the nostril in order to stop a nosebleed.

59. *Piqe'ah* is often used as an antonym to *heresh* (deaf), *shoteh* (mentally unsound), and *qatan* (a minor), referring not to high intelligence but to fully able, normal, adult (human) intelligence; but here I believe Rashi is correct that the adjective refers to extraordinary (animal) intelligence.

60. On the role of narrative—here a narrative snippet—within the Bavli's legal discussion, see Barry Scott Wimpfheimer, *Narrating the Law: A Poetics of Talmudic Legal Stories* (Philadelphia: University of Pennsylvania Press, 2011). Rav Pappa's ox also recalls the long tradition in Greek and Roman natural histories of remarkable animal anecdotes; see French, *Ancient Natural History* (above, n. 14), 206–7. A March 15, 2012, article in the *New York Times* suggests that the story of Rav Pappa's ox may have scientific plausibility—Benedict Carey, "Learning from the Spurned and Tipsy Fruit Fly," describes a study that found fruit flies turning to alcohol to self-medicate.

61. As the commentator Rashba puts it: "Behold 'he intended to shame' is not relevant to his ox" (s.v. *kegon she-nitkaven*).

62. Although the materials in the BT's pericope appear to be speaking to Rabbi Yohanan's position on setting fire on the Sabbath, they are probably unrelated. More likely

is that the rabbinic (amoraic) voices featured here, Rav Ivya, the students of Rav Pappa, and later Rava, are responding directly to the mishnah in *Bava Qamma*. The amoraim all appear to be bothered by the inexactitude of the parallel between the person and the ox, especially for the last two cases, when the person incurs the death penalty. In all likelihood, however, the mishnah is not assuming a tight parallel between the person and the animal in the array of cases it brings, and the amoraim are attributing to it a more rigorous compositional principle than it in fact possesses. When the mishnah speaks of the ox who lights a stack of grain, for example, it probably has in mind something similar to the dog it describes in Mishnah *Bava Qamma* 2:3, who drags a charcoal-baked cake to a stack of grain and accidentally lights it. The person lighting the fire, on the other hand, is flagrantly violating the Sabbath—and that is the point: a person can violate the Sabbath, but an animal cannot, at least from the perspective of his legal culpability for it. The later rabbis cited here, on the other hand, assume that the mishnah's contrast between people and animals is built on some implicit similarity within each case. If the person causes shame or knocks out the tooth of his slave, etc., the animal's parallel act must be closely comparable. Rav Ivya addresses the problem with respect to igniting a fire and comes up with the clever ox as a solution. Rav Pappa's students address the same problem with respect to shame, and as a solution the pericope draws upon an alternative understanding of shame payments that links them to intention to injure rather than intention to shame. Rava, whom I have not discussed and whose position is cited later in the pericope, addresses the same problem in yet another way, arguing that the person described by this mishnah is not in fact acting with full, conscious intention even though the mishnah may seem to imply that. The amoraim, all in their different ways, reconfigure the mishnah's contrast between human beings and animals in order to make each one a tighter fit.

63. See the active exchange from late June 2012 on H-animal, the animal studies listserv, about grammar checking and copyediting that refuses to use "human" grammar for animals.

64. For an intriguing parallel in contemporary thinking, see Frans de Waal's useful distinction between animalcentric anthropomorphism and humancentric anthropomorphism in *The Ape and the Sushi Master: Cultural Reflections of a Primatologist* (New York: Basic Books, 2001).

3

Language

Jeremy Schott

In the late sixth century, the East Syrian scholar Barhadbeshabba described the creation of the cosmos:[1]

> God . . . wrote a scroll of imperceptible light with his finger of creative power and with [his] command, [a scroll] that he had them [i.e., the angels] read with an audible voice: *Let there be light, and there was light* [Gen. 1:3]. . . . In a similar manner we have a practice after which we have a child read the simple letters and repeat them; we join them one to another, and from them we put together names that he may read syllable by syllable and be trained.

Barhadbeshabba's account of the creation of the material cosmos as a reading lesson or recitation illustrates the late ancient overdetermination of the cosmos as linguistic. The world was something to be heard, read, and interpreted. One could cite similar passages from across the late ancient gamut: the child Jesus's precocious knowledge of the cosmic mysteries of the alphabet, rabbinic discussions of the cosmic significance of the letters beth and aleph,[2] or the Qur'anic expression *umm al-kitab,* "Mother of the Book."[3]

Within this languaged cosmos, late ancients inherited and contributed to traditions of technical and theoretical knowledges concerning language. An account of these traditions would discuss the continued importance of the classical rhetorical tradition in late antiquity. Indeed, most of the extant rhetorical manuals were compiled in late antiquity, as was most of the extant corpus of Greek and Latin grammatical literature. One could also give an account of the creative debates among late ancient Platonists concerning linguistic naturalism and conventionalism, as well as the philosophies of language that informed early Christian Trinitarian and Christological discourses.[4] Such a narrative would trace the Great Chain of Being from its embodiment in human written and verbal language through to the semiotics of thought and the imagination, and beyond semeiosis to nondiscursive union with the One.

Yet the fact that Plotinus's image for the nondiscursivity of the noetic order of being is a text embodied in the dense material of stone—the hieroglyphics of Egyptian temple walls[5]—suggests that the Great Chain of Being did not unroll itself neatly like a freshly produced scroll. The Great Chain of Being was more like the fibers of a papyrus—woven and plaited, it formed a text that might yield to a discerning reader, yet like a papyrus it was subject to fraying and tearing. The well-worn book of the cosmos, like the tattered, sometimes impossible manuscripts of a Byzantine monastic library or the papyrus fragments of Tura, was often obscure and legible only with a great deal of anxious work.

This chapter takes the legibility and languagedness of the late ancient cosmos as a launching point. Rather than attempt a coherently unfolding, scroll-like account of late ancient specialist knowledges, however, this chapter explores the late ancient "book of the cosmos" as a vade mecum or enchiridion for late ancient practical knowledge and action.

ANIMALS

Late ancients knew language as a key basis of human community. That human beings were political animals was obvious, as Aristotle had explained, because "the human is the only animal that has the gift of speech."[6] In classical ethnography, language was an essential marker of ethnic and cultural identity.[7] But language also kept people apart. According to some, human beings had developed different languages because the earliest groups of them had developed in isolation from one another.[8] For others, linguistic diversity was to be lamented as a blemish on the human race and something to be overcome for the good of human community. As Augustine laments in *The City of God* (19.7):

> The diversity of languages separates man from man. For if two men meet, and are forced by some compelling reason not to pass but to stay in company, then if neither knows the other's language, it is easier for dumb animals, even of different kinds, to associate together than these men, although both are human beings. For when men cannot communicate their thoughts to each other, simply because of difference of language, all the similarity of their common nature is of no avail to unite them in fellowship. So true is this that a man would be more cheerful with his dog for company than with a foreigner.

Augustine's quip about human beings who converse with their dogs points to the fact that late ancient people, like many moderns, were interested in language beyond the limits of humanity.

Animals were also known to be naturally loquacious. As the third-century writer Aelian put it: "Nature has made animals with an immense variety of voice and speech, as it were, even as she has men."[9] Just as variety of languages is found among human beings, so too do the animals have various tongues: "Screaming, whistling, hooting, singing, warbling, twittering, and countless other gifts of Nature are peculiar to different animals."[10] Late ancient physiologists, for their part, understood how animals produced sound. Some animals, like human beings, communicated sonically, whereas others, such as fish, relied on nonverbal communication.[11]

Thinking about the possibilities of communication with animals, and animals' communication with each other, also served as a fruitful means for thinking through practical and ethical problems. For instance, the question of animal language figured crucially in discussions concerning the boundaries of the human community, a limit determined in large part vis-à-vis other animals. That boundary became particularly tangible whenever one thought seriously about food. *What may I eat?* was always also the question *What is part of my community?* The answer often lay in considering *What can I talk to, and what can talk to me?*

In the late third century the Platonist philosopher Porphyry of Tyre wrote *On Abstinence from Animals,* sometimes described as the most important ancient theoretical work on vegetarianism.[12] Porphyry wrote *On Abstinence* because his friend and fellow philosopher Firmus Castricius had lapsed from his commitment to a life of philosophical abstinence by "revert[ing] to consuming flesh" (*Abst.* 1.1.1).[13] To call the work a treatise on vegetarianism, however, would be an anachronism. The theme of Porphyry's treatise is neither proper diet, nor the prevention of cruelty, nor the rights of animals. It is, rather, an extended argument that abstinence from killing animate beings is integral to the cultivation of philosophical virtue. In the first two books of his reply to Castricius, Porphyry argued that "the eating of animate creatures contributes neither to temperance and simplicity nor to piety" (*Abst.* 3.1.1). Thus, book 1 concerns the virtues of justice (δικαιοσύνη) and self-control or moderation (σωφροσύνη), whereas book 2 explains that true philosophers can and should cultivate piety without animal sacrifice. Temperance, simplicity, and piety were political virtues. As Porphyry explained in *Launching Points to the Intelligible,* cultivating the political virtues aids the philosopher in disciplining her or his relationship to the world of sense perception; only through this discipline could a philosopher begin to ascend to higher levels of being.[14]

Whether or not one may eat animals is the subject of Book 3 of *On Abstinence.* Here again Porphyry considers the political virtue of justice. Should justice extend to the lower animates, or is it limited to the higher forms (e.g., human beings and gods: *Abst.* 3.1.4)? Stoics, for instance, claimed that "there can be no question of justice between us and other animals, because of unlikeness," an unlikeness marked, in particular, by other animals' lack of articulate (ἔναρθρος) speech.[15] Porphyry, in contrast, asserts that human beings and animals share in *logos,* for "every soul is rational" (*Abst.* 3.1.4). If the goal of the philosopher is ὁμοίωσις τῷ θεῷ, "likeness to god," Porphyry contends, he or she who preserves harmlessness is more like god. Abstaining from the killing of ensouled beings cultivates the political virtues by liberating the philosopher from becoming and from the things of the body (*Abst.* 3.27.2–11). Significantly, that can happen in part by recognizing the community of *logos* shared among human beings and other animates. And the way to do that is by reflecting on language—the phenomenal manifestation of *logos.*

Porphyry was arguably the most important late ancient theorist of language. His commentaries on Aristotle's *Categories* and *On Interpretation* were the basis of later Platonic studies of predication and meaning. His introduction to Aristotle's *Categories,* moreover, served as the standard introduction to philosophy of language and logic through the Byzantine period and the Western Middle Ages. As this list of his commentaries on Aristotle suggests, Porphyry held a largely Aristotelian view of language. This theory of language is encapsulated in Aristotle's short description of semeiosis at the opening of *On Interpretation* (16a4–8):[16]

> Now, what is in spoken sound are symbols of affections in the soul; and written marks, symbols of what is in spoken sound. And just as written marks are not the same for all men, neither are spoken sounds. But what these are in the first place signs of, affections of the soul, are the same for all; and what these affections are likenesses of, actual things, are also the same.

The Aristotelian description of signification and communication can seem commonsensical: we perceive things in the world, form thoughts or mental impressions about them, and use names that, according to the conventions of a given language, signify those thoughts. If we write those names in characters that signify the sound of the name, we merely add a fourth level to this process. To understand how we comprehend someone speaking or writing, we merely reverse the sequence: written signs signify spoken sounds, which signify thoughts, which in turn correspond to things in the world.

Although all recognized that animals possessed voices and made sounds, not all agreed that the voicings of animals were language. Epicureans, for instance, contended that animals' grunts, calls, barks, and so forth were natural and not conventional in the Aristotelian sense. Rather than seeing, for instance, a dog's barks as symbolic of thoughts, Epicureans understood a bark as the natural expression of fairly basic sensations or emotions. Epicureans considered this natural vocalization to be the basis for the development of prehistoric human language, the babbling of infants, and the neighing and yelping of animals. Prehistoric human beings, infants, and dogs do not think before barking or grunting. For Epicureans, such vocalizations were instinctual (*sensu*), not reasoned.[17]

For Porphyry, however, animals were languaged beings in precisely the same sense as human beings. In his commentary on Aristotle, Porphyry laid particular emphasis on the affections of the soul within Aristotle's schema. These affections, he explained, exist within the mind as an internal language.[18] Vocalization is a symbol of this internal, primary language. It was easy, then, to see that animals possess an internal language grounded in the things of the world. "Why," Porphyry writes, "should a creature have not first thought what it experiences, even before it says what it is going to say? I mean by 'thought' what is silently voiced in the soul" (*Abst.* 3.3.2).[19] Animals do not merely voice instinctual barks and grunts; instead, just as we can recognize that a human being speaking an unknown language aims to convey meaning through changes of articulation, intonation, pauses, and so on, "animals are heard to speak differently when they are afraid, when they are calling, when they are asking to be fed, when they are friendly," and so forth (*Abst.* 3.4.2). Animals, like different groups of humans, have their own conventional, symbolic sounds and gestures.

Consequently, human beings' seeming inability to understand animals should be chalked up not to animals' lack of language but to the vicissitudes of language itself. Squawks, bleats, barks, and so forth, are not spontaneous (*Abst.* 3.3.2). The fact that the spoken sounds of animals seem meaningless to us does not entail that they are not symbols of mental affections. Written and spoken *logoi* are conventional; therefore, even though *logoi* spoken or written in Indian, Scythian, or Thracian strike Greeks "like the calling of cranes," this does not entail that Indians, Scythians, or Thracians are not signifying the affections of their souls (*Abst.* 3.3.4–5):

> And if we do not understand them [i.e., animals], so what? Greeks do not understand Indian, nor do those brought up in Attic understand Scythian or Thracian or Syrian: the sound that each makes strikes the others like the calling of cranes. . . . Similarly in the case of animals, understanding comes to them in a way that is peculiar to each species, but we can hear only noise deficient in meaning, because no one who has been taught our language has taught us to translate into it what is said by animals.

Aristotelian conventionalism also provided a theoretical ground for translation. Aristotle's definition, as the late ancient commentators explained, considered spoken and written signifiers arbitrary. But if things and thoughts are the same for all people, then despite the arbitrariness of spoken and written language, there remains a solid basis for the chain of signification. Boethius, in his commentary on *On Interpretation,* gives an example: "For when a Roman, a Greek, and a barbarian see a horse at the same time, they also have the same thought that it is a horse; and the same thing is a subject to them, and the same thought is conceived from the actual thing" (*In Int.* 21.18–21).[20] Hence the possibility of communication among peoples with different languages: by tracing the chain of signification from the Latin, Greek, and "barbarian" words for "horse" to the actual horse, one finds that these different spoken sounds signify the same thought, "horse".

According to Porphyry, the possibility of translation extends to communication between human beings and animals as well. Porphyry paints an endearing vignette of his pet partridge (*Abst.* 3.4.7):[21]

> I myself reared, at Carthage, a tame partridge that flew to me, and as time went on and habit made it very tame, I observed it not only making up to me and being attentive and playing, but even speaking in response to my speech and, so far as was possible, replying, differently from the way that partridges call to each other. It did not speak when I was silent; it only responded when I spoke.

Porphyry's partridge is evidence that Aristotle's model of semeiosis applies to lower animals as well as to human beings. The partridge's ability to respond appropriately to Porphyry's speaking and his silence show that Porphyry and the partridge recognized each others' sounds as significant. Even voiceless animals provide evidence of translation and communication between human beings and animals. Porphyry tells of a pet lamprey that came to its owner when called by name. Certain eels and perch also come when called. These voiceless fish are able to link the spoken sound of their names to their inner language, which includes the concept of self, the concept of those beckoning, the verb *come,* and the direction *here* (*Abst.* 5.1–2).

If the Aristotelian schema of spoken sound–thought-thing applies to animals, moreover, then they should be able to learn human words. Porphyry suggests that translation should, at least theoretically, apply to animal language (*Abst.* 3.3.5). Many birds, Porphyry explains, like the partridge "imitate people and remember what they hear and, when they are taught, listen to their teacher" (*Abst.* 3.4.4). From earlier ethnographic sources Porphyry also knows of the *korokottas,* a kind of hyena in India that has learned to make humanlike sounds in order to lure people as prey (*Abst.* 3.4.5).

In their facility with imitation and their ability to use it to achieve their desires, animals bear a relation to human beings much like that of infants. Indeed, Augustine of Hippo understood the communication of human babies in the same terms as Porphyry explained interactions with his partridge. No one can remember his or her infancy, but one can observe the cries and gestures of infants (*Conf.* 1.6.8). Augustine saw in infants' cries and smiles evidence of internal language (ibid.):[22]

> Little by little I began to be aware where I was, and I wanted to manifest my wishes to those who could fulfill them as I could not. For my desires were internal; adults were external to me and had no means of entering into my soul. So I threw my limbs about and uttered sounds, signs resembling my wishes.... When I did not get my way, ... I used to be indignant with my seniors for their disobedience, ... and I would revenge myself upon them by weeping.

An infant does not, as the Epicureans would have it, merely utter instinctual vocalizations upon experiencing different sense perceptions or emotions. An infant, in fact, is more like Porphyry's partridge, or rather, more like the scheming Indian *korokottas*. Whereas the partridge's coos and trills indicate its efforts to form a bond of communication with Porphyry, an infant plots. Like the *korokottas*, it uses its voice to work its (discursive) will upon human beings. As Augustine put it, "the feebleness of infant limbs is innocent; not the infant's mind": he points to the glaring and whining of a baby who would gladly kill his brother in order to monopolize his mother's milk (*Conf.* 1.7.11).

TORTUOUS ORACLES

For those who knew how to listen to and talk with them, animals, infants, and barbarians were all potential communication partners. Communication between human beings, between human beings and animals, and between human beings and infants was limited by the circumstances of embodiment, such as space and time. As Augustine put it, he began to communicate as an infant precisely because he was aware of his physical boundedness: "My desires were internal; adults were external to me and had no means of entering into my soul" (*Conf.* 1.6.8). But the possibilities of linguistic communication extended beyond the corporeal world of human beings, infants, and animals. Specialist literatures theorized God beyond the parameters of language. The Platonic One and the Christian God, as absolute being and beyond difference, could not, of ontological necessity, be a discursive being, much less one that talked or conversed. The divine, as incorporeal, transcended space and time, was omnipresent yet nonspatial. A human being could call a lamprey to come to him, but "How can I call on [God] to come if I am already in [Him]?" (*Conf.* 1.2.2). Intellectuals could imagine a One/God as silence and suppose that the gods "communicate with us in silence" (*Abst.* 3.5.5).

Yet, classical and late ancient literatures portray gods and God as fairly talkative. Gods communicated with animals as well as human beings; as Porphyry remarked, "birds understand them [i.e., the gods] more quickly than human beings do, and having understood pass on the message [i.e., to human beings] as best they can" (*Abst.* 3.5.5). Signs given by birds, oracles, dreams, prophetic utterances—all were possible communications from gods to human beings.

Those who were philosophically inclined inherited an already well-developed theology of oracles and other divine communications. No serious thinkers in late antiquity thought God or the gods talked directly to human beings in human language. Gods spoke to human beings through various media. Oracles were broadcast via human reporters—inspired priestesses, priests, prophets, those vouchsafed divine visions, and so forth. The content of oracles belonged to the gods, but the language—that is, the form and style—of oracles belonged to this human mediation. As the character Theon explains in Plutarch's *On Why the Oracles Are No Longer Given in Verse* concerning the oracle at Delphi and its priestesses:[23]

Let us think not that the god has crafted these oracles but that, with the god supplying the origin of action, each of the prophetesses is naturally disposed to be moved. For if it were necessary that the oracles be given in writing rather than in speech, I do not think that we should consider the characters to be written by the god and criticize the calligraphy because it is inferior to that of imperial scribes. For the voice, the articulation, the phrasing, and the meter belong not to the god but to the woman.

There were also somewhat less-mediated communications with the gods, such as dreams in which gods spoke to human beings or granted them visions of the future. According to some, these visions represented a closer contact with higher, more divine levels of reality, because the soul was freed from the burdens of sense perception during sleep.[24]

Oracles and prophecies were further mediated to other human beings in writing. Collections of oracles were an extremely popular genre in late antiquity: the Sibylline Oracles, the prophetic books of the Hebrew Bible, the Chaldean Oracles, Porphyry's *Philosophy from Oracles,* and the Qur'an are some of the best known. Modern scholars know divine communication through these collections and other oracles recorded in literary texts. These written compilations of divine communication, however, present the oracular as complete and timeless; subject to the necessities of exegesis, certainly, yet the modern obsolescence of the oracles can cast its shadow on antiquity. It is easy, for instance, to imagine the oracular in late antiquity not as communication but as a simple output machine. Static collections of oracles can suggest that they were given only to be recorded and interpreted. In practice, however, oracles and prophecies were but one component of fairly complex and by no means unequivocal conversations among gods and human beings.

The story of the emperor Julian's fiasco with Apollo's oracle at Daphne is one of the better-documented cases of oracular communication (or miscommunication) in late antiquity. In midsummer 362, Julian arrived in Antioch. The metropolis was a logical place to begin his preparations for the Persian campaign that he was planning for the following year. For Julian, though, Antioch together with its territory was also a landscape that vibrated and echoed with the gods. To the irritation of many Antiochenes, who wished he might spend more of his energies on issues of more pressing civic concern, he made a point of frequent visits to the temples in and around Antioch: the temples of Zeus Philios, Tyche, Demeter, and the temple of Zeus Kasios in the uplands outside the city. The jewel of Antioch was the temple and oracle of Apollo at Daphne. As a festival in honor of Apollo approached, "I thought that there, more than anywhere," wrote Julian to the Antiochenes, "I would enjoy your wealth and munificence" (*Misopogon* 361D).[25] Julian was dismayed that the city council had made no preparations for the festival. (The only sacrifice available was a goose that the priest of Daphne had brought from home!) Subsequently Julian consulted the oracle as to the cause of its decline. Apollo's oracular reply (χρησμός) was that ritual pollution was preventing his oracles (*De*

S. Babyla 81).[26] Julian proceeded to have the relics of the martyr Babylas, which had been interred at Daphne several years before on the orders of his half-brother the Caesar Constantius Gallus, translated back to the city. The Christians complied but sang defiant psalms during the procession. Not long after, a mysterious fire destroyed the cult statue of Apollo at Daphne and did major damage to the temple—only a few of the columns were left standing.[27]

Contemporary interpretations of the fire varied. Some, including Julian, assumed a case of arson (*Misopogon* 346B, 361B–C). Others, like John Chrysostom, in his young teens during the events of 362–63 but writing as a deacon in the 380s, contended that the fire was divine retribution from the Christian God; still others, that the fire was just the most recent evidence of the Antiochenes' neglect of Apollo and their heritage;[28] others yet, that someone had merely left votive candles burning unattended.[29] Modern scholars' interpretations of the events also vary. They serve as evidence of Julian's tragic efforts to restore traditional Hellenism, or, alternatively, as the tipping point of a crackbrained effort to build a church of paganism.[30] Julian's efforts to restore Daphne and the Antiochenes' resistance have been read as evidence of both the decline of paganism and a pagan resistance. More recently, the fiasco over Apollo's temple and the translation of Babylas's relics has served as an excellent case study in conflict and competition over civic space, collective identity, and history.[31] This critically informed scholarship has greatly increased our understanding of social, cultural, and textual dynamics in Antioch, and in the late ancient world more broadly. The contemporary and near-contemporary accounts of these events, however, present them as the unfolding of a tortuous conversation with and about Apollo and Babylas.

Julian had been privy to divine communications at least since his troops had acclaimed him Augustus in Paris. He was reluctant to accept the acclamation and prayed to Zeus for a sign. The god answered: he should accede to his troops' will.[32] Divine revelation, in fact, had been crucial to the neo-Flavian dynasty's self-understanding and public presentation. Julian's uncle Constantine the Great had also been granted special revelations, at least once from Apollo and often from Christ.[33] By Julian's day, everyone knew that Constantine had liberated the Roman Empire from the tyrant Maxentius thanks to a vision vouchsafed before the decisive battle of the Milvian Bridge.[34]

According to Ammianus Marcellinus, who was in Antioch during the months before Julian's Persian campaign, the emperor was interested in Daphne precisely because he hoped to communicate with Apollo's oracle. According to tradition, at Daphne inspiration from Apollo came from the Castalian Spring, similar to its namesake at Delphi.[35] The spring had been blocked since the time of Hadrian; having received word from Apollo that he would become emperor, Hadrian had the spring sealed, hoping to cut off others' access to Apollo.[36] Julian ordered the spring reopened. In the meantime, Julian himself visited the temple of Zeus Kasios in the hills outside Antioch. With a regular festival of Apollo approaching, though, Julian hurried back to Daphne, thinking that perhaps the Antiochenes would offer due reverence to the neglected god.[37]

Though Apollo refused to give Julian his oracles, the gods had been communicating in the months preceding Julian's visit to Antioch. First, Felix, the *comes* of the imperial treasury, had died. Then the *comes* of the Orient, Julian's eponymous maternal uncle, had also died. The Antiochenes read the writing on the wall, mockingly reading the inscriptions bearing Julian's imperial title (*FELIX IULIANUS AUGUSTUS*) as an omen that the Augustus would follow Felix and Uncle Julian to the grave.[38] Earlier, on the kalends of January 362, one of the priests presiding at the temple of Genius had dropped dead as he ascended the temple steps with the emperor. Though the crowd knew that this pointed to Julian's coming demise, they patronized the emperor, arguing that "this surely pointed to [the impending death of] Sallustius, the elder of the two consuls."[39] Then an earthquake hit Constantinople. The experts tried to convince Julian that the gods were communicating a bad omen for his planned invasion of Persia. Julian, perhaps, was invested in Daphne because he hoped to receive better word from the gods around Antioch.

After arranging for the lavish sacrifices that the Antiochenes had neglected, Julian finally received a reply from Apollo: "Daphne is a place full of the dead, and this prevents my oracular response" (*De S. Babyla* 81).[40] The response was simple but not unequivocal. Which "dead" did the oracle mean? Antiochenes had been burying their dead along the road leading south from Antioch for generations. More recently, the cemeteries near Daphne had become popular among Christians. Did Apollo want Julian to order the removal of all burials in and around Daphne? Julian knew that Apollo meant something more specific in his oracle, something that Julian was meant to understand. In his oracles to the Athenian tyrant Pisistratus, Apollo had ordered the removal of burials from around his oracle on Delos. Indeed, Julian took Pisistratus's purification of Delos as a model for his response to the oracle at Daphne. He who received an oracle need not work out the god's message from whole cloth; a good recipient looked to precedent. Hellenic gods and Hellene men, it seems, shared a Hellenic cultural tradition, what we moderns call a "mythology" or an "intertextual network" of poetry, drama, and prose. Apollo could assume that Julian would know to track down his enigmatic allusions to Herodotus and Thucydides—what we moderns call "intertextual references"—in his oracles.[41]

Julian understood that the pollution Apollo spoke of was Babylas, the third-century Christian bishop whose body Julian's half-brother Gallus had translated to Daphne. Gallus's action had been bold; he not only had had the body moved but had had it interred within the *temenos*, the sacred precinct, of Apollo. Apollo called upon Julian, as the leader of the Hellenes, to undo this pollution.

The Christians threatened Julian as they processed Babylas's relics and the heavy sarcophagus back to its original resting place within a cemetery just outside the city.[42] As they walked they sang Psalm 96 (LXX), with its menacing refrain "Let all who worship carved images be shamed!" The singing was prescient of the coming fire and Julian's embarrassment; the crowd's chant called out an imminent warning to Julian and made a request of the Christian God. The Christians' procession, their God, and the emperor also shared a common language. Julian, who was raised a Christian and may have sung this psalm, could be expected to recognize that he was the intended target. Much as Julian translated his conversation with Apollo through the exemplum of Pisistratus, the Christians communicated their anger and supplication to God by recapitulating an ancient Israelite model. God, for His part, could be expected to hear the call of His people: "A fire will go out before Him and will burn his enemies before Him in a circle" (Ps. 96:3 [LXX]).

Julian planned to test the results of his efforts as soon as the site had been purified; priests and attendants, according to one source, prepared all night for the coming sacrifices.[43] After the suspicious fire, though, Apollo wasn't saying a thing. In *The Beard-Hater* (*Misopōgon*), his self-deprecating polemic against the Antiochenes, Julian wrote that he was not entirely surprised at the fire and Apollo's seeming abandonment of Antioch. The emperor claimed that he had been privy to a special revelation, unmediated by the oracle's attendants: "It seems to me that the god had abandoned the temple even before the fire, for upon first entering the temple, the statue gave me a sign—I call upon the great Helios to witness this to those who disbelieve" (*Misopogon* 361C).

Apollo wasn't talking, but Julian knew how to make men talk. He had Apollo's priest arrested and tortured (*De S. Babyla* 107). The priest's pained cries upon the rack pointed to the fact that nearly all communication with the gods was mediated, whether through priests and priestesses (and the streams and smoke that inspired them), the haruspices and the entrails of sacrificial animals, or birds and the augurs who read their flight. To talk with the gods one usually had to trust the words of other human beings. Because divine communication relied on human media and mediums, there was always a risk that a prophecy or oracle might well be nothing more than τερατεία, showy quackery, bullshit.

The torture of Apollo's priest was not without precedent in Antioch, a city whose people had been embarrassed before over oracular quackery. Fifty years before Julian's visit, the priests of Zeus Philios had been tortured into confessing their manipulation of that god's oracle. During Maximinus Daia's renewal of the Diocletianic persecution in 311–13, the *curator* of Antioch, Theotecnus, had reinvigorated the cult of Zeus Philios, adding impressive new ritual trappings designed to impress (and dupe): "Even before the emperor he paraded this bullshit [τερατεία], wherein he seemed to give oracles."[44] Under cover of this charade, Theotecnus pushed oracles that accorded with Maximinus's politics. In particular, he produced oracles identifying the Christians as a suspect minority—one that ought to be banished from the city.[45] The oracles became the basis for a petition from the Antiochenes, granted by Maximinus, that the Christians be banished from the city.[46] When Licinius defeated Maximinus, in 313 C.E., he arrested Theoctecnus and the priests of Zeus Philios; under torture they confessed that the oracles were faked.[47]

The tortured priest of Apollo at Daphne could name no culprit. Julian, though, had no more time to deal with Apollo and Daphne. He already had other divine communiqués to handle. In preparation for his Persian campaign, Julian ordered the Sibylline Books consulted. Envoys from Rome had arrived to report that the oracles indicated that the emperor should not leave his borders in the coming year.[48]

The fourth- and fifth-century sources concur that everyone who heard Apollo's oracle, Hellene and Christian, heard the same oracle. They agreed, too, about its ostensible meaning: Apollo was indicating that the presence of a dead body—probably Babylas's—was hindering his power to provide oracles. There was marked disagreement, however, as to the deeper intent and motivation behind Apollo's words.

Writing about two decades after the fire at Daphne, John Chrysostom contended that the main goal of Apollo's communication was to hide the truth that he had been defeated by the martyr Babylas. Apollo knew that he had lost his oracular abilities because "the force that resided in his neighborhood had curbed his speech" (De S. Babyla 80). Ashamed of his weakness, "he invented a pretext for his silence," namely his oracle to Julian concerning the pollution of the dead. Apollo's communication was not a genuine oracular communication but a ruse, a comic drama in which the god and the emperor each played his part (De S. Babyla 81).[49] It was a comedy of errors: the god hides his weakness in a vague oracle; the emperor knows the god's weakness but pretends to solve the oracle's enigma. In mutually deceiving each other, Apollo and Julian aim to dupe Antioch. The last laugh, though, is on the deceivers, as "the unhappy god soon realized that his wily artifices had been in vain. . . . For Babylas prayed that God would send down fire upon the temple of Daphne" (De S. Babyla 93).

Chrysostom draws sharp contrasts between Apollo's oracular communication and Babylas's powerful speech. Apollo is a liar, and a poor one at that; a good liar would "have taken refuge in other prophecies, of the sort [he] made many times before, ingenious as [he] is at inventing a thousand ambiguities to extricate [him] self from embarrassment" (De S. Babyla 87). A better fraud would have collaborated more effectively; he would "at least have confessed the truth for [his] priest's ears alone" (De S. Babyla 89). Babylas, in contrast to Apollo, is an honest and potent speaker. In life, he challenged emperors boldly and frankly (De S. Babyla 35). When "a certain emperor" (De S. Babyla 23) murdered a hostage entrusted to his care as part of a peace agreement with a neighboring power, yet dared to enter the church, Babylas denied him entry as an unrepentant sinner (De S. Babyla 30–33). Chrysostom's vocabulary is important here; Babylas enjoyed παρρησία, the frank or free speech that only the most honest and self-assured could display in the face of an emperor. Babylas's παρρησία was measured and controlled, unlike that of the Hellenes, "who are never measured, but always ... employ more or less παρρησία than is necessary" (*De S. Babyla* 37). In death, Babylas's body continued to speak: "When alive, Babylas's frankness [παρρησία] was intolerable to [the emperor Decius], so after his death, neither the emperor [Julian] nor the god [Apollo] could endure the influence of those remains" (*De S. Babyla* 90). Like a great public rhetor, Babylas unmanned Apollo with his παρρησία, depriving the god of his own ability to speak freely (*De S. Babyla* 75). Julian was a well-educated man, one who would recognize that the god had been rhetorically beaten; he "recognized no less than Apollo himself the strength of the saintly Babylas and his frankness [παρρησία] before God" (*De S. Babyla* 91).

Behind Apollo's words, others heard the malicious scheming of Julian's cadre of religious professionals. According to the Christian historian Philostorgius, when Julian repeatedly failed to obtain oracles from Apollo he called upon a theurgist named Eusebius. Julian "ordered him to render the idol fully alive and active."[50] Theurgy, for its part, was among other things a specialist mode of communicating with the gods. As the great theorist of theurgy, Iamblichus, explained it, a theurgist did not talk to the gods. When a theurgist used specific names and incantation formulas, he did not cause "the mind of the gods to incline toward humans"; rather, they purified the theurgist, "disposing the human mind to participation in the gods."[51] Theurgy, though, failed to produce oracles. In Philostorgius's account, it was Eusebius, not Apollo, who "replied that the truest reason why it and the other idols were silent was Babylas. . . . The gods abhorred his corpse and for that reason refused to visit their abodes."[52] Apollo had indeed communicated with Eusebius, privately, and "had told him clearly and explicitly that he could give no reply because of Babylas."[53] The theurgist understood Apollo's embarrassment and weakness—he wasn't muted by ritual pollution; rather, "it was obvious that a higher power had restrained the demons from acting."[54]

Modern scholarship tends to harmonize the varied accounts of Apollo's oracle into a narrative of a key battle in fourth-century culture wars. In such narratives, Apollo's oracle and the conflict that followed are indexes of profound social and cultural fault lines. But late ancient writers read these events in terms of human beings' centuries-old wrestling in conversation with the gods. Julian, classicizing Hellene that he was, accepted the vicissitudes of talking with gods. Like Pisistratus, he accepted the dynamics of oracular conversation. The truth of an oracle lay in listening to the gods' enigmatic messages and answering with action (sometimes heroic, sometimes tragic). John Chrysostom, for his part, knew that Apollo had communicated with Julian and the Antiochenes during fall 362. He also knew that Apollo was a liar, and twenty years on he still found himself disabusing Antioch of the god's lies. Apollo wasn't mute because of pollution or because his altars were neglected; he was silent because the power of Babylas's confession—his freedom of speech—had, like the pointed words of a superior rhetor, shamed and beaten

Apollo into silence. The theurgist Eusebius, according to Philostorgius—or Julian, according to Chrysostom—found himself playing spin doctor for Apollo in a raucous comedy of errors.

Still others knew that pain, or the threat of pain, could produce true statements from reluctant human beings.[55] The truth was out there and could be made to speak itself when force, or fear, or both were applied in the right manner. After the fire at Daphne, Apollo's priest was tortured to discover whether he had any information about the suspected arson. The priest, for his part, could say nothing, because he knew nothing. Apollo did not intervene, allowing his priest to suffer on the rack. The god might have been expected to intervene, as he had saved Croesus from being burned alive by the Persians when the Lydian king supplicated him.[56] According to Chrysostom, Apollo's failure to intervene signaled that the god, too, could name no arsonist, for the truth was that no human had set the fire. Drawing on his rhetorical training, Chrysostom knew how to exploit testimony derived from torture. Those trained in forensic oratory were aware that such evidence was a delicate topic. A good rhetor could "style torture an infallible method of discovering the truth" or "allege that it often results in false confessions," depending on which side of the evidence he found himself.[57] A great rhetor would exploit the nuances of confessions extracted under torture:[58]

> Whether torture should be applied, . . . who it is who demands or offers it, who it is who is to be subjected to torture, against whom the evidence thus sought will tell, and what the motive is for the demand. . . . It will make all the difference who was in charge of the proceedings, who was the victim and what the nature of the torture, whether the confession was credible or consistent, whether the witness stuck to his first statement or changed it under the influence of pain, and whether he made it at the beginning of the torture of only after it had continued for some time.

Apollo, the great prophet-god, surely must know the truth, but he says nothing as his servant suffers torture; consequently, in either case he stands convicted: on the one hand, for lying about his prophetic knowledge; on the other, as a defendant who withholds testimony.

A NOISY WORLD

For Barhadbeshabba, the cosmos was the most legible of all texts, written in the clearest of all languages. To be in the world, to listen to it, read it, was to live the life of angels. To be one of God's angels, to participate in creation, was to be schooled, to mimic the teacher's pronunciations and pen strokes.[59] For the Platonist Proclus, language was intimately rooted in the nature of being, and the knowledge of names was a point of contact with higher ontological levels. Since the authentic names of beings imitate their existence in Soul, and Soul is an image of Intellect, "the activity of naming . . . belongs not to any random individual but to one who sees the Intellect and the nature of real entities."[60] As the body of this chapter suggests, however, the late ancient world was much more cacophonous than an idealized grammarian's lesson or the contemplation of Intellect.

The cosmos could sound more like the learned banter of halakhic debate. For instance, Rabbi Eliezer the Great once argued that an earthenware oven might be rendered unsusceptible to ritual impurity if it were cut into a stack of sections, with sand placed between the sections, and then glued back together.[61] Such an oven would no longer be an integral utensil, and therefore would not be susceptible. The majority of the rabbis, however, disagreed with Eliezer, though he offered "all the arguments in the world." Eliezer called upon the cosmos:

> Said he to them: "If the *halakhah* agrees with me, let this carob tree prove it!" Thereupon the carob tree was torn a hundred cubits out of its place—others affirm, four hundred cubits. "No proof can be brought from a carob tree," they retorted. Again he said to them: "If the *halakhah* agrees with me, let the stream of water prove it!" Whereupon the stream of water flowed backwards—"No proof can be brought from a stream of water," they rejoined. Again he urged: "If the *halakhah* agrees with me, let the walls of the schoolhouse prove it," whereupon the walls inclined to fall. But Rabbi Joshua rebuked them, saying: "When scholars are engaged in a halakhic dispute, what have ye to interfere?" Hence they did not fall, in honor of Rabbi Joshua, nor did they resume the upright, in honor of Rabbi Eliezer; and they are still standing thus inclined. Again he said to them: "If the *halakhah* agrees with me, let it be proved from Heaven!" Whereupon a Heavenly Voice cried out: "Why do ye dispute with Rabbi Eliezer, seeing that in all matters the *halakhah* agrees with him?!"

Rabbi Joshua then uttered a famous retort: "It is not in heaven!"

The Talmud then asks, "What did he mean by this?" Because this bit of Talmud really speaks to the nature of Torah and halakhic consensus. As Rabbi Jeremiah explained, "the Torah was already given on Mount Sinai, and so we do not pay attention to a heavenly voice," or streams, or trees. The story demonstrates the privilege of majority consensus in halakhic dispute. As Rabbi Jeremiah points out, Rabbi Joshua's exclamation—"It is not in heaven!"—is a passage in the Torah, which continues, "after the majority incline" (Exodus 23:2). Rabbi Nathan later spoke with the prophet Elijah about the incident, asking him about God's reaction. "He smiled," Elijah reported, "and said, 'My sons have defeated me!'" Not even God can unwrite Torah or contradict halakhic consensus.

Though the rabbis knew where to listen for Torah and when to listen (or not) to the signs provided by trees, streams, and collapsing buildings, the narrative shows the need to mind one's own and others' words carefully. Because this bit of Talmud really speaks about the importance of not causing harm with one's words. The story about Rabbi Eliezer appears in this portion of Talmud for what its conclusion contributes to the talmudic discussion of verbal *ona'ah*—distress or pain suffered by a person through verbal insult.[62] After recounting the miraculous communication of trees and streams, the text describes how the rabbis anxiously debated how to inform Rabbi Eliezer that he had been excommunicated. Rabbi Akiba volunteered to report the decision to Rabbi Eliezer "lest someone who is unsuitable will go and inform him."

Ona'ah, or verbal wrong, can be avoided if the communication is handled with the right combination of comportment and euphemism. Rabbi Akiba announces the situation by dressing in black and sitting four cubits away from Rabbi Eliezer. These are signs that any rabbi would recognize. Thus Rabbi Eliezer's oblique reply: "What is the difference between yesterday and today?" and Rabbi Akiba's answer, "Rabbi, it seems to me that your colleagues are staying away from you." Despite Rabbi Akiba's best efforts, Rabbi Eliezer rent his garments, and "his eyes streamed with tears." Rabbi Akiba had feared that Rabbi Eliezer might suffer *ona'ah* and "as a result destroy the entire world."

Because this bit of Talmud really speaks about God's privileging of the prayers and tears of those who suffer *ona'ah.* Having been insulted and despairing, Rabbi Eliezer assumed the signs of mourning; he "rent his garments, put off his shoes, removed [his seat] and sat on the earth, whilst tears streamed from his eyes." God took notice, for "the world was smitten: a third of the olive crop, a third of the wheat, and a third of the barley crop. Some say, the dough in women's hands swelled up." Imma Shalom, Rabbi Eliezer's wife and the sister of the Nasi, Rabban Gamaliel, feared that Rabbi Eliezer's tears would prompt God to smite her brother. She watched him closely "lest he fall upon his face." The phrase refers to the daily practice of reciting the Amidah, or Eighteen Benedictions. The recitation was customarily followed by personal supplications, and Imma Shalom knew that Rabbi Eliezer's prostration could indicate that he was supplicating God to avenge the *ona'ah* that he had been made to suffer. Personal supplications were not recited at the turn of a month, on the new moon, *rosh ḥodesh.* Believing that the previous month was "defective," Imma Shalom had remained vigilant for twenty-nine days and thought she could relax her watch. Unfortunately, she had mistaken a full month for a defective one. The moon is a useful though not entirely accurate sign. When she realized her mistake, Shalom realized her brother was dead, for she knew that "all gates are locked, except the gates of *ona'ah.*"

But to read this bit of Talmud as only or primarily about the privileged status of two texts, or two communications—Torah and halakhic consensus—belies the cacophony that the narrative witnesses, because this bit of Talmud is really a story about messages and signs communicated from Torah but also from streams, trees, voices from heaven, the spirit of Elijah, and God. Human beings must grapple with that noisy cosmos. Natural phenomena like those that Rabbi Eliezer summons to support his halakhic opinion could also be signs that God is angry and that a community needs to institute a ritual fast. Much of the third chapter of Bavli *Ta'anit* (18b–26a), for instance, concerns how to differentiate natural phenomena that are legitimate signs from insignificant natural phenomena.[63] The collapse of a building, for instance, could be a sign of God's anger and a prompt for ritual fasting. Yet, some buildings are poorly constructed, or old, and may be expected to collapse naturally. Consequently, "the 'collapse' spoken of refers only to sound buildings but not to those already dilapidated; only to those that are not likely to fall in but not to those that are likely to fall in."[64] The presence of dangerous wild animals or animal attacks on human beings may likewise be signs. Yet one needed to be able to read the difference between animals' likely behaviors and those that might be considered out of the ordinary and therefore significant. The presence of a beast in the city might be significant, whereas one in the fields was not. One could expect to encounter a dangerous beast at night but not during the day. Reading these signs required a nuanced poetics:[65]

> [One could object,] "If the beast sees two persons and pursues them, it is a visitation," which implies that if it remains still it is no visitation. And then you add, "if it hides itself on seeing, then it is not a visitation"; this would imply that if it remains still it is a visitation! This is no contradiction. In the one case it speaks of [a beast] in a field near reedland; in the other, in a field not near reedland.

The Gemara's objection notes that there is a third thing, a third figure of speech, that may occur in an encounter with a beast not covered in the mishnah. A wild animal may neither flee nor pursue but remain still. The response explains the nuance. Animals feel safe when protective cover, like a reedland, is close by, and one encountering a beast in this situation could expect it to flee into the reeds. But if cover is available and the beast stares people down, this is out of the ordinary. Reading the cosmos, then, demanded a literacy that could discern changes in cosmic meter and diction, between the world's mundane or natural speech and its unnatural imperatives.

. . .

In this brief chapter I have attempted to trace some of the lineaments of a cosmos known through language. In the quotation that headed this chapter, Barhadbeshabba used the image of language to represent the interconnection, sense, and ultimate legibility of the cosmos. For him, the cosmic sympathies, like the cosmic cascade described by Catherine Chin elsewhere in this volume, were coherent and unified as a language is coherent and unified. Yet language is not a stable, coherent thing. The late ancient world was a noisy one, cut across by the centripetal and centrifugal forces of language. Polyphony extended beyond the horizon of human conversation to include nonhuman animals, the gods, and the natural world. Consequently, my story line has been circuitous—even disconnected at times—wending its way from Porphyry's ordered account of a philosophy of language, through the lies, spin, and oracles at Daphne, and finally to the dialogics of rabbinic writing. Contemporary late ancient histories are, among other things, metadiscourses about a late antiquity that was always already linguistic. Such histories are the off-spring of Aristotelian science and classical rhetoric; their aim has traditionally been to know and convince. They can flatten out or erase the polyphony of the late ancient world. Here I have tried to hint at another way of writing late ancient history: that is, as an account (a *logos,* to use a late ancient category) that embraces an aesthetic of the incomplete and unfinished. This is not the same as letting late ancients speak for themselves. Late ancients, too, obfuscated and overwrote tension and contradiction. Such, indeed, is the aim of John Chrysostom's or Julian's rhetoric surrounding the oracles at Antioch. Talmudic writing suggests another aesthetic for the writing of late ancient history, a writing that brings into dialogic relation (without necessarily resolving) the sometimes consonant, sometimes discordant voices that late ancient rhetorical and philosophical traditions eschew.

NOTES

1. Barhadbeshabba, *The Cause of the Foundation of the Schools* 348–49, trans. Adam Becker, *Sources for the Study of the School of Nisibis* (Liverpool: Liverpool University Press, 2008), 117–18, slightly modified.

2. The grammar teacher recognizes Jesus's supramundane origins from his knowledge of the cosmic significance of the letters of the alphabet: *Infancy Gospel of Thomas* 6:1–4, ed. and trans. B. Ehrman and Z. Plese, *The Apocryphal Gospels: Texts and Translations* (Oxford: Oxford University Press, 2011), 3–23. The world was created by means of the letter bet; the letter alef complains to God that it should have been used for the Creation, and God uses alef to begin the Torah given at Sinai: *Bereshith Rabbah* 1.10, trans. H. Freedman, *Midrash Rabbah: Genesis,* vol. 1 (London: Soncino Press, 1983).

3. The term *umm al-kitab* appears in the Qur'an at 3.7, 13.39, and 43.2–4. Taken together, "*umm al kitab* seems to signify a heavenly prototype, the substance, essence, or 'matrix' of all holy books," though interpretation of the phrase in each of these passages has differed in the exegetical tradition from antiquity to the present: S. Wild, "Mother of the Book," in O. Leaman, ed., *The Qur'an: An Encyclopedia* (London: Routledge, 2006), 418–19; see also D. A. Madigan, *The Qur'an's Self-image: Writing and Authority in Islam's Scripture* (Princeton: Princeton University Press, 2001).

4. In the late ancient commentary tradition, the loci classici for late ancient discussions of linguistic naturalism and conventionalism were, respectively, Plato's *Cratylus* and Aristotle's *On Interpretation* 16a4–8; for a recent detailed study of the place of philosophies of linguistic naturalism and conventionalism in Christian theological discourse, see Mark DelCogliano, *Basil of Caesarea's Anti-Eunomian Theory of Names,* Supplements to Vigiliae Christianae, vol. 103 (Leiden: Brill, 2010).

5. Plotinus, *Enneads* 5[8].6.1–9.

6. *Politics* 1253a7–10, trans. B. Jowett in J. Barnes, ed., *The Complete Works of Aristotle* (Princeton: Princeton University Press, 1984; rev. ed. 1995), 1986–2129.

7. See especially the work of Jonathan Hall, *Ethnic Identity in Greek Antiquity* (Cambridge: Cambridge University Press, 1997).

8. This idea is recorded, for instance, by Diodorus Siculus, *Bibliotheca Historica* 1.8.1–4 (ed. and trans. [slightly modified] C. H. Oldfather, *Diodorus Siculus: Library of History*, LCL 279 [Cambridge, Mass.: Harvard University Press, 1933]):

> The first men to be born . . . led an undisciplined and bestial life, setting out one by one to secure their sustenance and taking for their food both the tenderest herbs and the fruits of wild trees. Then, since they were attacked by the wild beasts, they came to each other's aid, being instructed by expediency, and when gathered together in this way by reason of their fear, they gradually came to recognize their mutual characteristics. And though the sounds that they made were at first unintelligible and indistinct, yet gradually they came to give articulation to their speech, and by agreeing with one another upon symbols for each thing that presented itself to them, made known among themselves the significance that was to be attached to each term. But since groups of this kind arose over every part of the inhabited world, not all men had the same language, inasmuch as every group organized the elements of its speech by mere chance. This is the explanation of the present existence of every conceivable kind of language, and, furthermore, out of these first groups to be formed came all the original nations of the world.

9. Aelian, *On Animals* 5.51, ed. and trans. A. F. Scholfield, *Aelian: On Animals*, LCL 446 (Cambridge, Mass.: Harvard University Press, 1958).

10. Ibid.

11. See, for example, Aristotle, *Historia Animalium* 535a29–b2 (only animals with lungs, larynx, and a tongue can produce voice); Diogenes Laertius, *Vitae Philosophorum* 7.158 ("hearing" is caused by the percussion of waves of air upon the ear); Galen, *De Usu Partium* 3 (Galen's vivisection of a pig, in which he demonstrated that the nervous system plays a role in the production of voice: by cutting the laryngeal nerves he was able to render the squealing subject silent).

12. See, for example, Wikipedia, where Porphyry is listed with Plotinus, Plato, and Pythagoras as representative of Greece in a nation-by-nation list of famous vegetarians (http://en.wikipedia.org/wiki/List_of_vegetarians; accessed May 7, 2012).

13. Ed. A. Nauck, *Porphyrii Philosophi Platonici Opuscula Selecta* (Leipzig: Teubner, 1886; reprint, Hildesheim: Olms, 1977); trans. Gillian Clark, *Porphyry: On Abstinence from Killing Animals*, Ancient Commentators on Aristotle (Ithaca: Cornell University Press, 2000).

14. Porphyry, *Sententiae* 32, ed. with French and English translations Y. Andia, L. Brisson, et al., *Porphyre: Sentences*, vol. 1, Histoire des Doctrines de l'Antiquité Classique, vol. 33 (Paris: Vrin, 2005), 334–35.

15. Diogenes Laertius, *Vitae Philosophorum* 7.55, 129, ed. and trans. (slightly modified) R. D. Hicks, *Diogenes Laertius: Lives of Eminent Philosophers*, LCL 185 (Cambridge, Mass.: Harvard University Press, 1931).

16. Trans. (slightly modified) J. L. Ackrill in Barnes, ed., *Complete Works* (above, n. 6), 25–38.

17. See, for example, Lucretius, *De Rerum Natura* 5.1056–90.

18. See, for example, Porphyry *apud* Boethius, *In Interpretatione* 29.29–30.10: "There are three [kinds of] speech, one written in letters, a second expressed vocally, the third composed in the mind" (trans. Andrew Smith in Richard Sorabji, *The Philosophy of the Commentators, 200–600 AD*, vol. 3, *Logic and Metaphysics* [Ithaca: Cornell University Press, 2005], 212). See also Plotinus, *Ennead* 1.2 [19] 3.27–28: "Voiced *logos* is an imitation of *logos* in the soul" (trans. Sorabji, ibid.).

19. Here Porphyry draws on the Stoic distinction between *logos endiathetos* (internal *logos*) and *logos prophorikos* (expressed/uttered *logos*); this terminology was also used by early Christians to describe the relationship between the Father and the Son.

20. Trans. Andrew Smith, *Boethius: On Aristotle "On Interpretation" 1–3*, Ancient Commentators on Aristotle (London: Duckworth, 2010), 82 (slightly modified).

21. Nauck, ed., *Porphyrii . . . Opuscula* (above, n. 13); trans. Clark, *Porphyry: On Abstinence* (above, ibid.); Clark points out that "unfortunately, the Greek does not provide a clear verbal distinction between transcribed [i.e., from a source text] and personal 'I'"; yet the fact that Porphyry is known to have spent time in Sicily makes it possible that what he reports here is autobiographical (*Porphyry: On Abstinence*, 166 n. 402).

22. Text: J. J. O'Donnell, *Augustine: Confessions* (Oxford: Oxford University Press, 1992); trans. Henry Chadwick, *St. Augustine: Confessions*, Oxford World's Classics (Oxford; Oxford University Press, 1998), with slight modifications.

23. Plutarch, *De Pythiae Oraculis* 397, ed. Frank Cole Babbit, *Plutarch: Moralia*, vol. 5, LCL 306 (Cambridge, Mass.: Harvard University Press, 1936); my translation.

24. As elaborated in detail, for instance, by Iamblichus, *De Mysteriis* 3.2–3. (Porphyry, on the other hand, questioned the certainty of unconscious communications; the passage of *De Mysteriis* just cited alludes to his objection and responds to it directly.) Text ed. and trans. Emma C. Clarke, John M. Dillon, and Jackson P. Hershbell, *Iamblichus: On the Mysteries*, Writings from the Greco-Roman World, vol. 4 (Atlanta: Society of Biblical Literature, 2003). Early Christians also differentiated between insignificant and revelatory dreams; Eusebius of Caesarea's comments on Isaiah's inspiration are characteristic (*Commentarius in Isaiam* 1.1; my translation):

> Now, he [i.e., Isaiah] says *vision;* this is not common sight gained by human eyes, but epoptic, prophetic vision of events in much later times, for just as if someone could see the approach of wars and the sacking and enslavements of besieged lands represented in color on a great tablet, in the same manner he seems to have seen things in a waking vision, not a dream, when the Spirit of God illuminated his soul.

25. Ed. and trans. Wilmer C. Wright, *Julian*, vol. 2, LCL 29 (Cambridge, Mass.: Harvard University Press, 1913).

26. Ed. Margaret Schatkin, *Discours sur Babylas*, Sources Chrétiennes 362 (Paris: Éditions du Cerf, 1990); trans. Marna M. Morgan in S. N. C. Lieu, *The Emperor Julian: Panegyric and Polemic*, Translated Texts for Historians, vol. 2 (Liverpool: Liverpool University Press, 1986; 2nd ed. 1989). Compare the other reports of the wording of Apollo's oracle, all remarkably similar: Libanius, *Orations* 60.5; Socrates, *Historia Ecclesiastica* 3.18.2; *Artemii Passio* 53).

27. Chrysostom, *De Sancto Babyla* 94; Libanius, *Orations* 60.7–10.

28. Ibid. 60.5.

29. Ammianus Marcellinus, *History* 22.13.3.

30. See, for example, Garth Fowden, *Empire to Commonwealth: Consequences of Monotheism in Late Antiquity* (Princeton: Princeton University Press, 1994), 52–56; Polymnia Athanassiadi, *Julian and Hellenism: An Intellectual Biography* (Oxford: Clarendon Press, 1981), 185–86; Glenn Bowersock, *Julian the Apostate* (Cambridge, Mass.: Harvard University Press, 1978), 79–93; Diana Bowden, *The Age of Constantine and Julian* (London: Elek, 1978), 99–102.

31. See, for example, Isabella Sandwell, *Religious Identity in Late Antiquity: Greeks, Jews, and Christians in Antioch*, Greek Culture in the Roman World (Cambridge: Cambridge University Press, 2007); Christine Shepardson, "Burying Babylas: Meletius and the Christianization of Antioch," *Studia Patristica* 37 (Louvain: Peeters, 2010), and "Rewriting Julian's Legacy: John Chrysostom's *On Babylas* and Libanius's *Oration 24*," *Journal of Late Antiquity* 2 (2009): 99–115; Wendy Meyer and Pauline Allen, *The Churches of Syrian Antioch (300–638 CE)*, Late Antique History and Religion, vol. 5 (Louvain: Peeters, 2012).

32. Julian, *Letter to the Athenians* 284C (ed. and trans. Wright, *Julian*, vol. 2 [above, n. 25]).

33. Vision of Constantine as *comes* of (or simply *as*) Apollo, *Panegyrici Latini* 6(7).21.4–5; on Christ's frequent granting of visions to Constantine, see Eusebius, *Life of Constantine* 1.47.3, whereas at *De Laudibus Constantini* 18.1 Eusebius mentions "thousands" of visions; the two classic accounts of Constantine's vision/dream before the battle of the Milvian Bridge are Lactantius, *On the Deaths of the Persecutors* 44.5, and Eusebius, *Life of Constantine* 1.27–30 (where Eusebius reports this version as one recounted by Constantine himself in the 330s).

34. See Raymond Van Dam, *Remembering Constantine at the Milvian Bridge* (Cambridge: Cambridge University Press, 2011), which draws on interdisciplinary work on memory to explore the varieties of oral, textual, and iconographic memories produced around Constantine's vision.

35. Sozomen, *Historia Ecclesiastica* 5.19.

36. Ammianus Marcellinus, *History* 22.12.8, ed. and trans. J. C. Rolfe, *Ammianus Marcellinus*, LCL 315 (Cambridge, Mass.: Harvard University Press, 1940; reprint 1986).

37. Ibid. 22.14.4.

38. Ibid. 23.1.5: "terrebatur omine quodam."

39. Ibid. 23.1.6.

40. Compare the other reports of the wording of Apollo's oracle, all remarkably similar: Libanius, *Orations* 60.5; Socrates, *Historia Ecclesiastica* 3.18.2; *Artemii Passio* 53).

41. Ammianus Marcellinus, *History* 22.12.8; Pisistratus's purification of Delos is narrated by Herodotus, *Histories* 1.64; Pisistratus interpreted Apollo's oracle as a command to remove all burials within sight of the temple. Later, during the Peloponnesian War (Thucydides, *Peloponnesian War* 3.104), the Athenians received another oracle from Apollo and interpreted it as a command to purify the entire island of Delos of burials. Julian, then, was in part trying to understand the Daphnean oracle in light of Apollo's history of equivocal requests for purification.

42. *Artemii Passio* 55.

43. Ibid. 56.

44. Eusebius, *Historia Ecclesiastica* 9.3.1; my translation. τερατεία conveys the marvelousness and, often, unbelievability of a wonder designed to distract or deceive; I suggest the contemporary English "bullshit" because τερατεία connotes a concern to persuade/dupe paralleled, for instance, in Harry Frankfurt's theory of bullshit (*On Bullshit* [Princeton: Princeton University Press, 2005]).

45. "And that one [i.e., Theotecnus], so as to flatter the ruler's pleasure, roused the demon against the Christians and said that the god ordered that the Christians be driven beyond the borders of the city and the country around the city, since they were his enemies"

(Eusebius, *Historia Ecclesiastica* 9.3.1, ed. E. Schwartz, T. Mommsen, and F. Winkelmann, *Eusebius: Werke*, vol. 2, *Die Kirchengeschichte*, Die Griechischen Christlichen Schrifsteller der Ersten Jahrhunderte, N.F., 6 [Berlin: de Gruyter, 1999]; my translation).

46. Eusebius preserves a copy of a rescript of Maximinus Daia answering a petition from Tyre, which, like Antioch, had requested that the Christians be expelled; the rescript states that it was "Zeus, highest and greatest, he who presides over your renowned city, . . . who inspired your souls with this salvific request" (Eusebius, *Historia Ecclesiastica* 9.7.7; my translation), suggesting that the oracle of Zeus Philios served as a goad for other cities in Maximinus's territory to submit petitions.

47. Eusebius, *Praeparatio Evangelica* 4.2.11.

48. Ammianus Marcellinus, *History* 23.1.7; the *quindecemviri sacris faciundis* were the Roman priestly college charged with the official care and interpretation of the Sibylline Oracles.

49. On the importance of theatrical imagery and metaphor in Chrysostom's rhetoric, see Blake Leyerle, *Theatrical Shows and Ascetic Lives: John Chrysostom's Attack on Spiritual Marriage* (Berkeley and Los Angeles: University of California Press, 2001).

50. Philostorgius, *Historia Ecclesiastica* 7.8a = *Artemii Passio* 53, trans. Philip Amidon, *Philostorgius: Church History*, Writings from the Greco-Roman World, vol. 23 (Atlanta: Society of Biblical Literature, 2007).

51. Iamblichus, *De Mysteriis* 1.12 (42.8–11).

52. Philostorgius, *Historia Ecclesiastica* 7.8a = *Artemii Passio* 53.

53. Ibid.

54. Ibid.

55. See, for instance, the Roman jurist Ulpian's definition of *quaestio,* or the formal process of judicial interrogation, which links investigation, torture, and truth: "By 'quaestio' we ought to understand torment and bodily pain for the purpose of extracting the truth" (*Digest* 47.10.15.41; my translation).

56. Herodotus, *Histories* 1.87.

57. Quintilian, *Institutio Oratoria* 5.4.1, ed. and trans. H. E. Butler, *The "Institutio Oratoria" of Quintilian*, vol. 2, LCL 125 (Cambridge, Mass.: Harvard University Press, 1939).

58. Ibid. 5.4.2.

59. Barhadbeshabba, *Cause* (above, n. 1) 348–52, trans. Becker, *Sources* (above, ibid.), 117–22.

60. Proclus, *In Cratylum* 16.

61. What follows is a summary of Babylonian Talmud *Bava Mezi'a* 59a–b, ed. and trans. I. Epstein, *The Babylonian Talmud* (London: Soncino Press, 1952), slightly modified.

62. The mishnah on verbal *ona'ah* is introduced at Babylonian Talmud *Bava Mezi'a* 58b.

63. Ed. and trans. Epstein, *Babylonian Talmud* (above, n. 61), slightly modified.

64. Babylonian Talmud *Ta'anit* 20b, trans. Epstein (above, n. 61).

65. Ibid. 22a.

4

Medicine

Heidi Marx-Wolf

This chapter begins with a case of mistaken identity, a historical confusion over the authorship of a work entitled *To Gaurus: On the Formation of Embryos.* Between 1840 and 1845, Minoïdes Mynas purchased the twelfth-century manuscript that was to become Parisinus supplementarius graecus 635 on behalf of Abel-Francois Villemain, French minister of public instruction, while on a trip to Mount Athos. The manuscript contains three works attributed to Galen: *On Marasmus,*[1] *Introduction to Logic,*[2] and *To Gaurus.* The attribution of this last work to Galen was eventually questioned by Karl Kalbfleisch in 1895, when he produced the first and, to date, only critical edition of the text.[3] For a number of convincing reasons, he argued that the third-century philosopher, polymath, and student of Plotinus, Porphyry of Tyre, was the most likely candidate for authorship.[4] This confusion of identity in the manuscript tradition raises a number of questions about the nature of medical knowledge in antiquity and the early Middle Ages, questions that serve as a point of entry to the topic at hand: namely the nature of late ancient medical knowing. We cannot be certain when the work was attributed to Galen. But it is not necessary to know that date in order to use this confusion to explore what it implies about the general theme of the present book. Having studied much of Porphyry's extant corpus in other contexts, both his complete and his fragmentary works, I was initially puzzled why he would write a work on what we may think of as a typically medical topic, namely embryology. I was also surprised that his level of engagement with contemporary biological and medical theory was sufficient to convince a late ancient or early medieval Byzantine compiler that the author was one of the most illustrious medical writers of classical antiquity. Upon reading the work, I realized that despite its sophistication as a piece of medical writing, *To Gaurus* is primarily philosophical, if not theological, in its argument. That argument serves as the basis for a certain understanding of the relationship between soul and body, incarnation, reincarnation, and astrology, all topics that exercised late Roman philosophers.

Kalbfleisch made his argument that Galen could not be the author of *To Gaurus* on the basis of key differences between this work and other of Galen's writings on embryology and reproduction. The main difference is that whereas Porphyry argues that the embryo is in essence a plant until the moment of birth—a position that, as we will see, leads him to some rather remarkable conclusions about the properties of the womb and the role of the mother in pregnancy and labor—Galen is what historians of medicine call a "gradualist."[5] He sees ensoulment as a process that maps onto the development of certain organs and their concomitant systems: liver, heart, and brain, to be specific. However, what is most striking about Galen's work *The Construction of the Embryo* is that it too is, in the end, more concerned with defending a philosophical position than with describing empirical knowledge gained through anatomical observation, dissection, and other medical procedures during which the doctor interacts with pregnant women, embryos, and infants.[6]

As this chapter will demonstrate, despite the differences in medical theory and philosophical content between the two embryological works, Galen and Porphyry participate in strikingly similar modes of conceiving of what goes on unseen in the wombs of women. Both writers are primarily engaged in defending key Platonic notions, although their respective arguments lead them to significantly different conclusions. Thus, one important facet of late ancient medical knowing is its transdisciplinary nature. By this I mean that medical writers, although they may at times identify distinctions between medical and philosophical modes of thinking, do not in practice observe or enforce such boundaries. This chapter will argue that this similarity between Galen and Porphyry can be accounted for in terms of a more general project in which both participate, namely the grand project that leads thinkers in the second and third centuries to favor polymathy and to endeavor to harmonize ancient writers with each other and with contemporary knowledge, as well as to totalize and systematize what is and can be known into a single, universal epistemological framework. The project of totalizing thus sheds light on what the activity of medical knowing is in late antiquity. Medical knowing is the process of recognizing the correct order into which the body and its parts and environments must be placed, but it is also the process of recognizing the correct order into which sets of prior knowledge about the body must be placed both in relation to each other and in relation to the experiences of everyday life.

THEORETICAL FRAMEWORK: THE ANTHROPOLOGY
OF SCIENCE AND MEDICINE

Coincidentally, at the same time as I was reading the respective embryological works of Galen and Porphyry, I was pregnant with my first child. It was just by chance that I happened to focus on embryology as my historical test case. The situation did, however, end up being strange, even comedic at times. For instance, while reading Porphyry on the plantlike nature of the fetus, the baby would be repeatedly banging a foot into my ribs, sticking its bottom way out on my left side, or hiccupping with little tics. At first this juxtaposition annoyed me and made me rather impatient with Porphyry. But it also forced me to ask the question how such a brilliant intellectual as Porphyry could fail so abysmally to take account of the very basic and obvious experiences of pregnant women in relation to their growing children. What was it about the nature of medical culture and knowing in the late Roman world that allowed for a situation wherein the experiential or so-called empirical could be so radically contravened by philosophical, theological, and metaphorical thinking? In fact, the juxtaposition of empirical knowledge and philosophical or theological reflection is precisely the problem. That juxtaposition assumes, like the sciences of today, that ancient medicine was a "culture of no culture."[7]

If the anthropology of science has taught us anything, it is that science in any epoch, including our own, is not "set apart from the rest of history and society," despite the claims of the modern sciences to "construct reality but not be themselves constructed by it."[8] Scholars such as Sharon Traweek and Emily Martin have challenged this impression by investigating the diverse cultures of the modern sciences and technologies. (The plurals are used very deliberately here.) Martin argues that, in this respect, "the distinctive anthropological concept of culture provides uniquely valuable insights into the workings of science in its cultural context."[9] Historians of science and medicine have been a bit slow to follow the lead of anthropologists in exploring their subjects as cultural phenomena. So although one could reasonably expect that a chapter on medicine in a volume on late ancient knowing may be about the state of medical knowledge in the late Roman period in comparison and contrast with our own time, periods of earlier antiquity, and subsequent epochs, this is not in fact what this chapter is about.

Indeed, this comparative approach has led historians of medicine to rather grim evaluations of late ancient medicine. The brief historical introduction of Oswei Temkin's *Hippocrates in a World of Pagans and Christians* relates the story of the gradual demise of the once-great Roman Empire, and with it a rich diversity of medical schools and their pagan, secular practitioners, and the increasing desecularization (read Christianization) of medicine.[10] Vivian Nutton follows Temkin in his basic assessment of the later Roman period insofar as he characterizes it in terms of a progressive narrowing from a plurality of medical schools down to a "near-monolithic Galenism."[11] The other trend that historians of medicine often comment on is the increased production of medical compilations in late antiquity. Many scholars have tended to evaluate this trend in negative terms. As Philip van der Eijk notes:[12]

> For many decades, the emergence and development of these texts in late antiquity was viewed as the literary testimony to the alleged stagnation of medical research and development. They were believed only to preserve old material without adding anything new—the "refrigerators of antiquity," as they have been called—and they were therefore quarried by fragment collectors and students interested in the reception of classical medicine in later times rather than studied for their own intrinsic interest.

As van der Eijk effectively demonstrates through his comparison of how texts from Oribasius, Aetius, and Paul of Aegina all compile and summarize sections of Galen's writing, these late ancient medical writers were by no means "mere mechanical cutters and pasters."[13] They "reflected on their practice, on the expectations of their patrons and readers, and on the practical purposes their work was meant to serve."[14]

If the main question to ask of late ancient medical knowing is not what did writers in this period know in comparison with earlier and later epochs, then what sort of question does a cultural study of medicine in this period pose? It asks such questions as, How was medical knowledge produced and disseminated, by whom, and under what circumstances and conditions? It also inquires whether knowledge claims were made and accepted primarily on the basis of erudition, of experience or practice, or of theorization, and whether the ability to theorize was based on contemporary logic, rhetoric, metaphorical thinking, or some combination of these. Furthermore, if we suspend the assumption that late ancient compendia and handbooks were produced because of cultural decline and devolution, we need to ask what kinds of conditions prevailed to make this form of knowledge production desirable. In other words, the questions that a cultural history of late antique medicine asks are tied to how medical knowing as an activity could occur and the intellectual and social resources that such knowing required.

This chapter cannot answer all these questions, but it will endeavor to provide a picture of how late ancient medical theorists engaged with their subject matter, with earlier authorities, and with their contemporary rivals by exploring the interesting case of mistaken identity with which it began.

WHY EMBRYOLOGY?

Although the larger points of this essay concerning late ancient medical knowing could be made using a different topic—for instance, the form and function of certain body parts or systems, or a specific illness and its treatment, such as melancholy—embryology is a particularly apt place to focus attention for a number of reasons. First, as Galen himself notes, it is a subject area common to both philosophers and medical writers:[15]

> Philosophers, too, have addressed the subject of the construction of the embryo but have provided no anatomical basis for their statements. And it is really little wonder that such people miss the truth—and also, incidentally, disagree among themselves.

Additionally, there are more interesting theoretical reasons for doing comparative embryology of the sort attempted here. First, in contrast to today, when medical professionals give the impression that what goes on in the wombs of pregnant women is immediately and empirically accessible to doctors and their various assistants by means of a panoply of monitoring techniques, in antiquity, the womb and its contents and processes were largely a mystery. However, and more important, embryos then and now were and are made to carry all kinds of cultural and social meanings. As Gwynn Kessler's book *Conceiving Israel: The Fetus in Rabbinic Narratives* demonstrates, philosophical, religious, and medical experts "call forth the fetus to articulate, essentialize, and embody that which is central" to social groups at critical junctures in their formation and existence.[16] The embryologies of antiquity are no exception in this regard. The main issues that most exercised medical and philosophical writers were: How does the body come to be ensouled, by what kind (or kinds) of soul (or souls), under the guidance of what sort of cosmic and spiritual agents, and for what reasons—as reward or punishment, as trial and purification, or as help to other creatures? Galen's concerns in *The Construction of the Embryo* are no exception.

GALEN'S *CONSTRUCTION OF THE EMBRYO*

As mentioned earlier, Galen argues for a gradualist theory of fetal development. But he is very particular about the order in which various organs and systems come into existence. Whereas in many of his other medical works, Galen's opponents are other anatomists, such as the Hellenistic Erasistratus or contemporary doctors in Rome who belonged to the Methodist or Empiricist schools, in this work Galen's main opponents are philosophers—Stoics, Epicureans, and Peripatetics. He claims to be superior in his knowledge to philosophers of these schools, whom we may also call gradualists, based on his anatomical exercises, on his frequent dissections and vivisections. He accuses them of speaking regarding things they cannot possibly know about based on the fact that their approach is purely theoretical. And yet, when he comes to argue that the liver must be the first organ to develop, in opposition to the view he attributes to the Stoics and Peripatetics that the heart is first, his reasoning is also purely theoretical. In other words, just when we would expect Galen to enforce the distinction between medical and philosophical knowledge, he turns to Plato's tripartite structure of the soul, as found in the *Timaeus*, as the pattern for his account of embryonic development. In the *Timaeus*, the liver is associated with the nutritive soul, the plantlike soul. The heart is associated with the passions; known also as the spirited part of the human being, it is characterized by and represents the form of life that human beings share with all animals. In many later Platonists, this animal soul is conflated or harmonized with Aristotle's definition of animal as characterized by locomotion. (That is, passion or emotion and locomotion are seen together to be characteristic of the difference between plants and animals.) This Aristotelian concept of locomotion will be very important to Porphyry's own embryological theory. Finally, the brain, the center of higher rational thought, develops and distinguishes human beings from other animals. Furthermore, Galen argues, it is the center of the nerves. This is contrary to the Stoic view, which holds that the heart is the first organ to develop and that it is also the center of the nervous system.[17]

In general, then, Galen marshals his observations as a medical practitioner and anatomist in the service of defending the Platonic tripartite structure of human nature as it maps onto embryological development in an endeavor to counter the views not of other medical theorists but of Stoic and Peripatetic philosophers.

Not only is he at pains to establish the plausibility and fitness of Plato's account; he also defends a certain understanding of Nature as providential and demiurgical. Here his opponents are not Stoics and Peripatetics but Epicureans.[18] Galen writes that when doctors describe the embryo as constructed by Nature, "they are making some utterance which amounts to more than a commonplace."[19] He calls on the philosophers to help him to identify what this Nature is:[20]

> Now I have shown that the structure of our bodies manifests an incredible degree of intelligence and power of the one who made it; and so I would hope that the philosophers could show me the identity of the maker. Is it a wise and powerful god, who has considered in advance how each animal's body should be constructed? And second, what is this power of his, by which he carried out the design he envisaged? Is it some sort of soul apart from that of the god?

Here Galen hopes that philosophy could help to defeat the position of the Epicureans, based as it was on Democritus's atomism, which held that "everything happens without design."[21] And here, too, Galen hopes that the philosophers will support the view that Nature is something like Plato's Demiurge in the *Timaeus* and further that this Demiurge delegates the creation of lesser animals to lesser gods, as we find in the Platonic work. Although Galen appears to be handing on the baton to philosophers and soliciting their aid, we should keep in mind the fact that he wrote a treatise entitled *Why the Best Doctor Is Also a Philosopher*, and we should also bear in mind that Galen was unabashed about emphasizing his superiority over his contemporary medical practitioners. Hence his appeal to philosophers for aid may not have been entirely sincere. We suspect that he may have felt himself perfectly capable of solving these quandaries all on his own.

At the very end of *The Construction of the Embryo,* Galen concludes what he knows and what he holds as belief:[22]

> So only this do I believe myself able to state definitely about the cause of construction within animals: that it involves an enormous degree of skill and intelligence, and that after this construction the body is managed throughout its life by three causes of motion: that from the brain through the nerves and muscle; that from the heart through arteries; and that from the liver through the veins.

In general, then, Galen's embryology is driven by a set of questions shared by medical theorists and philosophers alike, and his conclusions are guided by the application and interpretation of Platonic principles. Having observed this episte-mological state of affairs in the case of the second-century Galen, we find it less of a surprise that the third-century Porphyry writes on the same topic and does so in a way that also makes it impossible to distinguish medical, philosophical, and religious thinking.

PORPHYRY'S *TO GAURUS: ON THE FORMATION OF EMBRYOS*

As noted earlier, Porphyry's main aim in *To Gaurus* is to defend the view that the embryo or fetus is characterized by a plantlike existence until the moment of its birth. Despite the fact that Porphyry uses categories more like Aristotelian ones to distinguish various orders of soul—that is, his main distinction seems to be between the nutritive or generative soul and that associated with sensation, desire, and locomotion—or categories that are a hybrid between the Aristotelian and Platonic tripartite schemas, his ultimate understanding of these differences is, as James Wilberding emphasizes, Neoplatonic. In other words, it depends on a Plotinian understanding of participation and ontological hierarchy.

The way that Wilberding explains the Porphyrian interpretation is through the language of engagement (i.e., participation). Engagement means being "linked into the ontological hierarchy" through some connection to what is superior.[23] On Porphyry's account, the sole producer of the seed that enters the womb is the father's lowest soul (*phutikē*).[24] Once the seed enters the mother's womb, it is disengaged from the father and engaged by the mother's nature, which not only supplies it with suitable matter (the sole function of the mother in the Aristotelian account) but also helps to form it in the role of a demiurge.[25] So it becomes engaged to the mother's nature (*phusis*). In order to account for why the child can resemble both parents, Porphyry argues that this engagement can lead to changes in the seminal *phusis* supplied by the father in a number of ways. First, the mother's inherent *logos* can affect the fetus. (The association of *phusis* and *logos* here may be an example of the incorporation of Stoic elements into late Roman Platonism.) But the *logoi* of her *phantasia* can also affect the fetus, at least at the moment of conception. In other words, her thoughts at this very crucial moment also have profound implications for the development of the embryo. In this way, Porphyry's theory of engagement takes account of the popular ancient notion that at the moment of conception, if the mother forms an image in her *phantasia* of, for instance, a lover other than the father, or Alexander the Great, or conversely of something horrible and deformed, this image may affect the formation of the fetus through imprinting or sealing of this alternative *logos* on the unborn child. All this is asserted by Porphyry in order to lend support to his main argument: that the descended soul "has no role to play in the actual formation of the embryo."[26] This assertion amounts to denying that the embryo is in possession of a self-moving soul, and hence it must be, in essence, a plant.

In order to argue for this position, Porphyry elaborates on a number of plant-related metaphors. The first of these pertains to the way plants grow, rooted in moist media, deriving their nourishment thus, and not by ingesting food through the mouth.[27] Moisture, in the form of both water and blood, is associated with the nutritive or vegetative nature in other works of Porphyry, and it is part of the reason why he finds blood sacrifice so objectionable, given the fact that it makes damp and heavy otherwise more ethereal spirits, namely daemons, who then inhabit lower spheres of the cosmos than they should, creating havoc and disharmony.[28] The second metaphor he uses is of fruit, which when ripe drops from the tree.[29] In both these metaphors, the umbilical cord is of central symbolical importance to Porphyry's argument that the embryo is in essence a plant. In the first case, the cord is like the plant's root; in the second, it is the stem. Finally, Porphyry also talks about the relationship between embryo and womb as akin to a graft of one sort of branch onto another tree.

Not surprisingly, the idea that the embryo is merely a plant leads Porphyry to posit some rather interesting explanations for a number of the experiences women have while pregnant. He presents these in response to possible objections to his position. He summarizes these objections in the following passage:[30]

> But they say that embryos move locally and receive sensations or burning heat because they jump whenever the mother's belly encounters the burning air in the baths, and others have more generously posited that embryos even have the bizarre appetites to which the mothers are subject throughout the duration of the pregnancy.

In answer to these objections, Porphyry attributes some startling albeit not unprecedented qualities to the womb. Like certain of his predecessors, including Plato, Porphyry asserts that the genitals (including the womb) are unruly and self-willing, "like an animal that does not obey reason."[31] The genitals of men and women, on Porphyry's interpretation, have locomotion and appetite, and they are subject to representation.[32] In the case of women, he is referring to a traditional view that many female afflictions, especially psychological ones, can be accounted for by the unruly nature of the womb and its tendency to wander in the body, causing havoc of all kinds.[33] The question may be asked whether this view involves Porphyry in an interesting contradiction, namely that while denying the embryo an animal soul by denying it locomotion, he seems to posit an extra and distinct animallike soul for the genitals. Porphyry does not address this issue, but he does account for what women experience as fetal movement by using digestion as an analogue:[34]

> And how could it be owing to impulse and representation that spatial motions belong to embryos, which are rooted by the umbilical cord, when these motions are rather like the turning motion of the bowels and the vibration of organs in cases of flatulence?

In other words, what women have tended to experience as the fetus kicking and moving in the womb Porphyry explains as uterine gas. Digestion is analogous for Porphyry, because once food has passed through the throat, "there is no consciousness of the processes of digestion."[35] Like the growth and development of the embryo, the decoction, distillation, and general transformation of food into blood, *pneuma,* and other substances that enliven and sustain the body are hidden to us, inaccessible, and hence in need of interpretation by medical and scientific experts.

Porphyry reaches his conclusions about uterine movements based on how he conceives of the interaction between souls and bodies and his idea of engagement. Because he draws on a Plotinian notion of hierarchy, as described earlier, movement in the womb cannot be the result of the embryo's own faculties of emotion and representation. Although his conclusion may strike us as odd, and his digestive analogy as somewhat rude and demeaning, the question we should be asking in light of Porphyry's explanation is not how an educated polymath well versed in contemporary medical and biological theory could come up with such an account, which flies in the face of contravening empirical evidence. What is Porphyry's ultimate aim in defending the position that the embryo is a plant until the moment of birth? What are the larger debates in which he is involved?

Like Galen before him, Porphyry is involved in countering certain basic Stoic views. In general, Porphyry sees the Stoics as materialists, and hence he takes their position to be godless, in much the same way as Galen charged the Epicureans with impiety toward Nature or the Demiurge. Porphyry accuses the Stoics of generating everything "from the bottom up through different kinds and accumulations of motions," whereas the Platonists know that "one ought to proceed from the better to the lesser."[36] He uses Chrysippus's assertion that the air imparts *pneuma* to the child as an example of the Stoics' problematic materialism.[37] The term *pneuma* admits of a great deal of ambiguity and a wide variety of interpretations including breath, spirit, and air. Whereas the Stoics, on Porphyry's account, appear to argue that the embryo's soul emerges as a result of the material processes that occur as the child grows, he wishes to argue that the soul is received from higher spheres.

Furthermore, Porphyry is involved in an even more important ancient debate, one that concerns astrology and the very practical problem of how to determine the horoscope of an individual. This problem is best highlighted in ancient discussions of twins. As Véronique Dasen explains, the reason why questions about twins exercised medical, philosophical, and religious writers to the degree that they did was because of the way these questions brought together problems of embryology and astrology. The main question at issue was whether to take the horoscope of an individual at the moment of conception or at the moment of birth.[38] This debate served as fodder for detractors from astrology, such as Sextus Empiricus, who also used medicine to demonstrate the absurdity of the science. The gradualist view that conception is a long process also lent support to these skeptics. Porphyry circumvents the difficulty of the unreliable and fidgety calculus used by those who held the view that one's horoscope should be taken at the moment of conception by taking the view—which he attributes to those astrological masters the Chaldaeans—that the soul enters the body at birth.[39]

There are a number of facets of Porphyry's embryological and astrological theory that should be noted for the window that they provide us with onto late Roman medical knowing and its connection with religious and in particular astrological thinking. First, he asserts that the union of soul with body can happen only at the moment of birth, because the soul chooses a body appropriate to it, a body that must be fully formed in some sense. He describes this choosing in terms of the Platonic idea of cosmic harmony:[40]

> However, regarding the corporeal and irrational substance, what is lacking in terms of its being joined to [a captain] at birth is provided and afforded by the universe, [in the form of] any individual soul that comes to be present to [the body] that has been brought forth at just the right moment and comes to be in harmony with the instrumental body that is suited to receive it.[40]

In other words, the cosmos is a divine matchmaker between various types of souls and bodies.[41] Porphyry emphasizes this harmony by comparing it with contemporary scientific accounts of other natural processes, namely vision and magnetism.[42]

The second and related facet of Porphyry's account is explicitly astrological. Following the theory of the Chaldaeans, he claims that the souls that descend into suitable bodies do so via a stream "that moves and turns the cosmos and brings life to everything in it by sending them their own souls."[43] These souls descend through a portal in the East in this cosmic swirl, which is opened according to the degrees of the zodiac: "And every degree, when it came to be around at this eastern region, which is a portal of souls and the spiritual inlet of the universe, is given special powers."[44] Hence Porphyry follows what he takes to be the Chaldaean astrological view that souls descend to bodies at the moment of birth, not at conception, because it is only then that the body is sufficiently formed for the appropriate cosmic soul to know whether this body will be fitting or not. This is because, according to Porphyry, form is not just exterior shape; rather, it is the "full completion of the formation—the perfection of its exterior shape as well as of its inner parts and everything else, the sinews and bones, the arteries and veins: that is, the observed completeness of the production of all its organs."[45] Furthermore, sensation cannot be present in organs that aren't fully formed. But for the soul to be capable of representation it must have the proper sensory organs. Incomplete organs aren't obstructive to the vegetative power, because there the embryo is engaged by the mother's nutritive nature. But they would be obstructive for sensation and representation. This is the main difference between the existence of the soul apart from and in relation to the body. The soul without a body sees, senses, and desires as a whole, but once embodied it must do so through distinct parts and apertures.[46]

Porphyry's opinions on the subject of ensoulment and astrology are part of an even larger framework of Platonic and Homeric interpretation. (And indeed he seems to have seen Homer and Plato as in essential agreement.) Not only is he concerned, like many of his near contemporaries, including Origen (especially in his *On First Principles*), about the preexistence of the soul and how and why it comes to be united with a body. He is also exercised by questions about the afterlife and reincarnation (as is Origen). And he looks across a number of ancient sources for affirmation of what he holds as the correct view on these subjects. In the case of his embryology, he turns to the Chaldaeans. For his account of souls' entering and departing the sublunary sphere, in his work *On the Cave of the Nymphs* he turns to Homer; and in his work *On What Is in Our Power*, to Plato's Myth of Er. For his understanding of the afterlife, in his treatise *On the River Styx* he again engages in figural interpretation of Homeric myth.

In general, then, Porphyry's *To Gaurus* is important for understanding late ancient medical thinking because it reveals a high degree of continuity with earlier medical theory in terms of its engagement with philosophical and theological questions and concerns. It participates in a very broad, flexible, universal, even totalizing understanding of *scientia*. For both Galen and Porphyry, thinking about health, healing, the body, and life was inextricably bound up with thinking about divinity and cosmology. Both writers carry on a long lineage of medical and biological thinking that stretches all the way back to certain works in the Hippocratic corpus: for instance, *On the Sacred Disease,* a work equally as involved in making an argument about theodicy as a medical one. For Porphyry, however, thinking in a medical vein also means thinking about a range of spirits, about astrology and eschatology. In this respect, he represents something new or different about late ancient medical knowing—a more intense and global theologizing of medicine than we find in Galen's works. In Porphyry, we see how medical knowing concerns itself with ordering entire bodies of knowledge to create a systematic whole.

Hence, despite the similarity between Galen and Porphyry, we cannot understand the latter's own world of knowledge without noting a few key differences between these two thinkers. In general, Galen tends to align himself with two main ancient authorities, namely the Hippocratic works and Plato, and to leave most of his other sources uncited.[47] Porphyry, on the other hand, lived and wrote in what we may call a post-Ammonian, post-Plotinian thought world. Although we know little about Ammonius Saccas and have none of his writings, if ever he did write, Elizabeth Depalma Digeser has convincingly demonstrated that one of the main tenets of his school was a belief in and the pursuit of the harmonization of Plato and Aristotle.[48] Furthermore, starting in the second century and continuing into the third, philosophers increasingly sought to establish a lineage from Pythagoras through Plato to the present age. These totalizing programs changed the complexion of Platonic thought. And with Plotinus, we add another, more-mystical dimension to contemporary Platonism.[49] The third century is also a time when philosophers, theologians, and ritualists of various stripes began to develop totalizing discourses about the realm of spirits. These "daemonologies," as I call them elsewhere, aimed to identify and order the realm of spirits in clear, hierarchical ways, mapping moral taxonomy onto ontological difference.[50] Some of these discourses (for instance, Iamblichus's *On the Mysteries*) also sought to establish rules and procedures for interacting with these various spiritual levels. Whereas Galen's main religious or theological interest in his embryological works is in establishing that some sort of god or soul is the best way to interpret what medical practitioners and theorists refer to as Nature, Porphyry's own embryology is informed by a much more complex understanding of the spiritual realm and of how the human soul fits into it.

The transdisciplinary nature of late ancient medical knowing grows out of the social context of elite education in the Roman Empire. Not only would young men pursuing a career in medicine often spend time in various schools of philosophy as part of their formation; elite doctors often continued to frequent these schools to hear lectures and debates on philosophical topics. For instance, Porphyry tells us that within Plotinus's circle of hearers there were a number of important Roman doctors.[51] This social sphere shared between philosophers and doctors can also be seen in the life of Oribasius (ca. 320–ca. 400 C.E.), the personal physician to the emperor Julian. Not only did Oribasius serve as a close personal advisor to the emperor, whose theurgical tendencies were well known and emphasized in Eunapius's biographical account, but Oribasius also dedicated a handbook of medicine to Eunapius, calling him a *philiatros*. Van der Eijk translates this term as "amateur physician," but literally it means "lover of medicine."[52]

The tendency to take traditional medical topics and explore them through a theological lens is not a trend that ceases with the Christianization of the Mediterranean. To remain with embryology for a moment, Christian theologians reflected carefully on which ancient models would best explain and lend support to the difficult paradox of the incarnation. Not surprisingly, in the end, many settled on Aristotle's account that the father supplies the seed, the form, and the mother provides gross matter. The hybrid approach to medical knowledge found in both Galen's and Porphyry's works persists long into the Middle Ages and is beautifully demonstrated in Hildegard of Bingen's medical writings, focused on sexuality, reproduction, and embryology in the twelfth century, just prior to the rise of the university and scholastic philosophy and medicine.[53]

A FEW GENERAL THOUGHTS ON LATE ANCIENT MEDICAL KNOWING

Before concluding, I'd like to offer a few reflections on the broader question of the character of medical knowing in late antiquity. As noted earlier, this period has often been characterized in negative terms. Indeed, it suffered a fate similar to that of late ancient philosophy, which, based on its preoccupation with ritual and theurgy, was said to have devolved into superstition and decadence.[54] In the case of medicine, the main markers that scholars have used to argue for decline were what Nutton has called a "near-monolithic Galenism" and the preference for and production of medical synopses, handbooks, and compendia. There is no denying that Galen becomes the medical authority par excellence for the next thousand years. But a couple of questions need to be considered if we are to understand this trend. First, *In what sense is Galen an authority?* And second, *Why Galen and Galenism?*

In answer to the first question: Galen became an authority for late ancient and medieval medical writers in much the same way that Plato was an authority for both Galen and Porphyry. As we have seen, both writers use Plato as a guide but very much for their own purposes. Both of them are earnest about uncovering what Plato must have meant in his various writings. Plato's "likely story" in the *Timaeus* serves as the doctrinal basis for what Galen empirically experiences when it comes to the order of development of the human soul-body composite. For Porphyry, the Myth of Er serves as the basis for a complex astrological calculus. Plato has become infinitely interpretable because infinitely rich, and in possession of an infinitely rich truth. Galen never achieves quite this status for those who interpret and digest his work. However, this sense of authority informs those who do. And as van der Eijk demonstrates, use of Galen in late antiquity is anything but slavish and literal.[55]

As for the question *Why Galen?* here I'd like to put forth a hypothesis for consideration, namely that it is Galen's own fault that he achieved the status he did as an authority for later generations.[56] The shadow that the Pergamene doctor cast was of such magnitude that it made it difficult for subsequent writers and historians of medicine to escape it. Galen is one of the most interesting and colorful characters of the second century C.E. His education, his large corpus of writings, and his proximity to the imperial court make him as important a figure for the study of intellectual history as for the history of medicine. We are fortunate that he liked to talk about himself quite extensively. And it is his place as a second-century intellectual as much as his medical expertise that makes him relevant for our understanding of what came after him in later antiquity.

As the recent collection of essays *Galen and the World of Knowledge* demonstrates, Galen both participated in contemporary trends most often associated with the philosophical, rhetorical, and literary writings of the Second Sophistic and carried them over into the realm of medical discourse.[57] First, he extended the commentary tradition of his contemporaries into medicine by writing on many of the Hippocratic works. As the editors of the volume just mentioned note, Galen's techniques as a commentator are similar to those of contemporary writers on Homer and Aristotle. His main aim in writing extensive commentaries of this sort seems to have been part of a larger project to "systematize medicine."[58] Galen's ongoing efforts to digest, systematize, and universalize medical knowledge, from its Hippocratic roots to the writers of his own day, along with his own vexed and repeated efforts to impose order on his own works, which he always felt were getting away from him, likely gave the impression that medical knowledge could and should be distilled into more wieldy forms; and Galen's own efforts in this direction served as the basis for these attempts.[59] Rebecca Flemming argues that this totalizing project was an imperial undertaking on Galen's part, for it was after the fact of empire and as the direct result of the imperial process that the chaotic state of affairs that Galen attempted to remedy had come about in the first place. Hence Galen may well have given the impression that medical knowledge could be ordered systematically for universal, empirewide dissemination and use. It is he who convincingly argues that this sort of project is important and desirable. Thus, although we cannot describe late ancient medicine in terms of a "near-monolithic Galenism" without serious qualification, it should come as no surprise that Galen was as successful as he was at convincing if not his contemporaries then his heirs of his importance as a medical authority.

THEORETICAL REFLECTIONS REVISITED

As I mentioned earlier, reading Porphyry's views on the plantlike nature of the embryo while pregnant led to some interesting reflections and questions about the nature of late ancient medical knowing. Despite feeling some annoyance with Porphyry, I also found his idea of the soul choosing an appropriate body in the midst of the astral swirl of the horoscopic portals quite moving—not as a dogma to be believed but as a metaphor to be contemplated. During my final couple of months of pregnancy, it dawned on me that I really ought to supplement my reading of late ancient medicine and philosophy with some materials on parenting. This insight came to me after watching my husband try to teach my three-year-old nephew how to use an abacus—to no avail—and realizing that we understood pathetically little about early childhood development. My sister gave me a Waldorf-inspired book by Rahima Baldwin Dancy with the daunting title *You Are Your Child's First Teacher.*[60] Prior to my reading the book, my knowledge of Rudolf Steiner and his philosophy of childhood development was limited to the impression that children in Waldorf programs played with fairies in the woods and spent a lot of time mucking about with sand, water, and leaves rather than learning to read and write. I was surprised to find a very late Platonic philosophy undergirding the Waldorf view. Dancy, following Steiner and some of his students, thinks of birth and early childhood as a gradual process of incarnation: the incarnation of an ethereal spirit that chooses the parents even prior to conception. This process of choosing is facilitated by the child's own angel or tutelary spirit. The process of incarnating into this life, also described as awakening, involves some measure of the soul's forgetting its previous life as a spirit.

The strange and accidental conjunction of Porphyry and Rudolf Steiner in my own circumstances gave rise to reflections on how the histories of science and of medicine are often pursued today. To my mind, the best work in these histories takes account of the fact that any thinking about the cosmos, the human body, and nature is necessarily metaphorical. And as historians, it is our task to explore such systems of metaphors and how they in turn shape the everyday experience of being in the world, in a body, and living with and among other creatures, both human and not. To take an example from the health sciences: in antiquity, the main metaphors used to describe health and its opposite centered on ideas of balance and harmony of substances (humors) that were both internal to the body and yet integrally connected to the greater universe: the elements, the cardinal directions, the heavenly spheres, the Four Winds. Today our primary metaphors in the same domain are military: we have immune systems that are under constant attack from internal and external disease agents, and so forth. These metaphors are not neutral, as Emily Martin has demonstrated in her book *Flexible Bodies.* Her work in this book reveals how late-twentieth-century notions of fitness and flexibility in immunology have been deployed in the business philosophies of corporate and work culture in ways that serve to disadvantage and marginalize certain already-underprivileged groups.[61] In general, the metaphors we live by, in large part, serve to bound us as subjects and to sketch out the horizon of possibilities for thinking and acting. Although there is no way for people living in the postmodern world to live by the metaphors of the ancient past as they pertain to health and the body, people in antiquity may have had one distinct advantage over us in terms of how their world of knowledge was constituted, namely their ability to live and think without or across the disciplinary boundaries we tend to observe and police so ardently today, even in the somewhat recent push toward a more interdisciplinary intellectual and academic environment. Their unwillingness to clearly distinguish myth and science meant that ancient thinkers intuitively and in many cases explicitly grasped the metaphorical quality of theoretical, scientific, and philosophical reasoning. And if we are to get anywhere with late ancient medicine or a historical figure such as Porphyry, we too must engage this insight. Although I haven't been able to embrace either Rudolf Steiner's or Porphyry's theory of incarnation when I interact with my newborn child, on both philosophical and aesthetic grounds, metaphorically speaking, I could do a lot worse than regard my child as an ethereal spirit sent by an angel and still, as Wordsworth says, "trailing clouds of Glory" with heaven lying about him.

NOTES

1. Theoharis C. Theoharides, "Galen on Marasmus," *Journal of the History of Medicine and Allied Sciences* 26 (1971): 369–90.

2. Jürgen Mau, *Galen, Einführung in die Logik: Kritisch-exegetischer Kommentar mit deutscher Übersetzung* (Berlin: Akademie Verlag, 1960). Although this work is not notable for making significant advances in logic, it is the first example we have of an ancient textbook on the subject.

3. Karl Kalbfleisch, *Die neuplatonische fälslich dem Galen zugeschriebene Schrift "Pros Gauron Peri tou pôs empsukhountai ta embrua"* (Berlin: Verlag der Königlichen Akademie der Wissenschaften, 1895). All translations come from James Wilberding, *Porphyry: "To Gaurus on How Embryos Are Ensouled" and "On What Is in Our Power"* (Bristol: Bristol Classical Press, 2011).

4. In addition to the reasons given by Kalbfleisch, Tiziano Dorandi has recently lent further weight to the attribution. See Tiziano Dorandi, "Pour une histoire du texte du traité 'Ad Gaurum' attribué à Galien," in *L'embryon: Formation et animation,* ed. Luc Brisson, Marie-Hélène Congourdeau, and Jean-Luc Solère (Paris: Vrin, 2008), 123–37. I find no reason to question the work of Kalbfleisch and Dorandi on the question of Porphyrian authorship.

5. Some of the differences between embryological theories about ensoulment stem from differences in how writers understand the nature of the soul. For some, following an Aristotelian interpretation, soul is form in the sense of a developmental principle and the principle of motion. For someone like Porphyry, souls inhabit bodies and indeed form them, but they descend from other regions of the cosmos, following the Platonic understanding of the soul elaborated in works such as the *Phaedrus* and *Symposium.* By the time Galen and Porphyry are writing, the heritage of both Aristotle and Plato has become rather mixed. And Stoic interpretations of the soul have also impacted how Galen and Porphyry conceive of their subject.

6. Galen, *De Foetuum Formatione,* ed. Diethard Nickel, Corpus Medicorum Graecorum (hereafter CMG), vol. 5.3.3 (Berlin: Akademie Verlag, 2001). All translations come from Peter Singer, "The Construction of the Embryo," in *Galen: Selected Works* (Oxford: Oxford University Press, 2002), 177–201.

7. Jenelle S. Taylor, "Confronting 'Culture' in Medicine's 'Culture of No Culture,'" *Academic Medicine* 28 (2003): 556. See also Sharon Traweek, "An Introduction to Cultural and Social Studies of Sciences and Technologies," *Culture, Medicine, and Psychiatry* 17 (1993): 3–25, and *Beamtimes and Lifetimes: The World of High Energy Physicists* (Cambridge Mass.: Harvard University Press, 1988).

8. Emily Martin, "Anthropology and the Cultural Study of Science," *Science, Technology, and Human Values* 23 (1998): 26.

9. Ibid. 24.

10. Oswei Temkin, *Hippocrates in a World of Pagans and Christians* (Baltimore: The Johns Hopkins University Press, 1991), 1–7.

11. Vivian Nutton, *Ancient Medicine* (London: Routledge, 2008), 292.

12. Philip van der Eijk, "Principles and Practices of Compilation and Abbreviation in the Medical 'Encyclopaedias' of Late Antiquity," in *Condensing Texts—Condensed Texts,* ed. Marietta Horster and Christiane Reitz (Stuttgart: Franz Steiner Verlag, 2010), 519–54; quotation from page 521.

13. Ibid. 553.

14. Ibid.

15. Peter Singer, *Galen: Selected Writings,* 177 (CMG 5.3.3, p. 54); translation slightly modified.

16. Gwynn Kessler, *Conceiving Israel: The Fetus in Rabbinic Narrative* (Philadelphia: University of Pennsylvania Press, 2009), 28. It is interesting that Kessler juxtaposes Greco-Roman and rabbinic embryology by arguing that the latter theologizes whereas the former does not. She writes: "On a metatextual level rabbinic embryology that theologizes Greco-Roman embryology might very well in the process of imitating it make a mockery of it precisely because it overlooks God as the arbiter of life and breath, or soul" (p. 86). As this chapter demonstrates, the theological concerns of both Galen and Porphyry call this juxtaposition into question.

17. These arguments are concentrated in sections 1 to 4 of *On the Construction of the Embryo.* His mention of Stoic ideas on embryology comes at CMG 5.3.3, p. 78.

18. Galen's argument about Nature is found in section 6 of *On the Construction of the Embryo.* The frequent association of Nature and Plato's Demiurge in Galen's work has been noted by Rebecca Flemming. She writes: "The presence of a wise, powerful, skillful, and provident creator figure—alternately labeled 'nature' (*physis*) and 'demiurge' (*dēmiourgos*)—is absolutely key to Galen's thinking, to the medical and philosophical system he constructs and articulates" (Rebecca Flemming, "Demiurge and Emperor in Galen's World of Knowledge," in *Galen and the World of Knowledge,* ed. C. Gill, T. Whitmarsh, and J. Wilkins (Cambridge: Cambridge University Press, 2009), 59.

19. Singer, *Galen* (above, n. 15), 194 (CMG 5.3.3, p. 90).

20. Ibid., slightly modified.

21. Ibid.

22. Ibid. 201 (CMG 5.3.3, p. 106).

23. Wilberding, *Porphyry* (above, n. 3), 12.

24. Ibid. 11; Porphyry, *Ad Gaurum* 2.4, 3.1, 10.1, 10.5, 14.1.

25. Wilberding, *Porphyry* (above, n. 3), 14; Porphyry, *Ad Gaurum* 6.1.

26. Wilberding, *Porphyry* (above, n. 3), 14.

27. Ibid. 34; Porphyry, *Ad Gaurum* 3.2.

28. See chapter 3, "How to Feed a Daemon—The Demonic Conspiracy of Blood Sacrifice and the Moral Valencing of the Realm of Spirits," of my dissertation, "Platonists and High Priests: Daemonology, Ritual and Social Order in the Third Century CE," PhD dissertation, University of California, Santa Barbara, 2009.

29. Wilberding, *Porphyry* (above, n. 3), 34; Porphyry, *Ad Gaurum* 3.4, 13.4.

30. Wilberding, *Porphyry* (above, n. 3), 38; Porphyry, *Ad Gaurum* 5.1.

31. Wilberding, *Porphyry* (above, n. 3), 41; Porphyry, *Ad Gaurum* 8.2. Here Porphyry is quoting Plato, *Timaeus* 91b5–7.

32. Wilberding, *Porphyry* (above, n. 3), 41; Porphyry, *Ad Gaurum* 8.2.

33. Wilberding, *Porphyry* (above, n. 3), 41–42; Porphyry, *Ad Gaurum* 8.3–4. Here Porphyry is quoting Plato, *Timaeus* 91b7–d5. We may find this ancient notion of the wandering womb, which causes hysteria and emotional distress, to be quaint or even absurd. But as Emily Martin demonstrates in her book, now a classic in the anthropology of science, *The Woman in the Body*, late twentieth-century medical texts used metaphorical language about menopause and menstruation to much the same effect. According to one textbook, Allen Lein's *The Cycling Female: Her Menstrual Rhythm* (San Francisco: W. H. Freeman, 1979), the hypothalamus, which has got estrogen "addiction" from all those years of menstruation, experiences "withdrawal" in menopause, such that the hypothalamus begins to give "inappropriate orders." And in a diagram from a textbook by Ann McNaught and Robin Callander, *Illustrated Physiology*, 4th ed. (Edinburgh: Churchill Livingstone, 1983), menopause leads to "emotional disturbances" and "giddiness" along with a "decline in sexual powers" (Emily Martin, *The Woman in the Body: A Cultural Analysis of Reproduction* [Boston: Beacon Press, 2001], 42–43).

34. Wilberding, *Porphyry* (above, n. 3), 40, slightly modified; Porphyry, *Ad Gaurum* 7.1.

35. Wilberding, *Porphyry* (above, n. 3), 40; Porphyry, *Ad Gaurum* 7.2.

36. Wilberding, *Porphyry* (above, n. 3), 50; Porphyry, *Ad Gaurum* 14.3.

37. Wilberding, *Porphyry* (above, n. 3), 50.

38. Véronique Dasen, "Naître jumeaux: Un destin ou deux," in *L'embryon* (above, n. 4), 109–22, especially 110.

39. Wilberding, *Porphyry* (above, n. 3), 53–54; Porphyry, *Ad Gaurum* 16.5–6.

40. Wilberding, *Porphyry* (above, n. 3), 53, slightly modified; Porphyry, *Ad Gaurum* 16.5.

41. Porphyry even cites the "theologian of the Hebrews," who held that god breathed *pneuma* into the fully formed human soul. Wilberding, *Porphyry* (above, n. 3), 45; Porphyry, *Ad Gaurum* 11.1.

42. Wilberding, *Porphyry* (above, n. 3), 45; Porphyry, *Ad Gaurum* 11.2.

43. Wilberding, *Porphyry* (above, n. 3), 53; Porphyry, *Ad Gaurum* 16.5.

44. Wilberding, *Porphyry* (above, n. 3), 53; Porphyry, *Ad Gaurum* 16.5.

45. Wilbderding, *Porphyry* (above, n. 3), 49; Porphyry, *Ad Gaurum* 13.4.

46. Wilberding, *Porphyry* (above, n. 3), 49; Porphyry, *Ad Gaurum* 13.5.

47. For discussion of how Galen engages his sources, see Philip van der Eijk, "'Aristotle! What a Thing for You to Say!' Galen's Engagement with Aristotle and Aristotelians," in *Galen and the World of Knowledge* (above, n. 18), 261–81. See also Heinrich von Staden's article in the same collection, "Staging the Past, Staging Oneself: Galen on Hellenistic Exegetical Traditions," 132–56.

48. See chapter 1, "Ammonius Saccas and the Philosophy without Conflicts," in Elizabeth Depalma Digeser, *A Threat to Public Piety: Christians, Platonists and the Great Persecution* (New York: Cornell University Press, 2012), 23–48.

49. Zeke Mazur, "*Unio Magica*, Part I: On the Magical Origins of Plotinus' Mysticism," *Dionysus* 21 (2003): 23–52.

50. Heidi Marx-Wolf, "High Priests of the Highest God: Third-Century Platonists as Ritual Experts," *Journal of Early Christian Studies* 18 (2010): 481–513.

51. Porphyry, *Vita Plotini* 7.

52. Van der Eijk, "Principles and Practices" (above, n. 12), 529.

53. Margret Berger, *Hildegard of Bingen on Natural Philosophy and Medicine* (Suffolk: Brewer, 1999).

54. The most famous example of this evaluation of late Roman philosophy is found in E. R. Dodds, "Theurgy and Its Relationship to Neoplatonism," *Journal of Roman Studies* 37 (1947): 55–69. That article is reprinted with minor changes as appendix II: "Theurgy," in Dodds's *The Greeks and the Irrational* (Berkeley and Los Angeles: University of California Press, 1951), 283–311.

55. Van der Eijk, "Principles and Practices" (above, n. 12), 552–53.

56. It should, however, be noted that he does not yet have this sort of cachet in the third century, when Porphyry is writing. Although Porphyry addresses topics similar to Galen's, he does not appear even to be in conversation with the Pergamene doctor. One century later, though, when Oribasius is writing, Galen is the medical authority par excellence.

57. *Galen and the World of Knowledge* (above, n. 18), 6.

58. Ibid. 8.

59. As Rebecca Flemming notes "the taxic failure he observed around him in the medical circles of Rome disturbed him. But his own body of writings also lacked the order he extolled, hence he wrote a number of texts which endeavored to impose order on his own works." She argues that this was largely due to the fact that many of Galen's writings were occasional pieces: "The diversity inevitably produced by targeted compositions thus threatened to degenerate into promiscuous chaos" (Flemming, "Demiurge and Emperor" [above, n. 18], 243.

60. Rahima Baldwin Dancy, *You Are Your Child's First Teacher: What Parents Can Do with and for Their Children from Birth to Age Six* (Berkeley: Celestial Arts: 2000).

61. Emily Martin, *Flexible Bodies: The Role of Immunology in American Culture from the Days of Polio to the Age of AIDS* (Boston: Beacon Press, 1994).

5

Cosmos

Catherine M. Chin

The art historian Esther Pasztory describes a return from abroad as follows:[1]

> When I returned my apartment looked all wrong to me. I hated it. The morning after arrival I got up all exhausted and jet-lagged and before doing anything else, I started taking the pictures and textiles off the walls and moving them. A couple of hours later I found that I had rearranged everything, including the sculptures. . . . After a long absence the apartment did not reflect me in some way, and I was not comfortable in it until I brought us into accord.

Late ancient knowledge of the cosmos documents an intimate discomfort with being out of accord. The *kosmos*, as *kosmos*, is ordered and beautiful; Latin authors insist that the neatness of *mundus* is intellectually if not etymologically akin to the beauty of *kosmos*.[2] Accord is always very close by: late ancient writers on the cosmos follow their predecessors in assuming a general principle of sympathy between all the parts of this visible and invisible world that, in their order, are the cosmos.[3] "All things," says Plotinus, "must be enchained; and the sympathy and correspondence obtaining in any one closely knit organism must exist, first, and most intensely, in the All."[4] The doctrine of sympathy, moreover, requires Pasztory's "us": *I was not comfortable in it until I brought us into accord.* It is necessary for most late ancient cosmological thinkers that the cosmos is an agent and contains agents, some of whom are rational, some of whom are human, many of whom we today may choose to call inanimate.[5] These agents correspond with human beings and with each other. The late ancient cosmos, as cosmos, insists on a multiplicity of connected parts; action is a process of multiple actors coming into accord: "Man, like a tiny universe, is sustained by the everlasting fiery movement of the five planets and the Sun and Moon."[6] In a real, physical sense, then, the late ancient cosmos was made out of resemblances and connections: the microcosms and macrocosms that made up the cosmos were intricate sets of materially enchained reflections, constantly in the process of coming into accord.[7]

These multiple, reflecting, resembling actors were also, in a variety of ways, rational: the cosmos both contained rationality and in some accounts was itself a rational organism.[8] The presence of multiple knowing agents in correspondence made "knowledge of the cosmos" a matter not merely of human knowledge about the cosmos but of the cosmos itself knowing. The stars, for Origen, both know and freely obey the precepts of God and, further, serve as signs of terrestrial events; but this knowledge is merely part of the intellect of the cosmos.[9] That is, agents within the cosmos know, and their knowing is participation in the ongoing universal activity of mind. Theories of knowledge in late antiquity posit a congruence between the object known and the mind of the knower as the condition of knowledge;[10] but knowledge is consistently also a participation in the *logos* or intellect of the cosmos, so that the congruence that constitutes knowledge is simultaneously the congruence of mind embedded in cosmic order. The cosmos actively knows, and human beings know as part of this knowing. Universal knowing is itself a process of internal reflection and accord: in the same way that action is a matter of multiple actors coming into accord, knowing is the process of multiple intellectual objects, sensory or immaterial, coming into accord.[11] To know the past, the character, and the future of an individual, chart the corresponding stars or planetary bodies. To know the truth in language, find words that resonate with each other.[12] They are enchained.

Because all things are enchained, the cosmos is ultimately also mundane. Cosmological knowledge could function as restricted or hierarchical expertise in late antiquity, as in the cases of Plotinus and Origen, but the principle of universal correspondence, as well as its attendant ambiguities and discomforts, was widespread, as the flourishing of sympathetic practices sometimes called magic, sometimes called *technē*, sometimes called astrology, and sometimes called worship makes clear.[13] In this chapter I purposely do not differentiate among them; this is an essay in the embodied history of correspondences and in their movement toward accord. Knowledge about the cosmos, along with the knowledge possessed by the cosmos, was embedded in specific material acts and problems. The embedding of cosmic knowledge in actions, events, and problems, however, introduces a diffuse cosmic agency into late antique history and calls for a new kind of narrative to capture the presence of the invisible.

What I would call "cosmological historiography" follows three principles: first, that events are shaped by external invisible forces; second, that events and actions are necessarily the products of multiple interacting agents, only some of whom are human; and third, that all things, human and nonhuman, visible and invisible, seek to be brought into accord. In order to suggest the abundant invisible forces of late antique cosmic experience, I describe below three well-known related moments in the cosmological history of the later fourth century: the Priscillianist controversy, the magic trials under Valens, and the Milanese basilica crisis.[14] These moments represent three modes of cosmic knowledge: knowing, being known, and being used to know.

WORKS AND DAYS

Priscillian of Avila, it was agreed, possessed knowledge of the cosmos. Priscillian was executed around 385 under the authority of the usurper Magnus Maximus, who had come to the imperial throne in 383 through the assassination of the emperor Gratian. Priscillian's execution was legally justified on the ground of sorcery.[15] Among the ecclesiastical accusations that ultimately led to his imperial condemnation were charges of participating in sympathetic agricultural practices and of worshipping the planetary gods, specifically the gods of the week (the Sun, Moon, Mars, Venus, Mercury, Jupiter, and Saturn).[16] It is instructive to consider the context of these charges and Priscillian's response to them in some detail in order to see how cosmological knowledge was embedded in everyday practice and how the nature of its embedding could become controversial.

A sympathetic view of agriculture was widespread in late antiquity; among its other activities, the cosmos was partly responsible for food production. Photius of Constantinople's ninth-century *Bibliotheca* recommends reading the fourth-century collection of agricultural advice by Anatolius of Berytus, a correspondent of Libanius, although Photius cautions that "it contains some marvelous and incredible tales, full of Greek fables, which the pious husbandman should pass over."[17] Since much of Anatolius's collection is lost in its original form, it is not clear exactly which fables Photius thought impious, but one fourth-century Latin user and adapter of Anatolius's text, Palladius, relied on a number of sympathetic agricultural practices that appear to have been representative of late ancient farming techniques broadly understood. The cosmological expertise needed for farming, according to Palladius, assumes cosmic sympathy at the level of seasons and weather patterns that continue to be intelligible to contemporary farming, but it also pursues correspondences, both astronomical and terrestrial, that reveal the overall location of food production within an enchained system. For example: "All sowing should be done on a waxing moon, but all reaping or gathering on a waning moon."[18] Or, similarly, a terrestrial correspondence: "The view of the Greeks is that if a cloud of *locusts* suddenly arises, it can pass over as long as all humans stay hidden inside their buildings."[19] This kind of agricultural correspondence was not universally rejected by Christians; no less an authority than Cassiodorus recommends Palladius to his readers, and Isidore of Seville also quotes him.[20] Palladius's popularity—the text's abundant copying and translation—during the Latin

Middle Ages suggests that the cosmological sympathy described in the text cannot be dismissed as the product either of unlearned farmers or of non-Christians; instead it seems clear that Palladius's ideas found a warm reception in the agricultural corpus of the educated Christian West.[21]

The tenth-century *Geoponika,* compiled under Constantine Porphyrogenitus, likewise uses Anatolius as one of its main sources, and few of its sources appear to postdate the sixth century.[22] The *Geoponika* ascribes a number of its agricultural recommendations to Zoroaster, signaling the persistence of agricultural-cosmological embedding, which is perhaps best epitomized in such constellations of advice as: "If the moon is in Leo when the rising of Sirius takes place, there will be a plentiful harvest of wheat, olive oil, and wine; all other supplies cheap; clamour, killings, appearance of a king, mildness of air, invasion by one people of another; there will also be earthquakes and tidal waves. . . . If in Taurus, much rain, hail, wheat rust, many vendettas."[23] The convergence of agricultural practice and astrological knowledge is fully in line with a generalized notion of sympathy and hence with the ability to know terrestrial events through the physical experience of related cosmic powers. By the same token, the fact of cosmic resonance, in this system, creates knowledge of cosmic powers through the physical experience of terrestrial events: the bodily pleasure of "mildness of air" or the physical tension of "vendetta" is enchained to the position of the moon and becomes a bodily knowing, a physical tie between the moon and the human being.[24] Although this sympathy may have manifested in a variety of ways, the fact that it would manifest was not in serious doubt. The lunar phases or positions of the planets relative to the fixed stars, along with the physical presence of blight and vendettas, are simply basic to the functioning of the cosmos. The procession of days consisted of patterns, agricultural, meteorological, and bodily, that structured what could be known and that structured the physical sensations in which they were known.[25] Thus knowledge of the cosmos and its effects was embedded in the direct bodily sensation of daily life and its participation in the yearly, monthly, and weekly patterns of agrarian existence.

In the first of the Würzburg tractates that constitute our primary direct evidence for Priscillian and his ideas, Priscillian clearly rejects the accusation that he is involved in the worship of planetary gods.[26] Instead, he offers an extended explanation, deity by deity, of how adherence to Christianity gives one access to a greater cosmic power than that attributed to the traditional gods:[27]

> Let those who love gold create for themselves a golden age of Saturn: for us, "divine wisdom is more precious than all gold and silver and precious stone"; let those whose only dwelling is the fire of Gehenna say that their God is the sun. . . . For us, all things that are under the sun are vain.

The list continues in a similar vein for each planet. As to the charges of agricultural magic, of tying the fortunes of crops to the waxing and waning of the moon, Priscillian is similarly vehement, calling it a charge "damnable even in report, not to mention in deed."[28] His argument is that wrong understandings of divine power are crassly material:[29]

> Let them believe, as children of the devil and perdition, that they are sated by the rain of the devil: for us it is God who makes all things, who summons water from the sea, and pours it on the surface of the whole world and grants the pouring of the morning and the evening rain. . . . But our God is Jesus Christ, who said: All that is under the sky is mine.

It is important that in each of these cases in *Tractate* 1, Priscillian is proposing a competing attribution for traditional cosmological activity rather than an outright rejection of the idea of cosmic sympathy overall. For Priscillian, it is wrong and worthy of condemnation to attribute ultimate efficacy to forces that may mistakenly be considered gods but that are under the control of the Christian God. Priscillian does not deny that he has knowledge of the cosmos, but he does suggest that this knowledge must be refracted through the prism of greater, Christian, cosmic powers.

Priscillian's argument could be read either as straightforwardly antiastrological (the planetary gods are not gods; those who believe that they are should be condemned) or, following Orosius, as an admission that Priscillian "affirmed the validity of astrology" (planetary forces do have effects).[30] The ambiguity suggests that the question whether Priscillian favored astrology or agricultural magic should be reframed as a question of where and how Priscillian considered cosmological knowledge to be embodied. Priscillian's position is reminiscent of his contemporary Zeno of Verona, whose *Tractate* 1.38 on the rebirth offered by baptism describes sacramental rebirth as an effective replacement, sign by sign, of the powers resident in the zodiac.[31] In this light, Priscillian's explanation of the Christian God's power over rain, the planets, or the elements is less a rejection of astrology or cosmic sympathy than it is the correction, under a Christian cosmological scheme, of a series of false attributions. The knowledge that is the bodily tie between the human and the cosmic body becomes a tie between the human being and the Christian God, imperfectly reflected in the cosmic body. This becomes clear if we compare Priscillian's rejection of the gods of the week in *Tractate* 1 with a slightly more direct passage in *Tractate* 6, in which he explains that Christian baptism makes Easter "our first month and day, not the one in which we appear in the world, but the one in which, after Egypt has been defeated . . . , we are renewed in God through the divine birth."[32] Thus the Christian "recognizes that he came not to be bound by time, but to win, and by believing understands that the entire fact that the sun during the day and the moon during the night wane or wax is not the command of our captivity, but the effective [*operabilis*] system of nature, and all that we lived, when we return to our origin, will be called the Easter of the Lord, not the work of the world [*opus mundi*]."[33] For Priscillian, then, the question is not whether the patterns of the cosmos are terrestrially efficacious but, first, whether that efficacy should be attributed to the cosmos itself or to the Christian God as its author, and second, in what ways the Christian God will realign those patterns and effects with the lives of those who become tied to him in the wake of their baptism. It is in the baptized Christian that true agriculture takes place: "so that he may cultivate what was infertile in himself, after it had been made fertile by the word of the Lord, as he received the grace of divine preaching."[34] Priscillian's bodily tie to the patterns of the calendar and agrarian life is now a tie to God.

The Priscillianist controversy was thus not strictly about the degree to which Priscillian and his followers may or may not have practiced sorcery or engaged in sympathetic astrology and agriculture. Yet neither are concerns about the efficacy of cosmic systems absent from the issues at stake, nor are they merely a screen for social, ecclesiastical, doctrinal, or political maneuvering. The physical ties between human bodies and cosmic forces are real. The Priscillianist controversy was a dispute over how knowledge was embedded in the cosmos: that is, over the nature of the physical connections and reflections that constitute cosmic knowledge. The position that Priscillian's accusers claimed that he took was that planetary powers were inherent and attributable to the planets themselves and were thus to be known directly through calendrical or astronomical experience or agricultural manipulation, without reference to Christian authority; on the other hand, the position Priscillian seems to have taken is that such powers were only provisionally associated with the planetary system under the oversight of the Christian God and thus were more appropriately known and surpassed through the lens of Christian sacramental and liturgical practice, which is itself cosmically efficacious. As Priscillian says of Jesus:[35]

> He is the only one who, as is written in the prophet, "is able to connect the bond of the Pleiades and to open the barrier of Orion," [and] by knowing the changing of the firmament and destroying the wheel of generation he regained the day of our birth through the renewal of baptism.

Priscillian's bodily sensation is tied to what is above the stars.

Priscillian's defense of his cosmic knowledge was unsuccessful, but as the robust afterlives of Anatolius's and Palladius's agricultural works suggest, this was likely not because the agricultural or calendrical manifestations of cosmic sympathy were problematic to Christian orthodoxy. Yet Priscillian's execution was nonetheless the resolution of an intolerable cosmic knowing: his encounter with Magnus Maximus and the circumstances of the imperial house preceding Maximus's usurpation bring into focus a much more dangerous aspect of cosmological knowledge, to which I will now turn.

SPEAKING LOUDLY IN PUBLIC

Although Priscillian's execution is generally seen as motivated by Maximus's desire to demonstrate his own orthodoxy,[36] as a recent claimant to the imperial throne Maximus had good reason to be concerned about a secretive Christian sorcerer interested in a new astrological order that realigned the powers of the previous cosmic system. Maximus's coemperor, Theodosius, had come to power in 379, as was widely recognized, in fulfillment of a magical prediction made by a band of conspirators in 371.[37] Indeed the reign of the family of Valentinian prior to Maximus's usurpation was marked by a highly public sense of cosmological uncertainty and by attempts to constrain or deflect the knowledge accessible to human participants in the cosmic order. The notorious magic trials of the early 370s, as narrated in Ammianus Marcellinus's *Res Gestae,* provide insight into the primary complication of cosmological knowledge for political life in the late ancient world, namely the problem of being known.

The pervasiveness of mind, the multiplicity of knowing agents in the cosmos, and the distribution of knowledge across sympathetic agents meant that to participate in cosmic knowing was also to be known. This is most visibly a problem in accounts of late antique predictions, astrological and otherwise, concerning the life or future of the emperor, and such predictions are a focal point for Ammianus's narrative, although they are not the only proscribed forms of cosmological knowledge. Two moments in Ammianus's account are particularly instructive: the most extended narrative of the magic and treason trials, taking up most of *Res Gestae* 29.1, is the story of Theodorus, who is incorrectly identified by magical means as Valens's successor: "When we then and there inquired, 'What man will succeed the present emperor?' . . . and the ring leaped forward and lightly touched the two syllables ΘEO, adding the next letter [i.e., Δ], then one of those present cried out that by the decision of inevitable fate Theodorus was meant."[38] Theodorus becomes the center of a conspiracy and is ultimately executed along with many others. Similarly, at *Res Gestae* 29.2.27, Ammianus writes: "Among the papers of a distinguished townsman . . . the horoscope of a certain Valens was found; when the person concerned was asked why he had cast the nativity of the emperor, he defended himself against the charge by saying that he had had a brother named Valens and that he had died long ago." These accounts illustrate the most obvious political problem of cosmic knowledge, that of the physical vulnerability of being known. The inevitable consequence of cosmic sympathy is that all agents, including the emperor, are continuously objects of knowledge, at times to other human beings but on a more basic level to the cosmos itself.

The close connection between cosmological discovery and the physical vulnerability of objects of knowledge is further suggested by Ammianus's connection between the torture and execution of those accused of magic and the burning of forbidden books.[39] At *Res Gestae* 28.1.26, Lollianus is condemned for "having written a book on destructive magical arts." At 29.1.23, the trial of Theodorus begins "Accordingly, when the highest officials ... had been called together, the racks were made taut; the leaden weights were brought out along with the cords and the scourges," and in the immediate aftermath of Theodorus's execution, Ammianus claims that "innumerable writings and many heaps of volumes were hauled out from various homes and under the eyes of the judges were burned in heaps as being unlawful, ... although the greater number were treatises on the liberal arts and on jurisprudence."[40] The ravaging of books and bodies exposes the potential violence of the physical tie that is cosmic knowledge. Moreover, the fact that these particular executions and book burnings are fundamentally mistaken, according to Ammianus, only reinforces the power of correct cosmic knowledge and the vulnerability of those known by it: "After these various deeds of injustice ... and the marks of torture shamefully branded upon the bodies of such free men as had survived, the never-closing eye of Justice, the eternal witness and avenger of all things, was watchfully attentive. . . . The truth of the oracle was confirmed, which had predicted that no crimes would go unpunished."[41] In Ammianus's narrative, Valens, while condemning those who would be his successors, is moving inexorably toward his own death at the battle of Adrianople.

It is not unreasonable in such a system for Firmicus Maternus, earlier in the century, to advise would-be astrologers that they must themselves operate in a manner that allows them constantly to be known—that is, to be constantly physically accessible: "He who daily speaks about the gods or with the gods must shape his mind to approach the likeness of divinity. Therefore study and pursue all the distinguishing marks of virtue and ... be easy of access. . . . See that you give your responses publicly in a clear voice, so that nothing may be asked of you that is not allowed either to ask or to answer."[42] Speaking loudly in public is not merely a statement that the astrologer is not performing illicit acts but is a demonstration of being physically known and knowable, just as the object of the astrologer's inquiry is known and knowable. Similarly, Firmicus's insistence that the emperor's horoscope cannot be known is a clear wish, on one level, to avoid a political or legal problem but is also an attempt to solve a real cosmological problem: if the emperor is not physically vulnerable, how can the emperor be cosmically known? Firmicus's answer is an appeal to cosmological patterns above the level of the stars: "For the emperor alone is not subject to the course of the stars, and in his fate alone the stars have no power of decreeing. Since he is master of the whole universe, his destiny is governed by the judgment of the Highest God."[43] Firmicus retains the cosmological fact that all things are known, but he limits the accessibility of some knowledge to the two most appropriately aligned knowers, God and the emperor.

The physical reciprocity between knowing and being known is an inevitable by-product of the multiplicity of knowers within a sympathetic, mind-infused cosmos. Yet as Ammianus's narratives make clear, this multiplicity also introduces potential ambiguities in acts of knowing. The condition of being known can itself lead to instances of dissonance in need of resolution. As Ammianus reports of the man who cast the horoscope of Valens but claimed it was the horoscope of his long-dead brother: "They did not wait for the truth to be discovered, and he was tortured and butchered."[44] Just as it is possible to know incorrectly, it is possible to be incorrectly known. The unstated truth of Ammianus's story of Theodorus is that the magical prediction is in fact correct: ΘEOΔ- did succeed Valens, but ΘEOΔ- was Theodosius. The truth of cosmic knowledge is thus persistently embedded in false cognates. Human misunderstanding is a cliché in accounts of ancient oracles, but its use in Ammianus makes clear that the punning nature of the cosmos had not lost its wit or power by the late fourth century. Valens's own death is foreshadowed in Ammianus's aside that "the truth of the oracle was confirmed, which had predicted that no crimes would go unpunished." In the same way as late ancient theorists of language both worried about ambiguity and found etymological truth in it, interpreters of cosmic signs assumed multiple layers of possible true and untrue meaning in the levels of macrocosm and microcosm.[45] As Firmicus Maternus acknowledges, "all knowledge that has to do with divine skills is handed down to us in a form hard to understand."

The potential for ambiguity in the correspondence of cosmic actors and elements means that cosmic knowledge may resemble many things but requires time (that movement of cosmic bodies) to achieve its correct correspondence. It also suggests that events and actors persistently tend toward correspondence over time. The reader of the *Res Gestae* knows, as the cosmos knows, that ΘEOΔ- will be Theodosius, but Valens, Theodorus, and the conspirators do not know this. The ambiguous nature of cosmic signs returns us to Priscillian's cosmos. Priscillian, like Ammianus, believes in the ambiguous signification, the punning nature, of cosmic signs. For Priscillian, what appear to be the planetary gods are in fact the days of Christian creation; what appears to be the day of birth governed by the zodiac turns out to be the day of rebirth governed by baptism. Magnus Maximus is thus not merely like Valens in his concern over sorcery and the cosmic order; from the Priscillianist vantage point, he is like Valens in refusing to allow ambiguous cosmic signification to be resolved into correct correspondence. In his refusal to be known, Maximus mistakes the meaning of cosmic signification and thus does not know the Priscillianist cosmos. The connection between acknowledgment of one's status as known and correct knowledge of correspondence is perhaps best indicated in Firmicus's insistence that the best astrologer is unafraid of the public performance of his craft. Willingness to be known is a sign of cosmic knowledge.

"THEY SAY THAT THE PEOPLE ARE
SEDUCED BY MY SONGS"

At around the same time as Priscillian was killed for exposing a potentially treasonous sympathy, another difficult bishop was deploying cosmic resonances in
defiance of imperial wishes. Over the course of 385–86 Ambrose of Milan—who
had rebuffed Priscillian's attempts to ally with him a few years earlier and yet
deplored Priscillian's execution—came under increasing imperial pressure to
allow one of the Milanese basilicas to be used for Homoian liturgy. He famously
refused, and during a particularly tense period in the confrontation between the
bishop and the court, he encouraged Nicene Christians in Milan to occupy the
basilicas in protest. Augustine's later account of the Milanese basilica crisis in the
Confessions includes the important detail that "it was then that the practice of singing hymns and psalms was introduced, in keeping with the usage of the Eastern
churches, to revive the flagging spirits of the people during their long and cheer-
less watch."[46] Indeed, in the sixth book of his *De Musica,* Augustine's analysis of the
soul's reception of music's numerical properties is centered on a discussion of one
of Ambrose's most famous hymns, "Deus Creator Omnium."[47] The deployment of
cosmological resonance in terrestrial music brings us to the third moment that I
would like to discuss in the cosmological history of the late fourth century, wherein
the human participants in cosmic knowledge are neither knowers nor known but
are themselves technologies of the cosmos's knowing. In this moment, the experience of music gains Ambrose a basilica.

It is a commonplace in ancient and late ancient writing on music both that
music is capable of physical effects and that music is a necessary part of cosmic
structure. Plato's *Timaeus,* following Pythagorean number theory, posits musical
intervals as basic building blocks of cosmic creation,[48] and Plotinus carries this
idea forward in his argument that "all music . . . must be the earthly representation
of the music there is in the rhythm of the Ideal Realm."[49] Boethius's *De Institutione
Musica* explicitly and concisely connects Platonic musical creation with both terrestrial music and human action: "What Plato rightfully said can likewise be
understood: the soul of the universe was joined together according to musical
concord." He continues: "For when we hear what is properly and harmoniously
united in sound in conjunction with what is harmoniously coupled and joined
together within us and are attracted to it, then we recognize that we ourselves are
put together in its likeness. For likeness attracts, whereas unlikeness disgusts and
repels."[50] Here not only does terrestrial music resemble cosmic music; it also acts
sympathetically upon human listeners, in that it creates attraction between human
actors, musical intervals, and the music of cosmic structure. Human beings here
are acted upon by the correspondence that makes up the process of cosmic knowing. The agency of the sounds themselves is suggested in Boethius's discussion of

dissonance slightly later: dissonance consists of sounds that are "unwilling to blend together," in which "each strives somehow to be heard unimpaired."[51] This striving affects and impels its listeners: Boethius adjudicates between competing theories on whether physical hearing or rational thought is primarily responsible for the soul's response to music, arguing that hearing "serves as an exhortation," although "the ultimate perfection and the faculty of recognition consists of reason."[52] The hortatory power of music, like its power to attract or to repel, clearly establishes that human beings are understood not to be the primary agents in this occasion of cosmic resonance. They are merely one set of the vehicles or instruments through which that resonance passes.

Ambrose was fully aware of the sympathetic resonance of song and music. In his *Epistle* 75A, of 386, the *Sermo contra Auxentium,* he addresses the criticism that he is using music for his own ends: "They assert that the people have also been deceived by the spells of my hymns. I am obviously not denying that. They are indeed a mighty enchantment. There is nothing more powerful."[53] Ambrose's explicit connection, in response to Homoian charges, between the resonance of music and the power of "enchantment" or incantation makes clear that cosmic sympathy was understood by both Ambrose and his opponents as a force in the struggle for control of the basilicas; it is worth noting that an accusation of sorcery in defiance of imperial wishes so close to the time of Priscillian's trial and execution would have highlighted the real political and indeed physical force found in the sympathetic action of the cosmos. More important, in Ambrose's letter, agency is very directly attributed to the sounds that act upon people and their environments: "There is nothing more powerful." The potency and popularity of Ambrose's hymns has been attributed to their metrical and stanzaic regularity, in particular the consistent use of the eight-stanza form, with its echoes of the Christian numerical significance of the eighth day of creation, the resurrection.[54] The content of several of the authentic hymns, similarly, with their emphasis on the passage of time between day and night, the rising of the stars, and the ties between the natural markers of time and the process of Christian salvation, in sum suggests a direct connection between Ambrose's hymns and the idea of a much broader cosmological resonance.[55]

The connection between sound and building is also made clear in *Epistle* 75A. At *Epistle* 75A.19–21, Ambrose explains that Jesus's driving the money changers out of the temple (Lk 19:37–46) was preceded, indeed precipitated, by song: "Doubtless you heard in today's reading how when Christ was riding on the foal of an ass the children kept shouting aloud, and the Jews were becoming angry. . . . They see children singing [*concinentes*] the glory of Christ—because it is written *out of the mouths of babes and sucklings you have perfected your praise. . . .* And so, enticed [*invitatus*] by these acclamations [*laudationibus*], Christ enters his temple, and takes up a scourge, and drives the money changers out of the temple."[56] The recovery of the holy building is here attributed to the children's singing; even Christ is moved to action by the song. Of course the relation of cosmic resonance to physical buildings is also a trope of late ancient visual and architectural culture. The poem ascribed to Ambrose on the octagonal baptistery at Milan plays on the cosmic symbolism of the number eight;[57] and although the connection between the domed church and the dome of heaven is not common before the sixth century, aquatic and astral motifs in late ancient floor decoration suggest that the physical experience of movement in and around a building served as a reflection of being in cosmic order.[58] Thus Ambrose's conflation of musical and architectural resonance in *Epistle* 75A reveals how far resemblances between microcosms and macrocosms could be expected to drive action at a physical level in the late fourth century. The production of the appropriate resonance impels the action that results in physical possession of the basilica.

The Milanese basilica crisis was a movement toward resonance. According to Ambrose, of course, the resonance was not of his own making but was divine. The power of his hymns, like his success in retaining the basilica, lies in the power of the Trinity: "For what is more powerful than the glorification [*confessio*] of the Trinity, which is celebrated day after day by the voices of the whole people?"[59] This presumption of human coagency, or of the instrumentality of human beings in divine effects that are occurring simultaneously on a cosmic and on a terrestrial scale, reveals the possibility of being acted upon as part of a larger cosmic system that is in the process of knowing something in and through its system of resemblances.[60] Ambrose emphasizes his own passivity in the face of divine action— "Am I really to bring back into the temple someone whom Christ has excluded?"[61]— but the humanly incarnate Christ, too, has been moved (*invitatus*) by the songs of the children. What is more, Ambrose adds, the passage on Jesus's entry into Jerusalem continues: "He replied, 'If these should be silent, the stones would cry out.'"[62] This judicious quotation transforms the account in Luke into a description of a cosmic knowing so powerful that it can use either animate or inanimate objects, or even the incarnate Logos, as its means of creating resonance. Ambrose and his congregation are here simply the technology of a cosmic knowledge that, in knowing and asserting the Trinity, uses human sounding boards to correct the difficult physical situation in Milan.

CONCLUSION: COSMOLOGICAL HISTORY

In book 3 of the *Matheseos*, Firmicus Maternus offers some memorable details about the variations of planetary effects on human lives, depending on whether those lives are influenced predominantly by one planet or by a conjunction of planets. For Mercury: "Mercury, located exactly on the ascendant in signs in which he rejoices, in a daytime chart, makes philosophers, teachers of the art of letters, or geometers: often he makes those who measure heavenly phenomena or study them so that they can contemplate the presence of the gods, or men skilled in sacred writings."[63] By contrast, "Mercury together with the Sun on the ascendant by day will make powerful kings and leaders; but if found together in this house by night, they make the fathers of low class and low occupation. [Those born at this time] will work for the government but in obscure and wretched jobs according to the nature and quality of the signs."[64] As Firmicus well knows, the presence of multiple agents in the cosmos working either jointly or in opposition to determine the outcome of human lives makes the telling of individual human stories a dizzyingly complex undertaking;[65] his lists of possible horoscopes are effectively short collections of overlapping, contrasting, conflicting, complementary, and vague narratives of human existence. This profusion of narratives, carefully delineated and collected, similar but never entirely the same, is one way of writing cosmological history.

It is also possible to narrate at least some events of the Western Roman Empire in the 370s and 380s cosmologically, as a cascade of cosmological events, doublings, and conflicts of higher and lower powers: Valens condemns the innocent and uncovers a true conspiracy; the forecast at the heart of the conspiracy is true, but the conspirators act according to wrong knowledge. Continued fear of treason and sorcery lead Magnus Maximus, himself a usurper, to the execution of Priscillian, accused of worshipping the gods of the days when he urges Christians to transform themselves into a holy week ruled from above the stars. Priscillian's trial, in turn, lies in the background of Homoian charges against Ambrose's admitted incantations to retain the basilicas of Milan. All these events involve human agents acting in accord with what they consider to be forces aligned in the cosmos; whether or not the modern narrators of their stories believe in the efficacy of those forces, or whether or not the human beings involved would have agreed on which forces were in the ascendant moment by moment, the events of those stories are shaped by cosmic powers. By virtue of knowing the cosmos, the human beings in this history also know themselves to be variously actors, acted upon, and caught up as instruments in the actions of invisible others.

· · ·

I have tried here to understand the invisible forces of cosmic sympathy as they influenced a related series of events in the later fourth century, particularly the force that sympathetic knowledge, in its varied human and nonhuman forms, exerted to bring these events and their constituent parts into accord. Yet ultimately the accord into which such narratives may be brought is nonverbal, bodily, and aesthetic: Pasztory's rearrangement of her apartment is an aesthetic material cognition.[66] Perhaps more appropriately to late antiquity, Boethius defines consonance simply as "a mixture of high and low sound falling pleasantly and uniformly on the ears."[67] The system of this pleasure is cosmic knowledge.

NOTES

1. Esther Pasztory, *Thinking with Things: Toward a New Vision of Art* (Austin: University of Texas Press, 2005), 20–21.

2. On the etymology of *kosmos* and *mundus*, see Jaan Puhvel, "The Origins of Greek *Kosmos* and Latin *Mundus*," *American Journal of Philology* 97 (1976): 154–67; see also the more recent survey of Katharina Volk, *Manilius and His Intellectual Background* (Oxford: Oxford University Press, 2009), 18–23.

3. On the origins and influence of the idea of cosmic sympathy, see the useful survey of Katerina Ierodiakonou, "The Greek Concept of *Sympatheia* and Its Byzantine Appropriation in Michael Psellos," in Paul Magdalino and Maria Mavroudi, eds., *The Occult Sciences in Byzantium* (Geneva: Palme d'Or, 2006), 97–106, which covers much of the relevant Stoic and later Platonic material.

4. *Enneads* 2.3.7, trans. Stephen MacKenna, *Plotinus: The Enneads*, rev. ed. (Burdett, N.Y.: Paul Brunton Philosophic Foundation, 1992), 109.

5. On the problem of the inanimate, however, see Jane Bennet, *Vibrant Matter* (Durham: Duke University Press, 2010), especially chapter 2, "The Agency of Assemblages," 28–38.

6. Firmicus Maternus, *Matheseos Libri VIII*, 3, proem 3, trans. Jean Rhys Bram, *Ancient Astrology, Theory and Practice: "Matheseos Libri VIII" by Firmicus Maternus* (Bel Air, Md.: Astrology Classics, 2005).

7. See Michel Foucault, *The Order of Things: An Archaeology of the Human Sciences* (New York: Random House, 1970), chapter 2, 17–25, on the Early Modern variations on this system of resemblances. Although it is common to see Stoic and Neoplatonic cosmologies sharply differentiated as "materialist" and "nonmaterialist," Stoic influence on Neoplatonic thought was considerable: see especially Andreas Graeser, *Plotinus and the Stoics* (Leiden: Brill, 1972).

8. For a detailed survey, see Heinz R. Schutte, *Weltseele: Geschichte und Hermeneutik* (Frankfurt: J. Knecht, 1993).

9. For discussion, see Alan Scott, *Origen and the Life of the Stars* (Oxford: Oxford University Press, 1991), chapter 8, "Origen and the Stars," 117–33.

10. This may be either in a materialist, imprinted sense, in Stoic-influenced epistemologies, or, more commonly, in the discernment of resemblances through recollection, in Platonic epistemologies: see especially Plotinus, *Enneads* 5.3.3, and Proclus, *Elements of Theology* 180, 195.

11. As one modern theorist of cognition puts it: "Thinking consists of bringing these structures [of knowledge] into coordination so that they can shape and be shaped by one another": Edwin Hutchins, *Cognition in the Wild* (Cambridge, Mass.: MIT Press, 1995), 316.

12. See John Henderson's excellent *The Medieval World of Isidore of Seville: Truth from Words* (Cambridge: Cambridge University Press, 2007).

13. On the problem of magic as a scholarly category, see especially Naomi Janowitz, *Magic in the Roman World: Pagans, Jews, and Christians* (London: Routledge, 2001), chapter 1, "Greco-Roman, Christian, and Jewish Concepts of 'Magic,'" 9–26; and David Frankfurter, "Dynamics of Ritual Expertise in Antiquity and Beyond: Towards a New Taxonomy of 'Magicians,'" in Paul Mirecki and Marvin W. Meyer eds., *Magic and Ritual in the Ancient*

World (Leiden: Brill, 2002), 159–78; but see also C. A. Hoffmann's historiographical survey of magic and defense of the term, "Fiat Magia," at pages 179–94 of the same volume. For an excellent discussion of the problems involved in scholarship isolating "ritual" practices as objects of study, see David Frankfurter, "Ritual as Accusation and Atrocity: Satanic Ritual Abuse, Gnostic Libertinism and Primal Murders," *History of Religions* 40 (2001): 352–80.

14. I use "abundance" following Robert Orsi's advocacy of writing "abundant histories" in the study of religion, in which the invisible and miraculous are counted as part of the experience of the persons involved: Orsi, "Abundant History: Marian Apparitions as Alternative History," *Historically Speaking* (2008): 12–16.

15. For a detailed narrative, see Henry Chadwick, *Priscillian of Avila: The Occult and the Charismatic in the Early Church* (Oxford: Oxford University Press, 1976), chapters 1 and 3, 1–56 and 111–69; on the historiography of the controversy, particularly with reference to its importance in Spanish historiography, see F. J. Fernández Conde, *Prisciliano y el priscilianismo: Historiografía y realidad* (Gijon: Ediciones Trea, 2007), chapters 2 and 4, 21–33 and 65–85. On the importance of astrological doctrine in reading Priscillian's *Tractates,* see Gabriella Bianco, "Tematiche astrali nei Trattati di Würzburg," *Studi e Materiali di Storia delle Religioni* 13 (1989): 223–34.

16. See the discussion in Virginia Burrus, *The Making of a Heretic: Gender, Authority and the Priscillianist Controversy* (Berkeley and Los Angeles: University of California Press, 1995), 61–69.

17. Photius, *Bibliotheca,* codex 163 (trans. J. H. Freese, *The Library of Photius,* vol. 1 [London: MacMillan, 1920], 239); on the identity of Anatolius, see Scott Bradbury, "A Sophistic Prefect: Anatolius of Berytus in the Letters of Libanius," *Classical Philology* 95 (2000): 172–86.

18. Palladius, *Opus Agriculturae* 1.34, trans. John G. Fitch, *Palladius: The Work of Farming* (Totnes, Devon: Prospect Books, 2013), 60.

19. Ibid. 1.35; trans. Fitch, 63.

20. Cassiodorus, *Institutiones* 1.28.6; Isidore, *Etymologiae* 17.10.8.

21. For the transmission history of Palladius, see R. H. Rodgers, *An Introduction to Palladius* (London: Institute of Classical Studies, 1975), 14–71. Chadwick, *Priscillian* (above, n. 15), 52, suggests that agricultural magic is fundamentally the province of the uneducated: "It was one thing for illiterate peasants to practice country magic, another for this to be believed of a prominent teacher soon to be appointed bishop of Avila." Fritz Graf implicitly groups agricultural magic with lower-class status in his discussion of Pliny's account of an agricultural-magic trial in which the defendant is a freedman: *Magic in the Ancient World,* trans. Franklin Philip (Cambridge, Mass.: Harvard University Press, 1997), 62–65.

22. John L. Teall, "The Byzantine Agricultural Tradition," *Dumbarton Oaks Papers* 25 (1971): 39–44.

23. *Geoponika* 1.8; trans. Andrew Dalby, *Geoponika: Farm Work, a Modern Translation of the Roman and Byzantine Farming Handbook* (Totnes, Devon: Prospect Books, 2011), 61.

24. Hutchins, *Cognition* (above, n. 11), 141: "When a knowledgeable navigator hears or sees this bearing, he may know which direction he is currently facing and may actually feel the direction indicated by the bearing as a physical sensation. For example, a navigator facing west may hear '059' and experience a sense of the direction to the right of directly behind."

25. For an overview of patterns of days in late antiquity, see especially Michele Salzman, "Pagan and Christian Notions of the Week in the Fourth-Century-CE Western Roman Empire," in R. M. Rosen, *Time and Temporality in the Ancient World* (Philadelphia: University of Pennsylvania Museum of Archaeology and Anthropology, 2004), 185–216; and C. Pietri, "Le temps de la semaine à Rome et dans l'Italie chrétienne (IVe–VIe s.)," in *Le temps chrétien de la fin de l'antiquité au Moyen Âge, IIIe–XIIIe siècles* (Paris: CNRS, 1984), 63–97.

26. I use the Latin edition of Marco Conti, *Priscillian of Avila: The Complete Works* (Oxford: Oxford University Press, 2010), but I have modified some of Conti's English translations for clarity. For a discussion of the cosmological significance of the charge of Manichaeism, see Burrus, *Making of a Heretic* (above, n. 16), 69–76.

27. Priscillian, *Tractates* 1.232–36; trans. Conti (above, n. 26).

28. Ibid. 1.380–81.

29. Ibid. 1.392–95 and 409–10, trans. Conti (above, n. 26).

30. See discussion in Bianco, "Tematiche astrali" (above, n. 15), and Tim Hegedus, *Early Christianity and Ancient Astrology* (New York: Peter Lang, 2007), 339; for other Christian views that reorient astrological knowledge along a Christian cosmological scheme, see especially Nicola Denzey, "A New Star on the Horizon: Astral Christologies and Stellar Debates in Early Christian Discourse," in Scott Noegel, Joel Walker, and Brannon Wheeler, eds., *Prayer, Magic, and the Stars in the Ancient and Late Antique World* (University Park: Pennsylvania State University Press, 2003), 207–21.

31. For a detailed analysis, see Hegedus, *Early Christianity* (above, n. 30), 353–70.

32. *Tractate* 6.162–66 trans. Conti (above, n. 26).

33. Ibid. 6.180–84: Burrus, *Making of a Heretic* (above, n. 16), 63, translates *operabilis* here as "working" rather than as "effective" or "efficacious," and thus reads the passage as "the working order of nature": i.e., the natural order. I suggest that Priscillian's subsequent worry that events in human lives ("all that we lived") could be considered the *opus mundi* ("work of the world" or "work of the cosmos") rather than the "Easter of the Lord" lends a more astrological, "efficacious" meaning to *operabilis*.

34. *Tractate* 5.112–14 trans. Conti (above, n. 26).

35. Ibid. 1.432–34.

36. See discussion in Chadwick (above, n. 15), *Priscillian,* chapter 3, 111–32.

37. Perhaps the best account of the magic trials and their setting during the reign of Valens is Noel Lenski, *Failure of Empire: Valens and the Roman State in the Fourth Century A.D.* (Berkeley and Los Angeles: University of California Press, 2002), chapter 5, 211–63.

38. Ammianus, *Res Gestae* 29.1.32; on the rise of astrology in the late Republic and the early imperial period, see Tamsyn Barton, *Power and Knowledge: Astrology, Physiognomics and Medicine in the Roman Empire* (Ann Arbor: University of Michigan Press, 1994), 27–71, and Volk, *Manilius* (above, n. 2), 127–37.

39. Ammianus, *Res Gestae* 29.1.41.

40. Cf. the repetition of the charge at *Res Gestae* 29.1.4; see also two later laws that stipulate the burning of magical and astrological works, *Codex Theodosianus* 16.5.34.1 from 398 and ibid. 9.16.12 from 409.

41. Ammianus, *Res Gestae* 29.2.20.

42. Firmicus Maternus, *Matheseos Libri VIII* (above, n. 6) 2.30.1–3. See also the discussion of magic accusations in Silke Trzcionka, *Magic and the Supernatural in Fourth-Century Syria* (London: Routledge, 2007), 64–80.

43. Firmicus Maternus, *Matheseos Libri VIII* (above, n. 6) 2.30.5.

44. Ibid. 29.2.27.

45. On ambiguity, see especially Catherine Atherton, *The Stoics on Ambiguity* (Cambridge: Cambridge University Press, 1993); on etymology, Henderson, *Medieval World* (above, n. 12), especially chapters 12–14, 149–73.

46. Augustine, *Confessions* 9.7 trans. R.S. Pine-Coffin, *Saint Augustine: Confessions* (London: Penguin, 1961), slightly modified.

47. *De Musica* 6.17; Brennan, "Augustine's *De Musica*," *Vigiliae Christianae* 42 (1988): 273–74; on Augustine's ambivalence about musical manipulations, see Richter, "*Carmina autem quaecumque in laudem dei dicuntur hymni vocantur* (Isidore of Seville, *Etymologiae* 6.1)," *Journal of Late Antiquity* 2 (2009): 116–30.

48. *Timaeus* 35b–37c.

49. *Enneads* 5.9.11, trans. MacKenna (above, n. 4).

50. Boethius, *De Institutione Musica* 1.1, trans. Calvin M. Bower, *Boethius: Fundamentals of Music* (New Haven: Yale University Press, 1989), slightly modified.

51. Ibid. 1.8.

52. Ibid. 1.9.

53. Ambrose, *Epistle* 75A.34; trans. J.H.W.G. Liebeschuetz, *Ambrose of Milan: Political Letters and Speeches* (Liverpool: Liverpool University Press, 2005); see Liebeschuetz 159 n. 2 on the double meaning of *carmen* as "song" and "spell."

54. See Maurice P. Cunningham, "The Place of the Hymns of St. Ambrose in the Latin Poetic Tradition," *Studies in Philology* 52 (1955): 509–14; Carl P.E. Springer, "The Hymns of Ambrose," in Richard Valantasis, ed., *Religions of Late Antiquity in Practice* (Princeton: Princeton University Press, 2000), 347–56; Jan den Boeft, "Ambrosius Lyricus," in den Boeft and Anton Hilhorst, eds. *Early Christian Poetry: A Collection of Essays* (Leiden: Brill, 1993), 77–89; that the basilica controversy was also a controversy over Easter and baptism (see Marcia L. Colish, "Why the Portiana? Reflections on the Milanese Basilica Crisis of 386," *Journal of Early Christian Studies* 10 [2002]: 361–72) reinforces the importance of the resurrection symbolism.

55. Den Boeft, "Ambrosius Lyricus" (above, n. 54), 86–89.

56. Ambrose, *Epistle* 75A.19–21 trans. Liebeschuetz (above, n. 53), slightly modified; cf. Brennan, "Augustine's *De Musica*" (above, n. 47), 268, on the "sing-song" child's voice that precipitates Augustine's conversion.

57. See Deborah Mauskopf Deliyannis, *Ravenna in Late Antiquity* (Cambridge: Cambridge University Press, 2010), 88–89.

58. Ra'anan Boustan, "Angels in the Architecture: Temple Art and the Poetics of Praise in the *Songs of the Sabbath Sacrifice*," in Boustan and Annette Yoshiko Reed, eds., *Heavenly Realms and Earthly Realities in Late Antique Religions* (Cambridge: Cambridge University Press, 2004), 195–212; Kathleen E. McVey, "The Domed Church as Microcosm: Literary Roots of an Architectural Symbol," *Dumbarton Oaks Papers* 37 (1983): 91–121; Jodi Magness, "Heaven on Earth: Helios and the Zodiac Cycle in Ancient Palestinian Synagogues," *Dumbarton Oaks*

Papers 59 (2005): 1–52; Fabio Barry, "Walking on Water: Cosmic Floors in Late Antiquity and the Middle Ages," *The Art Bulletin* 89 (2007): 627–56; Nicholas Temple, "Baptism and Sacrifice: Cosmogony as Private Ontology," *Architectural Review Quarterly* 8 (2005): 47–60.

59. Ambrose, *Epistle* 75A.34.

60. Ambrose's cosmos, in Neoplatonic fashion, here inclines toward knowledge of God.

61. Ambrose, *Epistle* 75A.21.

62. Ibid. 19.

63. Firmicus Maternus, *Matheseos Libri VIII* 3.7.1, trans. Bram (above, n. 6), slightly modified.

64. Ibid. 3.8.1.

65. See Barton, *Power* (above, n. 38), 92–94, on the utility of complexity.

66. Pasztory, *Thinking with Things* (above, n. 1), 21: "This thinking deals with crucial issues of identity and relation to others and the cosmos, and it is definitely problem-solution oriented."

67. Boethius, *De Institutione Musica* 1.8, trans. Bower (above, n. 50), 16.

6

Angel

Ellen Muehlberger

The material remains of the culture of late antiquity—the art, the texts—locate angels as exceptional creatures existing with and among human beings yet different from humanity in ways that expand and complicate the range of possibilities available to both species. Late ancient cultural products of all sorts conveyed the message that angels were special but also familiar. When a person attending a Christian ritual in late fourth-century Ravenna looked up, he saw the faces of human figures looking back at him from the mosaics on the walls of his church. He also saw the faces of angels, in form much like human beings but with additional appendages, wings, that were theirs alone. When a curious reader perused one of the many collections of stories about ascetic feats accomplished in Egypt that were produced in the fifth and the sixth century, he learned that angels often appeared in the company of ascetic practitioners, frequently there to help out by exercising abilities that no human being, even the most disciplined, could claim. So, when the modest monk Amoun of Nitria needed to ford a river but would not disrobe to do so, an angel appeared in order to carry him across, dry and dressed.[1] Even the more pedestrian letters that survive from ascetic leaders support extraordinary expectations about how angels could act among human beings: when the head of an ascetic collective needed to know the nighttime activities in his community but loyalty and dignity required that he not pry, an angel appeared to reveal to him the secret practices taking place among monks in their cells at night.[2] When a city dweller decided to go through the initiation that would prepare him to participate in the central ritual activities of his community, he was trained to see in his mind's eye the angels who attended the service—spectators just like the human participants surrounding the person who performed the ritual.[3] And when a budding mystic studied the paths of others to learn how to gain entrance into the heavens, he came to understand that angels guarded the entrance to specific levels of heaven, their extraordinary divine status granting them the power to be guides to less adept, human travelers.[4] In all these cases, readers of texts could infer how angels acted and on what motivations, learning from their inferences that angels were very much like the human beings with whom they mingled; and yet angels displayed novel characteristics. Those novel characteristics were often so closely aligned with unexpected events that occurred in late ancient texts—heavenly tours, miraculous actions—that a modern reader may be tempted to conclude that angels were simply narrative devices, employed in late ancient religious literature to mark the intractable problem surpassed or the divine made accessible.

That temptation could be amplified by the fact that the majority of what we can retrieve of late ancient knowledge about angels is itself preserved in narrative form. Such sources as those that I have just listed were all rhetorical constructions in which angels acted as characters. Shortly put, they were stories or could be read as stories, their words establishing situations and landscapes in which angels appeared and acted. Late ancient thinkers rarely engaged questions about angels in any other rhetorical register besides narrative. There was no industry of persuasive or polemical treatises aimed at establishing the nature of angels as there was an industry of persuasive or polemical treatises written to establish one or another understanding of the nature of God.[5] In expository terms, angels were undertheorized in late ancient culture, particularly when compared to other, highly theorized divine beings like God but also when compared to other topics, such as the constitution of the human person or the proper exercise of a virtuous life. Though forensic philosophical methods were not frequently employed in late antiquity to explore the meaning and essence of the category "angel," we can still imagine how late ancient people may have known angels otherwise than in the narrative form. Two possibilities that are attested from late antiquity are direct visionary experience and magical collaboration; yet the media through which we know about them limit the information that they deliver. For example, angels may have been known to appear directly to human beings, establishing contact and a certain level of intimate knowledge, but the late ancient sources that point to such experiences are already narrativized. Recorded in stories, whether in first-person or third-person voice, such experiences are not available for us to investigate in any other form. For a second example, angels may have been known to be conjurable through ritual practices undertaken by individuals; and indeed they appear frequently in the magical material that survives from late antiquity. Yet even these sources allow us scant perspective on how such angels may have been known to those who conjured them. The form in which their presence survives, the spell, was itself a type of narrative in waiting, a formula containing of the hope of future behavior by certain characters, linked to the establishment of certain conditions and proffering certain results. Thus the kinds of sources that could allow modern readers to explore other, nonnarrative ways of knowing angels in late antiquity—conjuring, deriving them logically, taking up bodily practices to induce their presence: these are things not accessible to us in the remains of late ancient culture in forms that convey the alternative ways of knowing that visionary experience or magic seems to indicate. And so the material by which we can investigate late ancient ways of knowing about angels comprises largely stories—texts that present angels in action among other agents, inaugurating new actions and responding to others' activities.

The preponderance of narrative sources from late antiquity seems to limit our ability to reconstruct how and what late ancient people knew about angels (or truly, what any people in the past knew about subjects in their world). And indeed, even late ancient people recognized the insufficiency of language to convey knowledge of those beings that exist in the divine realm, angels included. But the fact that angels appear in narrative at all allows us to discern something blindingly important about late ancient knowing, about angels conceived as subjects and objects of knowledge, and about the way that we as moderns make sense of intellectual cultures equipped with actors and categories of being not viable in our own culture. Among the insights that acceptance of the narrative nature of most late ancient sources delivers is this: such representatives suggest that interaction with humanity was possible for angels. Though many texts from the late ancient period recount interactions among divine beings, few are the texts that focus on angels' interactions with each other.[6] Instead, the relationship between angels and humanity is almost always on display; in the absence of philosophical treatises that define it otherwise or narrative scenarios that offer an alternative, such a fact suggests that interaction with humanity was the angels' primary mode of action.

This chapter explores the parameters and consequences of that relationship, seeking to illuminate how late ancient assumptions about angels fostered particular cultural perspectives and products among human beings. My argument explores late ancient knowledge of angels and our estimation of it in two parts. In the first, I demonstrate that the presence of angels in narrative reveals that they had the capacity to communicate with humanity, an observation that on its face seems simple but in fact leads to several complex realities about both species. Late ancient thinkers, in ways both explicit and implicit, followed the potential for communication to rarified logical ends. They understood angels to share a common psychology with humanity yet held them to be a different class of being, with natures and motivations often beyond human understanding. Angels were not precisely the same as human beings, but they were familiar to them. The best way to conceptualize this relationship is to say that for late ancient Christians, angels were in the same ontological circle as human beings. As I explain, an ontological circle is a shifting cultural construction that can comprise members of different species but one wherein all members possess the potential for real contact with each other and thus for consequential communication, resulting in positive or negative outcomes. In the second part, I describe the consequences of the late ancient disposition of imagining angels as members of the same ontological circle as human beings. Although angels do illumine possibilities and limitations for humanity, they are far more than just tools "to think with," as an oft-adopted scholarly phrase would have it. Instead, they occupy a place of potential and, as messengers, bring new ethical models to humanity. Knowledge of angels in late antiquity, and contact with them, produced and reproduced cultural forms that ultimately changed ways of being human in that they introduced new forms of moral life and religious devotion.

THE ONTOLOGICAL CIRCLE

In the fourth and fifth centuries, both Christian and non-Christian writers participated in a trend of philosophical thought that removed God, the highest divine being, from similarity with the material world and any beings associated with it. Whereas intellectuals influenced by Platonic traditions had long assumed a division between what was material and what was immaterial, and followed that assumption by locating the divine in the immaterial, late ancient thought experiments redefined the highest divinity as even more remote from the material world. For although many ancient ideas about the immateriality of the highest god included a corollary assumption about limited contact with the world, God appearing to a few select human beings in only a handful of situations, late ancient philosophers pushed the highest god out of the realm of incomprehensibility toward the truly alien. At the start of the fifth century, for example, the Christian writer Augustine argued that it was inaccurate to think that God, the highest divinity, had appeared to human beings in material form throughout history. For him, Christian writings, especially the Epistles of Paul the Apostle, described a single moment when God chose to interact with humanity in one particular form, by sending the incarnate Christ. The incarnation was so definitive for Augustine that he vacated centuries of Christian reading practice to declare that God, the highest god, had not appeared in the material realm before the birth of Jesus—this despite numerous descriptions of God interacting with humanity in the books Augustine held to be sacred scripture, especially the books of the Old Testament. Similarly, for the philosopher Proclus, active in the latter half of the fifth century, it was not just inaccurate but inadequate to think, as had previous philosophers, that the highest divinity could be described even as a separate being, a god who existed in the realm of the immaterial and who communicated with the world through words or ideas. Instead, the highest divinity was so far beyond the human capacity to understand that it was necessary for Proclus to make a concession to the limited nature of the human mind. He advised that those seeking to understand the highest god should conceive, as best a human being could, a One residing "beyond being" and thus beyond any contact with (however far removed from) the material realm, characterized by multiplicity, decline, and the lack of the Good.[7] For both Augustine and Proclus, developments in the qualities by which they defined the divine world had pushed them to conclude that God was irretrievably separate, essentially unable to be in contact or communicate with the world, because of the dissonance existing between his unity and the world's multiplicity. They both felt so strongly about the discontinuity between the nature of the highest god and the nature of the rest of existence that they self-consciously argued for the abrogation of the methods by which their own teachers and traditions had understood that god.

Yet neither man gave up the premise that there was some type of contact between the material world and the divine world. As the highest being was philosophically removed from communication with existence, angels were elevated to maintain the possibility of contact between the remainder of the divine world and humanity, and even to manage that contact. For Proclus, angels were necessarily lacking in evil, because they kept contact with the multiple gods below the One, interpreting and conveying knowledge of them to the order below. As he argued, "the class that is the interpreter of the gods stands in continuity with the gods, knows the intellect of the gods, and reveals the divine will." That class "is nothing other than the good proceeding and shining forth first from the beings which remain inside the One."[8] At the same time, for Augustine, angels accomplished the visitations of God to the material world before the incarnation, executing their duties as a clerk would make announcements for a judge.[9] Those angels have no will of their own and exist solely to enact the material appearances of the divine. In both cases, as the highest god was being written out of contact with humanity, neither writer abandoned the prospect that human beings could communicate with some part of the divine world. Consequently, their theories maintained that the quintessence of angels was that they were in contact with humanity.

Augustine and Proclus were heavy thinkers, developing philosophical theories of the divine, but even late ancient readers unengaged in philosophy had resources by which they could arrive at much the same conclusions about angels; the most accessible of these resources were the narratives that I discussed at the start of this chapter. Reading a narrative is an act of the imagination, which forces a reader to entertain the possibilities that the characters of the text are compatible enough to exist in the same space and perhaps to communicate. In this way, any act of reading is an instance of cultural training, porting its own philosophical and epistemological lessons, implicit though they may be. To understand how and what reading teaches, consider what a reader could learn from a simple dialogue. What follows is an exchange between Mary, the woman about to become the mother of Jesus, and Gabriel, an angel who comes to announce to her the events that will happen to her (Luke 1:28–38, New Revised Standard Version):

And he came to her and said, "Greetings, favored one! The Lord is with you." But she was much perplexed by his words and pondered what sort of greeting this might be. The angel said to her, "Do not be afraid, Mary, for you have found favor with God. And now, you will conceive in your womb and bear a son, and you will name him Jesus. He will be great, and will be called the Son of the Most High, and the Lord God will give to him the throne of his ancestor David. He will reign over the house of Jacob forever, and of his kingdom there will be no end." Mary said to the angel, "How can this be, since I am a virgin?" The angel said to her, "The Holy Spirit will come upon you, and the power of the Most High will overshadow you; therefore the child to be born will be holy; he will be called Son of God. And now, your relative Eliza-beth in her old age has also conceived a son; and this is the sixth month for her who was said to be barren. For nothing will be impossible with God." Then Mary said, "Here am I, the servant of the Lord; let it be with me according to your word." Then the angel departed from her.

Though this story originated in the late first century, it was circulated and reimag-ined extensively in late antiquity, entering late ancient discourse, especially Chris-tian discourse, again and again: in texts that situated it and other Christian stories from the New Testament gospels with respect to Jews and Jewish religious culture; in explorations of the Holy Spirit and its place in the Trinity; in homilies reflecting on the birth of Christ; in discussions about and advice to virgins; as a lens for interpreting older stories of announcement from the Old Testament; and, of course, in commentaries on the gospel of Luke itself.[10] What does not immediately stand out but does come gradually to impose on the reader is the fact that Mary and Gabriel are engaged in a conversation. They exchange greetings; they size up each other's responses; they respond to likely but unstated emotional responses of their interlocutor. They possess common communication skills; to verge toward the technical for a moment, those skills depend on the ability of each to hold a theory of mind for the other. Mary has a theory of mind for Gabriel, estimating that when she asks him about what seems an impossible situation he will compre-hend and answer her question. But Gabriel also holds theory of mind for Mary, for as the story narrates, he sees her reaction to his appearance, understands what it means, and takes the initiative to reassure her: "Do not be afraid." Though it was an extremely popular story in late antiquity, readers rarely subjected its characters to the same kinds of interpretive adjustments that, say, Augustine applied to appearances of God. Readers of the gospel of Luke—and there were many—engaged in worldmaking when they read the text, representing to themselves a realm in which productive, emotionally complex contact between human beings and angels was possible, even expected.

Angels in this realm of contact followed the logic of interaction with beings in the material world, even if they did not always follow the normal expectations for the human capacity for action in the material world. Though the angel comes to

Mary with miraculous news, he delivers it in a regular, if frightening, conversation, an exchange whose development nevertheless follows the rules of more normal conversation. Even in the miraculous stories that I recounted at the start of the chapter, angels do extraordinary things. They accomplish those things that human beings could be able to do were they only powerful enough: the monk could cross the river if only he were not hampered by his code of conduct; the monastic leader could have discovered the secrets of his monks were decorum not an issue. I mean to say that angels do not appear in late ancient texts in order to accomplish truly unimaginable acts or introduce truly novel situations. Their actions were surprising but not incomprehensible; their motivations were legible to others—both to the other characters in their own narrative contexts and to the readers who engaged these stories. Indeed, angels produce acts that meet expectations in most cases yet exceed or defy them in one or two aspects.[11] As I mentioned above, this limited exceptionalism may signal to the skeptical reader nothing more than the convenience of angels as plot devices, but the consistent inclusion of angels in narrative in reality reinforces how truly normal angels are to late ancient readers in their abnormality. Perhaps the best indication of their normality is the consistent application of moral evaluation to angels: Proclus, Augustine, and other late ancient thinkers judged angels in moral terms, drawing a boundary between evil angels and good ones. By including them both in the logic of interaction and in the expectations of interaction that obtain among human beings, such intellectual projects signal that the nature of angels was understood to be quite close to that of humanity.

In certain instances, angels were not just close to humanity; they were expected to interact with human beings immediately, by voicing their words inside the minds of human beings. Magical texts often point to this expectation. For example, consider this spell for garnering a companion angel, which is preserved in a Greek magical papyrus. It ensured the person who executed the spell a guide and guaranteed that no observer could tell the difference between the beneficiary of the spell and the angel he had gotten to direct him:[12]

> When you go abroad, he will go abroad with you; when you are destitute, he will give you money. He will tell you what things will happen both when and at what time of the night or day. And if anyone asks you "What do I have in mind?" or "What has happened to me?" or even "What is going to happen?" question the angel, *and he will tell you in silence. But you will speak to the one who questions you as if from yourself.*

Identified as a "mighty angel," this guide meant safety and financial security for the one who conjured it, but it also meant knowledge of the future, mind-reading abilities, and, perhaps best of all, no way for others to detect its presence. The conjurer would naturally seem to have the abilities that in reality were the result of the angel's help. More important, although we may assume that an angel got by magic would then assist with one or two discrete acts of more magic, it appears that this is not the case with the "mighty angel" garnered by this spell. Instead, the intent of the spell is to acquire, seemingly permanently, such a personal guide, seer of the future, and internal helper as we all might want. Whether the spell was successful or not is immaterial, because even simply reading the spell taught a reader that angelic companions existed to be harnessed. And consulters of spells were only one of many groups to hold this expectation; personal angelic companions were a regular, if infrequent, topic in certain types of Christian literature. Evagrius of Pontus, for instance, was part of a tradition that considered angels a normal part of the program of ascetic advancement for monks.[13] Angels were assets to those attempting the difficult practices that Evagrius taught his students. In his treatise *On Prayer*, Evagrius describes how an angel can, "with a single word, [put] an end to every opposing activity within us." Its presence "moves the light of the mind to an unerring activity," so that "the mind stands thereafter free of all turmoil, acedia, and negligence."[14] Angels could communicate so closely as to incline the mind toward certain dispositions and could meld with one's desires in order to reveal all the answers a human being could ever wish to know, from the motivations of others to the events of the future.

These moments of communication between angelic and human subjectivities signal a peculiar late ancient assumption, namely that the two species, though different, were psychologically similar. Evagrius's theory of the deep compatibility between the two is the most detailed and precise late ancient evidence for this assumption: during his time as an ascetic, Evagrius elaborated a complex working theory of the common psychological constitution of angels and of human beings—and of demons, for that matter. All these were rational beings, having the faculty of the intellect in common; what distinguished them from one another was the peculiar mixture of other components; angels were predominantly composed of intellect, whereas human beings were less so, yet their practices of fending away the passions helped them cultivate their intellect.[15] For Evagrius in particular, angels were capable of immediate congress with the human mind because of their sympathy to the human intellect, a faculty that they shared with humanity. Angels could communicate directly with human beings and could even seem to speak inside human minds, then, because they were of one kind with and continued to share a basic nature with humanity.

Other writers were more cautious, positing a close similarity between angels and humanity only in the distant past or the distant future. Christian thinkers who narrated the origins of the cosmos often aimed to explain the contemporary state of humanity, and their explanations often hinted at the latent potential within humanity either to have been or to have become something else. Gregory of Nyssa's treatise *On the Making of Humanity*, written in the late 370s C.E., argued that God originally intended human beings to participate in a rational existence like the one that angels enjoyed. It was only after humanity's disobedience became evident that human beings were changed and given passions that overrode their originally rational nature. According to Gregory, at the resurrection humanity would return to unity with the angels and with God.[16] Whereas this version of the beginning of the world suggested that the actions of humanity had precipitated the different statuses of angels and of human beings, still other explanations located the cause in the actions of angels. In contrast to Gregory, Augustine of Hippo suggested that angels had received their status, different from humanity both morally and ontologically, as a result of the choices that they exercised at the start of the world. Angels were currently stable in their essence and their will, never departing from the will of God, but this was a result only of their having not abandoned God when other angels did. That is to say, angels acquired their status only because of the choices they exercised, or rather did not exercise, at the beginning of time.[17] Although Gregory and Augustine gave different reasons for the contemporary division that they posited between the nature of angels and the nature of humanity, they shared an understanding that there was a moment in the archaic past when angels and humanity were essentially similar. Put a different way: many late ancient people, whether Christians or non-Christians, philosophers or lay readers, assumed that angels were in a certain sense kin to humanity. I mean not that ancient people included angels in their tightly conceived kinship structures but that they recognized angels as related familiars. Either human beings and angels continued to be in a close relationship, possessing psychologies similar enough to each other to work in concert to advance toward unity with God, or they were at some other point in history close, until their actions separated them and made them distinct in essence in the present.

ANGELS, HUMANITY, AND THE ETHICAL
PRODUCT OF KNOWING

The observations that I have made in the previous section about angelic communication with humanity, and the diverse ways that late ancient Christian thinkers imagined congruity with angels, translate in reality to a more precise theoretical observation. Together they suggest that in a wide range of late ancient Christian discourses angels and human beings were known to occupy the same ontological circle. By "ontological circle" I refer to a cultural construction that comprises all beings whose constitutions, as defined by the culture they inhabit, are alike enough to allow communication among them. The members of such a circle are independent of one another; they can all exercise agency to some degree. Furthermore, members of the same ontological circle are not necessarily members of the same species as categorized by the culture in which they take shape. The combination of differences among members and their similarities allows for productive, even unpredictable, interactions. Indeed, the beings in any given ontological circle have real contact with one another; that is to say, the circle is not the precipitate of a thought experiment but is the set of implicit or explicit assumptions in a culture about the types of interaction possible among beings in the world.

The parameters of an ontological circle are constructed and thus vary from one cultural context to another. In the contemporary North American context, some animals share the ontological circle with human beings, particularly domestic animals. The theorist Donna Haraway has written extensively about the relationship between humanity and multiple "companion species," operating on the assumption that human beings are accompanied by, even constituted with, any number of other organisms, as are all other types of life.[18] Haraway is one important early voice in a wider contemporary turn among scholars toward investigating animal-human relationships as imagined in the products and processes of different cultures. Yet there are several other configurations of the ontological circle to be explored; that is to say, human beings have often been paired with animals in an ontological circle—Beth Berkowitz's chapter in this volume is an excellent illustration of the complex negotiations that such pairings can inspire—and yet other cultural contexts have included other types of nonanimal agents among the actors in the ontological circle: agents who were immaterial, or artificial, or alien.[19] In all these cases, what is common is this: existing as members of the same circle with other beings holds the promise of transformation, the potential of surpassing the capacity of any individual member or even kind, as well as the threat of unforeseen consequences of interaction. As a logical result, part of a culture's construction of its circle is the development of rules about how to manage contact among members, especially members otherwise thought to be of different kinds. The exchange between members is therefore often culturally regulated in an intense way, to the point that the transfer of certain kinds of information among members—a natural eventuality of the communication common to members of the same circle—and even physical contact, especially sexual contact, are problematized. Indeed, the persistence of explicit rules about contact with other beings in a culture can often signal the implicit assumption of an ontological circle, in that such rules necessarily imagine both that the contact is possible and that such contact is not under the full control of the human member. Insistent talk about other species, especially about the types of contact that are taboo, is as much a negative marker of the existence of an assumed ontological circle as the positing of the possibility of communication is a positive one. In late antiquity, for example, tales about angels and their interaction with humanity warned about the corruptive potential of the knowledge that they shared and the moral consequences of sexual contact with them.[20] Those specific late ancient contexts in which angels were assumed to be likely to come into contact with human beings were often flush with instructions about how to deal with angelic visitors. The resulting structures harnessed the power of interactions, now guarded, among members. For late ancient people, meaningful contact with angels was unpredictable in its outcomes yet often productive, resulting in new cultural forms. Understanding that angels existed in the same ontological circle as human beings in much of late ancient culture allows us to understand the transformative potential latent in the contact between them.

When taken as members of the same ontological circle as human beings, angels introduce their own capacities into the field of potential from which all in the circle may draw. For instance, in the stories that I shared at the start of this chapter, angels accomplished miraculous things, creating situations and results that had remained out of the reach of the human actors in their midst. Yet the promise of sharing the ontological circle with angels extended further, bearing the suggestion that some aspects of angelic existence could also obtain for others in the circle. We know, for example, that late ancient Christians assumed that angels had an extensive capacity for vision, one that outstripped the human faculty of sight. They were capable of seeing other divine beings, which human beings could not see.[21] Given how closely angels and humanity were held to be related, it is not surprising that this widespread assumption about angelic vision led to deliberate exploration of what such sensibilities meant for humanity. A collection of homilies from late ancient Syria, now identified with the single author Pseudo-Macarius, explored the latent potential of angelic visual acuity. For this homilist, Ezekiel's vision of the special angels known as cherubim was the fodder for an entire discussion of the nature of angels, which was completely visual: angels were "entirely eye," or "entirely vision." He urged readers to understand this fact not just as a distinctive feature of the angelic class but as a trace that pointed toward a real transformation available also to them. Speaking directly to the most advanced religious practitioners, he explained: "When you become a throne of God and the heavenly charioteer has mounted you, and your whole soul has become a spiritual eye, . . . then you too are a living being."[22] The constitution of human beings was close enough to angels' that human beings might become like them, gaining the sensibilities that angels already possessed. Being part of the same ontological circle as angels, then, allowed writers like Pseudo-Macarius to imagine how they might extend normal human faculties to develop in new, unpredicted ways. The expansion of human possibilities—in this case, of vision, or of developing the intellect, or of someday returning to the unity of rational thought that God originally designed—all these are possible only if humanity is ontologically contiguous with angels, in contact with them. We need to be meaningfully like those other beings that we interact with for the promise of angelic transformation to be real.

While contiguity among members is the foundation of ideas that expand the potential of members of the same ontological circle, at the same time it means that actions taken among the members have consequences. Being part of an ontological circle means being exposed to the ideas and influences of the other members.

As I have mentioned, the possibilities that such a state brings are also paired with dangers; those dangers exist because the mores and motivations of the others in one's ontological circle are not always well known. As nonhuman beings, angels work by their own unpredictable processes. On the one hand, this is just a logical observation: if angels worked and acted like human beings, they would be human beings. But on the other, there is evidence from antiquity to prove that ignorance of the nature of angels was an assumption commonly voiced in late ancient discourse—that it was historically a part of late ancient knowledge of angels. For each late ancient thinker who tried to describe angelic vision, angelic appearances, angelic creation, or angelic morality, there was another who simply threw up his hands and admitted ignorance with respect to angels, their abilities, and their motivations.[23]

Even that ignorance, though, was culturally productive. If I am right that Christians considered themselves part of the same ontological circle as angels, and if they regularly reflected on how much they did not know about angels, then late ancient Christian culture as a whole entertained two seemingly opposite ideas: that angels were like human beings and that angels could act in ways and produce things radically different from how humans acted and what humans could produce. Let me put this point in visual terms by describing the ontological circle for a moment as a physical shape in which all members stand side by side. Ignorance about angels and their abilities created a perspective in which the Christian stood in an exceptionally large ontological circle with other beings, yet the complete contours of that circle, especially the distant place where the curves of the circle joined to form the whole, were hidden from him. In theory, the circle is complete, but in practice much of it exists over the horizon, hidden from view, so that the effect is not so much a circle of known beings but an open-ended curve in which some members can be imagined but must necessarily remain unknown in their basic essence.[24] I speculate that this quality underlies the intensity that infuses talk of communication among members of the circle—it is at once exhilarating and frightening to think oneself part of a group some of whose members are partly or entirely obscure in their existence and essence. Simply thinking of different kinds of beings with whom one may interact lacks the charge that characterizes descriptions in late antique literature of meetings between angels and human beings. Knowing as late ancient people did that there are beings like you whose nature remains mysterious, truly incomprehensible, is transformative in a way that no thought experiment could ever be.

The proof of my claim lies with the evidence from late antiquity detailing the role of angels as messengers. The Greek word *angelos* meant "messenger," and many angelic visitors to humanity were understood to be passing information. Gabriel, for example, when he appeared to Mary, was there to inform her; his visit did not induce or change her situation. In some parts of late ancient culture, this function of angels dominated. Late ancient Christians in particular began to write about angels as permanent channels of illumination and knowledge, tethering the divine world to the material through a series of interlocking levels of existence, each capable of being in contact only with the levels adjacent to it. In figurations like that created in Pseudo-Dionysius's *Celestial Hierarchy,* angels were ordered by their closeness to God and vesseled knowledge in sequence among themselves, from highest to lowest, and from the lowest angel to the most advanced human beings. Understanding angels as divine messengers in this way, messengers that can filter and channel information from two discontinuous realms, has extensive practical and cultural ramifications.

As late antiquity progressed, however, the most significant purpose of angelic visits shifted from conveying information to impelling human beings to write new narratives. Two examples from late ancient monastic culture illustrate the change. Sometime in the fourth century, a man named Pachomius received a text from an angel, along with a set of instructions:[25]

> One time when he was sitting in his cave an angel appeared to him and told him: "So far as you are concerned, you conduct your life perfectly. It is in vain for you to continue sitting in your cave! Come now, leave this place, and go out, and call the young monks together, and dwell with them. Rule them by the model that I am now giving you." And the angel gave him a bronze tablet on which [the following rule] was engraved.

The angel gave Pachomius a message, but he also insisted that Pachomius begin to institute a community governed both by his authority and by the authority of the rule granted to him. According to this text, the beginning of the Pachomian federation, a large but loose association of monastic communities, can be traced to a prodding angel whose delivery of a communiqué was both direct and directive. Pachomius's experience was repeated: There is evidence that Shenoute of Atripe, the leader of the White Monastery, also received instruction from an angel to write a rule and to gather monks. The document in which Shenoute meets his messenger is badly damaged, but it appears to have an angel speaking directly to Shenoute, saying, "Write! Write!"[26] And write Shenoute did—his collected works reveal the intimate details of the community that he founded, both through rules that he instituted proscribing behavior and through accounts of punishments that he ordained. Both Pachomius and Shenoute headed monasteries or federations of monasteries that were remarkably large in their late ancient contexts, with populations in the thousands. Beyond their absolute numbers, though, the communities that these men founded bore quite an influence on subsequent expressions of Christian monasticism.[27] The monastic systems that these men created changed the landscape of Upper Egypt, remaking the world in which the men and women who joined their federations lived and the villages that supported their communities.[28]

That is to say, angels not only came with messages but in these cases inspired the composition of new texts; and with those new texts, often elaborate, came the creation of entire ethical systems, new habitats in which new human endeavors could flourish.

One more example will make plain the transformative potential of this way of envisioning interaction between angels and human beings. It is difficult to think of a late ancient event with larger cultural consequences than the meeting of the angel Jibril with Muhammad.[29] Jibril, the faithful spirit, pressed Muhammad to recite messages that he had been receiving; Muhammad began to recite and in so doing began the project of revealing the Qur'an to humanity. This account appears in some forms in the Qur'an itself, in other forms in the hadith collections, those accumulated traditions reported about Muhammad by his close companions. In the Qur'an, a discussion of the prophet's authority in Surah 6 makes it clear that the revelation of the Qur'an was not simply a matter of Jibril's delivering a previously composed message from God. Rather, it was a collaboration between the angel and the human being. Muhammad was a necessary actor in the Qur'an's inception: a piece of paper conveying the details of God's will or an angel speaking them would not have worked.[30] The result of the collaboration between Jibril and Muhammad was, like the *Rules* of Pachomius and the *Canons* of Shenoute, adopted by an early community of believers as an important document, one that held open a new way of being, something unprecedented and thus requiring careful preservation. That is because the Qur'an, like the *Rules* of Pachomius and the *Canons* of Shenoute, lent itself as a divine scaffold for the enactment of a creative discourse of instructions for living. All these angelic products were ethical documents that encouraged the formation and continuation of ethical communities, in turn anchored in the authority of their message. This is my observation—that the presence of angels in the ontological circle of human beings creates new, unpredicted, and pluripotent options for living for all who are in the circle.

Yet it seems that at least some late ancient people reached the same conclusion. Let me close by citing a story that circulated about Muhammad and his understanding of his experience with the angel. Among the ahadith collected in the ninth century by the Iranian scholar Muslim ibn al-Hajjaj is a vignette about a second visit by Jibril, this time to a group of people. Muhammad and several friends were approached by a man in white clothing and with raven hair—a stranger, whom none of them recognized, yet whose body and appearance showed none of the usual wear and tear to indicate that he was a traveler. Familiar yet alien, he quizzed the prophet about several topics: about submission, about faith, about beauty, about judgment. Muhammad patiently and piously answered his questions. The questioner left, and after a while Muhammad asked his close friend Umar: "Do you know who that was?" Umar demurred, and Muhammad said: "That was Jibril. He came to teach you your religion."[31] This story, the hadith of Jibril, is often presented in pious Islamic sources as the only hadith that one needs to know. It tells us what we need to know about how angels were conceived of in late antiquity and about the deep effects of their being considered to exist in the same ontological circle as human beings. Whereas in the narrative setting of the first century Gabriel appeared to Mary to deliver a bit of news and to prepare her for her experiences, Jibril, understood within the parameters of late ancient knowledge about angels, came to Muhammad to force him to recite a new plan for humanity. Their work together was at once conservative, recalling humanity to an original message from God, and creative at the same time, in that it gave voice to a new cultural form in which human beings could exist and could relate to the divine.

NOTES

1. Palladius, *Lausiac History* 8 (trans. Robert T. Meyer, *Palladius: The Lausiac History,* Ancient Christian Writers, vol. 34 [Westminster, Md.: Newman Press, 1965], 43).

2. The Pachomian leader Theodore was known to have angelic informants who helped him keep an eye on monks; see the *Letter of Ammon* 20 and 26 (ed. and trans. James E. Goehring, *The Letter of Ammon and Pachomian Monasticism,* Patristische Texte und Studien 27 [New York: de Gruyter, 1985], 171, 175–76).

3. See my discussion of catechetical training in visualization and the place of angels among spectators to Christian ritual in *Angels in Late Ancient Christianity* (New York: Oxford University Press, 2013), chapter 6, "Bringing Angels into the World," 176–202.

4. The text of *Zostrianos,* bound together with the *Letter of Peter to Philip* in Nag Hammadi Codex VIII, was alluded to by Plotinus in his work *Against the Gnostics* (*Enneads* 3.8, 5.8, 5.5, and 2.9); thus it was known among both philosophers and whatever Christians hid the Nag Hammadi cache.

5. There are a few exceptions: Proclus, Pseudo-Dionysius, and Augustine, who will all be discussed below.

6. Isaiah 6 is one exception; Pseudo-Dionysius's *Celestial Hierarchy* seems another, but as we will see, that text is as much about humanity as it is about angels.

7. Proclus, *Platonic Theology,* proposition 138.

8. Proclus, *On the Existence of Evils* 14 (ed. and trans. Jan Opsomer and Carlos Steel, *Proclus: On the Existence of Evils,* Ancient Commentators on Aristotle [London: Duckworth, 2003], 68).

9. Augustine, *On the Trinity* 3.23 (ed. W. J. Mountain, *Sancti Aurelii Augustini "De Trinitate" Libri XV,* Corpus Christianorum, Series Latina, vol. 50 [Turnhout: Brepols, 1968], 152).

10. In order: Eusebius's *Demonstration of the Gospel,* Didymus the Blind's *On the Trinity,* homilies on the day of Jesus's birth from Gregory of Nyssa and John Chrysostom, in advice about and to virgins from Ambrose of Milan and Gregory of Nyssa, in interpretations of the Old Testament from Theodoret of Cyrrhus and Procopius of Gaza. Ancient commentaries directly on Luke abound as well.

11. Cognitive studies of religion have long observed the way that most divine beings fulfill the grand majority of expectations that we hold for human behavior, with one or two

extraordinary ways of acting or being. See, for example, Pascal Boyer, *The Naturalness of Religious Ideas: A Cognitive Theory of Religion* (Berkeley and Los Angeles: University of California Press, 1994), particularly chapter 4, "Natural Ontologies and Supernatural Furniture," 91–124.

12. K. Preisendanz, ed., *Papyri Graecae Magicae* (Leipzig: Teubner, 1928), 1.171–78 (ed. and trans. Hans Dieter Betz, *The Greek Magical Papyri in Translation, Including the Demotic Spells,* 2nd ed. [Chicago: University of Chicago Press, 1992], 7), emphasis mine.

13. For a longer discussion, see "Angels as Equipment for Living: The Companion Angel Tradition in Evagrian Christianity," in my *Angels* (above, n. 3), 89–118.

14. Evagrius of Pontus, *On Prayer* 74–75 (trans. Robert E. Sinkewicz, *Evagrius of Pontus: The Greek Ascetic Corpus,* Oxford Early Christian Studies [Oxford: Oxford University Press, 2003], 201).

15. Sinkewicz, *Evagrius* (above, n. 14), xxxvii–xl, has a longer description of Evagrius's program.

16. Gregory of Nyssa, *De Opificio Hominis* 17. See J. Warren Smith, "The Body of Paradise and the Body of the Resurrection: Gender and the Angelic Life in Gregory of Nyssa's 'De Hominis Opificio,'" *Harvard Theological Review* 99 (2006): 207–28.

17. Augustine, *Enchiridion* 9, summarizes his view of how angels came to enjoy their special status.

18. Donna Haraway, *The Companion Species Manifesto: Dogs, People, and Significant Otherness* (Chicago: Prickly Paradigm Press, 2003).

19. For an introduction to the force of animal studies in the humanistic disciplines, see Cary Wolfe, "Human, All Too Human: 'Animal Studies' and the Humanities," *Proceedings of the Modern Language Association* 124 (2009): 564–75. A large portion of the issue in which this article appears is dedicated to work in animal studies in a wide range of cultural and theoretical contexts. See also Posthumanities, the monograph series that Wolfe edits with the University of Minnesota Press.

20. For an extended discussion of taboo contact, see Annette Yoshiko Reed, *Fallen Angels and the History of Judaism and Christianity: The Reception of the Enochic Literature* (Cambridge: Cambridge University Press, 2005).

21. See, for example, Gregory of Nazianzus, *Orations* 2.13, in which he explains that higher divinities can see what lower divinities cannot.

22. Pseudo-Macarius, *Homily* 1.12 (trans. George A. Maloney, *Pseudo-Macarius: The Fifty Spiritual Homilies,* Classics of Western Spirituality [Mahwah, N.J.: Paulist Press, 1992), 44, slightly modified.

23. I offer a theory about this ignorance in the conclusion to my *Angels* (above, n. 3), 203–14.

24. John Crowley's essay "A Well without a Bottom" offers another physical metaphor, by which he indicates what I mean by the "hidden" or "distant" contours of the ontological circle: *Lapham's Quarterly,* July 1, 2012, http://www.laphamsquarterly.org/essays/a-well-without-a-bottom.php?page = all, accessed July 1, 2012.

25. Palladius, *Lausiac History* 32 (trans. Meyer, *Lausiac History* [above, n. 1], 92, slightly modified); cf. Gennadius, *De Viris Illustribus* 7, which does not speak of tablets but still has Pachomius producing the rule under the guidance of an angel.

26. Shenoute, *Canon* 1 (XC 59:45; for more information about White Monastery Codex XC, see Stephen Emmel, *Shenoute's Literary Corpus,* vol. 1, Corpus Scriptorum Christianorum Orientalium, vol. 599 [Louvain: Peeters, 2004], 128–31).

27. For an estimate of their size, see Ewa Wipszycka, *Moines et communautés monastiques en Égypte (IVe–VIIIe siècles),* Journal of Juristic Papyrology, Supplement 11 (Warsaw: Journal of Juristic Papyrology, 2009), 419–29.

28. Bentley Layton, "Rules, Patterns, and the Exercise of Power in Shenoute's Monastery: The Problem of World Replacement and Identity Maintenance," *Journal of Early Christian Studies* 15 (2007): 45–73.

29. Hussain Kassim, "Nothing Can Be Known or Done without the Involvement of Angels: Angels and Angelology in Islam and Islamic Literature," in *Angels: The Concept of Celestial Beings—Origins, Development, and Reception,* ed. Friedrich V. Reiterer, Tobias Nicklas, and Karin Schöpflin, Deuterocanonical and Cognate Literature (Berlin: de Gruyter, 2007), 645–60, at 648–49.

30. Patricia Crone, "Angels versus Humans as Messengers of God: The View of the Qur'ānic Pagans," in *Revelation, Literature, and Community in Late Antiquity,* ed. Philippa Townsend and Moulie Vidas, Texts and Studies in Ancient Judaism 146 (Tübingen: Mohr Siebeck, 2011), 315–36, contextualizes the claims of Sura 6:8–10 as an argument between Muhammad and the polytheists, who expected something different in their messenger.

31. Muslim ibn al-Hajjaj, *Sahih Muslim,* book 1.1.

7

God

Lewis Ayres

At first glance this chapter may seem to be a conservative outlier in a collection showcasing new questions: a historian of early Christian doctrine writes about Augustine's understanding of the relationship between God and creation! And yet, through exploring the complexities of just a few texts, I hope to show that historians cannot hope to grasp the dynamics of knowing in late antiquity without attending to how Christians viewed Christian belief as implying particular conceptions of knowledge and shaping habits of seeking understanding. Christian theology should be seen not as a separate branch of late antique knowledge, with a content separate from other branches of knowledge, but as itself a means of structuring the activity of knowing overall. In particular, the development of Nicene theology offered new ways for Christians to articulate both the task of knowing and its goal. As Nicene theology defined specific ways of speaking about God in Trinitarian terms, so too it described a Trinitarian order in the world in which Christians spoke about and sought after God. The texts that I consider offer different angles of view onto a knot of themes revealing the inseparability of imagining God and imagining the created order. Although I focus exclusively on Augustine of Hippo (354–430 C.E.), I do so because he presents one of the most compelling examples of the Nicene Christianity of the late fourth and the early fifth century. This focused study should then stimulate others concerned with different authors and movements within the Christian tradition.

We can make no progress into this field without noting first that Augustine envisages God as Trinitarian, and in both the texts with which we shall be concerned it is not God but the Word of God who is Augustine's focus.[1] In fact one of my central arguments will be that one of the main ways in which Augustine reveals the inseparability of imagining the divine and imagining creation is through a slow intensifying of his theology of the Word and of all things as existing in that Word. This deepening and intensifying culminates in an account of the incarnate Word's mission as revealing the true nature of God's providential ordering and of the reformation of desire that should accompany our striving for knowledge of Creator and creation.

AD ME AURES, AD ILLUM COR

In order to show Augustine's complex interweaving of themes I will structure this chapter by following closely the arguments to be found in just a few short sections of text. I do so because how Augustine attempts to draw his audience into a particular mode of knowing in faith is to be seen not simply in the positions he espouses but in the shape of his literary (and, in the case of some of these texts, originally spoken) performance. I will begin with the first of Augustine's *Tractates on John*.[2] At the outset Augustine comments not directly on John but on another text that has just been read, 1 Corinthians 2:14: "The natural man [*animalis homo*] does not perceive the things that are of the Spirit of God." The discussion that begins here provides a foundation for the rest of his exposition, and we must follow it closely. What is it, Augustine asks, that those who are natural do not understand? In this context, he answers, the natural do not understand John's prologue, the words that speak directly of God.[3] But Augustine immediately disrupts this simple disjunction between understanding and not understanding.

All understanding, Augustine tells us, rests on divine aid—but Augustine's concern is not so much with the individual as with the individual in the communal context of the church. John was, Augustine tells us, inspired, he was a mountain to which we should look. The language of mountains is taken from Psalm 71:3: "Let the mountains receive peace for your people, and the hills justice." The mountains are, Augustine tells us, "eminent souls," whereas the hills are "little souls." As a mountain John has received peace in order to announce it to us; he has seen something of wisdom itself, but he did so by ascending, by beginning to be an angel.[4] Through raising up such mountains God calls to us and enables us all to rise beyond the state of mere men. But in order to be a human being moving toward being a god—Augustine quotes Psalm 81:6—we must first recognize that we are only human beings; we must know who and what we are in order to ascend toward the heights in humility.[5] Thus, at the very beginning of his discourse Augustine insists that the task of describing the divine (more precisely, the task of interpreting scripture's revelation of the divine) does not simply result in a changed account of the world but is wound up with the task of imagining that world and the character of humanity within it. An exhortation toward considering God is also an exhortation toward reimagining oneself.

Returning to Augustine's text, we find him now insisting that we cannot understand from where John has risen unless we understand to where he has risen. We cannot look to the sky or to the angels: of these Psalm 148:5 tells us, "He spoke, and they were made." But, Augustine continues, "if 'he spoke, and they were made,' it was through the Word that they were made," and John could not reach to the Word unless he moved beyond all that was made though the Word.[6] If we are to look toward the Word whom John announces, we must raise our eyes not to the mountain as such but to John's meaning.[7] Drawing together the idea that we must look through the text to understand its meaning and the biblical call for us to look up toward the mountain, Augustine instructs us not to raise our eyes to the mountain as if the mountain itself were our help. The mountains receive from the Lord's fullness ("de plenitudine eius": John 1:16), from the light that enlightens everyone: "My help is from the Lord, who made heaven and earth."[8] Because the mountains receive from the source of all, they do not seek to teach in a manner that might indicate that they are themselves able to enlighten; and thus, if we wish to understand their words, we must lift our eyes in such a way that we drink from the same source as the mountains. Augustine's rhetoric plays on the ambiguities of looking from afar, looking up and toward. God has providentially structured a community and a tradition within which there are mountains, so that there can be looking in this differentiated sense—the sort of looking to which we are accustomed. And yet God is not far off, God is not above the mountains but beyond them, and so we must learn to look afresh. In other words, Augustine presents scripture as using the spatial language of physically viewing mountains to heighten the paradox that we are called to be attentive to what cannot be represented in physical terms—not because it is farther off still but because it transcends such categories. Similarly, one should not be misled by Augustine's calls to look within as if "within" named another space: "within," rather, provides a privileged site for imagining the divine transcendence and yet presence but not a site that enables comprehension. Thus, coming to imagine the divine transcendence is interwoven with newly imagining the created and the historical as semiotic; but this is also to see how what appears is used by a grace known to us through the concepts and narratives of faith.[9]

As Augustine has slowly explained how we are to look toward the mountains, his exhortation depends on our grasping some basic features of a Nicene theology of the Word of God. The Word transcends all, and all is created through him. This transcendence can be understood only by learning to think of a reality beyond our material and temporal categories. But as we have begun to see, exposition of this doctrinal position is inseparable from Augustine's different modes of recommending how we must imagine ourselves. He continues:[10]

"But perhaps you will say this," he says, "that I am more present to you than is God. Perish the thought! He is far more present.... Turn your ears to me, your heart to him ["ad me aures, ad illum cor"], so that you may fill both.... Let each one of you so lift that he sees what he lifts and where he lifts. What did I mean, "what he lifts and where he lifts"? Let him see what kind of heart he lifts up—for he lifts it up to the Lord—in order that it may not fall.

Thus, at one level looking toward God is always a looking for what does not appear as a visible object, and for that whose mode of presence is unique. But at the same time, our looking is always conditioned by the state of our hearts; how far they are able to look toward the Lord and beyond the supposition that the material is constitutive of reality. In other words, though, this is also to suggest that only those who are able to look toward the Lord who is already present can look at, and at the same time beyond, the material and the temporal, which God orders, in order to lead us onward. Seeing, desire, and faith are interwoven.

In these preliminary paragraphs of the first two sermons, then, Augustine has begun to interweave two themes, presence and providence. Taking the theme of presence first, we should not miss that a Nicene conception of the Word has already begun to be visible as what makes possible Augustine's argument. All things, we have already seen, were made through the Father's eternal speaking of the Word; but this Word must thus transcend all categories of mutability, temporality, and space that mark the created, because it is the Father's Word, coeternal with the Father. But Augustine's notion of divine presence is also a comment on the created order. The more we understand how God transcends the created order, the better we will understand its (and hence our own) quality as revealers of the divine; the better we will understand our own stability and lack of it. And this theme unrolls as a discourse on some aspects of divine, providential care. God orders visible mountains toward which we may look for guidance, and thus the search for a sustained and growing attention to divine presence may travel a providentially ordered road toward, and yet not stopping at, visible markers laid out for us. I have named providence here, but it is important to realize how easily we could also speak of grace; for Augustine, God's enabling of individual human ascent toward God, and God's creating and shaping of a world that may encourage such ascent, are two sides of a coin.[11] Between these two themes—presence and providence—tension will constantly spark, and between them God and the created order are mutually imagined.

IN ARTE VITA SUNT

What we have seen so far is introductory, and Augustine now deepens his account by setting out in turn three aspects of the Nicene theology of the Word that makes his discourse possible. These three together form the lens through which he suggests we may best see more of the interrelationship between Creator and creation, and more of the forms of attention that should follow. In each case Augustine offers explanation and exhortation, exhorting us to imagine our world in the light of the Nicene faith and exploring how things should seem if we do so. His three aspects are these:

1. The creation reveals the Word as the design, art, or word of the Father;
2. All things are created and ordered through the Word—but the true nature of this ordering is revealed in the incarnation;
3. All things find that they are fully life only in the Word.

Allow me to say a little about each in turn. When the word "God" is spoken, Augustine claims, there is a fleeting spark of understanding.[12] The soul is compelled to assert that God is immutable; the mind conceives a plan (*consilium*), a collection of thoughts. The word that we naturally think of in the cheapened and wounded state of the natural person is the sound that comes from the lips. But we may recognize a very different word within: this word is a thought or collection of thoughts. It is also the plan that we conceive as the foundation for a creative act. It is, stretching the likeness toward its theological end, "an offspring of your mind" ("filius cordis tui").[13] We have with us, then, the possibility of thinking beyond the fleeting quality of our spoken words if we attend to what is present with us.

Through the course of these sentences Augustine has gradually shifted his focus away from the inner and the spoken word toward the idea of the plan or design conceived in the mind before an external product is constructed. That he does so is not surprising: throughout his writing Augustine fills out the notion of the divine Word by reference to the divine Wisdom. Through the course of this tractate we see Augustine linking together a number of biblical titles and themes: the Word is Wisdom, Life, and Light. Elsewhere in his corpus Augustine makes much also of the Second Person as Son, as only-begotten, as Image, as Truth, as Justice, and as the one who is both Way and Homeland. But there seems to have been for him a special linkage between Word and Wisdom. The theme of Wisdom in Augustine's thought shows evidence of an early drawing on the Plotinian notion of *intellectus* (probably under the guidance of his readings in Ambrose) to explore not only what it might mean to speak of the Word of God *in se* but also how (against both Manichaeism and Skepticism) the created order can be envisaged as rational and providentially governed. An early and careful reading in the biblical book of Wisdom—especially insofar as verses such as 11:21 suggested ways of developing the theme of a cosmos ordered by and in the Word—helped to cement the title "Wisdom" in the foundations of his theology.[14]

But let us return to the tractate. Once he has introduced the concept of the inner word or plan, Augustine emphasizes that the inner design is seen only in the building, even though through the building we admire the skill and vision of the architect. What, he asks, should we see when we look to the building of which we are part, the *fabrica mundi,* the structure of the world? Augustine immediately answers: "If human design is praised because of some great building, do you wish to see what a design of God [*consilium Dei*] is the Lord Jesus Christ—that is, the Word of God?"[15]

Augustine is here exhorting, suggesting that indeed we should wish to see in faith the Word as the *consilium Dei*. Augustine is claiming not that we can easily see the Word but that this is the sight that the faithful Christian should aim toward. Were we to see the Word as the Father's *consilium*, we would see the created order as reflecting the Word that the Father has eternally spoken, the Word who is eternally with the Father, the Word who is eternally God. At one level, Augustine seems to have taken much away: he has insisted that we can look toward the Word only when we recognize the complete transcendence of God, when we begin to move beyond the temporal and the material images that have become our natural home.

And yet, at another, more fundamental level, Augustine gives. Gradually a foundation is being provided from which we can learn to imagine the creation as pointing us toward the Father, revealed as one who speaks all from eternity in his Son. In the same paragraph Augustine incorporates a Platonic commonplace: an exhortation to recognize the sheer mystery of the material cosmos culminates in a call to recognize the need for the ordering action of intelligible forming realities. But here that commonplace is adapted to Trinitarian needs: we should recognize that through the Word all things from the angelic to the most basely material were created and imbued with order and beauty, with powers of growth and interrelationship that amaze and perplex. Recognizing all this should draw us into a new tension of faith, a tension in which awareness of our failure to see beyond the material stimulates—and is stimulated by—belief in the Word as the Father's own.

The rational and the mysterious interact in complex ways here. Augustine adapts from earlier Platonic traditions of ascent to shape accounts of what is involved in abstracting from the material to imagine the intelligible, but he seeks to locate such practices within an account of faith that presumes the impossibility of moving beyond the basic temporal and spatial language used in the revealed text—and the centrality of that language in shaping the goal of our abstraction. But an account of faith is, for Augustine, an account that quickly turns to one of hope and love, and to one of mystery and humility. Faith shapes desire and the path along which the exercising of the intellect may be of benefit; but only when we grow in the ability to experience what is as mysterious to us, and thus to wonder at and be humble before the one we believe to be the source of all, and the governor of all, can we think and interpret rightly Creator or creation.[16]

But another note has already been sounded, which will now be heard more and more clearly. Augustine described the *consilium Dei*, the design of the Father, as "the Lord Jesus Christ—that is, the Word of God." All that has been said about the Word's presence so far will be increasingly shaped by attention to the incarnate mission of Christ, and thus we come to the second of the three aspects that I identified a little while ago. All things were made and are ordered through the Word, Augustine emphasizes, and he now names Arians and Manichees as those who miss this fundamental truth. The defective Christologies of these groups, Augustine alleges, were accompanied by a defective understanding of how Creator and creation relate. Arians fail because they place the Word within the created order; Manichees fail because they do not see that all things are created and encompassed by the Word. Only one who recognizes the Word as coeternal with the Father can, for Augustine, recognize the transcendence of the Word and the mystery of the Word as distinct and yet also as lacking nothing of what it is to be the one, true God.[17] Once again, imagining the creation and imagining the Word are intertwined. But then Augustine juxtaposes two statements and draws us toward the significance of the incarnation. On the one hand, the God who creates also arranges ("qui creauit, ipse disposuit"), so that everything has a place and a commensurate purpose, even the seemingly most base. On the other hand, although we rightly would reprove God were the worm placed in heaven, "God almost does this, and he is not to be reproved" ("et tamen prope hoc facit Deus, et non est reprehendendus").[18]

How does God do this? Human beings are born of flesh and are no better than worms. A catena of texts follows, demonstrating not only that scripture speaks of human beings as worms but also that the Lord and the Son of Man is a worm (Ps. 21:7; Job 25:6). The Lord himself, though he is God, deigns to become a worm to lead those who cannot yet chew solid food: "For no shape, no structure, no union of parts, no substance whatsoever, . . . can have weight, number, and measure unless it is through that Word."[19] At one level Augustine's point is a simple one: it is through the same Word that the creation exists, is governed, and is ordered toward redemption. At another level, the point is more complex: the vision of divine ordering that we have must be shaped by attention to how God orders all things in the incarnate dispensation, not only according to an intuitive sense of ontological value.[20] As we grow in understanding of faith's content, our practices of attention to the world must subtly but decisively change. Only in attention to the Word's becoming flesh, becoming a worm for us, do we see the full depth of God's ordering. In this light we take extra care not to despise what seems at the bottom of the created heap, and in this light we must take care to remember that the relative importance and revelatory quality of the order we most commonly see is grasped only in the light of God's most important ordering toward redemption. Our understanding of Father and Son, and of creation itself, grows in perceptive intensity the more we recognize how the nature of creation is most fully revealed in the mystery of the incarnation.

And so we come to the third aspect that Augustine highlights. How should we understand, he asks, "what was made in him was life"? Continuing his polemic agenda, Augustine directly rejects the Manichaean interpretation that everything that was made in him may be described (in some sense) as life. Rather, we must read the verse as saying that everything that has been made "in him is life."[21]

Augustine plays further with the collection of images used earlier. The chest existing in the carpenter's creative intelligence is a perfect idea coeval with the mind: the created chest exists externally and is mutable. Similarly, all things that have been made through the Word and exist externally exist also in the Word, where they may be described not so much as living but as life. The sun, the moon, the earth:"Externally," Augustine summarizes, "they are bodies; in [the Word's] creative knowledge they are life" ("sed foris corpora sunt; in arte uita sunt").[22]

Augustine's formulation here provides yet greater density to his vision of the created order's relationship to the Word. Augustine does not (here, although we will see an instance of his doing so later) turn to the language of all things' participation in the Word, nor does he say that all things reflect the Word's perfection. Instead Augustine chooses a language that strikingly focuses on the dependent character of our existence in his theology and aids him in setting out the character of the desire and attention that follows from correct Trinitarian faith. Thus the form of life that things in the created order exhibit is truly understood only when it is seen as revealing that all things find not only their source but also their true existence in the Father's eternal speaking of the life and truth that is the Word. This language also reveals more of the link between Augustine's account of God's providential ordering and his view of creation. Augustine does not think that we can make much useful headway by conceiving of God as creating a world within its own internal laws or principles and then also and subsequently intervening. Rather, all that is, all that appears to us as distinct, sequential, ordinary, and extraordinary, finds its true existence, and hence unity and simultaneity, in the eternally spoken Word. Once again, faith shapes us toward the recognition of mystery, but note how Augustine's account of existence in the Word and his call for humility before grace in the process of redemption mesh; acceptance of the need for divine graceful assistance in the process of redemption inculcates a sense of reality's dependence on the divine that should be ours as created beings who grasp the true nature of existence.

Augustine moves into the final section of this homily. If we cannot grasp what Augustine has said, what should we do? "He who cannot grasp it, let him nourish it in his heart that he may be able to. With what is he to nourish it? Let him nourish it with milk, so that he may arrive at solid food. Let him not withdraw from Christ, born through flesh, until he arrives at Christ born from the one Father." Because we are (and are made after) the image of God, because we have the rational mind, we may see or perceive wisdom: that is, light. This light is our life; we must know ourselves as beings who find their own light when they look beyond this world into the Word. But we cannot see, because we are blind men in the sun: "Wisdom is present; but it is present with a blind man. It is absent to his eyes, not because it is absent to him but because he is absent from it." And thus we must cleanse ourselves until we see, for "blessed are the pure in heart, for they shall see God" (Matt. 5:8).[23]

Augustine has, then, offered us three aspects of a Nicene theology of the Word that add depth and focus to his initial concerns. The unique presence of the divine has been given form as the creating and ordering presence of the eternally spoken Word, who is our true life. Presence and providence (or grace) remain central: Augustine's initial picture of God raising up visible mountains to lead us toward the presence of the one who illuminates but is not above has been given color and depth through meditation on the truth that we grow in knowledge of the manner of that ordering when we attend to the Word's becoming flesh. Only on that basis do we see the character and true significance of the order that appears in creation. Throughout, by focusing on the relationship between Word and creation Augustine has also set down further contours of appropriate creaturely desire and tension. Throughout also, Augustine has worked by recommending and displaying an imaginary complex in which God is rethought as the world is rethought. A Nicene theology of the Word as coeternal with God and also as that wherein creation finds its true life is the axis around which all turns. It is noticeable that as Augustine's picture grows in specificity, the more evident it becomes that recognition of the mysterious forms an integral part of the whole. We can see here how a specifically Nicene theology offers not simply a content of knowledge but an order and structure for the process of knowing, based in the order and structure of the divinely created world.

DEUS . . . MUNDO INFUSUS FABRICAT

I have spent a good deal of time with just one of Augustine's sermons in order to give a sense of how he interweaves exposition of (Nicene) Christian faith's content with an account of the habits of thought that are for him intrinsic to that faith. In the rest of this chapter I will comment far more briefly on some key sections of the second of Augustine's tractates on John and then turn to a different but contemporary text, *On The Trinity*.

The next Sunday Augustine returned to the first chapter of John, this time taking his treatment as far as John 1:14. We know that these two sermons were part of an extended series and that in between Augustine preached on a number of Psalms, the most important of them being 121. There he meditated at length on what it means when attaining Jerusalem is paralleled with attaining a share (*participatio*) in what is *idipsum*, the identical, the selfsame. Augustine sees what is eternally *idipsum* as eternally, actively remaining what it is, not merely being statically unchangeable.[24]

This language is now the backdrop for Augustine's second tractate on John. Our own mutability, our own experience of being torn asunder, and hence our inability to maintain our own existence now stands out in sharper contrast. The Word is now not only our Life but also our stability.[25] The striving for true Life that we should feel is, from this angle, also a striving for rest and stability. But faith's existential tension should for Augustine sit alongside hope that the Word, the *idipsum*, will take us across the sea of the world to our homeland. And thus Augustine insists very clearly here:[26]

> It is better, then, not to see with the mind what is and nevertheless not to depart from the cross of Christ than to see it with the mind and to despise the cross of Christ. Beyond this it is good, indeed best, if it can be done, that a person both sees where he must go and holds fast the means by which he is to be conveyed.

Having spent a good deal of time reprising his discussion of the Sunday before, Augustine now asks what it means to say that "he was in the world, and the world was made through him." To answer, he takes up again the analogy of the carpenter. The carpenter makes a chest external to him, but "God constructs while infused in the world. He constructs while situated everywhere" ("Deus autem mundo infusus fabricat, ubique positus fabricat"). And then, a few sentences later, "By the presence of his majesty he makes what he makes; by his own presence he governs what he has made" ("praesentia maiestatis facit, quod facit; praesentia sua gubernat, quod fecit").[27] Augustine's account of creation's existence—and our appropriate response in faith—has taken another step forward. Creation is created and governed by being in the presence of the Father acting through Son and Spirit. To understand the character of our existence and our journey home toward true life and stability we need to grasp the immediacy of the one whom the fallen think they must struggle to see from afar. At the same time, new aspects of our imagining of the world in faith have been sketched; desiring God as the one who transcends all is now accompanied by an intensified sense of our own instability and lack of ontological self-governance.

EX INTIMO AC SUMMO CAUSARUM CARDINE

There is much more that may be drawn from Augustine's second tractate on John, but I want to leave it there in order to turn briefly to one more text from Augustine, book 3 of *On the Trinity*. Augustine's express concern in this book is with how God has appeared in the Old Testament theophanies, those events in which a figure appears who seems to be a visible divine agent or visible representative of the divine. Genesis 18, Exodus 33, and Daniel 7 offer particular, important examples. To explain his view of these events Augustine offers a minitreatise on God's action within creation that offers much material for this discussion.

I want to begin by noting a theme that is, I suggest, anti-Platonist in intent. Although there is a complex set of causal relationships between God and his creation, and although God has created in part through setting in motion a set of *rationes seminales* in the created order as structuring principles, Augustine insists that God is the supreme cause, "the most intimate and highest hinge of causality." The word I translate "hinge," *cardo,* is indeed pivotal.[28] It would be possible to translate *cardo* "apex" and to speak of God as the apex of causality, but this is not quite Augustine's meaning.

To understand, let us begin with what may seem a tiny argument. Augustine spends some time with the breeding activities of Jacob's sheep in Genesis 30. One question bothers him: How did the sheep who saw the striped sticks that Joseph put before them transmit this coloration to their unborn offspring? Augustine's initial answer draws on a number of Platonized Stoic themes: the soul animates the body, giving it a certain spiritual affinity for the soul, which is thus able to imprint upon the body what it thinks or sees internally. How? Because there exist in the Word—or better, we may gloss, the Word exists as—certain appropriate reasons ("congruae rationes") that enable such things to happen and that are the ultimate cause of their actually happening. Exactly what the powers of the soul are need not detain us, Augustine emphasizes, provided that we rule out the idea that soul is itself the creator of matter and accept that every subordinate cause is and is able to be a cause "through [or "by means of"] the intelligible and unchangeable Life" ("ab intelligibili et incommutabili vita"), which not only exists above all but also reaches down to the earthly depths.[29]

Augustine insists that because of the manner in which all causality ultimately stems from the intelligible Life, nothing other than God, Word, and Spirit can be acclaimed Creator. Once again, neither must we accept a variety of creative forces without unified command nor must we envisage God intervening to overturn or set aside his own laws: all that causes does so ultimately because of reasons that rest in the Word.[30] This, obviously enough, is not only a point about how we envisage causality (though it is that); it is also another attempt to inculcate acceptance of the impenetrable and mysterious into the life of rationality and of faith. Because all finds its true life in the Word, and because all events find their true nature in the Word's life, faith in the Word should be accompanied by a growing awareness of the sheer mystery of divine purpose and glory. God is thus the hinge of causality and not its apex, because God does not only stand at the highest point in a causal series. Through eternally speaking all things, their purposes and sequences in the Word, through acting from eternity to give human actions their reality—causing and allowing—the Father's purposes are what the meaning of every event turns on.

Allow me to draw out one more theme from book 3 of *On the Trinity,* one that speaks both of time and of the Eucharist. Augustine suggests that we imagine the harmony intrinsic to how God governs by thinking of the heavenly country itself.[31] There the will of God melts all into one by a spiritual fire, and it is thence and in a manner directly analogous that the will of God directs all. How does that will direct? By the Word, who creates and directs all through the Spirit of Life. The initial tractates on John focused so much upon the Word because of the text with which

Augustine was engaged; here we see the pneumatological also revealing its importance. It is the Spirit of Life, the Spirit of Christ, the Spirit in whom God unites all
who burns all into harmonious unity. We see the tip of a dogmatic iceberg here:
Augustine's account of how all is worked through the Son and in the Spirit. For our
purposes here, let me say only that to draw attention to the Spirit's work is not to
demote the Word; it is to give yet greater density to the Word as the pivot around
which Augustine's theology of the Trinity and his theology of creation turn.[32]

But back to the text. When Augustine states that all is created and directed in the
Spirit of Life, he immediately emphasizes that God turns all to his purpose. Thus
Paul, even though he groaned, was weighed down by the body, and sought to be
with Christ, was able through the Spirit to preach the gospel by means of signs, by
voice, by letter, and by the Eucharist.[33] It is this last that becomes Augustine's focus.
The character of the Eucharist as sacrament reveals how it was possible for Paul to
preach: although the taking of the fruits of the earth and the blessing of them occur
at human hands, these become so great a sacrament only because the Spirit of Life
is at work. Just as God effects everything in the Eucharist by bodily movements—
the movements of his ministers—he makes use of sensible and visible effects in the
created order to signify his presence and reveal himself. The Eucharist is thus
offered as perhaps the site in which the members of the body of Christ learn the
purpose of creation and learn how to attend to the divine causality.

The centrality of the Eucharist, as an example of how the heavenly and eschatological court of God reveals itself among us, points us toward the Christological.
Now, in some ways the Christological is heard only sotto voce in book 3 of *On the
Trinity*, because Augustine is saving his reflections on the sending of the Word for
book 4, where he will consider the uniqueness of the incarnation in relationship to
all other theophanies. And yet, as we see with this Eucharistic passage, Augustine
must occasionally preempt that discussion, because it is from the rock of the incarnate Christ that we can see with real penetration how God interacts with the created order.[34] Thus, again, toward the end of book 3, when Augustine summarizes
the principle that the Old Testament theophanies were the work of angels appearing in created forms at the will of God, he turns to the first chapter of Hebrews.[35]
Augustine quotes first "to which of the angels has he ever said, 'Sit at my right
hand'?" and then "For all these things happened to them as a type" to emphasize
that his concern is not merely with demonstrating a distinction between the Old
Testament theophanies and the incarnation but with showing that all appearances
of God have a direction: all point toward Christ, and all are to be understood as
comprehensible only in that light.

My use of "comprehensible" in the last sentence was something of a mistake:
once again mystery must attend. Augustine thinks we can be clear that God did
not appear in his own substance (for it is invisible) and that angels taking created
forms were probably the immediate agents of revealing. We can, however, be

certain that the angels did so at divine command. But the mechanism by which God works through his angels should not concern us greatly: much is hidden, and we can be wise only according to the measure of faith. Drawing attention to the Eucharist similarly serves not to render all clear but to shape our attention to the divine action and presence as governing all toward an end, as never less than more present to us than we are to ourselves, and as present under the rubric of mystery. One may say that the more we follow Augustine's intensification and deepening of his theology of the Word, the more we see his meditations on presence and providence (or grace) converge. Augustine's account of divine presence and of God's governing of causality are increasingly situated in his account of the temporal ordering of all toward eternal life with God, and in turn all causality and ordering is most fully viewed through an entering into the central mystery of salvation.

CONCLUSION

It would have been possible to shape this essay around an exploration of Augustine's particular debts to and adaptations of Platonic and Stoic traditions. And yet, I decided to focus on the structure and interweaving of Augustine's theological arguments in order to give some sense of how a Nicene theologian of the period thinks with (and also against) that Platonic and Stoic background. Only thus do we get a clear sense of the difference that Christianity could make to the imagining of the world and the divine. Augustine presents a particularly easy subject for such an investigation. When we draw out the links between Augustine's articulation of the doctrine of God and his articulation of his theology of creation, we do not need to claim that we draw out a subtext unknown to the bishop himself.

As a summary we may perhaps imagine the argument that we have traced through these three texts as a series of concentric circles, each successive outer layer shaping and governing the principles espoused within those circles that are now encompassed. At the most basic level, Augustine calls his audience to imagine God as transcendent, intelligible, and unchanging. Doing so reflects one version of a theme echoing down the Platonic tradition and has the inevitable result of suggesting a reconsideration of the reality and character of the sensible.[36] Yet at least two more circles must be identified; Augustine's exploitation in aid of a new conception of knowing must be understood as both Trinitarian in form and governed by his vision of the Word's incarnation.

In the first case, I say "Trinitarian" because how Augustine describes the relationship between Creator and creation flows from his conception of God as Trinity. Thus, as we have seen, Augustine shapes an account of all things' finding their true existence in the Word, who is coeternal with the Father. The complex relationship between Word and world is governed by the Word's transcendent status (being fully all that it is to be the one God), by the distinction between the created and the uncreated (in such a way that the Word's existence is ultimately beyond our comprehension), and by the shape of a desire distorted by sin and yet intrinsic to our existence as beings whose true life is spoken from eternity in God's Word and whose true end is found in that Word. In these texts, the Word for the moment took center stage, although the brief passage I considered from *On the Trinity* 3 revealed Augustine offering also an account of God's Spirit as what draws all things together toward their source and home.

In the second case, just as Augustine's Trinitarianism governs his adaptation of Platonic and Stoic conceptualities (and is of course also shaped by them), so too does Augustine's attention to the incarnation act as a further governing principle. But here it is important to note the direction of his thought. At one level, incarnational thinking governs, because it provides further principles to which we must be attentive: our conceptions of divine ordering must be attentive to God's subverting of seemingly obvious hierarchy in the dispensation of the incarnation. But at another level, and one toward which Augustine constantly draws the Christian seeking to understand the divine, God's act in the incarnate Christ shapes our growing in understanding through the continued presence of Christ in his body. In this chapter we saw this theme take form as Augustine's call for us to be attentive to how the Eucharist reveals and hides, how God uses it for our transformation. The focus on the Eucharist that we saw here is partnered by a wider insistence on charity practiced in the knowledge that our reformation finds its source and constant root in our being incorporated into the sacrificial love and identity of Christ. Thus the works of mercy, for Augustine, take on an epistemological function. But here the language of discrete circles shows its only partial utility: Augustine's account of ecclesial life is itself resolutely Trinitarian. The life of charity to which Augustine exhorts intellectual and nonintellectual alike is one understood only when it is undertaken in confession of thankfulness for the immediate work of the divine Spirit, who gives us what may from another angle be named as our merits.[37]

Thus the more one attempts to characterize how Augustine sees the task of reimagining the world, the more one is drawn into the depths of his theology. There are, of course, many dimensions to the study of late ancient knowing, and the conversation between those of us interested in the topic needs to be engaged from many angles. But I hope this chapter has suggested one set of ways in which the development of Christian belief in late antiquity was also a development in Christian conceptions of knowing and imagining the world. I have focused on one particular vision of Nicene Christianity and on an author who seems to have been peculiarly conscious of the manner in which the Nicene faith implied and even demanded a reimagining of the cosmos as creation and of the Creator as the source and omnipresent life of all. However, my account should be taken not to describe all Nicene thought but as an invitation to explore continuities and differences among the full range of Nicene traditions. Indeed, it is also an invitation to explore similarities and distinctions between Nicene Christianity and other Christian doc-trinal traditions of, before, and after this period. And pushing the possibilities yet one step farther, I suggest that my account is also, then, an invitation to find ways of exploring how the theological visions of these Nicene experts shaped or did not shape the belief and practice of others in the Christian community and beyond.[38]

NOTES

An earlier version of this chapter was presented to a symposium in honor of Robert Wilken at Baylor University in March 2012. I wish to thank Hans Boersma, Matthew Levering, and Jens Zimmerman for their invitation. I wish also to thank Kyle Eastwood for his calming influence on the writing process.

1. For introductions to Augustine's account of the Trinity, see my "Augustine and the Trinity," in Matthew Levering and Gilles Emery, eds., *Oxford Handbook of the Trinity* (Oxford: Oxford University Press, 2011), 123–37; Michel René Barnes, "Re-reading Augustine's Theology of the Trinity," in Stephen T. Davis, Daniel Kendall, and Gerald O'Collins, eds., *The Trinity: An Interdisciplinary Symposium on the Trinity* (Oxford: Clarendon Press, 1999), 145–76. For my own more extensive treatment, see *Augustine and the Trinity* (Cambridge: Cambridge University Press, 2010).

2. The best introduction to Augustine's *Tractatus in Evangelium Iohannis* is provided by the introduction and notes attached to the most recent edition of M. F. Berrouard, *Augustin d'Hippone: Homélies sur l'évangile de saint Jean,* Bibliothèque Augustinienne, vols. 71–75 (Paris: Desclée de Brouwer, 1993–2004). All abbreviations for works of Augustine are those of Cornelius Mayer, Robert Dodaro, et al., eds., *Augustinus-Lexikon* (Basel: Schwabe, 1989–).

3. *Tractatus in Evangelium Iohannis* 1.1 (Corpus Christianorum, Series Latina [hereafter CCSL] 36 [Turnhout: Brepols, 1954]: 1).

4. Ibid. 1.2–4.

5. There is not space here to comment at length on the character of Augustine's exegesis, but for our purposes it is important to note that Augustine reads the significance of the scriptural text, and the task of interpreting it, within the conception of God's use of the text that follows the contours of God's use of history and the created, as sketched throughout this chapter. In this regard *Confessions* 12.14.17–32.43 is a continually fruitful point of departure. For scholarly introductions to this complex of concerns, see John Cavadini, "The Sweetness of the Word: Salvation and Rhetoric in Augustine's *De doctrina christiana,*" in D. Arnold and P. Bright, eds., *"De Doctrina Christiana": A Classic of Western Civilization* (Notre Dame: University of Notre Dame Press, 1995), 164–81. On Augustine's allegorical patterns of reading, see Michael Cameron, "The Christological Substructure of Augustine's Figurative Exegesis," in Pamela Bright, ed., *Augustine and the Bible* (Notre Dame: University of Notre Dame Press, 1997), 52–73, and now idem, *"Christ Meets Me Everywhere": Augustine's Early Figurative Exegesis* (New York: Oxford University Press, 2012). Isabelle Bochet's *"Le firmament de l'écriture": L'herméneutique augustinienne* (Paris: Institut d'Études Augustiniennes, 2004) is also seminal.

6. *Tractatus in Evangelium Iohannis* 1.5 (above, n. 3).

7. Ibid. 1.6.

8. Ibid. 1.6 (CCSL 36: 3–4).

9. Jeremy Schott's chapter in this volume, "Language," may be read alongside my own at this point, if only to illustrate the different ways in which late antique thinkers meditated upon how language might function. Overt discussion of naming and reference in non-Christian philosophical traditions was certainly taken up by Christian authors, but Christian authors also sustained a discussion of the sacramental character of discourse that had roots in the rhetorical tradition, in ancient conceptions of the enigmatic and symbolic, and also in a theology that saw the divine Word as having become flesh and as speaking in human language to draw us toward a knowledge of the divine. For discussion of Augustine's own engagement with non-Christian traditions of linguistic theory, see, as a point of entry into a complex scholarly labyrinth, the work of the late Robert Markus, perhaps beginning with his *Signs and Meanings: World and Text in Ancient Christianity* (Liverpool: Liverpool University Press, 1996). On the sacramental function of language and its relationship to the Latin rhetorical tradition, see Robert Dodaro, *Christ and the Just Society in the Thought of Augustine* (Cambridge: Cambridge University Press, 2004), chapters 4 and 5, 115–81.

10. *Tractatus in Evangelium Iohannis* 1.7 (CCSL 36: 4).

11. Fundamental in this regard is the discussion of the manner in which grace works that Augustine developed some years before in his *De Diversis Quaestionibus ad Simplicianum* 1.2.2. For secondary discussion I point initially to two classic pieces: William S. Babcock's "Augustine's Interpretation of Romans (A.D. 394–6)," *Augustinian Studies* 10 (1979): 55–74, and James Wetzel's *Augustine and the Limits of Virtue* (Cambridge: Cambridge University Press, 1992).

12. *Tractatus in Evangelium Iohannis* 1.8 (above, n. 10).

13. Ibid. 1.9 (CCSL 36: 5). On the developing notion of the inner word in Augustine's thought, see my *Augustine and the Trinity* (above, n. 1), 194–96, 290–93.

14. See A.-M. La Bonnardière, *Le livre de la Sagesse,* Biblia Augustiniana, Ancien Testament (Paris: Études Augustiniennes, 1970). Other papers in this volume also address questions of cosmic ordering and how Platonic and Stoic traditions were central to late antique construals of this order: see the chapters by Catherine Chin and Heidi Marx-Wolf. By the end of this section of the chapter I hope it will be clear how Augustine's theology of the Incarnation shapes his adaptation of this common philosophical background and specifically of the patterns of attention that we should cultivate if we are to comprehend divine use of it.

15. *Tractatus in Evangelium Iohannis* 1.9 (above, n. 13).

16. One of the most important recent discussions of the value of faith in this respect is to be found in Dodaro, *Christ and the Just Society* (above, n. 9), chapters 4 and 5, 115–81. (I make use of this material in my own account of Augustine's Christological epistemology in *Augustine and the Trinity* [above, n. 1], chapter 6, 142–74.) Augustine also carefully links the process of recognizing the necessity of faith in our knowing to the practice of charity within the Christian community as the unavoidable school of humility. See, for example, John Cavadini, "Trinity and Apologetics in the Theology of St Augustine," *Modern Theology* 29 (2013): 1–37; Lewis Ayres, "'Where Does the Trinity Appear?': Augustine's Apologetics and 'Philosophical' Readings of the *De Trinitate,*" *Augustinian Studies* 44 (2012): 109–26.

17. Cf. my *Augustine and the Trinity* (above, n. 1), 193–98.

18. *Tractatus in Evangelium Iohannis* 1.13 (CCSL 36: 7).

19. Ibid.

20. Augustine's point here may be read as partly anti-Platonic in intent even as he draws on fairly traditional Platonic and Stoic themes. In Plotinus, *Enneads* 1.6, for example, the recognition of the intelligible to which Plotinus exhorts us is a call to what subsequently will seem intuitive. Augustine himself is capable of very similar argumentation (especially in anti-Skeptical moments), but his deepest reflections revolve around a careful reorientation of how we conceive of providence's use of the ordered cosmos.

21. Augustine's argument here rests on a textual variant not present in modern editions of the Greek text of John's gospel.

22. *Tractatus in Evangelium Iohannis* 1.17 (CCSL 36: 10).

23. Ibid. 1.19.

24. *Enarrationes in Psalmos* 121:5 (CSEL 95.3 [Vienna: Austrian Academy of Sciences, 2001], 90–91). For discussion, see Jean-Luc Marion, "*Idipsum:* The Name of God according to Augustine," in George Demacopoulos and Aristotle Papanikolaou, eds., *Orthodox Readings of Augustine* (Crestwood, N.Y.: St. Vladimir's Seminary Press, 2008), 167–89. In my *Augustine and the Trinity* (above, n. 1), 200–208, I have attempted to use Marion's insights without succumbing to his fear of "being."

25. *Tractatus in Evangelium Iohannis* 2.2.

26. Ibid. 2.3.

27. Ibid. 2.10 (CCSL 36: 16).

28. *Trin.* 3.9.16 (CCSL 50 [Turnhout: Brepols, 2001]: 143), "ex intimo ac summo causarum cardine."

29. Ibid. 3.8.15 (CCSL 50: 142–43).

30. Ibid.

31. Ibid. 3.4.9–10.

32. On Augustine's consistent insistence that the Father works through Son and Spirit, see my *Augustine and the Trinity* (above, n. 1), chapter 7, 177–98. On the theological necessity, for Augustine, of allowing Son and Spirit overlapping roles, see Robert Dodaro, "Augustine on the Roles of Christ and the Holy Spirit in the Mediation of Virtues," *Augustinian Studies* 41 (2010): 145—63, and my "Augustine on the Spirit as the Soul of the Body; or, Fragments of a Trinitarian Ecclesiology," *Augustinian Studies* 41 (2010): 165—82. On the Trinitarian dimensions of Augustine's theology of creation, see also Marie-Anne Vannier, "*Creatio*," "*Conversio*," "*Formatio*" *chez S. Augustin* (Fribourg: Éditions Universitaires Fribourg Suisse, 1991); Scott A. Dunham, *The Trinity and Creation in Augustine: An Ecological Analysis* (Albany: SUNY Press, 2007).

33. On the importance of the Eucharist in Augustine's conception of the life of faith, see John C. Cavadini, "Eucharistic Exegesis in Augustine's Confessions," *Augustinian Studies* 41 (2010): 87–108.

34. For seeing from the rock who is Christ, see Augustine's exegesis of Exodus 33 at *Trin.* 2.16.27–17.31.

35. Ibid. 3.11.22–23.

36. Although Augustine certainly knew Porphyry from around 391 C.E., I am one of those who think that at its root Augustine's Platonism shows the influence of Plotinus and Ambrose. In the case of the latter, his *De Isaac vel Anima* provides a good window onto

themes Augustine probably encountered in Ambrose's catechetical lectures; in the case of the former, it seems likely that Augustine knew *Enneads* 1.6 (or some portion of that text), and there we find a useful parallel exhortation to the recognition of the sensible order as exhibiting form and as pointing to forming realities that transcend the sensible. I offer some remarks on the character of Augustine's debts to Platonism at *Augustine and the Trinity* (above, n. 1), 13–20, 200–217 (with specific reference to the theme of divine simplicity).

37. On the importance of the Eucharist here, see Cavadini, "Trinity" (above, n. 16).

38. In the specific case of Augustine there is also much to be learned by exploring the themes that he addresses and does not address in different genres. How are the themes that are the focus in works such as *De Trinitate* and *De Civitate Dei* related to what we find in the *Sermones ad Populum?* In this regard I await with particular interest the project on Augustine's preached theology being undertaken by Patout Burns. See also John Cavadini, "Simplifying Augustine," in John Van Engen, ed., *Educating People of Faith: Exploring the History of Jewish and Christian Communities* (Grand Rapids: Eerdmans, 2004), 63–84.

PART TWO

Putting Things in Order

8

Emperor

Matthew Canepa

The rise of the Sasanian Empire (ca. 224–642 C.E.) and its constant rivalry with Rome introduced a political phenomenon that the ancient world had arguably never experienced before on such a scale: two powerful and stable imperial structures that both claimed universal status coexisting over the course of centuries in intimate communication with each other.[1] By the age of Husraw I (r. 531–79) and Justinian I (r. 527–65), the courts considered the ritualized diplomatic equilibrium that had developed to be not only the established order of things but, when it suited them, primordial and divinely ordained. Many aspects of late ancient Mediterranean and Western Asian history were affected by their relationships with each other, the peoples and states caught between the empires, and with other, more distant foreign powers.

Given their centrality in the political structures and cultures of the late antique and early medieval worlds, it should come as no surprise that the institutions, ideologies, rituals, and artistic and architectural creations of the Roman emperor and Sasanian king of kings have consistently generated important scholarly debates.[2] Scholarship has analyzed the structures of imperial institutions, their relationship to Christian or Zoroastrian hierarchies or theology, and their developmental trajectories. This essay follows a different line of inquiry and asks how subjects living in the late antique Mediterranean and Western Asia knew their sovereign—and how those sovereigns understood themselves. While theological, legal, or poetic discourse provides a view into the variety of ways power was formulated, writing an intellectual history entirely from such evidence does not access the way power was actually practiced and experienced—how the sovereigns themselves wielded it and how those subject to it understood its source. This essay aims to show how imperial theoretical formulations were made tangible and how cosmologies of power were translated into visual, bodily, and spatial experiences.

The Roman and Sasanian sovereigns succeeded in consolidating greater and greater control over the political, social, and religious economies of their societies. This developed according to unique pathways and at a different pace in each empire. The founder of the Sasanian Empire, Ardaxshir I, and his son Shabuhr I drastically curtailed the power and privileges that provincial kings enjoyed under the Arsacid Empire. They began a process by which most provincial dynasties were replaced by members of the Sasanian dynasty and eventually governors answerable only to the king of kings. In the Roman Empire, the reign of Diocletian was pivotal in reorganizing and establishing direct imperial control over the provinces. Although they couched their changes in the language of tradition and conservatism, both empires witnessed many changes as greater power concentrated in the hands of the sovereign and his officials.

Individuals living in and on the peripheries of the Iranian Plateau, Mesopotamia, and the Mediterranean knew that the world was ruled and ordered by two powerful empires. Settled and nomadic peoples on the peripheries and interstices considered Rome and Iran sources of wealth and political legitimacy as well as a constant source of meddling, subversion, and military threats. As one empire's knowledge of and engagement with the world outside its borders grew, the worldview of the other transformed and expanded to counter the extended geopolitical and ideological threats of its rival. The end result was a greatly expanded understanding of the world within Rome and Iran, with economic and political agents of both empires regularly operating in parts of the world that formally existed as terra incognita for both.

Although they presented themselves to internal audiences as universal sovereigns, the idea that the Roman and Sasanian empires were part of the natural order of things, their coexistence divinely ordained to rule and pacify the earth, developed as a recurring theme in diplomatic communications between the two imperial courts. Even in the midst or aftermath of the nearly constant overt or covert conflicts that arose between them, the sovereigns of the Roman and Persian empires repeatedly acknowledged this formulation of the order of things in their dealings with each other, either grudgingly or enthusiastically. Although each pressed military advantages over the other, extracted indemnities and tribute,[3] and periodically seized portions of the other's possessions in the borderlands, neither ever attempted a war of annihilation—that is, not until the very end, with disastrous ramifications for both. Husraw II's full-scale invasion of the Roman Empire and siege of Constantinople was driven by a new and unprecedented attempt to fully conquer the other empire and rule as Roman emperor and Persian king of kings.[4] It was a drastic departure from the previous four centuries of equilibrium and was ultimately fatal for both Husraw II and the Sasanian Empire.

PARADOXES IN KNOWING POWER

Two themes repeat throughout all our visual, literary, epigraphic, archaeological, and numismatic evidence. The first is relentless, bombastic, insistent, and totalizing: the Roman emperor and the Sasanian king of kings were sacred creatures, who ruled in the place of God on earth and were invincible. Although individual sovereigns could be both challenged and overthrown and, in Rome, the office could be shared, the institutions of monarchical rule themselves were never seriously challenged in the late Roman or Sasanian empires. Nevertheless, another theme that creeps in and lingers over many reigns is equally insistent: whereas the office was sacred, individual emperors were complete bastards—even demons incarnate. This paradox is present in the literary productions of elites and in the slogans and chants of large urban populations.

Groups or individuals within the empire could critique, chide, and even challenge the sovereign's actions. They could appeal to philosophical reason, panegyrical flattery, religious morality (especially significant in the Roman Empire with the coming of Christianity), or, in Iran, ancient social traditions in order to challenge, temper, or guide the sovereign's actions.[5] The veiled critiques of contemporary rulers in the biographies of earlier emperors in the *Scriptores Historiae Augusti* or bitter reproaches of Procopius's *Secret History*, demonstrate how elites living in late antiquity could accord their individual ruler little respect despite the office's sacred status. Populations of cities or provinces could riot and attack the emperor's images or his agents or they could simply ridicule him, as the Antiochenes did Julian during his stay in their city, or as the circus factions would periodically taunt Justinian I during hippodrome chants. Such resistance would occur even as the selfsame soldiers, courtiers, and even members of the urban crowds would genuinely acclaim him and marvel at the experience of viewing him or even being allowed near his presence. Marginalized religions like Christianity or Manichaeism accepted the power of the emperor or king of kings as a given, yet even after persecution would eagerly incorporate the power of the emperor or king of kings into their cosmology as a beneficent force when given the protection or support of the state. Although the prophet Mani described Shabuhr I as "more tyrannical and harsher than some princes" and "an evildoer and sinner in all lands," he immediately proclaimed that his "soul would find life," since he had offered him his protection.[6] It goes without saying that Romans living in Amida or Antioch facing attack and deportation by Shabuhr I or Husraw I or Armenians massacred by Shabuhr II would curse their names, as would Sasanian subjects witnessing the devastation that Julian brought to Mesopotamia or Heraclius's wholesale and systematic destruction of some of the Sasanian Empire's most magnificent and holy sites, buildings, and cultivated land during his counterinvasion in response to Husraw II.

What is crucial to keep in mind is that although their subjects could revile them (often losing their lives for it), those subjects never doubted that they were dealing with an ancient force with incredible power. Although certain sovereigns might face challenges of popular riots and elite revolts, or even be overthrown and replaced by an inner circle or even a rival, in neither the late Roman nor the Sasanian Empire was any alternative mode of governance ever proposed or imposed. An emperor was known to be part of the immutable order of things, and the world could no longer be seriously conceived of without one.

PROCESSES OF KNOWLEDGE CREATION IN LATE ANTIQUITY

Understanding what people in late antiquity knew about the sovereign demands that we consider multiple perspectives and abilities to know, from the sovereign himself and his inner circle, to hostile populations, or even to those who might observe at a great geographical or social distance with little hope of or care to engage in the process. We should focus not on the products of individual cognition but rather on a complex, overlapping set of communicative processes. These processes extended well beyond introducing, repeating, or modifying ideas discursively in the realm of text and speech, though these were indeed important. If we are truly to access what was expressed and known, we must extend our focus to include the major media of communication and individual or collective reflection: the built and natural environments of important landscapes, cities, and structures; physical and visual modifications to these environments; and the overlapping webs of ritual activity that animated them. Such an inquiry focuses on an inherently reflexive set of processes wherein the sovereign expressed—or rather, imposed—an idealized formulation of knowledge on individuals. In all instances, the sovereign expected and expended a great amount of resources to ensure that the viewers or participants would become inculcated with or at least act according to an ideologically correct formulation of reality. These individuals, who varied according to social place and political alliance with the emperor and could be either passive observers or active participants, also could communicate feedback to the sovereign, even if just by attacking the urban monuments and images that were the visual and spatial manifestations of his power. Given the constant succession of riots, usurpations, and subtle resistance, an ironic conflict between how individuals behaved publically and what they secretly understood or believed appears to have been deeply interwoven through most individuals' understanding and experience of power in late antiquity. Evidence from both the Roman and Sasanian empires indicate that what was known was subject to constant negotiation and, at times, even violent negation.

DISCOURSE

Just as did those living in late antiquity, modern historians, by reading or hearing the discursive messages that they or their agents promulgated through a variety of media, have come to know that the Roman and Sasanian emperors were sacred.[7] Even statements in documents as dry as law codes were inflected with these expressions. Each in his own way, every Roman or Persian sovereign was eager to shape and control his culture's perception of him in relation to the past. Specially commissioned historical works, such as the works of Procopius, or epic histories, such as the late Sasanian *Xwadāy-nāmag* ("The Book of Lords"), reflect varying attempts to present authorized explanations of recent events or the past.

The Sasanian court created a powerful new formulation of Iranian sacred kingship. Like the late Roman emperor, the Sasanian kings of kings was inherently divine, though only a member of the Sasanian family could be king and an evil king could lose his divine legitimacy.[8] Even though terse, titles from coin legends and inscriptions clearly express the understanding of the early Sasanian court. Shabuhr I proclaimed himself to be "the Mazda-worshipping Lord Shabuhr, king of kings of Iran and non-Iran, of divine lineage [or "nature"]" (Middle Persian *mazdēsn bay Šābūhr šāhān šāh ī Ērān ud Anērān kē čihr az yazdān*). By at least the fourth century the court presented the Sasanian kings as part of the cosmic order of things quite literally. They began to share in the divine quality of the sun, moon, and stars. From records in Greek, Latin, and Armenian sources, late Sasanian royal titulature expanded to describe the king as "a god manifest among men," "partner with the stars, brother of the sun and moon," "the divine, good, father of peace, ancient, . . . fortunate, pious, and beneficent, to whom the gods have given great fortune and a great kingdom, giant of giants, formed in the image of gods,"[9] "king of kings, master of dynasts, lord of nations, prince of peace, savior for mankind, among the gods a righteous and immortal man, a god manifest among men, most glorious, victorious, who rises with the sun and gives eyes to the night."[10]

In addition to historical texts, which seem to reproduce official letters rather faithfully, the later, more grandiose Sasanian titulature is imprinted on many other genres and literatures. These range from panegyric,[11]

> Even he who boasts himself the friend of the sun, who watches the lofty horns of the waning moon and reveres and takes omens from the night wandering blaze of stars, is subdued by fear of you.

to sermons in provincial Roman churches:[12]

> Today the Holy Apostle says, "Do not be conformed to this world." Do you think that Saint Paul is exhorting us to take the form of the elements with this statement? To be like the kings of the Persians who place a globe below their feet so that they may be

thought of as treading on the heavenly vault and pretend occupy the place of God? Even now, with a shining head they sit in an image of the sun so that they may not appear human; with horns stuck to them as if they were pained to be men, they feminize themselves in the midst of the moon. They assume various forms of stars so that they may lose the shape of a man, and yet they gain nothing of the radiance of the heavens.

Armenian sources also bear the imprint of this relentless and evidently effective barrage of Persian royal cosmological propaganda:[13]

King of earth and sea, whose person and image—as it truly is—are of our gods, and whose fortune and fates are above those of all kings.

The Sasanians created a new ideology of kingship that encompassed or super-seded all previous Iranian traditions. They relentlessly delegitimized the claims of the Arsacids and later dismantled those of the Kushans and of the Hephthalites in Chorasmia. The Sasanian kings of kings presented themselves as the latest in a long line of ancient Iranian kings stretching back to the dawn of time and all oth-ers as usurpers or frauds. The Sasanians claimed they were reinvigorating a divinely created imperial order thrown into disarray by Alexander; and although the Ach-aemenids were present in this line, they were not its source but merely a conduit leading back to much older Iranian dynasties. The focus on Iran in calling their kingdom *Ērānšahr* and themselves "king of kings of Iran and non-Iran" (*šāhān šāh ī Ērān ud Anērān*) reflects an innovation—or rather, a new emphasis on an ancient, epic worldview. Centuries before, Darius I had thought it important to identify himself as an Iranian (*Ariya*) of Iranian lineage (*Ariyaciça*), as well as a Persian and an Achaemenid. However, the Sasanians' formulation of *Ērānšahr* was the first time Iranian identity overtly defined an overarching, official political expression. The Sasanians made the ancient concept of Iranian lands politically current, con-necting the present empire with the religious worldview of the Avesta, a process that would deepen in later centuries.

The early Sasanian kings claimed the physical remnants of the Achaemenid pat-rimony in their home province while integrating themselves discursively into Iran's mythological history and dynasties, especially that of the heroic Kayanids.[14] Sasa-nian kings took Kayanid titles in the fourth century and eventually claimed the dynastic name *kay* as well. By the late empire the Sasanians' universal history, the *Xwadāy-nāmag* ("The Book of Lords") presented a continuous royal genealogy that overtly traced their dynasty through the half-remembered Achaemenids to the mythological Kayanids while accounting for the existence of the Romans and powers of the Central Asian steppe, such as the empires of the Hephthalites or Türks.[15]

The Roman emperor developed an institutional sanctity whose appeal and influence rivaled that of the Sasanians. The language and expressive means by which the late Roman emperors articulated divinely inspired sovereignty evolved continuously from the Tetrarchy to their Christian successors, despite the rise of the new religion. Such formulations reached the public in a variety of forms—from official letters, preambles, acclamations and legal works, to coin legends and inscriptions. Diocletian and Maximian made known their divine nature in official documents as well as panegyrics in terms that reflect the Tetrarchic theology, the chief element of which was the idea that they were not only divine themselves but the creators of gods ("deorum creatores"), referring to their unique ability to make legitimate emperors and thus divinities.[16] An inscription in present-day Albania dedicates a milestone to "those begotten by the gods and the creators of gods, our lords Diocletian and Maximian, invincible Augusti."[17] Panegyrical evidence similarly proclaims the Tetrarchic conviction that the emperors acted with divine virtue. The *Panegyrici Latini* contain several allusions to the emperor's deeds as enactments of Hercules' labors or Jupiter's triumph over the Titans. Expressing the new Christian understanding in the sixth century, Justinian I proclaimed in a legal preamble: "The two greatest gifts that God in His infinite goodness has granted men are the Priesthood and the Empire. . . . Both powers emanate from the same principle and bring human life to its perfection."[18]

The titles by which the Roman and Persian sovereigns were known had deep roots in the cultural and political currents of the Mediterranean and Western Asia, but they also reflected contemporary innovations. In the Latin-speaking West and still among the courtly and military elite in Constantinople, the Roman emperor was commonly referred to by such titles as *Imperator, Augustus,* and, officially after Diocletian, *Dominus.* However, continuing a tradition inherited in the eastern Mediterranean from the Hellenistic monarchies, in the Greek East the emperor was known in common parlance and learned discourse simply as *Basileus,* a title that eventually became official in the seventh century. As the Roman emperors became Christian, the precedent of Constantine the Great completely overshadowed those of Augustus, Trajan, or Hadrian, with Constantine I's status as a saint in the Eastern church reinforcing the living emperor's status. The letters and sermons of bishops turned to biblical precedents, both positive and negative, for understanding the current emperor. The reign of Heraclius represents an important turning point, when the emperor's own imagery and court poetry evoked the imagery of Old Testament kingship, especially that of David, to interpret contemporary events and the emperor's place in them, a process that became more and more important in the Byzantine Middle Ages. Whereas imperial legitimacy and the divine favor that it implied rested almost entirely on a candidate's ability to become and remain emperor, after Constantine an emperor's election and survival was seen as reflecting the Christian God's will. The emperor, by virtue of becoming emperor and defeating all rivals, was considered chosen by God, God's representative on earth. The emperor could unproblematically represent himself as heritor of both the ancient traditions and power of Rome and the multifarious traditions of Christianity.

KNOWLEDGE AND THE NATURAL, BUILT, AND EXPRESSIVE ENVIRONMENT

The Roman and Sasanian sovereigns expended considerable resources to create and maintain environments that inculcated their sacred, eternal, and victorious status to their own populations, their subject peoples, and to each other. The process involved a variety of interdependent expressions, including discursive statements, visual media both large and small, additions to and manipulations of urban and natural environments, and a wide, overlapping array of ritual performances. The populace would encounter a relentless barrage of messages in cities where the emperor or king of kings resided or at especially holy or historically significant sites throughout their empires. The audience hall, palace, and portions of the city that interfaced with the palace were the site of some of the most intense efforts of creating and displaying an ideologically correct manifestation of royal cosmology. Sacred or ritually charged spaces were equally important sites of royal display and performance. In Sasanian Iran these included major fire temples and royal hunting estates (Middle Persian *dastgird*), and in the Roman Empire the hippodrome and imperially sponsored or frequented churches. These all worked together to instruct internal and external populations what they should know about the emperor.

Late ancient Western Asia and the Mediterranean both yielded cultural landscapes and cityscapes that were instrumental for establishing, defining, and maintaining power.[19] These built or natural environments were dynamic entities subject to constant modifications and change, and they were agentive in and of themselves in shaping cultural forms. As the accumulated and collective features and significances of a landscape or cityscape served as repositories and engines of (real or imagined) cultural memory, they were a primary medium where successful sovereigns negotiated relationships with the recent and ancient past. Conversely, by radically changing these environments or creating new ones to rival them, sovereigns could actively manipulate the order of things. In addition to text and speech, power was formulated, experienced, and known in late antiquity through expressive events and the built and natural environments.

Official discursive expressions could appeal intellectually to certain members of the population, but the statements that likely made the deepest impression were the short formulations seen often on coin legends, on inscriptional titles, and (for the vast majority) heard in acclamations chanted by the army or in public ceremonies. Alluding to the complex ritual environments that informed and conditioned their reception were the state-managed acclamations that were performed at special celebrations.[20] On the occasion of the completion of the Theodosian legal code, in 438, the Roman Senate began their acclamation of Theodosius II with the following:[21]

> Augustuses of Augustuses, the greatest of Augustuses! [repeated eight times]. God gave You to us! God save You for us! [repeated twenty-seven times]. As Roman emperors, pious and felicitous, may You rule for many years! [repeated twenty-two times]. For the good of the human race, for the good of the Senate, for the good of the State, for the good of all! [repeated twenty-four times]. Our hope is in You; You are our salvation! [repeated twenty-six times].

The senators did not chant this for the personal entertainment of the emperor, who was in his palace in Constantinople during the performance. Although individual members of the Roman Senate may have personally harbored subversive thoughts, the collective chanting manifested a certain experiential knowledge and ensured that it was current in Rome as it was in Constantinople. Among the most evocative examples are the nighttime chants praising their respective sovereigns that the opposing Roman and Persian camps traded through the dark at the siege of Amida. They show how deeply ingrained and vital the knowledge of the emperor could be from the perspective of soldiers on a battlefront. The Persians chanted that Shabuhr II was truly, king of kings and victorious while the Romans chanted back that Constantius II was lord of all things and of the universe.[22]

VISUAL AND BODILY KNOWLEDGE

One of the most direct and most powerful ways people in late antiquity knew an emperor was through his image, whether on a coin, in colossal statuary, on silver plate, in ivory, a wall painting, or a rock relief:[23]

> It is an axiom of royal practice, observed, if not by all other men among whom royalty exists, certainly by the Romans, that the rulers should be publicly honored by their statues. Neither their crowns and diadems and bright purple, nor the number of their bodyguards, nor the multitude of their subjects is sufficient to establish their sovereignty; but they need adoration in order to seem more supreme: not only the adoration directed to them personally, but also that made to their images and portraits, in order that a greater and more perfect honor be rendered to them.

They had the power to manifest the imperial presence through deference, ritual obeisance, and the threat of severe punishment should they be defaced. The city of Antioch faced annihilation for destroying the emperor Theodosius I's images and dragging them through the street. For this act they anxiously expected the same fate as Thessaloniki, where the same emperor slaughtered nearly seven thousand people for disobeying his commands and killing his officials. Images manifested the imperial presence throughout the empire and beyond. The vestments or crowns of client kings, empresses, and consuls carried the image of the emperor. Imperial images stood behind judges, and honoring an imperial image with candles and ritual obeisance demonstrated individual and group loyalty even after the coming of Christianity. Saint Basil's oft-quoted explanation of the Trinity, invoking how imperial images work, articulates in words what the majority of inhabitants of the empire knew through vision and practice:[24]

> For the Son is in the Father, and the Father is in the Son inasmuch as the former is like the latter, and the latter like the former, and in this lies their unity. . . . How then, if they are one and one, are there not two Gods? Because the imperial image, too, is called the emperor, and yet there are not two emperors: neither is the power cut asunder, nor is the glory divided. And as the authority that holds sway over us is one, so the glorification that we address to it is one and not many, since the honor shown to the image is transmitted to its model.

Even in the city of Rome in the seventh century, icons of the emperor in Constantinople would be duly received, processed through the city accompanied by officials and tapers, and installed in the Oratory of San Cesario on the Palatine Hill, the image taking the place of the actual emperor on this site of the ancient imperial residence.[25]

One of the most vital ways individuals in living in late antiquity understood imperial power was through the body, both that of the sovereign and their own. People knew the emperor's nature and his will through experiencing or viewing ritual obeisance, material reward, or violence. The bodies of both emperors were thought to manifest their divine nature through a visible glow. The iconographic conventions to represent this converged after the first century of the empires' coexistence and overlapped with the divine iconographies of several late antique religions. According to official fact established in the Tetrarchy and continuing until the end of the empire, the Roman emperor carried a "light that surround[ed] his] divine head with a shining orb," which came to be represented in artistic form as a nimbus.[26] The Sasanian dynasty developed the ancient Iranian idea of *xwarrah* or *farrah* (from Avestan *xvarənah-*), "Divine Royal Fortune," which inhabited, and thus linked them to, every rightful Iranian ruler since the first kings of humanity. It was the spiritual force empowering the rightful Iranian sovereign that manifested as a bodily glow, especially around the head.[27] As with the Roman emperor, in Persian visual culture a disk nimbus artistically expressed the king of king's *xwarrah*. Textual sources repeatedly insist on the Roman and Sasanian sovereigns' official radiance. Several sources comment that the Roman and the Sasanian sovereign's courtly dress and accoutrements, covered in jewels and precious metals, had the effect of manifesting a dazzling glow to those in their presence:[28]

> [Constantine entered the chamber] like some heavenly messenger of God, clothed in raiment that glittered as it were with rays of light, reflecting the glowing radiance

of a purple robe, and adorned with the brilliant splendor of gold and precious stones. . . .

While standards preceded him on each side, he himself sat alone upon a golden chariot in the resplendent blaze of shimmering precious stones, whose mingled glitter seemed to form a sort of shifting light.

Such statements are often enough encountered that one could wonder whether they arose just as much from culturally conditioned expectations bordering on hallucinations as they did from rich court costumes or aulic technologies and stage management.

Violence, as expressed either through law or on the battlefield, offered the most immediate and inescapable knowledge of a sovereign's will. Criminal law was Zoroastrian in the Sasanian Empire, and as the magi were also the judges, the will of the sovereign was enforced by the same means as the will of God. Punishment was considered salutary, and torture was part of the normal operating procedures of criminal trials. The most common punishment mentioned in Sasanian law books is the lash, with crimes rhetorically distinguished in severity by the number of blows, even up to absurd levels. Amputation of the nose was recommended for adultery. More spectacular punishment methods existed too, especially when connected with apostasy.[29] An apostate's tongue could be torn out and his jaw broken in the course of a trial. Decapitation by the sword was the most common method of capital punishment, often preceded by amputation of the convict's fingers, arms, and legs. Crucifixion was reserved for thieves and sorcerers. Some were hung by their feet until dead. Thieves and Christians were trampled by elephants, as befell the entire city of Susa under Shabuhr II. Techniques applied more rarely included burning convicts alive with naphtha, cutting them to pieces, stoning them, or gouging out their eyes with hot nails. *The Letter of Tansar* refers to execution by the donkey or the cow: animal-shaped cauldrons filled with molten lead.[30]

The bodies of usurpers and rebels, as literal embodiments of disorder and rebellion, could be subject to horrific punishment in both empires. The purpose of the penalty, of course, was not simply to punish the usurper but to discipline society through the spectacle of his dismembered and mutilated body. In the Roman Empire, the ceremonial parading and ostentation of a usuper's head and, later, body parts became an especially important conclusion to any clash between rivals for the imperial throne. When Constantine defeated Maxentius in 312, the victory parade through Rome, the city that had been his residence for years, was dominated by Maxentius's severed head raised high on a spear. Less spectacular defeats of usurpers could be similarly celebrated. Although Constantius II's rival Magnentius committed suicide, his head was sent around to multiple cities in multiple provinces.[31] When Theodosius I defeated Eugenius, the usurper's head was paraded before his troops and then sent through Italy as proof that the rival emperor was no more.[32] When Priscus Attalus was captured, in 416, Honorius mutilated his right hand and had him ritually trampled.[33] The most spectacular of such displays was after Heraclius's successful usurpation of Phocas, when Heraclius had the former emperor ritually trampled and then ordered his body mutilated, with its right arm and genitals paraded on poles and the body burned.[34] People in the Roman Empire knew who their emperor was quite literally, by seeing who had tried and failed to challenge or resist him. They knew that an emperor was no longer by seeing his mutilated body. In contrast, given the sanctity of the Sasanian family, rivals or deposed Sasanian kings of kings would simply disappear from view, either suffocated by ashes or imprisoned in a "Tower of Oblivion," his body inviolate even in disgrace.

SPATIAL KNOWLEDGE

The late Roman imperial court carefully orchestrated courtroom ceremonial in order to minutely express and define the relationship between the emperor and subjects to inculcate an experience of his sanctity. Just as the emperor was sacred, so was anything closely associated with him, from the hippodrome to his bedchamber to his writing desk, extending the imperial sanctity to a wider material and spatial field. As both the emperor and his environment were sacred, they demanded changes in behavior from emperors and subjects alike. The emperors orchestrated and described any contact with their sacred presence in religious terms: their appearance was a divine epiphany; admission to the audience hall was a privileged visit to the inner sanctum of a temple, and ritual acts performed there were called sacred rites.[35] Permanently and metonymically linked to the office of emperor, the adoration of the emperor's purple cloak (*paludamentum*) was the preeminent ritual act for honoring both the office and the particular emperor.[36] This act of physical obeisance (Latin *adoratio,* Greek *proskynēsis*) changed form several times between the third and the seventh century, in terms both of who was allowed to perform it and of the ritual itself.[37] Under the Tetrarchy the *adoratio purpurae* required bending the knee and kissing the emperor's purple *paludamentum;* it was portrayed as a privilege enjoyed only by those of the highest rank, who were admitted to the emperor's presence hierarchically.[38] Those of lower rank performed *adoratio* without the kiss of the cloak. The masses might only glimpse the emperor in quickly moving processions when he entered a city in an *adventus,* in a space like the Roman Forum or Constantinople's Forum of Constantine at the heart of a solemn procession of officials, courtiers and bodyguards or enthroned in the imperial box of the hippodrome amidst the roar of acclamations. Those who were fortunate to attend the Divine Liturgy at an imperial church, might glimpse him through the chancel barrier and clouds of incense while receiving communion at the high altar with the patriarch and clergy.

One of the Latin panegyrics written for Maximian suggests 291 as the terminus ante quem for the use of *adoratio* in Tetrarchic court ceremony, describing a joint ceremony held by Diocletian and Maximian, and giving us a glimpse of the hierarchy and the sacred terms:[39]

> What a spectacle your piety created when those who were going to adore your sacred features were admitted to the palace in Milan: you both were gazed upon, and your twin deity suddenly confused the ceremony of single veneration! No one observed the hierarchy of deities according to the usual protocol; they all stopped still to spend more time in adoration, stubborn in their duplicate pious duty. Yet this private veneration, as if in the inner shrine ["interioribus sacrariis"], stunned the minds only of those whose public rank gave them access to you. But when you passed through the door and rode together through the middle of the city, the very buildings, I hear, almost moved themselves, when every man, woman, and tiny child and aged person either ran out through the doors into the open or hung out of the upper thresholds of the houses.

The use of both lights and incense and the requirement that all in the emperor's presence keep absolute silence were strictures aimed at heightening the experience of awe and sanctity.[40] The Roman imperial court was often described as a vision of the divine realm. Recalling his experience of an imperial banquet, Eusebius exclaimed: "One might have thought that a picture of Christ's kingdom was thus shadowed forth, and a dream rather than a reality!"[41]

The Sasanian court skillfully cultivated a complex interaction among architectural space, ritual practice, and the visual environment in order to make their assertions of the Sasanian king of kings' cosmological centrality tangible. The Sasanian palace and audience halls were not just an expression of Sasanian political cosmology but were where that cosmology was celebrated and performed. Although they were intended to celebrate ancient traditions, the Sasanians patronized innovative palace and sacred architecture. Their early creations pushed the limits of domed and vaulted brick or rough stone architecture. The supreme monumental expression, the Ayvān-e Kīsra at Ctesiphon, was truly one of the great monuments of late antiquity, surpassing all other structures but the great church of Hagia Sophia in size and engineering. The experience of an audience with the Persian king was awe-inspiring and was intricately stage-managed to maximize its impact. The Sasanian king of kings concealed himself behind a veil until ready, and the audience seeker would wait outside until bidden to enter by the master of ceremonies, ensuring an element of surprise in the envoy's experience of the king of kings.[42] A golden chain suspended a superhumanly heavy golden crown over the throne, which the king of kings appeared to bear easily.

The Sasanian king of kings reigned at the center of the Iranian world, which, according to Sasanian cosmological knowledge, was the center of the earth, with the lands of all other peoples constellated around it. The late Sasanian kings of kings translated this cosmological formulation into a tangible reality in their audience hall:[43]

> In the collection of customs of the reception hall of [Husraw I] was [one that dictated that], inside [the throne room], a golden chair was placed to the right of his throne [*takt*], and in this manner golden chairs were placed also to the left and to the rear, thus three chairs. One of the chairs was for the king of China, another was for the king of Rome, and the third was that of the [Hephthalite] king.

The ritual space of the throne room was a symbolic map of the world that made all important nations of the earth and the elements of Iranian society visible, placing them in their cosmologically correct conformation. No reigning king ever took his place on one of these golden thrones. The kings intended such spatial and performative experiences primarily for their internal courtly audience. The important point is that the late Sasanian worldview was represented and, in a sense, animated before the eyes of the king and court.

The natural environment played an especially important role in Sasanian Iran. Although the Roman Empire was equally concerned with extracting agricultural wealth and converting it to taxes, much of this occurred well out of the view of the emperor and the urban elites. In contrast, Sasanian sovereigns used the landscape and the processes of cultivation and extraction in a performative way. In cultivating massive irrigation and agricultural projects they created monuments that brought people and natural resources together in a way that not only served a functional purpose but also produced ecological spaces wherein the royal power was continually practiced and displayed. These range from vast plantations to private hunting and garden enclosures accessible only to the king and court. Mesopotamia was the most important of these regions in the early empire, though later city foundations and the reforms of the sixth century brought new lands elsewhere in the empire under the control of the central administration. In Mesopotamia in particular, the Sasanian court's efforts to expand agriculture and trade in order establish a more stable tax base drove the development of landscape.[44] This period experienced a most remarkable expansion of agriculture in the Sasanian era.[45] Achieving an unprecedented scale and organizational capacity, the Sasanians created "large dendritic systems of canals bringing whole sub-regions of the plain into coordinated control."[46] Newly founded cities often anchored these possessions, though sometimes royal estates (*dastgirds*), often veritable cities in and of themselves, could also control areas of agricultural, commercial, or hydraulic exploitation.[47]

In addition to their military and economic functions, engineering works like bridges and roads, and hydraulic installations, like canals, dams, weirs, and mills, which constellated around and supported the city, could also function as impressive monuments. The most dramatic examples of hydraulic works survive in Khuzestan. Many of them are closely associated with Shabuhr I's foundation of

Weh-Andiog-Shabuhr (Gondēšāpur). The techniques of Roman engineers captured by the king of kings are especially noticeable on a 400-meter-long weir on the Dez River and a roughly 550-meter bridge and dam on the Karun River at Shushtar, with similar works at Pa-ye Pol and Ahvaz.[48]

CONCLUSION

Although official legal or religious formulations provide some explanation of what people in late antiquity knew about their sovereigns, the knowledge that made the deepest impact in individuals' daily lives and understanding of the world was manifest through nondiscursive, visual, ritual, and environmental expressions. The sovereign was a constant element in late antique people's lives, yet he was known almost entirely at several removes. The vast majority of the empires' populations never laid eyes on the bodies of their sovereigns. Yet, in both the Roman and the Sasanian case, the image of the sovereign was ubiquitous, appearing on coins, in statuary placed in privileged places, and, in the Sasanian Empire, integrated into the environment with rock reliefs. Although most never heard the sovereign's voice, the words of the emperors were visible in inscriptions and enforced through their officials, judges, and armies. The mutilated bodies of those who challenged or defied the royal will were evidence of the emperors' power. The majority of the population never saw their sovereign in audience, but royal palaces dominated the empires' most important urban environments, and public processions linked to more intricate and intimate rituals in palaces or sacred structures ensured that many were aware of the courts' magnificence.

The sovereigns of Rome and Iran tightly controlled their cultures' historical narratives while shaping the natural and urban environments to reinforce knowledge of those narratives. They controlled their cultures' perceptions of history by adding new structures or monuments to august urban and ritual spaces. The Roman emperors continued to add monuments, even if on a small scale, to the Forum Romanum through the seventh century, even though the urban space of Constantinople soon took on greater importance. In carving their images into the cliff of the Achaemenid necropolis of Nasqsh-e Rostam, early Sasanian kings of kings gained control of a powerful site that provided a touchstone for provincial connection to the Achaemenid heritage. Through patronage the sovereigns created and controlled some of the holiest sites of the Mediterranean and Western Asia. In sites that had not seen previous monumental building, Roman imperial patronage under Constantine I created a monumental sacred topography in the Holy Land, and the Sasanian court built the most important, most venerated fire sanctuary of late antiquity, Adur Gushnasp.

Sacral kingship, in essence, was the other great religion of late antiquity and one that the two empires both practiced, both in competition and in unison. After the first tumultuous century, as the two empires came to terms with each other, their own relationship became retrojected into the distant past. The presence of the Roman and Iranian sovereigns was a necessary and primal reality, which the world had always known, and continually needed, to be ordered and pacified. Internal propaganda generated within both empires placed each sovereign at the center of the world, yet their diplomatic protocols and communications reveal that even in times of conflict the constant existence of each one's brother king was deeply interwoven into the natural order of things. With centuries of diplomatic exchange engendering competition and appropriation, the two empires' ritual systems, visual cultures of power, and even courtly realities became more and more similar. The two courts competed in idioms that were not only mutually intelligible but had in fact merged. This yielded a continuity of practice and understanding of what it meant to be a king and how to be one that extended from the Atlantic to Central Asia. Rivals and clients on their peripheries and in their interstices appropriated their court cultures and court practices—in essence, the theoretical and practical knowledge of being a king.

NOTES

1. Matthew Canepa, *The Two Eyes of the Earth: Art and Ritual of Kingship between Rome and Sasanian Iran* (Berkeley and Los Angeles: University of California Press, 2009).

2. Foundational and influential works on the Roman emperor from these perspectives: Andreas Alföldi, "Die Ausgestaltung des monarchischen Zeremoniells am römischen Kaiserhof," *Mitteilungen des Deutschen Archäologisches Institut, Römische Abteilung,* 49 (1934): 3–118; idem, "Insignien und Tracht der römischen Kaiser," *Mitteilungen des Deutschen Archäologisches Institut, Römische Abteilung,* 50 (1935): 1–177; André Grabar, *L'empereur dans l'art byzantine: Recherches sur l'art officiel de l'empire d'Orient,* Publications de la Faculté des Lettres de l'Université de Strasbourg, vol. 75 (Paris: Les Belles Lettres, 1936); Otto Treitinger, *Die oströmische Kaiser-und Reichsidee nach ihrer Gestaltung im höfischen Zeremoniell* (Jena: Frommann, 1938); Wilhelm Ensslin, *Gottkaiser und Kaiser von Gottes Gnaden,* Sitzungsberichte der Bayerische Akademie der Wissenschaften, Philosophisch-Historische Klasse, 1943, vol. 6 (Munich: Verlag der Bayerischen Akademie der Wissenschaften, 1943); Herbert Hunger, *Proimion: Elemente der byzantinischen Kaiseridee in den Arengen der Urkunden* (Vienna: Böhlaus,1964); Fergus Millar, *The Emperor in the Roman World, 31 BC–AD 337* (Ithaca: Cornell University Press, 1977); Michael McCormick, *Eternal Victory: Triumphal Rulership in Late Antiquity, Byzantium and the Early Medieval West* (Cambridge: Cambridge University Press, 1986); idem, "Emperors," in *The Byzantines,* ed. G. Cavallo (Chicago: University of Chicago Press, 1997), 230–54; Gilbert Dagron, *Empereur et prêtre: Étude sur le "césaropapisme" byzantin* (Paris: Gallimard, 1996); Frank Kolb, *Herrscherideologie in der Spätantike* (Berlin: Akademie Verlag, 2001). Representative of specific studies or sections of larger works on Sasanian Iran: Arthur Christensen, *L'Iran sous les Sassanides,* 2nd ed. (Copenhagen: Munksgaard, 1944); Richard N. Frye, "The Charisma of Kingship in Ancient Iran," *Iranica Antiqua* 4 (1964): 36–54; Gherardo Gnoli, "L'Iran tardoantico e la

regalità sassanide," *Mediterraneo Antico* 1 (1998): 115–49; Zeev Rubin, "The Sasanid Monarchy" in *The Cambridge Ancient History*, vol. 14 (Cambridge: Cambridge University Press, 2000), 638–61; Abolala Soudavar, *The Aura of Kings: Legitimacy and Divine Sanction in Iranian Kingship* (Costa Mesa, Calif.: Mazda Publishers, 2003); Josef Weisehöfer, "King, Court, and Royal Representation in the Sasanian Empire," in *The Court and Court Society in Ancient Monarchies*, ed. A. J. S. Spawforth (Cambridge: Cambridge University Press, 2007), 58–79; Dietrich Huff, "Formation and Ideology of the Sasanian State in the Context of the Archaeological Evidence," in *The Sasanian Era*, ed. V. S. Curtis and S. Stewart (London: I. B. Tauris, 2008), 31–59; Touraj Daryaee, "Kingship in Early Sasanian Iran," in Curtis and Stewart, *Sasanian Era*, 60–70; Antonio Panaino, "The King and the Gods in the Sasanian Royal Ideology," *Sources pour l'histoire et la géographie du monde iranien (224–710)*, ed. R. Gyselen (Bures-sur-Yvette: Groupe pour l'Étude de la Civilisation du Moyen-Orient, 2009), 209–56; Canepa, *Two Eyes* (above, n. 1), 1–5.

3. In relation to Yazdegerd II and the protection of the Caucasus, see Henning Börm, "'Es war allerdings nicht so, daß sie es im Sinne eines Tributes erhielten, wie viele meinten . . .': Anlässe und Funktion der persischen Geldforderungen an die Römer (3. bis 6. Jh.)," *Historia* 57 (2008): 327–46.

4. Richard Payne, "Cosmology and the Expansion of the Iranian Empire, 503–628 CE," *Past and Present* 219 (2013): 1–31.

5. "A king is one who truly rules over anger and envy and pleasure, who commands all things under the laws of God, who keeps his mind free, and who does not allow the power of pleasures to dominate his soul. Such a one I would gladly see ruling peoples and earth and sea and cities and peoples and soldiers. For the person who has put the reasoning power of his soul in charge of his passions will rule over men as well with the divine laws, so that he will be to the ruled as a father, frequenting the cities with all kindness": John Chrysostom, *Comparatio Regis et Monachi* 2 (ed. J.-P. Migne, *Patrologia Cursus Completus, Series Graeca*, vol. 47 [Paris, 1862], 388), trans. David G. Hunter, *Two Treatises on Monastic Life* (Lewiston, N.Y.: Edwin Mellen Press, 1988), 70–71; cf. Ambrose, *Epistola* 57. Andrew Wallace-Hadrill, "The Emperor and His Virtues" *Historia* 30 (1981): 298–323; Ilaria Ramelli, *Il basileus come nomos empsychos tra diritto naturale e diritto divino: Spunti platonici del concetto e sviluppi di età imperiale e tardo-antica* (Naples: Bibliopolis, 2006), 102–31. *Tansarnāma*, trans. Mary Boyce, *Muḥammad ibn al-Ḥasan Ibn Isfandiyār: The Letter of Tansar*, Literary and Historical Texts from Iran, vol. 1, Persian Heritage Series, no. 9, Serie Orientale Roma, vol. 38 (Rome: Istituto Italiano per il Medio ed Estremo Oriente, 1968), 23.

6. *Shabuhragan* (Mani's "Book Dedicated to Shabuhr") BT 11, text 11.2.

7. Discussed in greater depth in Canepa, *Two Eyes* (above, n. 1), 100–106.

8. Ibid.

9. Menander Protector, frag. 6.11.177–83; trans. R. C. Blockley, *The History of Menander the Guardsman* (Liverpool: Francis Cairns, 1985), ARCA Classical and Medieval Texts, Papers, and Monographs, col. 17, 63; "particeps siderum, frater solis lunae" (Ammianus Marcellinus 17.5.3). P. Huyse, "Die sasanidische Königstitulatur: Eine Gegenüberstellung der Quellen," in *Eran und Aneran: Studien zu den Beziehungen zwischen dem Sasanidenreich und der Mittelmeerwelt*, Oriens et Occidens, vol. 13, ed. J. Wiesehöfer and P. Huyse (Stuttgart: Steiner, 2006),

181–201; A. Panaino, "Astral Characters of Kingship in the Sasanian and Byzantine Worlds," *La Persia e Bisanzio: Atti dei Convegni Lincei* 201 (2004): 561–62.

10. Michael Whitby and Mary Whitby, *The History of Theophylact Simocatta* (Oxford: Clarendon Press, 1986), 114 (ll. 4.8.5); on the "official correspondence" preserved in non-Iranian sources, Huyse, "Sasanidische Königstitulatur" (above, n. 9), 193–97. In the remembrance of the *šāhnāma*, the Sasanian kings bear such expansive titles as *šāh-e jahān*, *šahhriyār-e zamin*, *šāh-e geti*, "king of the world," or *jahāndar*, "conqueror of the world": Abka'i-Khavari, *Das Bild des Königs in der Sasanidenzeit: Schriftliche Überlieferungen im Vergleich mit Antiquaria*, Texte und Studien zur Orientalistik, vol. 13 (Hildesheim: Olms, 2000), 47 and 143.

11. Flavius Corippus, *In Laudem Iustini Augusti Minoris* 30, trans. A. Cameron (London, Athlone, 1976), 85.

12. Peter Chrysologus, *Sermo* 120 (ed. J.-P. Migne, *Patrologiae Cursus Completus, Series Latina*, vol. 52 [Paris, 1862], 527); A. Panaino, "The Bagan of the Fratarakas: Gods or 'Divine' Kings?" in *Religious Themes and Texts of Pre-Islamic Iran and Central Asia*, Beiträge zur Iranistik, vol. 24, ed. C. Certi, M. Maggi, and E. Provas (Wiesbaden: Reichert, 2003), 208; Andrea Gariboldi, "Astral Symbology on Iranian Coinage," *East and West* 54 (2004): 31–53.

13. Movses Khorenats'i 1.9, 3.17, 3.26, 3.42, 3.51; Huyse, "Sasanidische Königstitulatur" (above, n. 9), 193.

14. Matthew Canepa, "Technologies of Memory in Early Sasanian Iran: Achaemenid Sites and Sasanian Identity," *American Journal of Archaeology* 114 (2010): 563–96.

15. E. Yarshater, "Iranian National History," in *The Cambridge History of Iran* (Cambridge: Cambridge University Press: 1983), 359–476; T. Daryaee, "Memory and History: The Construction of the Past in Late Antique Persia." *Name-ye Iran-e Bastan* 1 (2001–2): 6; "Sasanians and Their Ancestors," in *Proceedings of the 5th Conference of the Societas Iranologica Europaea, Ravenna 6–11 October 2003*, ed. A. Panaino and A. Piras, vol. 1 (Milan: Mimesis, 2006), 287–93; "*Imitatio Alexandri* and Its Impact on Late Arsacid, Early Sasanian, and Middle Persian Literature," *Electrum* 12 (2007): 89–94; Yarshater, "Iranian National History," 402–11; Richard Payne, "The Reinvention of Iran: The Sasanian Empire and the Huns," in *The Cambridge Companion to the Age of Attila*, ed. M. Maas (Cambridge: Cambridge University Press, 2014), 282–99.

16. Kolb, *Herrscherideologie* (above, n. 2), 168–70.

17. Inscription on a milestone near Dyrrhachium: "Diis genitis et | deorum creatoribus | dd. Nn. Diocletiano et | [Maximiano invict]is AUGG(ustis)," ibid. 169–70.

18. Justinian I, novel 6, March 6, 535, trans. Francis Dvornik in Michael Maas, *Readings in Late Antiquity: A Sourcebook* (London: Routledge, 2000), 7.

19. Adam Smith, *The Political Landscape: Constellations of Authority in Early Complex Polities* (Berkeley and Los Angeles: University of California Press, 2003), 272.

20. Canepa, *Two Eyes* (above, n. 1), 101–2.

21. *Gesta Senatus Romani de Theodosiano Publicando* 5, trans. Maas, *Readings* (above, n. 18), 9, slightly modified.

22. Ammianus Marcellinus 19.2.11.

23. Gregory of Nazianzus, *Oratio* 4.80, trans. Francis Dvornik, *Early Christian and Byzantine Political Philosophy: Origins and Background*, vol. 2 (Washington, D.C.: Dumbarton Oaks, 1966), 686–67, slightly modified.

24. Basil the Great, *De Spiritu Sancto* 17.44, trans. Cyril Mango, *Art of the Byzantine Empire, 312–1453: Sources and Documents* (Englewood Cliffs: Prentice-Hall, 1972), slightly modified.

25. Andrea Augenti, "Lo splendore del vuoto: I palazzi senza imperatori," in *Aurea Roma: Dalla città pagana alla città cristiana* (Rome: L'Erma di Bretschneider, 2000), 93.

26. *Panegyrici Latini* 10.3.2., trans. C. E. V. Nixon and Barbara Saylor Rodgers, *In Praise of Later Roman Emperors: The Panegyrici Latini* (Berkeley and Los Angeles: University of California Press, 1994), 57–58.

27. *Bundahišn* 14.7–8, ed. B. T. Anklesaria (Bombay: British India Press, Byculla, 1908).

28. Eusebius, *Vita Constantini* 3.10.

29. János Jany, "Criminal Justice in Sasanian Persia," *Iranica Antiqua* 42 (2007): 347–86; Christelle Jullien,"Peines et supplices dans les *Actes des Martyrs Persans* et droit sassanide," *Studia Iranica* 33 (2004): 243–69.

30. *Tansarnāma*, trans. Boyce (above, n. 5), 23.

31. Ammianus Marcellinus 22.14.4.

32. McCormick, *Eternal Victory* (above, n. 2), 45.

33. Ibid. 56–57.

34. Nikephoros 1.40–41.

35. Alföldi, "Ausgestaltung" (above, n. 2), 33.

36. Kolb, *Herrscherideologie* (above, n. 2), 39.

37. This discussion is adapted from Canepa, *Two Eyes* (above, n. 1), 149–53, where it is explored in much greater detail.

38. *Codex Justinianus* 9.51.1; W. Ensslin, "The End of the Principate," in *The Cambridge Ancient History*, vol. 12, *The Crisis of Empire*, AD 193–337, ed. A. K. Bowman, P. D. Garnsey, and Averil Cameron (Cambridge: Cambridge University Press, 1939), 352–82, esp. 363.

39. *Panegyrici Latini* 11.11.1–4; trans. Nixon and Rodgers, *In Praise of Later Roman Emperors* (above, n. 26), 96, slightly modified.

40. A. Dieterich, *Der Ritus der verhüllten Hände* (Leipzig: Teubner, 1911), 440–48; Alföldi, "Ausgestaltung" (above, n. 2), 33; Hanns Gabelmann, *Antike Audienz und Tribunal-szenen* (Darmstadt: Wissenschaftliche Buchgesellschaft, 1984).

41. Eusebius, *Vita Constantini* 3.10.

42. Pseudo-al-Jāḥiẓ, *Le livre de la couronne*, trans. C. Pellat (Paris: Les Belles Lettres, 1954), 56–57; al-Masʿūdi, *Murūj al-dahab*, trans. C. de Meynard, *Les prairies d'or*, vol. 4 (Paris: L'Imprimerie Impériale, 1865), 2.158; Christensen, *L'Iran sous les Sassanides* (above, n. 2), 44. See Kayanid King Kay-Husraw as referenced in Ferdowsī, *Šāhnāma* (hereafter ŠN), ed. E. E. Bertels, *Shākh-nāme: Kriticheskii tekst*, 9 vols. (Moscow: Izd-vo Vostochnoĭ Lit-ry, 1960–71), 5.382.2472; 5.386.2542; 5.387.2563–64; 5.390.2607; 5.390.2610; See Kayanid King Lohrāsp as referenced in ŠN 6.56.757, and many similar passages; Abkaʾi-Khavari, *Bild des Königs* (above, n. 10), 78, 179.

43. *The Fársnáma of Ibnu'l-Balkhí*, E. J. W. Gibb Memorial Series, new series, vol. 1, ed. G. Le Strange and R. A. Nicholson (London: Luzac, 1921), 97; Matthew Canepa, "Distant Displays of Power: Understanding Cross-Cultural Interaction among the Elites of Rome, Sasanian Iran, and Sui-Tang China," in *Theorizing Cross-Cultural Interaction among the Ancient and Early Medieval Mediterranean, Near East and Asia*, Ars Orientalis, vol. 38, ed. M. Canepa (Washington D.C.: Smithsonian, 2010), 131–32.

44. M. Morony, "Economic Boundaries? Late Antiquity and Early Islam?" *Journal of the Social and Economic History of the Orient* 47 (2004): 184–88.

45. Robert McC. Adams, *Land behind Baghdad: A History of Settlement on the Diyala Plains* (Chicago: University of Chicago Press, 1965); idem, "Intensified Large-Scale Irrigation as an Aspect of Imperial Policy: Strategies of Statecraft on the Late Sasanian Mesopotamian Plain," in *Agricultural Strategies,* ed. J. Marcus and C. Stanish (Los Angeles: Cotsen Institute of Archaeology, UCLA, 2006), 17–37; idem, "Ancient Mesopotamian Urbanism and Blurred Disciplinary Boundaries," *Annual Review of Anthropology* 41 (2012): 1–20.

46. Robert McC. Adams, "The Limits of State Power on the Mesopotamian Plain," *Cuneiform Digital Library Bulletin* 1 (2007): 2.

47. Canepa, *Two Eyes* (above, n. 1), 127–29. T. Daryaee, *Sasanian Persia: The Rise and Fall of an Empire* (London: I. B. Tauris, 2009), 127. Karim Alizadeh, "Borderland Projects of Sasanian Empire: Intersection of Domestic and Foreign Policies," *The Archaeology of Sasanian Politics* (eds. M. Soroush and R. Payne), special issue of the *Journal of Ancient History* 2.2 (2014): 93–115. Eberhard W. Sauer, Hamid Omrani Rekavandi, Tony J. Wilkinson, and Jebrael Nokandeh, *Persia's Imperial Power in Late Antiquity: The Great Wall of Gorgān and Frontier Landscapes of Sasanian Iran* (Oxford: Oxbow Books, 2013), 304–81.

48. ŠN, trans. R. Levy, *The Epic of the Kings: Shah-nama, the National Epic of Persia* (London: Routledge and K. Paul, 1967), 284. Also reflected in Mas'ūdī, *Murūj* (above, n. 42), 1.227; Ṭa'ālebī, *Ḡorar,* ed. and trans. H. Zotenberg, *Histoire des rois des Perses* (Paris: Imprimerie Nationale, 1900), 494, 527; D. Huff, "Bridges, Section i: 'Pre-Islamic Bridges.'" Encyclopaedia Iranica Online (1989): www.iranica.com.org/articles/bridges#pt1.

9

Ordo

Michael Kulikowski

Outside the governor's palace in Constantina, the provincial capital of Numidia, in the interior of modern Algeria, or possibly in the city's forum, a bronze tablet was erected at some point between late 361 and mid-363. In it, the *vir clarissimus* Ulpius Mariscianus, *consularis* (governor) of Numidia, laid out the order in which the population of the medium-sized provincial town of Thamugadi (modern Timgad) could salute or greet the governor when he made his formal entry into town. This *ordo salutationis* shaped the way all involved knew what to make of their world, and it was vitally important to all of their prestige.[1] It ensured that a new governor would never mistakenly greet first someone of lower status than whomever he greeted second, although he ought to have known such rules by heart. More important, it reified—literally turned into a bronzed thing—the social hierarchy of the city; it ordered this hierarchy, rendered it an object of social knowledge, and made it impossible for anyone to challenge it, though few, if any, would have chosen to do so. Every local community in the empire had its own hierarchies, and though the Greek- and Latin-speaking parts of the empire might refer to individuals' ranks in different words, their respective vocabularies displayed a remarkably universal sense of stable local hierarchy—and an inability to conceptualize the world and know one's own place in it without such a hierarchy.

Very few monumental texts comparable to this one of Constantina survive, but we know enough about the formalities of imperial government's interaction with the provincials that nothing in the *ordo salutationis* comes as much of a surprise: this is how rulers and ruled learned to understand the structures of their lives. Somewhat more interesting to the modern historian is the location in which the decree of Ulpius Mariscianus was found—bronze inscriptions of antiquity are very rare, bronze being the sort of commodity far more often melted down for reuse than preserved; and so the *ordo* does not survive at Constantina. Instead, the text of the decree is preserved in the city to which it was directed, Thamugadi, but inscribed on marble rather than bronze as in its original. There it stood outside the curia, the building in which the town council (*curia*) of Timgad met to run the town in a solemn and fixed fashion that hardly altered as years went past. Beside this impressive testament to the Roman social order stood another, (to us) even more impressive monument. Three large marble blocks, each inscribed with two columns, decorated the grand audience hall of the curia. Reworking disused inscriptions from an earlier age, the fourth-century masons labored hard to make them look good. The stonecutters, too, took care to produce a kind of monumental lettering that recalled classical inscriptions on bronze. They also mapped out the spacing of the letters and words (the inscription's *ordinatio,* or what modern type-setters call "kerning") with far greater care than fourth-century readers were generally used to. And with good reason. At the top of the first block, one read:

ALBVS ORDINIS COL.
   THAMG.

THE ALBUM OF THE CURIAL ORDER OF THE COLONY
   OF TIMGAD

The name of the colony whose *curiales* so lovingly display themselves is carefully chiseled and expertly centered, larger than the rest of the words. After it, the great men of the *colonia* are listed, first the *viri clarissimi,* then the *viri perfectissimi,* then the rest of the curial order, according to their prestige: the *sacerdotales,* the *curator,* the *duoviri,* the *flamines perpetui,* the *pontifices, augures, aediles, quaestores, duovi-ralici,* and then the *curiales* who had not, or not yet, held any special office, ending in the *praetextati,* the children of *curiales* who had not yet entered the *ordo* but who were admitted to its sessions and could listen to curial deliberations before taking up their actual positions in the *ordo.* At the very head of the list, among the *viri clarissimi,* stand men designated as patrons of the city, at least one of whom was not even a resident, Vulcacius Rufus, a relative of Constantine I and great senator of Rome who had earlier served as governor of Numidia. *Viri clarissimi* were members of the senatorial *ordo* of the empire at large; the *perfectissimi,* a fourth-century relic of the old imperial *ordo equester.* The *sacerdotales,* at the end of their local careers, had held annual elected priesthoods that for the rest of their lives entitled them to stand at the head of their local *ordo,* above the ordinary decurions and just below the *honorati* of senatorial or nearly senatorial rank. But their status was not heritable, and their children were mere *curiales,* as they themselves had been before their careers took them higher. Then at the end of the list come other names, those of Christian clergy and of imperial officials who must have had some relation to the curial order—some share the names of men inscribed in the curial list—but who had taken on other roles. All in all, there are 263 names in the list, with perhaps twenty more now missing, and there are several cases where three generations of a single family appear in their respective spots.[2] Most of these men disclose their African background in the cognomina native to the region: Victorinus, Victorianus; Faustus, Faustinus, Faustinianus; Donatus, Donatianus; and so on.[3] Many add a *signum* to their name, *signa* being a sort of nickname that became fashionable throughout the Latin Empire in the fourth century. In this minor backwater of the Roman Empire, in a corner of modern Algeria that is now too dangerous for most scholars to visit, the *ordo* (governing elite) of the colony is graphically mapped in order (*ordo*) of rank that is underscored by the ordering (*ordinatio*) of the text, a text that was in turn displayed near to and undoubtedly in sight of the text of the order (*ordo*) in which the great men of the city might be allowed to address the governor of the province when he visited. Everything was in keeping with the law enunciated by the great Severan jurist Ulpian: "In albo decurionum in municipio nomina ante scribi oportet eorum, qui dignitates principis iudicio consecuti sunt, postea eorum qui tantum municipalibus honoribus functi sunt."[4]

Nothing else so well illustrates the obsession of the late Roman world with the precise organization of rank and precedence. It was how Romans knew the world, their place in it, that of their neighbors, that of their kin, their clients, and their slaves. This mental mapping by reference to rank is embodied for us in the rich semantic field of the noun *ordo* (genitive *ordinis*).[5] That field is almost too fertile for the modern scholar to encompass, but it is worth thinking of the various meanings that the word *ordo* could bear. At root, after all, it meant no more than "line" or "row," as in a row of seats in the theater—in one of those many historicosemantic overlaps that the word encourages, the *ordo equester* was in 63 B.C.E. assigned its own *quattordecim ordines* in the theater, setting it apart from the other census groups of the state.[6] From there, the word *ordo* could be used to distinguish almost any regular group in society, or any body of people within the social order; hence, to adlect a man into the Senate without any special status was an *adlectio in amplissimo ordine,* the Senate as construed at its widest. By contrast, if someone was forced to know his place, or prevented from rising above his station, he was *in ordinem coactus.* Similarly, though, the word could also literally refer to a line of soldiers; as far back as the time of Plautus and in historical writers it regularly meant "unit," as of soldiers, a pregnant association in the late antique era, in which all society was increasingly militarized and imperial service was called *militia.*[7] In all this, the common abstract usage of the word—by which thoughts were conveyed in order or succession, benches thus arranged, preferences ranked—could hardly be separated from its many concrete uses: the abstract sense, of things being put in order or arranged as they ought to be, could never be erased or avoided.

Latin, in fact, could use the ablative singular (*ordine*) to convey the same sense of satisfaction that German conveys by "in Ordnung." Not for nothing did the Severan jurists speak of *ordo* in their efforts to systematize a Roman law that had developed willy-nilly from now irrelevant Republican structures into the machinery of world government or Macrobius explain how he would reduce the jumble of his learning to good sense, "in ordinem."[8]

So central are the concepts subsumed within the single word *ordo* to the late Roman construction of social knowledge that one may be surprised to discover that *ordo* had no antonym. No single word could function as a privative to its sense of harmonious structuring. *Ordo* was one word with an encompassing, approving semantic field. All the many things that could challenge that fundamental unity were specific and differentiated, and their multiplicity was part of their threat. The many forms of the single lexeme were confronted by numerous different derogations, so that the legal, social, and cultural order of the world was beset on all sides by myriad challenges that might disorder them. What strikes the historian of late antiquity is how consistently this nexus of ideas is transmitted from earlier Roman culture into the world of the later empire, how consistently the fundamental building blocks of Roman sociopolitical culture were sustained as ideas even into a period when their reality was becoming unsustainable. The deep conviction in the stability of a social order always threatened with dissolution is an almost immutable feature of Roman elite discourse.[9] One could never forget the social order, because, as Lactantius reminds us at the very beginning of the fourth century, one would never forget the *ordo* from which one came.[10] What follows will consider just three aspects of this phenomenon, each as it touches on the lexical, semantic, and epistemological fields of *ordo* and each as it functioned meaningfully in the lives of late Roman people who used this concept as a structure within which to know their world. We will begin with the legal and social distinctions among *honestiores* and *humiliores,* an essential part of the late Roman world's daily reality. Second, we will consider the meaning of *libertas,* a concept that had since the earliest times been inseparable from the social order and the proper "ordering of things." Finally, we will consider how threats to public order, real, potential, and imagined, provoked a consistency of response, something encapsulated in a famous short episode of Ammianus Marcellinus.

In a context like this, it is impossible to ignore the influence of Michel Foucault on the scholarship of late antiquity, and indeed on historical scholarship more generally, so that that even those who have never read his works have by now absorbed parts of his analytical vocabulary.[11] There can be no question that the semantic field of *ordo, ordinis,* carries with it the entire array of Foucauldian implications of discipline, punishment, and surveillance. The corporate nature of the *ordo,* in which individuals (or individual parts) were both distinctively within and functionally indivisible from their larger unit; a consequence of this fact is how the social orderings implied in the word's semantic field were always more than a technology for disciplining the individual body.[12] As result, even when it is individuals within an *ordo* who are in question, they are never wholly dissociable from their *ordo,* in the same way that in any given moment any given individual necessarily served as a synecdoche for his or her *ordo* and thus for *ordo* in the sense of social ordering.[13] Our discussion, then, can begin from the distinction between the *honestiores* and the *humiliores,* because it both objectified the abstractions of *ordo* and in consequence created a predictable locus of social threat.

HONESTIORES AND HUMILIORES

The distinction of the *honestiores*—the good, the "honest," the "better"—and the *humiliores*—the vile, the humble, the lowly—was one of the basic structuring devices of imperial Roman society, and one of the key means by which people knew their world and thus operated within it. Such social distinctions were essential to the social order. As we noted in Lactantius, one always remembered one's *ordo,* especially if it was a privileged one. Adjectives like *senatorius* come with *ordo* unspoken ahead of them.[14] How easy it must have been to recall one's status in the social order when it was known to be so venerable: new senators acceded to a *reverendus ordo.*[15] They offered largesse, games, and entertainment to the people, who acclaimed them for their beneficence—the major and minor magistrates, even the grand women of the city, all reminded daily of their importance.[16] How hard, by contrast, it was for the lower orders to forget their *ordo,* hedged about with restrictions and frequent degradations.

At the apex of society, among the best of the *honestiores,* was the *ordo senatorius.* It may surprise a scholar of the early empire to realize how little the semantic assumptions of that *ordo* had changed over time despite the actual political transformation that it had undergone between the second and the fourth century, with a comprehensive blurring of the distinction between inherited rank and officeholding. One might have expected this blurring to have attenuated the implicit high imperial order, but it did not. Instead, the equestrianization of imperial government that began in the second century and was fully accomplished by the middle of the third leveled status assumptions downward.[17] That is to say, as the last traces of the Augustan and Flavian senatorial aristocracies disappeared, more and more equestrians were appointed to formerly senatorial offices, not least to the great provincial commands. This mattered. Service in the *ordo equester* had always been just that, service, or *militia,* with its military connotations. Just as in the military, the holding of particular offices brought with it a particular rank defined by its formal salary grade.[18] By contrast, the remunerations of senatorial office were not a subject of polite conversation, and as late as the 210s it was fatal for an emperor's reputation to imply that a senator might find the money associated with a *dignitas* as important as the holding of it.[19] Thereafter, however, equestrians penetrated the *dignitates* of the senatorial order, and they brought with them into the *ordo senatorius* their own assumptions. By the middle of the third century, equestrian emperors were no longer the embarrassment that they had once been, and the vast majority of formerly senatorial offices were in the hands of equestrians. The word *dignitas,* of ancient Republican heritage, shed most of its special meaning, as office was less and less the expected privilege of rank and came just as often to confer rank. On account of such elisions, the equestrian *ordo* itself ceased to exist as a census category by the fourth century, merged into an *ordo senatorius* that now held office in the manner and with the attitudes of the old equestrian order.

For all that, however, the implicit force of the word *ordo* as conveying social privilege and thus the right "ordering of things," its force as a lens through which to know about one's world, grew more intense, not less, perhaps because a new (and originally equestrian) sense of orderly official rank-hierarchy could now appropriate the rhetoric of honor and privilege of the old *reverendus ordo senatorius.* Hence a paradox of the fourth century: the senatorial order was vastly larger than before, socially and geographically much more diverse, and more open than ever to penetration from below. And yet it also retained a rhetorical ideology, and to some degree a reality, of social privilege and superiority in very nearly the same way as had its early-imperial forerunner.

Within the category of *honestiores,* the new late antique *ordo senatorius* formed the social apex, pragmatically equestrian in outlook but with an old senatorial sense of social distinction. The category of *honestiores,* however, included others of less exalted status, and it is among these that we get a somewhat better sense of how a concept of *ordo* articulated late ancient ways of knowing the world. The *curiales* of the cities—the ones who display themselves with such pride in the marbles of Timgad—fell nearer the bottom of that *honestiores* hierarchy. Although at the top of the album there are a couple of members of the senatorial order, even the most distinguished of the other men named—the priestly *sacerdotales* and *pontifices*—were distinguished only within their own small world, in a province that was on the whole quite rustic, far from the cosmopolitan world of Carthage and Africa Proconsularis. Inside this small world, their brilliance would be plain for all to see; they would be fêted and constantly attended to and in possession of the best properties and of the best luxuries that their estates could offer. When outside their small world, however, they would have been aware of how bounded and limited their distinction really was. That is because members of the *curiae* (or of the *boulai* of the Greek world) had a privileged social position but one that was also somewhat precarious—indeed, became more precarious as the fourth century wore on and the absence of a direct connection to the hierarchy of imperial government became ever more of a liability.

The Timgad album makes clear how real the corporate pride of *curiales* remained in the fourth century, but it tells us nothing about their actual power. We get a better sense of the power that *curiales* had in the lives of their cities several decades earlier, at the end of the third century, when (it is surprising to discover) our evidence comes not from any curial source but rather from the canons of the church council at Elvira.[20] This long collection of canons is one of the richest, most extensive illustrations of local Roman social relations in the transitional period between the Severan and Constantinian empires.[21] The Elvira canons are almost exclusively disciplinary rather than theological, and because they are firmly rooted in a local urban context, with little sense of the larger provincial or imperial universe, they demonstrate the centrality of *curiales* to the functioning of their local communities. This is particularly true of the penitential canons, wherein the legal powers associated with curial officeholding worried the gathered bishops quite a lot. That is to say, the same offices that gave magistrates authority over their fellow citizens also gave them punitive powers, and those might end with a Christian magistrate shedding the blood of a fellow Christian: that they might do so attracted the gravest penalties and explains why magistrates could not enter a church during their term in office.[22] Equally central to pre-Constantinian urban life were the traditional priestly offices, which situated the city and its *ordo* within the larger social and indeed cosmic order of the empire. Unsurprisingly, the nineteen bishops at Elvira are harsh toward any who believed that their Christianity was compatible with the holding of traditional pagan priesthoods or who married their daughters to pagan priests.[23] Clearly, there were many local worthies whose time-honored expectation of and right to the dignities of officeholding outweighed any fear of pollution from pagan rituals. If that changed over time—and very little evidence for municipal cults survives from later in the fourth century—it is nevertheless interesting to see how thoroughly what we may call "curial thinking," or curial ways of knowing, not only survived the Christianization of the empire but were to some extent embedded in it. But that they were thus embedded is made clear during the fourth and fifth centuries, when the conduct of church councils came to mimic the precise, rank-obsessed sequences of speaking and voting characteristic of the *curiae*. We can see this at Serdica and again in the various African councils of the late fourth and early fifth centuries that preserve much of the framework of discussion along with the canons themselves.[24] We see this not only in the hierarchy of those who could speak but also in the presence of *consistentes*, clerics whose only role at a council was to stand—not sit: stand—and listen to proceedings, in the same manner that precedence was formerly asserted within a curial *ordo*.[25]

Whether revealed in the inscriptions of Timgad or the canons of church councils, the proceedings of fourth-century *curiae* are very distant echoes of old Republican urban institutions, echoes of long-gone systems of knowledge about society that have been repurposed but have not lost their meaning in a different world. It is worth noting that the fourth-century traces of this older Roman past are most visible here, at the in-between level of the *curia* and not at that of the *ordo senatorius*. That should not surprise us. The enactment and reenactment of time-honored privilege is most essential to those whose grasp on privilege is most tenuous, and the privileged status of *curiales* came under increasing threat during the fourth century.[26] That threat can be explained simply, in that the indispensable administrative role played by the *curiae* in the functioning of empire remained while at the same time both opportunities and incentives to leave the curial order grew more numerous. At one basic level, Roman imperial government existed to convert agricultural revenue from the land into military salaries via taxation. Decurions had since the beginning of the imperial period been essential to the collection of the empire's tax revenue (as Eastern *bouletai* had been since the time of the imperialist Republic) and its transmission to the higher levels of Roman officialdom.[27] A shortage of *curiales* meant a potential loss of taxes, and that in turn could be a major threat to the security of an imperial government, something that had not changed in the fourth century. On the other hand, because the imperial government was enormously larger than it had been previously, there were more opportunities to move up and into its ranks—and because imperial service had come to provide greater access to wealth and power than did local government, the incentive to enter into imperial service was correspondingly greater. That is not to imply that there was any generalized rejection of curial status—the modern historical trope of a "flight of the *curiales*" is an exaggeration, if not a fabrication.[28] In fact, there is plentiful evidence for the continued dominance of the curial class, be it the rhetorical and resentful "quot curiales, tot tyranni" of the moralist Salvianus or the completely offhand evidence of a hymn by Paulinus of Nola that casually contrasts the plebs and *ordo* gathered to worship Saint Felix in language that is also omnipresent in late imperial laws.[29] That is, the hierarchy of local, curial government remained a primary structure of knowledge about the world.

Nevertheless, the fact remained that imperial service was demonstrably more privileged and better rewarded than curial status. In the Greek world, there is good evidence that imperial bureaucrats, who owed their status to contemporary officeholding, were able to displace old bouletic families, disrupting ancient patterns of landholding, because only imperial officials had guaranteed access to the supply of gold coin.[30] It is no wonder, given the importance of *curiales* to the empire's finances, that imperial legislators should fear curial flight, whether it was in reality a common phenomenon or not. In light of that fear, however, restricting the mobility of *curiales*, binding them legally to their *ordo*, and making them collectively responsible for the financial obligations of their towns and territories was a sensible precaution, one that hedged their status about more and more strictly in the course of the fourth century.[31] Doing so, however, had a predictable if at the time seemingly unexpected consequence: as curial status became more restricting and subject to the high-pitched rhetorical bombast of late imperial legislation, the mere fact of restriction threatened to derogate from the privileged status of *curiales*, to push them further to the margins of the *honestiores*.

The sedulous status display of those who remained in the curial *ordo,* the massive care taken by the magistrates and decurions of Timgad, thus makes sense. They had to assert to what degree they remained members of a privileged elite—had to insist that the old status structure through which they and those around them understood the world remained intact. That assertion mattered on many levels, and not merely symbolically or as a matter of wounded pride. Rather, with reduced status came increased risks: of humiliation and also to life and limb. In late imperial society, actions permitted to one *ordo* were forbidden to others. So too with penalties: high status exempted one from punishments to which only the lower orders might be subject.[32]

PENALTY, PUNISHMENT, AND THE REPRODUCTION OF SOCIAL ORDER

Socially differentiated punishment is by no means historically limited to the Roman Empire, but it was an omnipresent feature of late Roman life and meant something more than the disciplining of individual bodies. Our clearest evidence comes with reference to the penalties for treason (*maiestas*), the omnipresent threat of which was an ineluctable corollary of autocracy. The late-third-century jurist Paulus shows in his *Sententiae* how the vast late ancient category of *maiestas* affected the upper and lower orders in different ways. The penalty of exile (interdiction from fire and water), which had once been traditional, he tells us, was now replaced by death: death by wild beasts for *humiliores,* less horrible capital punishment by decapitation for *honestiores.*[33] Torture was normal for *humiliores* in the investigation of even minor offenses and could be used against even the highborn in the case of *maiestas.*[34] This distinction, of differing penalties for identical crimes, permeates the evidence for the third and fourth centuries and lies at the heart of the "didactic symbolism" of late Roman criminal law.[35]

There is space here for just two examples. We can begin with the treatment of the followers of Priscillian executed for *maiestas* under Magnus Maximus. The heresy of Priscillian has been much studied from a variety of theological and historical perspectives, but the basic facts of the case have been straightforwardly understood for decades.[36] Priscillian was a well-born Spanish churchman with deep ascetic convictions who expounded doctrines that several Spanish bishops believed to be heretical. After being ordained a bishop in circumstances of questionable legitimacy, Priscillian was summoned to Gaul to defend himself in a council of bishops but exercised his right of appeal to Caesar. The case was transferred to Trier, where the new emperor, Maximus, himself of dubious legitimacy, had Priscillian and his followers condemned for sorcery. Magic was *maiestas,* and if *maiestas* was a general preoccupation of imperial Rome, fourth-century emperors were especially paranoiac about the treasonous applications of magic.[37] Priscillian was executed by decapitation, along with two fellow priests, Felicissimus and Armenius. The rich Bordelaise widow Euchrotia was likewise killed.[38] Others were executed in Spain and elsewhere.[39] All had been tortured, as even the wellborn might be in treason cases.[40] But their executions were honorable and quick. That point is worth stressing. Differential punishment served to police the boundaries of social order so that, even in transgression, its hierarchy was maintained.

A different logic had been at work almost two centuries earlier, when the wellborn Perpetua was thrown to wild beasts when an honorable decapitation would properly have befitted her social position.[41] The goal here was just as much the reinforcement of the social order through differential punishment, but that was to be achieved by its symbolic rupture. That is, there was a didactic purpose to subjecting an aristocratic lady like Perpetua to the degrading death of the *humiliores,* and Carthaginian spectators, highborn and low, were being read a public lesson: a Christian stood outside the social order and beyond the protections that it offered one of Perpetua's exalted status. The penalty also demonstrates the astuteness and at times cunning irony with which Roman authority handled threats. After all, when Christian ideology was taken at face value, it valorized the eirenic disruption of the imperial social order, putting the last first and slaves on terms of equality with masters. In the arena at Carthage, the teeth and claws of wild beasts showed precisely where that led.

That said, such an exemplary and humiliating rupture of what people thought they knew about social boundaries in punishment could happen only occasionally if it was to successfully police the social boundaries that affirmed elite power. Thus, on the whole, criminal *honestiores* required—and received—careful treatment, for it was easy to offend against the rights due to the higher orders. If a senator charged with a serious crime was surrounded by an armed guard, the offense against his *dignitas*—and thus the *dignitas* of his *ordo*—was of greater significance than was the putative crime.[42] Among his many other indictments of the brutish Valentinian, Ammianus Marcellinus singles out the incivility of allowing the lowborn imperial official Maximinus ("obscurissime natus") to terrorize the Roman Senate in pursuit of magic and treason charges.[43] The historian does not suggest that the senators were innocent of these crimes or were in any way above suspicion. The problem, rather, was that an official with no social standing threatened and then actually inflicted punishments that were inappropriate to men of senatorial rank. By contrast, Ammianus tells his readers directly that the lowborn victims ("squalidas personas") were unworthy of mention; their *ordo* rendered their deaths appropriate and unmemorable.[44]

Maximinus's reign of terror at Rome helps to remind us of the delicate balancing act required of fourth-century government: an authoritarian emperor ruled in part because of the terror that the machinery of the state could inspire, and so the threat of extending the humiliation of that terror beyond the lower orders was an essential tool of social control.[45] It might be resented, and the extension of low-status punishment to high-status figures is a preoccupation of the elite evidence, but those same elites were complicit in state terror, because the existence of qualitative boundaries enforced their own status and kept the lower orders in their place. The alternative to state terror was worse: a world turned upside down, in which social distinctions were not instantly and always legible. If the barriers between *ordines* became invisible, or even began to fade, the lower orders might overwhelm their betters. So it was that Symmachus, as urban prefect, urged the young Valentinian II to tread softly in demanding the *munera* owed by the *negotiatores* of horses: even an emperor as fearsome as Valentinian I had found to his cost that imposing a small burden ("munus exiguum") on men of that sort ("huic hominum generi") threatened riot.[46] Symmachus knew whereof he spoke and had every reason to fear the lower orders. It was, after all, his father, Lucius Aurelius Avianus Symmachus, whose house was burned to the ground after "a certain cheap plebeian" ("vilis quidam plebeius") spread a rumor that the elder Symmachus would rather quench his lime kilns with his wine than sell it below its value.[47] The younger Symmachus, who is nothing if not a proxy voice for elite Roman opinion, needed constant contact with the imperial court to ensure its support in regulating and containing the behavior of lower *ordines*.[48]

Elites were complicit in a violent and coercive system that might sometimes be turned on themselves, because that occasional price was worth paying if it reinforced the status of their *ordo* and themselves. Nor was theirs a one-way relationship to the emperor and the imperial state. Elite complicity in systematized violence and coercion also implied consent to a given emperor's reign, a symbolic agreement that the social order was being maintained in a legitimate and valuable fashion. The withdrawal of this consent could and did get emperors killed. Thus the ruling orders of the West, pagan and Christian alike, collaborated not once but twice in the overthrow of Valentinian II's government in favor of one that might be more sympathetic to the privileges of their *ordines*.

LIBERTAS

Upper-class complicity in a savage ordering of things sheds light on another semantic field, *libertas,* that was closely connected to *ordo* in the fourth-century elite view of the world and that is worth brief consideration here. Until the end of the Roman period, the word *libertas* had two overlapping semantic fields, one a state of individual existence and one a form of government, the latter always primary. Modern and abstract conceptions of liberty have no place in Roman thought. The first meaning of *libertas* was the right of people to live under Roman law, and by the late imperial period that meant living under the law as subjects. The other meaning was individual, freedom from constraint by others though not from constraint by the state. In the Republic, *libertas* meant government by the Senate and also the right of Roman aristocrats, and particularly the great *nobiles,* to live as they pleased, jockeying among themselves as a privileged class of the great and the good, with none among them able to exercise overwhelming power over the rest.[49] The clearest statements of this aristocratic Republican definition come in Cicero's late *Philippics.*[50] Threatening this *libertas* was what got Caesar assassinated, and it is what the monster Antonius will destroy altogether.[51] In reality, of course, it was Caesar's heir who destroyed that old *libertas* with the willing collaboration of the surviving *ordo senatorius.*[52]

By the later empire, that individual meaning of *libertas* as an absence of constraint had not disappeared, but it was now most frequently pejorative—when Symmachus warns of riots, he speaks of "libertas plebis," the illicit license of the plebs, what earlier would have been called *licentia.*[53] This *libertas* went with mad arrogance and pride, *superbia.*[54] The lower orders would, as it were, take liberties. Controlling them, stopping their doing so, was a large part of what the social order was for. And so it was a matter of surprised comment when, during the emperor Constantius's ceremonial visit to Rome, the plebs refrained from exercising the presumptuous *libertas* expected of them, which in turn meant that the emperor was able to behave with a good grace that did not come naturally to him.[55] That is, when his plebeian subjects refrained from the undesirable *libertas* characteristic of their *ordo,* Constantius was able to govern as a good emperor should.

Government, of course, is the other main sense of *libertas.* By the fourth century *libertas* as government meant living as subjects of an emperor, from whom law flowed. Already in the early second century, deficiencies in the law were to be supplied by the emperor, subsuming in his own person the lawmaking capacity of the *senatus populusque Romanus.* Freedom, in the eyes of the great Severan jurists, was something permitted to subjects by an emperor. Subjects had rights, and jurists spent a great deal of time articulating them, especially after the so-called Antonine Constitution made it necessary to extend the use of Roman law to the entire population of the empire; but there was never any question whence came a subject's rights.[56] *Libertas,* then, was the freedom to live under an emperor and his laws. Where the emperor's law held sway, *libertas* was necessarily present. Thus, after the elder Theodosius had put down widespread but unspecified civil disturbances in Britain, it could be said that the province had returned to *libertas.*[57] So, too, when several Spanish provinces fell to barbarian invaders in 409, they were, according to Hydatius, reduced to *servitudo.*[58] The Spanish chronicler was claiming not that the provincials were actually enslaved but rather that they were deprived of the *libertas* that came from living under imperial government.

As the evidence from Hydatius shows, the traditional semantic fields of *libertas* lasted an extraordinarily long time, even into the period when the social structures needed to sustain them—a functioning imperial government—had ceased to exist.

That is just one way in which the concept of *libertas* intersects with that of *ordo*: both still functioned in late antiquity within an ideological framework that went back to the late Republic, a conceptual longevity that is remarkable, if not unique.[59] But *libertas* is also connected to the idea of *ordo* in other ways: in its individual sense, it was the expected characteristic of specific *ordines*, whether the great *nobiles* of the Republic or the sordid plebs of the fourth century. In its larger, constitutive sense, *libertas* existed only where there was Roman government, and Roman government existed only where the social order existed, predicated on its social *ordines*. Where *ordo* did not exist, *libertas* could not, and Romans knew it.

THE ARREST OF PETER VALVOMERES

This digression on what *libertas* meant in the autocratic world of the later empire brings us back to the ideological sense of order and rightness that permeated its society—that things are as they should be when order in its largest sense is maintained, with each *ordo* keeping to its place (*ordo*) within the framework of the *libertas* granted it by the emperor, a *libertas* constrained by social rank (*ordo*).[60] We began with perhaps the best-known example of this inclusive fourth-century sense of *ordo,* as graphically depicted in the hierarchy of the Timgad album. We can close with one of the most famous episodes of disorder in fourth-century history. At almost the same time as the *vir clarissimus* Ulpius Mariscianus was giving his legal authority as governor to the *ordo salutationis* of Timgad, the other side of the Roman social order was being enacted in the city of Rome. A rioter, mob leader, threat to *ordo* (order) and to the *ordo* (curial order: Senate) of Rome was arrested. This episode, a minor and commonplace event by Roman standards, became thanks to the great twentieth-century literary critic Erich Auerbach the only thing most people know about the *Res Gestae* of Ammianus Marcellinus.[61] The arrest of Peter Valvomeres is one of the most graphic rhetorics of scene in the whole of late ancient literature.[62] Ever since Auerbach wrote about it more than half a century ago as a microcosm of the late ancient social drama, generations of scholars have gone back to this episode, which takes up little more than forty lines of Ammianus. Some have read it as evidence for how the late Roman state used ritual violence to control the population and delineate the comforting boundaries of social order.[63] Others have treated it as part of a dossier documenting not just the violence of late ancient society but the cruel sadism of Ammianus himself.[64]

In fact, this story of Peter Valvomeres tells us something quite complicated. On the one hand, it is a straightforward account of social disorder and its repair; on the other, because of its place in Ammianus's narrative structure, it is evidence for a much wider set of anxieties about the threat that Christianity posed to the traditional social order. Thus, although modern analysis has moved far beyond Auerbach, there is no question that he was right to sense the sheer importance of this brief and easily summarized episode. As Symmachus showed us above, public order in the city of Rome was the responsibility of the *praefectus urbi* and a constant challenge for him. Symmachus was careful not to provoke the urban crowd, not to give any excuse for the *libertas plebis,* but there were times when no amount of caution could prevent an outburst of rioting. The urban prefect of 356, Flavius Leontius, experienced both sides of this, first having provoked the crowd by arresting a charioteer whom the people loved—rioters eventually forced his release—and again mere days later, when a wine shortage brought people back into the streets. Leontius, of whom Ammianus very much approved, rode his official carriage out into the crowd, in which he recognized a giant red-haired man, supposedly notorious as an agitator.[65] "Are you Peter Valvomeres?" Leontius asked, and having been answered with bold effrontery ("sonu . . . obiurgatorio"), he had the offending rioter strung up on hooks and beaten until his flanks were torn open ("exaratis lateribus").[66] Huge and sinewy as Peter was, his tormented screams had exactly the terrorizing effect that they were meant to, and the crowd dispersed without further incident. This is a triumph of the social order, the correctness of which Ammianus demonstrates by recording Peter's future conduct and fate: after his banishment to Picenum by Leontius, he went on to rape a woman of high birth, for which he was executed, no doubt in the humiliating way that a member of the lower orders should have been. The disruption of the social order, the fearsomeness of the plebs, which Peter here embodies metaphorically, is safely resolved and reordered by the application of violence to his single physical body, which can stand in for the crowd as a whole. It is, for Ammianus, an entirely satisfactory result.

Up to that point, Ammianus's account seems susceptible of a fairly simplistic Foucauldian reading of punishing bodies to discipline social class, but the historian does not end his story there. It is the second half of the chapter that makes his larger point about the late Roman social order and how untoward novelty disrupts.[67] As is well known, Ammianus structures his narrative in blocks that alternate irregularly (and not annalistically) from Western to Eastern affairs, interspersed with digressions or excursuses but never failing to include narrative blocks on the city of Rome and its prefects.[68] These are the structural elements of Ammianus's historical construction, and the blocks themselves carry meaning. It is a basic mistake to dip into any one section of Ammianus without taking the whole of it into account. Leontius's urban prefecture is one of these building blocks; to read the story of Peter Valvomeres' arrest and ultimate fate without reference to the rest of the section risks missing part of its point. In Ammianus, Leontius's prefecture is a story in two halves each of which resolves into two parts. The first half of the chapter is the paired riots, over the arrest of the charioteer and over the wine shortage (15.7.1–2); in the latter riot Peter is arrested and tortured (15.7.3–5). The second half of the chapter pairs two churchmen, Liberius of Rome and Athanasius of Alexandria. As we have seen, the first half closes with the proof that Peter was a threat to the social order, whose violent treatment at the hands of Leontius was fully justified by his eventual execution for rape. The second half opens with the arrest of the bishop Liberius for his failure to endorse the imperial and episcopal condemnation of Athanasius. By implication, the pope's arrest is paired with Peter's, and if the one is justified, so by implication is the other.

But there is more. If Liberius was arrested justifiably for his defiance of the emperor, then the man whose condemnation he refused to endorse was probably even worse. Athanasius, Ammianus tells us, was a man puffed up beyond his social station ("ultra professionem altius se efferentem"). He also foretold the future by signs and omens, something again beyond his station because he was neither pontifex nor augur nor haruspex. In pointing out that particular offense, Ammianus was imputing to Athanasius the same crime of magic-as-*maiestas* as would later get Priscillian executed.[69] The imputation is no accident: Ammianus says that Athanasius's coreligionists did not approve of his using divination to predict the future, and the historian knew full well that Christianity condemned pagan religion, including augury and prophecy, as the magical work of demons. Athanasius, then, is a magician, and ipso facto a traitor, a threat to the social order in either Christian or Roman terms. That is all Ammianus says of Athanasius—it is all he needs to say—but he concludes his account of Leontius's prefecture by returning to Liberius (15.7.9–10). Liberius's defiance of the emperor meant his punishment was just; but for the emperor's men to impose it, the bishop had to be kidnapped and taken out of Rome under cover of night ("noctis medio"). This could be done, Ammianus tells us, only with the greatest difficulty ("cum magna difficultate") for fear of the urban mob, with whom Liberius was very popular ("aegre populi metu qui eius amore flagrabat"). That is the punch line, although to Ammianus and some of his intended audience it is anything but funny. On the contrary, we are back at the original locus of social disruption, *libertas plebis,* the freedom of the vile urban mob. On account of Liberius, the mob threatens not merely an urban prefect but the emperor and the very system of justice. That is more than a thug like Peter Valvomeres can do. That Ammianus disliked Christianity has now been proved, and he rarely introduces Christians into his narrative save to damage or ridicule them.[70] But the narrative of Leontius's prefecture is more than Christian-baiting, and it reveals something deeper: an anxiety that Christianity worked at the intersection of a traditional form of disorder, plebeian riot, and a new one—religious leaders beyond the reach of the Roman state.

Ammianus chose to juxtapose two events of Leontius's prefecture, and only two. It was a reasoned decision, revealing of his own understanding of the world and a way to direct his readers' knowledge of it. But though he wished to demonstrate the problems that Christians caused, his juxtaposition also reflects a social reality. Christianity did have the capacity to disrupt the old social order, in a way that public cults of the sort condemned by the canons of Elvira never could, because they were part of the very fabric of that social order. Because it was originally apocalyptic, Christian ideology extolled the poor, not the powerful, placed the last first, and questioned the rich man's ability to go to heaven. However many highborn Christians there were in the fourth century, the religion was meant to challenge the hierarchy of ancient status. Vettius Agorius Praetextatus, when he joked to Pope Damasus that he would become a Christian if they made him bishop of Rome, knew exactly what he was saying: for him, even so late in the history of the Christianization of the empire, it seemed impossible to be wellborn and a Christian.[71] High office in the church was something, but it was an ersatz thing, and Praetextatus could make his joke precisely because he would not have converted even had they made him bishop of Rome. Ambrose, another man of high birth, entered the church directly as a bishop, and he was chosen precisely for his birth, not necessarily for his piety. But until good birth became a prerequisite for episcopal office, which it was not until after the empire had ceased to function in the West and the aristocracy replaced its magistracies with miters, the revolutionary principles of Christianity had the potential for social disruption. Its disregard for traditional status, even when more theoretical than actual, was threatening. Ammianus understood this, and he was of course proved right. In the end, Christianity was every bit as disruptive as his anxieties suggested it might be. It is impossible to deny what Gibbon, with all his Enlightenment prejudice, already knew: barbarism and (Christian) religion did cause the fall of the empire, each offering an alternative social model that helped create the European Middle Ages.

· · ·

How does contemplating the word *ordo* and the many different elements of its semantic field enhance our understanding of late ancient knowing? Is there a critical-theoretical perspective that illuminates the uses of *ordo* and in turn helps us understand the world of late antiquity? The foregoing pages can at best be a sketch that suggests other paths forward. There are many more and probably better sources available to illustrate what has been outlined here; there is also no simple way to feed the semantic field of the late antique *ordo* through a Foucault or Bourdieu machine and achieve dramatic insights. *Ordo* and other status-keyed words that it kept in its lexical orbit (e.g., *senatus, plebs, honestior, humilior*) were all at the same time a machinery for ordering knowledge about the world, for fixing the objects of that knowledge in the places where they belonged, and for mapping social relations into a pattern in which all *ordines* acquiesced, for the perpetuation of the status quo. In keeping with the programmatic goals of the present volume, however, one may suggest that there is no aspect of late Roman life that participants did not view through the filter of rank and social status. The socially neutral did not exist. It is, of course, true that status-neutrality is a rarity, perhaps an impossibility in any culture past or present. But historical articulations of status are infinitely varied, and not every culture is willing to admit their valence.[72] (Contrast, for instance, the respective comfort levels of English, American, and German discussions of class.) Roman concern for *ordo* in all its many status connotations was not merely pervasive but frankly so. The language itself filtered social knowledge into normalizing ranks and constructed a world that was healthy when everything was in its place (*in ordine*) and stability (*ordo*) was guaranteed by each one's keeping to his station (*ordo*). We can see this in the confident but also nervously assertive monolith of the Timgad album; in the tension between the evident power of the curial *ordo* of Elvira and the dictates of its members' new religion; in the exemplary punishments of the Priscillianists and of Perpetua, each in its contrasting way reasserting social hierarchy; and in the brutal torture and later execution of Peter Valvomeres, a man who threatened public order in the manner of his social *ordo* but who was controlled by that public order in a way that the Christian bishops with whom he is contrasted could not be in the end—with fatal results for the empire. We can come to know the late imperial world better if we bear in mind the filter through which late Romans knew their own world. More important, we should always remember to look for that filter before we draw conclusions from the traces that they have left us.

NOTES

1. Edition in André Chastagnol, *L'album municipal de Timgad* (Bonn: Habelt, 1978). The *ordo salutationis* is followed by a list of the *sportulae* due to those in attendance on the governor's *adventus,* particularly the *advocati.*

2. Ibid. 70–74.

3. Ibid. 57.

4. *Digest* 50.3.2.

5. The essays in Claude Nicolet, ed., *Des ordres à Rome,* Histoire Ancienne et Médiévale, vol. 13 (Paris: Publications de la Sorbonne, 1984) are fundamental for the early imperial period. Benjamin Cohen, "La notion d'*ordo* dans la Rome antique," *Bulletin de l'Association Guillaume Budé,* ser. 4, 1 (1975): 259–82, considers only the social or "class" meanings of the word, though it is excellent on that point and demonstrates that, within that semantic field, what separates Latin *ordo* from any of related words for "social group" (*genus,* for instance), is the presumed intervention of a civic government.

6. Suetonius, *Augustus* 44.1.

7. Plautus, *Amphitryo* 241. Sara Elise Phang, *Roman Military Service: Ideologies of Discipline in the Late Republic and Early Principate* (Cambridge: Cambridge University Press, 2008), examines the social ideology of *disciplina* in the context of military service.

8. On the jurists and their activity after Caracalla, see Tony Honoré, *Emperors and Lawyers,* 2nd ed. (Oxford: Clarendon Press, 1994), 33–138. Macrobius, *Saturnalia,* praef. 6: "nos quoque quicquid diversa lectione quaesivimus committemus stilo, ut in ordinem eodem digerente coalescat." It is no accident that the characters in his invented symposium should all be *nobilissimi,* members of the *ordo senatorius.* The essays in Jason König and

Tim Whitmarsh, eds., *Ordering Knowledge in the Roman Empire* (Cambridge: Cambridge University Press, 2007), concern themselves with multiple different examples of this sort of *ordo*, which reduces the diversity of knowledge to comprehensible shapes.

9. For the corporatism of Roman social conceptions, recognized already by Theodor Mommsen in the *Staastrecht*, see Claude Nicolet, "Les ordres romains: Définition, recrutement, et fonctionnement," in Nicolet, ed., *Des ordres à Rome* (above, n. 5), 7–21.

10. Lactantius, *De Opificio Dei* 1.9: "memento et veri parentis tui et in qua civitate nomen dederis et cuius ordinis fueris: intellegis profecto quid loquar." Date of the treatise from Michel Perrin, *Lactance: L'ouvrage de Dieu créateur,* 2 vols., Sources Chrétiennes, vols. 213, 214 (Paris: Éditions du Cerf, 1974), vol. 2, 231.

11. The same thing is obviously true of the many other theorists so often linked as together part of a linguistic and cultural turn. The *AHR* Forum "Historiographic 'Turns' in Critical Perspective" in *American Historical Review* 117 (2012): 698–813, provides a vital summary of this lumping.

12. Cohen, "La notion d'*ordo*" (above, n. 5), 272, illustrates this point in discussing the *accensi,* freedmen *apparitores* of Republican magistrates, who were part of an *ordo* so long as their patron was in office but ceased to be the moment he was not, in this way contrasted to, e.g., *publicani,* who as free men existed as an *ordo* irrespective of the status of anyone else: that is, a *publicanus* was always both within and indivisible from his *ordo*, and an *accensus* was not.

13. Nicolet, "Ordres romaines" (above, n. 9), 16.

14. Note, of course, that belonging to one's *ordo* was as restrictive as it might be honorable: proud as the members of Timgad's curial order might be, it was illegal for them to choose to leave that order, as *curiales* who moved into other service sometimes found. (Symmachus, *Relationes* 38.5: "sed cum Venantii stratoris inlicitam usurpatamque militiam Marcellus argueret, quod decurionum adscriptus albo, ut gesta docuerunt, adversum leges ad Palatina castra transisset . . ." Venantius, in other words, was a member of the curial order, and by entering palatine service, *militia,* he had contravened the law.) In general, *Codex Theodosianus* 12.1 shows the development of legislation binding *curiales* to their station.

15. Symmachus, *Relationes* 46.1: "siquidem convenit principes et parentes humani generis edoceri, quid reverendo ordini vel senatorum novorum accessus adiciat vel glebae excusationibus detrahatur."

16. See Ammianus Marcellinus 28.4.33 on the acclamation of benefactors.

17. The best narrative analysis of how the empire changed between the second and fourth centuries is at present David S. Potter, *The Roman Empire at Bay: AD 180–395* (London: Routledge, 2004). On the history of the *ordo equester,* Arthur Stein, *Der römische Ritterstand* (Munich: Beck, 1927), is still essential.

18. The military evidence is collected in Alfred von Domaszewski, *Die Rangordnung des römischen Heeres* (Cologne: Böhlau, 1967).

19. See Cassius Dio 79.22.3 on the offense given by the first equestrian emperor, Macrinus (r. 217–18), for offering the wellborn Aufidius Fronto, who was in line for the proconsulship of Asia, a million *sestertii* to forgo the *dignitas* and remain in Rome. Part of the reason Macrinus did not last long was that he failed to understand the residual touchiness of senatorial honor.

20. These date to just before the Diocletianic persecutions, as Louis Duchesne, "Le Concile d'Elvira et les flamines chrétiennes," in *Mélanges Léon Renier,* Bibliothèque de l'École des Hautes Études, Sciences Philologiques et Historiques, vol. 73 (Paris: Fieweg, 1887), 159–74, established beyond question. Despite that proof, too many scholars still repeat the Constantinian date ascribed to the canons by the seventh-century compilers of the *Collectio Hispana* in which their text is transmitted (Gonzalo Martínez Diez, ed., *La collección canónica hispana,* vol. 4, *Concilios galos, concilios hispanos: Primera parte,* Monumenta Hispaniae Sacra, Serie Canónica, vol. 4 [Madrid: CSIC, Instituto Enrique Flórez, 1984], 234).

21. There have been occasional doubts about whether the extant canons of Elvira represent an actual council or a compilation of rulings from various sources, but the way different topics flow naturally one from another without much of a systematizing hand is actually good evidence for the ebb and flow of actual conciliar debate: see Manuel Sotomayor, "Consideraciones sobre las fuentes para el estudio del cristianismo primitivo en Andalucía," in *La Bética en su problemática histórica,* ed. C. González Román (Granada: Universidad de Granada, 1991), 299–311.

22. Elvira 56, ed. Martínez Diez, vol. 4 (above, n. 20), 259–60: "Magistratus vero uno anno quo agit duumviratum, prohibendum placet ut se ab ecclesia cohibeat."

23. Elvira 2–4, 17, 55. The best edition is Martínez Diez, vol. 4 (above, n. 20), 233–68.

24. See Hamilton Hess, *The Canons of the Council of Sardica, A.D. 343: A Landmark in the Development of Early Canon Law* (Oxford: Clarendon Press, 1958), 24–41, on the curial and (local) senatorial procedures reflected at Serdica. The Sixth Council of Carthage is the best African example, with its *allocutiones, responsiones,* and standard *X. . . . episcopus dixit* (ed. Gonzalo Martínez Diez, *La collección canónica hispana,* vol. 3, *Concilios griegos y hispanos,* Monumenta Hispaniae Sacra, Serie Canónica, vol. 3 [Madrid: CSIC, Instituto Enrique Flórez, 1982], 387–426; and vol. 4 [above, n. 20], 233–68).

25. In general, see Michael Kulikowski, *Late Roman Spain and Its Cities* (Baltimore: The Johns Hopkins University Press, 2004), 39–43. These *consistentes* were the imperial development of the *pedarii,* senators whose only means of participating in senatorial government was during the ballot division (*pedibus in sententiam ire*). At the church councils, the *consistentes* would have mirrored the function of *praetextati* in a curial setting.

26. I dispense here with explicit appeal to Pierre Bourdieu's theories of *habitus* and social violence (for which the interested reader may consult Bourdieu's *Language and Symbolic Power,* ed. John B. Thompson [Cambridge, Mass.: Harvard University Press, 1991]), but both are relevant in terms of cultural reproduction that construct acquiescence in the social order and its hierarchy, which necessarily involves the subordination of some to others.

27. That was true whatever form Roman taxation took in a particular province at any given moment before Diocletian's attempt at standardization.

28. E.g., standard reference works: *Oxford Classical Dictionary,* 3rd ed., 437–38; A. H. M. Jones, *The Later Roman Empire, 284–602: A Social, Economic, and Administrative* Survey (Norman: University of Oklahoma Press, 1964), 737–57; Alexander Demandt, *Die Spätantike: Römische Geschichte von Diocletian bis Justinian, 284–565 n. Chr.* (Munich: Beck, 1989), 408–9 ("Das Curialenproblem . . .").

29. Salvianus, *De Gubernatione Dei* 5.18; Paulinus of Nola, *Carmina* 21.796, which is a very ancient locution: cf. Cicero, *Philippics* 13.6, "ordini populoque." For legal texts, see

among many others, *Collectio Avellana* 3.2: "quare participato examine cum venerabili sacerdote intimatisque omnibus et magnificentissimo ordini et Christiano populo," who are all consulted over the construction of Saint Paul's Basilica at Rome.

30. Because gold *solidi* were the only legal tender for certain transactions, like the payment of tax, those with ready access to gold (officials) could engage in a profitable form of arbitrage from those with less ready access (*bouletai*): see Jairus Banaji, *Agrarian Change in Late Antiquity: Gold, Labour and Aristocratic Dominance* (Oxford: Oxford University Press, 2001), at length, though he was building on the prescient insights of Gunnar Mickwitz, *Geld und Wirtschaft im römischen Reich des vierten Jahrhunderts n. Chr.* (Helsinki: Societas Scientiarum Fennica, 1932), about the role of the *solidus* in the transformation of the late Roman world.

31. See particularly the laws in *Codex Theodosianus* 12.1, of which there are an astonishing 192.

32. Jones, *The Later Roman Empire* (above, n. 28), 516–22, remains the basic account of differential punishment. Also, Jill Harries, *Law and Empire in Late Antiquity* (Cambridge: Cambridge University Press, 1999), 135–52. The problem was exacerbated by a tendency (on which see Jill Harries, "Violence, Victims and the Legal Tradition in Late Antiquity," in *Violence in Late Antiquity: Perceptions and Practice,* ed. H. A. Drake et al. [Burlington: Ashgate, 2006], 96–98) to conflate or elide the differences between civil and criminal jurisdictions and between torts and crimes.

33. Paulus, *Sententiae* 5.29.

34. See, e.g., Paulinus Diaconus, *Vita Ambrosii* 20.1, for a magician under torture.

35. Ramsay MacMullen, "Some Pictures in Ammianus Marcellinus," *The Art Bulletin* 46 (1964): 452; this didactic symbolism matches the "gestural and pictorial vocabulary" (Eric Auerbach, *Mimesis: The Representation of Reality in Western Literature,* trans. W. Trask [Princeton: Princeton University Press, 1953], 57) of late antique writing, in law as well as literature.

36. The literature in Spanish is large and repetitious. Henry Chadwick, *Priscillian of Avila: The Occult and the Charismatic in the Early Church* (Oxford: Clarendon Press, 1976), remains the single best treatment in English, though its approach to religious belief in general shows its age. Virginia Burrus, *The Making of a Heretic: Gender, Authority, and the Priscillianist Controversy* (Berkeley and Los Angeles: University of California Press, 1995), improves on the sociology of the Priscillianist movement but does not otherwise supersede Chadwick's narrative, to which readers should refer for primary source citations.

37. Harries, *Law and Empire* (above, n. 32), 128–32.

38. Ausonius, *Professores Burdigalenses* 37–38; *Panegyrici Latini* 2(12).29.2.

39. Chadwick, *Priscillian* (above, n. 36), 144, has the list and the citations.

40. *Panegyrici Latini* 2(12).29.2 is graphic.

41. Text in Herbert Musurillo, *The Acts of the Christian Martyrs* (Oxford: Oxford University Press, 1972), 106–31.

42. Symmachus, *Relationes* 49.2: "agens in rebus Africanus accusationem professus Campano et Hygino clarissimis viris violentiae crimen obiecit. continuo, ut severitas exigebat, reos custodia militaris dissimulata dignitatis reverentia circumdedit." In other words, strict procedure meant that a charge of violence required an armed guard, but to insist on one for senators was a grave derogation of their dignity.

43. Ammianus Marcellinus 28.1.5–57. Although its assumptions about how faction worked in the later empire have been superseded, the analysis in A. Alföldi, *A Conflict of Ideas in the Late Roman Empire* (Oxford: Clarendon Press, 1952), 48–95, remains compelling.

44. Ammianus Marcellinus 28.1.15: "non omnia narratu sunt digna, quae per squalidas transiere personas."

45. Christopher Kelly, *Ruling the Later Roman Empire* (Cambridge, Mass.: Harvard University Press, 2004), is the best treatment of late Roman government in practice.

46. Symmachus, *Relationes* 14.2.

47. Ammianus Marcellinus 27.3.4.

48. Note, equally, how in Macrobius 1.1.3 the information that is being put "in ordinem" is special knowledge, "latens clam vulgo" (hidden from the common herd).

49. See the classic and valid statement of Ronald Syme, *The Roman Revolution* (Oxford: Clarendon Press, 1939), 155: "The *libertas* of the Roman aristocrat meant the rule of a class and the perpetuation of privilege," with Chaim Wirszubski, *Libertas as a Political Idea at Rome during the Late Republic and Early Principate* (Cambridge: Cambridge University Press, 1950), 88. The book remains the definitive study of Republican *libertas* despite a view of political parties that has been largely superseded.

50. E.g., the words of personified Wisdom in *Philippics* 13.6: "Tu vero ita vitam corpusque servato, ita fortunas, ita rem familiarem, ut haec libertate posteriora ducas itaque his uti velis, si libera re publica possis, nec pro his libertatem, sed pro libertate haec proicias tamquam pignora iniuriae " The Senate fights for liberty; Antony "servum se illius [viz. Caesaris] quam collegam esse malebat" (*Philippics* 13.17).

51. Cicero makes Antony's crowning of Caesar at the Lupercalia the cause of Caesar's murder: "Tu, tu, inquam, illum occidisti Lupercalibus" (*Philippics* 13.41). It should, of course, be noted that even the Republican *libertas* coexisted with an authoritative *res publica*, obligation to which meant that unfettered freedom was never part of the Roman conception of *libertas*: F. Schulz, *Principles of Roman Law* (Oxford: Clarendon Press, 1936), 140–63.

52. To continue with Cicero, it is ironic that what Octavian brought with lasting success was what Cicero half praises in Caesar's case—that is, safety, not freedom:"Caesare dominante veniebamus in senatum, si non libere, at tamen tuto" (*Philippics* 13.18).

53. Symmachus, *Relationes* 14.2: "cum munus exiguum huic hominum generi mandare temptasset, motus libertate plebis abstinuit." At 23.13, too, Symmachus uses *plebs* in its most pejorative sense:"nomina testium plebeiorum danda promisit, credo, ut per moram." In other words, no one would call plebeian witnesses unless to waste time. For *licentia*, see Tacitus, *Dialogus* 40: "Licentia quam stulti libertatem vocant."

54. Ammianus Marcellinus 14.9.6: "libertatem . . . superbiam," words he often links, as in the passage quoted in the following note.

55. Ibid. 15.10.13: "et saepe cum equestres ederet ludos, dicacitate plebis oblectabatur, nec superbae nec a libertate coalita desciscentis, reverenter modum ipse quoque debitam servans."

56. Ulpian, it has plausibly been argued, pioneered theories of human rights: Tony Honoré, *Ulpian: Pioneer of Human Rights*, 2nd ed. (Oxford: Oxford University Press, 2002).

57. Ammianus Marcellinus 30.7.9: "in libertatem et quietem restituit placidam."

58. Hydatius 41 (ed. R. W. Burgess, *The Chronicle of Hydatius and the Consularia Constantinopolitana* [Oxford: Clarendon Press, 1993]).

59. Harries, "Violence, Victims and the Legal Tradition" (above, n. 32), is unusual, and unusually perceptive, in recognizing that a Republican cognitive framework survived into late antiquity ("The Roman Republic was alive and well in the time not only of Augustus and Nero but also of Augustine and Theodosius" [p. 101]).

60. Full (*aequa*) *libertas* had never been possible at Rome, because of the claims made by *dignitas*: Cicero, *De Republica*. 1.43: "Et cum omnia per populum geruntur quamvis iustum atque moderatum tamen ipsa aequabilitas est iniqua, cum habet nullos gradus dignitatis."

61. Ammianus Marcellinus 15.7.1–5. Auerbach, *Mimesis* (above, n. 35), 50–60.

62. See Joaquín Martínez Pizarro, *A Rhetoric of the Scene: Dramatic Narrative in the Early Middle Ages* (Toronto: University of Toronto Press, 1989), for the idea of a rhetoric of the scene in late ancient and early medieval prose.

63. John Matthews, "Peter Valvomeres, Re-Arrested," in Michael Whitby, Philip Hardie, and Mary Whitby, eds., *Homo Viator: Classical Essays for John Bramble* (Bristol: Bristol Classical Press, 1987), 277–84.

64. See Timothy D. Barnes, *Ammianus Marcellinus and the Representation of Historical Reality* (Ithaca: Cornell University Press, 1998), 100–102, for Ammianus's sadism, which may be thought to suffer from the biographical fallacy. The Peter Valvomeres episode occurs throughout the book, most sustainedly at pp. 11–15.

65. Ammianus Marcellinus 15.7.4: "vasti corporis rutilique capilli."

66. Ibid. 15.7.4, 15.7.5.

67. Ibid. 15.7.6–10.

68. Barnes, *Ammianus Marcellinus* (above, n. 64), 32–42.

69. Ammianus Marcellinus 15.7.7–8.

70. This was the main achievement of Barnes, *Ammianus Marcellinus* (above, n. 64), 79–94.

71. Jerome, *Contra Johannem Hierosolymitanum* 8 (ed. J.-P. Migne, *Patrologia Cursus Completus, Series Latina*, vol. 23 [Paris, 1862], 377C): "Homo sacrilegus, et idolorum cultor, solebat ludens beato papae Damaso dicere: Facite me Romanae urbis episcopum et ero protinus Christianus."

72. See the important discussion of William V. Harris, *Rome's Imperial Economy: Twelve Essays* (Oxford: Oxford University Press, 2011), 15–26 (first published in 1988).

10

Christianization

Edward Watts

In the twenty-first century it is deceptively easy to think that Rome's move from a pagan empire to a state in which Christianity played the dominant role followed a clear and well-defined path. In truth, in 312 it was as easy to conceive of a Christian Roman Empire as it was to imagine a Roman imperial rail network. Both these things are, after all, the products of innovative technologies imagined by bright thinkers and then implemented over time by a determined, capable, and sophisticated political and social system. Though Christianity's eventual dominance of the Roman state is often seen as a natural result of Constantine's conversion, its triumph over traditional religion actually represents an extremely difficult intellectual, political, and social achievement. Christianization needed to be imagined before it could be implemented. Once conceived, its implementation depended upon the political will of the emperor and his calculations about what his subjects would accept. In addition, all these things were fluid. Both imperial attitudes toward traditional religion and ideas about the shape of a Christian empire evolved at an inconsistent pace throughout late antiquity.

This essay will examine the intersection of the intellectual, political, and social processes that propelled the Roman Empire toward a state in which Christianity exercised a dominant role. Space constraints demand that the discussion largely concentrates on the first century following the conversion of Constantine, but even within this period of time one can see how much the late Roman imagination helped to set the terms according to which the Christianization of the Roman world progressed. This essay will have five parts. The first considers the Roman physical and social environment that Christians sought to remake. The second examines ideas about the shape of a Christian empire that emerged during and immediately following the reign of Constantine as well as the influence that these ideas had upon imperial policy. The third and fourth sections consider how these concepts and their implementation evolved under later fourth-century emperors. The third section focuses upon Constantius II, Jovian, Valentinian, and Valens. The fourth section does the same for Gratian, Theodosius I, Honorius, and Arcadius. The essay concludes by considering the dynamic interplay between ideas of what a Christian empire should look like and the challenges revealed when the implementation of these ideas failed to create the Roman state envisioned by Christian thinkers.

IMAGINING A CHRISTIAN ROMAN EMPIRE

In order to properly appreciate the intellectual challenge of simultaneously defining a Christian Roman Empire and charting a course that might lead to it, one must consider the physical, spiritual, and political landscapes inhabited by Christians at the time of Constantine's conversion. These posed significant barriers to the creation of a Christian state. The most daunting such obstacle was the persecution of Christians that the empire had launched in 303, which was petering out in 312.[1] This was a substantial practical problem, but Christians could easily imagine it away. The church had, after all, lived through extended periods of toleration in the third century and seemed to be stumbling toward another one again. Christians knew how to imagine a world that tolerated Christianity and chose not to persecute it.[2] This was, however, never anything more than a midpoint in the process through which a Christian future would emerge. Roman Christians instead imagined themselves waiting patiently for the moment when the tangible reality of the Roman rule would one day be superseded by a "heavenly and angelic empire" governed by Christ.[3]

This focus on a process of development through which the earthly empire of Rome would ultimately give way to a heavenly empire of Christ made it extremely difficult for Roman Christians to begin to imagine a Roman world dominated by Christianity. A range of factors made this task so difficult, but none was more important than the particular Christian combination of reticence and passivity that had developed over three centuries of living in a hostile Roman world. During that time, some Christians had faced prosecution and death because of their failure to participate in traditional Roman sacrifices, but most quietly absented themselves from the processions, sacrifices, and events that conflicted with their beliefs without attracting too much attention.[4] The decision to refrain from religious participation became more problematic in 250, when the emperor Decius issued an edict requiring every person in the empire to offer a public sacrifice to the gods.[5] Whatever Decius's intent, this was the moment in Roman history when imperial policy and imperial legislation first punished abstention from traditional religious life.[6] Christian refusal to perform the one sacrifice required of all residents of the empire would now be noted—though their continued absence from all other traditional religious activities remained unremarkable.[7] The Tetrarchic persecution of the early fourth century that attacked Christian leaders and Christian property was more comprehensive, though it again would have done nothing to change a pattern of behavior that simply encouraged Christians to disengage from the traditional religious world around them, hope to remain unnoticed, and look forward to Christ's heavenly empire.[8] This was deeply ingrained behavior, and when Roman persecution of Christians ended, Christian patterns of silent withdrawal from traditional religious life could not immediately disappear. Any move toward a Christian empire of this world required Christians to venture confidently out into the licit religious marketplace with a plan to use imperial power to enhance Christianity's standing.

The empire into which these Christians were born had long belonged to the old gods and was filled with physical reminders of their power. An early fourth-century Alexandrian *Notitia* that catalogs the types of buildings in five sectors of the city lists almost twenty-five hundred temples in the city, nearly one for every twenty houses.[9] Each of these temples contained images of gods. The Tychaion, for example, was "completely adorned from floor to ceiling" with statues and other images of the gods as well as those of quasi-divine historical figures like Alexander the Great and Ptolemy Soter.[10] The Tychaion was located across the street from a major bath complex and at a crossroads where two porticoed streets met. Between the statues found in the bathhouse, those housed in the niches of the porticoes, and those housed in the Tychaion, there were easily upwards of a hundred different images of gods in and around this one intersection. If this picture is then extended across the rest of the city (a city with upwards of 130 major intersections), we can begin to get a sense of how many sacred images filled the public spaces of an ancient city. To these tens of thousands of publicly displayed images, there were many thousands more displayed in Alexandria's homes, depicted on its coins, and worn as amulets or signet rings.

This Alexandrian document suggests the overwhelming architectural presence of the divine in later Roman cities. Another document, a calendar listing the holidays and festivals celebrated in Rome in 354, gives a sense of how frequently the gods and their servants appeared publicly.[11] It classifies fully 177 days of the year as holidays or festivals.[12] Overall the calendar marks the public celebrations of the cults of thirty-three different gods and goddesses, a number that does not include the various commemorations of imperial birthdays and divinized emperors.[13] Some gods and goddesses had multiple days in their honor. So, for example, the calendar contains eleven festival days that involved the cult of the Egyptian god Isis.[14] Although only the devotees of the gods or goddesses being celebrated took part in every part of these long, loud, and colorful festivals, many people throughout the city dressed for the occasion, watched and marched in one of the processions, or attended a related spectacle.[15] It was again far easier for Christians to envision a world replaced totally by a heavenly Christian empire than to consider a process through which the actual loud, messy, and overwhelmingly pagan cities, towns, and countrysides of the Roman Empire could be rendered Christian.

Constantine and his successors, of course, could not control the cosmic progression to a completely new, divine empire. They did control the real Roman world, however, and found themselves in a position to move it toward a new, Christian form. Unfortunately, no one knew quite what form a Christian Roman Empire ought to take or how one could practically create it. These emperors faced two related problems. First they needed to figure out what to do with the millennia-old traditional religious practices and infrastructure that they had inherited. Then they had to decide how imperial Christianity would interact with these traditional religions. These two linked concerns meant that Christian sovereigns not only had to imagine what a new, Christian religious order would be like, but they also had to decide what pagan elements of the Roman world could, if necessary, be allowed to remain. Only when emperors knew what Christianization was could they begin to articulate policies that might bring it about.

THE CONSTANTINIAN DYNASTY

This intellectual process of envisioning a Christian empire began in earnest during the reign of Constantine I, and it finds its clearest articulation in book 2 of Eusebius's *Life of Constantine,* a work written soon after the emperor's death.[16] At 2.44 Eusebius discusses a *nomos* (literally, a law) issued soon after Constantine took control of the eastern half of the empire in 324. This *nomos* forbade provincial governors and their superiors from offering sacrifice.[17] Eusebius then continues by stating: "Soon after this, two laws were promulgated about the same time, one of which was intended to restrain the idolatrous abominations that in time past had been practiced in every city and country; and it provided that no one should erect images, or practice divination and other false and foolish arts, or offer sacrifice in any way."[18] A second law connected with this one ordered officials to build churches according to specified dimensions "as though it were expected that, now that the madness of polytheism was wholly removed, pretty nearly all mankind would henceforth attach themselves to the service of God."[19] This was a model based upon Deuteronomy, the only historical parallel that Eusebius could find in which a polity governed by biblical law claimed to eradicate traditional polytheist religious practices.[20] In Eusebius's mind, Roman paganism, like Canaanite religion, would simply die away if sacrifice was restricted. A Christian empire would naturally emerge, filled with churches and believing congregations, but only as a result of Roman depaganization.

This path to a Christian empire proved far easier to articulate than to implement. The Roman legal system in the imperial period depended upon a dialogue between ruler and ruled in which the sovereign and his advisors primarily offered legal remedies to local challenges and conditions.[21] Legal initiatives either originated with the emperor's own inspiration (*spontaneus motus*) or, much more frequently, as a response to some situation that a prefect or a bishop had brought to the emperor's attention.[22] The situation and proposed remedy were then discussed within the imperial consistory, a body of advisors that included praetorian prefects, the *magister officiorum* (head of the palace administration), the two counts of the treasuries, the quaestor, and a number of counts of the consistory.[23] The consistory first discussed the matters brought to its attention. If it agreed that a legal remedy was necessary, it asked the imperial quaestor to draft a law. The consistory then discussed the text of the law before passing it along to the emperor for his signature. Once the law was issued, it was distributed to praetorian prefects and, eventually, to provincial governors so that they could disseminate it and implement it in ways appropriate to local conditions.[24]

The system, of course, offered ample scope for policy initiatives undertaken by emperors, but these were implemented across the empire only to the degree that elite opinions and local conditions permitted. Emperors needed to move slowly and consider carefully to what extent their subjects would tolerate interventions in their daily lives. There were considerable checks built in to control this process. The consistory was designed to produce frank discussions of these laws that could guard against imperial caprice and prevent the implementation of policies that would prove too disruptive. This usually worked, and when it did not, elites in the consistory or senate could often convince the emperor to moderate laws.[25] Prefects and local governors could also selectively implement laws either by silently ignoring them (an all-too-common aspect of Roman administration) or by providing instructions locally tailored for their implementation. The most effective emperors charted new social directions not by using coercion but by communicating their preferences and creating legal mechanisms that could advance their goals without prompting resistance. The laws that emperors issued and how they communicated their preferences, then, reveal both what policy objectives emperors desired and how prepared they thought society was to accept those policies.

Constantine's policies related to traditional religion show an emperor acutely aware of this dynamic.[26] The *Life of Constantine*, which treads a careful line between a descriptive account of Constantine's actions and a prescriptive treatise laying out the actions expected of an ideal Christian sovereign, speaks about "successive laws [*nomoi*] and ordinances [*diataxeis*]" that forbade everyone "to sacrifice to idols, dabble in divination, have cult statues erected, conduct secret rites, or to pollute cities with gladiatorial games."[27] Eusebius records that Constantine removed "the venerable statues of brass" from pagan temples so that they could be "exposed to view in all the public places of the imperial city [Constantinople]."[28] Eusebius also notes that he ordered the destruction of four temples, three devoted to the goddess Aphrodite and one to Asclepius. One of the temples of Aphrodite was located on the supposed site of Christ's resurrection. It was replaced by a church. Two others dedicated to Aphrodite were centers of ritualized prostitution, a practice that he deemed "unlawful commerce of women and adulterous intercourse."[29] Only the fourth of these, a temple of Asclepius in the city of Aegae, was closed without obvious reason.

Eusebius claims that the removal of statues, the destruction of temples, and the restrictions on sacrifice were all legally sanctioned by the emperor. This, then, seems to be the ultimate plan for what imperial power could do to eliminate paganism. And yet, even imperial power had its limits. Aside from the ban on gladiatorial games that Eusebius mentions in passing, nothing shows up in surviving legislation to indicate that Constantine issued laws ordering any of these things. They are known only from Eusebius's text—and Eusebius's account does not agree with other literary evidence. The Antiochene orator Libanius (who was born in 314) wrote in the late 380s that "Constantine made absolutely no changes in the traditional forms of worship" and elsewhere blames Constantine's son Constantius II for first prohibiting sacrifice and closing temples.[30]

Scott Bradbury has proposed an interesting way to resolve the apparent contradictions between the Constantine profiled by Eusebius, the emperor who appears in the *Theodosian Code,* and the figure mentioned in Libanius's oration. Bradbury argues that Constantine's prohibition of sacrifice appeared in an imperial letter.[31] Imperial letters did have the force of law, but they usually served only to state the basic principles guiding imperial policy. They did not often specify steps to implement these policies, nor did they lay out penalties for disobedience. Eusebius's discussion of the *nomoi* against sacrifice issued by Constantine contains neither any specified penalties nor any people actually punished for violating these laws. These were statements of legal principle, but they were deliberately left without enforcement mechanisms. Thus Libanius is likely correct when he says that "Constantine made no changes in traditional forms of worship." Although Constantine opposed much of traditional worship on principle, he apparently did nothing more to deter its practice than to suggest that he found it distasteful.[32]

Similarly, Constantine's actions against statues and temples can have much more nuance than Eusebius allows. Whereas Eusebius sees religious meaning in Constantine's importation of statues of gods to his new capital, Constantinople, it is just as likely (as Sarah Bassett has suggested) that these represent artistic adornments to the city chosen for their beauty.[33] A sense of context and proportion is also useful when considering the temple destructions. The Roman Empire was packed full of temples. Temples, even large and impressive ones, regularly fell into disrepair and were either abandoned or torn down. The Alexandrian Serapeum, described as the second-greatest temple in the world by a fourth-century author, was actually a second-century-C.E. reconstruction executed after the Ptolemaic Serapeum had essentially been condemned.[34] Traditional religion had been practiced in the Mediterranean region for millennia and paganism's sacred buildings often showed their age. It is not surprising that an emperor would sanction the destruction of an existing temple. What was new, of course, was Constantine's decision to replace an existing temple with a church devoted to the Christian God. These four temple destructions each had different impacts. Whereas the three temples of Aphrodite seem not to have been missed, the destruction of the temple of Asclepius at Aegae elicited speeches of mourning and other impassioned reactions from devotees of traditional religion well into the 360s.[35] This may, then, have been a case where Constantinian religious initiatives went farther than the public was willing to tolerate.

For the next fifty years the model of imperially supported depaganization described by Eusebius in the *Life of Constantine* would set the parameters for both Christian ideas about how a Christian empire could be achieved and what policies emperors enacted. Following Eusebius, it seems that intellectual and political approaches to depaganization worked within a rather well-defined spectrum of possibilities related to the continued legality of sacrifices and access to temples. Christian thinkers continued to push emperors to fully and completely ban sacrifices, close the temples, and open the empire to full Christianization. The lessons of Constantine were well learned, however, and Constantius II, Jovian, and Valentinian I and Valens all seem to have pursued these goals only as far as they thought was politically tolerable. This made the emperors seem less aggressive than many Christians wanted, but with more extreme positions framing the limits of the debate, this measured approach preserved for emperors a useful appearance of moderation.

CONSTANTINE'S SUCCESSORS

Constantine's successors generally seem to have followed the Eusebian notion that imperial depaganization represented an essential core component of Roman Christianization. Like Constantine, however, they proceeded cautiously. They set legal limits on traditional religious practices while simultaneously shielding administrators from the reactions that the full implementation of those policies would provoke. As Libanius suggests, Constantine's son Constantius II began practically implementing the legal principles that Eusebius ascribed to Constantine. The *Theodosian Code* preserves a series of laws issued by Constantius that lay out a series of applications of Constantinian antipagan principles. They began in 341 with a simple prohibition of sacrifice that restates Constantine's *nomos* and adds an unspecified penalty.[36] In 356 Constantius took the additional legislative step of prescribing actual penalties for sacrifices. *Theodosian Code* 16.10.6, a law of

February 20, 356, proclaimed "if any persons should be proved to devote their attention to sacrifices or to worship images, We command that they be subjected to capital punishment." A further expansion came on December 1 of the same year, likely in response to the imperfect (or incomplete) implementation of *Theodosian Code* 16.10.6. This additional law, *Theodosian Code* 16.10.4 (misdated in the manuscripts to 346),[37] ordered that "all temples should be immediately closed in all cities and access to them forbidden so as to deny to all abandoned men the opportunity to commit sin." The law then continues by restating the ban on sacrifice and the imposition of capital punishment upon violators. It concludes with an interesting new provision: "The governors of the provinces shall be similarly punished if they should neglect to avenge such crimes." This last provision, then, suggests that Constantius may have pushed far enough beyond the limits of what was palatable that some of his governors decided not to implement the law. Indeed, disregard for the law seems to have been widespread. Not only did public festivals involving sacrifice continue throughout the empire, but also there is no record of anyone being charged under this law.

Constantius pursued a more cautious policy toward temples. Although he did mandate their closure, he also issued a legal instruction that "the buildings of the temples outside the walls shall remain untouched and uninjured. For since certain plays or spectacles of the circus or contests derive their origins from some of these temples, such structures shall not be torn down, since from them is provided the regular performance of long-established amusements for the Roman people."[38] Constantius seems to have understood that temple destructions might so seriously disrupt life in the Roman world that they would provoke a reaction. At the same time, Constantius did transfer to the Christian church some temples belonging to the emperor, including the large Caesareum (a temple honoring the divinity of the emperors) in the city of Alexandria.[39] It is also clear from other evidence that Constantius and his officials permitted people to take materials and statuary from temples and use these materials to build or decorate their private property. No surviving Constantian legislation encourages this sort of activity, but private possession of temple property was retroactively criminalized and punished by Constantius's successor, the pagan emperor Julian. Oddly enough, the frenzied appeals from people, both pagan and Christian, who were penalized by Julian's law suggests that Julian, not Constantius, may have been the one who forced people to adjust their behavior uncomfortably.[40]

Constantius's measured moves toward the depaganized empire envisioned by Eusebius attracted criticism from Christians claiming to be frustrated that he was not moving aggressively enough. In the 340s, Firmicus Maternus repeatedly urged Constantius and his brother Constans to ban sacrifice and overthrow pagan temples.[41] In *De Errore* 16.3, for example, Maternus describes temples as tombs that keep the "ashes of the dead, so that the daily blood of victims may commemorate their bitter end." He appeals to the emperors to utterly eradicate and destroy these practices through "the severest laws of your edicts, so that the deadly error of this delusion no longer stains the Roman world."[42] Later he informs the emperors that "the benevolent Godhead of Christ has reserved the extermination of idolatry and the overthrow of the pagan temples for your hands. . . . Rejoice in the destruction of paganism."[43] This goal is near because "only a little is lacking that the devil should be utterly overthrown and laid low by your laws and that the horrid contagion of idolatry should die out and become extinct."[44] Maternus anticipated the objection that such a legislative remedy might be too politically painful and responded by saying that "it is better for you to save them against their will than to let them follow their wishes into death. Sick people like what is not good for them, and when ill health takes control, the sufferers make perverse demands."[45]

Maternus's comments show that in the 340s temple closings and a ban on sacrifices remained at the center of Christian ideas about how a world free from paganism might be created. Maternus's work also shows that the dynamic between Christian thinkers and imperial leaders had changed upon the ascension of Constantine's sons. Unlike Eusebius, Maternus directly criticizes imperial hesitancy to move directly and forcefully against traditional religion. This criticism suggests that a consensus had begun to develop among radical Christians about what steps needed to be taken to extinguish traditional religion. Because these steps had been identified, Maternus expressed a growing impatience with the emperors who were unwilling to take them. His impatience, though, reflected positively upon the political strategy adopted by the emperors and their advisors. Constantius and Constans had carved out a position between the extreme calls of Christians for temple closings and the idea that traditional practices should continue without interruption. Their policies would make it through the consistory and levels of imperial bureaucracy without great resistance and thus enabled the emperors to push for change at the pace that they chose without appearing beholden to Christian extremists.

It would have been hard for Christians arguing about the pace at which the final elimination of paganism should proceed during the reign of Constantius to imagine how quickly the imperial religious dynamic would change upon the ascension of Julian. Julian, of course, reversed the policies of Constantine and his sons that restricted traditional religious activity and replaced them with others that offered robust imperial support to traditional cults.[46] He reinstated sacrifices, removed temples from the imperial *res privata,* and offered generous financial support to cult activities. He also changed the conversation that Christian thinkers and authors were having about traditional religion. Julian took power as a young man, and had he not been killed during his Persian campaign, he could reasonably have been expected to govern for at least a generation—and possibly for longer.[47] Christian thinkers of the 360s thus spent more energy pondering their narrow escape from Julian and less considering the appropriate pace of Christianity's imminent triumph.[48]

One sees the effect of this intellectual shift in the policies pursued by Julian's Christian successors Jovian, Valentinian I, and Valens. Julian's dramatic recalibration of imperial religious policy not only changed the conversation among Christians; it also took momentum away from imperial depaganization efforts. In his short reign, Jovian reversed Julian's unpopular law restricting the ability of Christians to teach but otherwise seems to have done little with respect to religious policy.[49] Valentinian and Valens, for their parts, never managed even to move imperial policy back to where Constantius had left it. Although they reappropriated temple properties, they did not sanction the destruction of any temple buildings. Libanius states that Valens revived a ban on sacrifice, but the loss of the law doing this makes it impossible to determine when in his thirteen-year reign this happened.[50] It is also unclear exactly what ban was revived. Libanius makes clear that incense offerings were still permitted by Valens. More interesting is Theodoret's comment that "the slaves of [pagan] error even went so far as to perform pagan rites. . . . The rites of Jews, of Dionysus, and of Demeter were now no longer performed in a corner, as they would be in a pious reign, but by revelers running wild in the forum."[51] If this is true, it is possible that the renewed ban on sacrifice was closer to the laws of the early 340s that prohibited sacrifice without specifying penalties than it was to those of the mid-350s in which a severe penalty is mandated.

There is other evidence to suggest that laws enacted by Constantius in the 350s were no longer politically palatable in the period after Julian. In 364 Valentinian and Valens issued a law that prohibited nocturnal sacrifices, a reiteration of a restriction first issued by Constantius in 353.[52] Valentinian and Valens's ban required only that violators be subjected to unspecified "suitable penalties," a provision that made it unlikely to be enforced anyway. Although Constantius's stronger law went into effect without significant challenge, Praetextatus, the proconsul of Achaea, convinced Valentinian to rescind the order because it "would make life unbearable for the Hellenes if it was intended to prevent the divinely prescribed practice of the most sacred mysteries."[53] After hearing about the resistance that this was likely to produce, Valentinian "abandoned the proposal and allowed everything to be done according to national custom."[54] Facing no significant Christian pressure to reinstate the law, neither Valentinian nor Valens attempted to revive it.[55]

GRATIAN AND THE THEODOSIAN DYNASTY

Valentinian and Valens were the last Roman emperors born during the lifetime of Constantine and the last whose policies toward traditional religion fit within the model of depaganization articulated by Eusebius. For sixty years following the conversion of Constantine, Christians imagined a world in which a ban on sacrifice and the closure of temples would drive traditional religion to extinction. Although Constantine and Constantius made occasional gestures toward closing temples, imperial policy during this time largely concentrated on the most palatable ways to limit pagan sacrifice. The Christian empire that Maternus imagined loomed just around the corner in the 340s remained a mere aspiration in the later 370s.

Gratian, Theodosius I, and their advisors resolved to realize this vision with a series of aggressive actions against sacrifices, priesthoods, and (eventually) temples. Their laws and actions were issued jointly, though it is difficult to say how closely they were coordinated. Nevertheless, the early 380s saw both Eastern and Western imperial sovereigns initiate actions against what they thought were the foundations of traditional religious practice. Around 380, Gratian took a series of actions that undercut the financial and practical foundations of traditional Roman religion. None of his actions is preserved directly in the *Theodosian Code,* but it is clear that he assumed control over whatever temple property was held freely and refused to provide the funds necessary for major public celebrations of traditional rites in Italy.[56] The Altar of Victory was famously removed from the senate house in Rome; sacrifices again seem to have been restricted, and old cults like that of the Vestal Virgins seem to have ceased operation as a result.[57]

Theodosius's early actions against traditional religion are both better attested and more clearly in line with the path toward a Christian empire envisioned by early fourth-century thinkers. The assault began in December 381 with a law making illegal both diurnal and nocturnal sacrifices while also forbidding anyone to approach a temple.[58] A law issued in November 382 further clarified the situation. It concerned a temple that contained images that "must be measured by the value of their art rather than by their divinity."[59] These images, the emperor declared, were to be protected, and the temple that contained them was to remain open, "but in such a way that the performance of sacrifices forbidden therein may not be supposed to be permitted under the pretext of such access to the temple."[60] With this law Theodosius effectively rendered temples tourist attractions and decreed that any cultic activity within them was now forbidden.

Theodosian policy, of course, went beyond what this legislation spells out. The emperor issued no laws ordering the destruction of temples, but he tacitly sanctioned this activity. The most notorious instances occurred during the praetorian prefect Cynegius's inspection tour of Syria, Mesopotamia, and Egypt in 386–88, when men accompanying the prefect attacked rural shrines and temples.[61] All this activity was done in such a way that the emperor could claim ignorance, but Christian thinkers understood what Theodosius was aiming to do. Theodoret prefaces the segment of book 5 of his *Ecclesiastical History* that discusses temple destructions with a short analysis of the actions taken against traditional religion by previous emperors. Constantine, Theodoret wrote, "issued a general prohibition against the offering of sacrifices to idols. He had not, however, destroyed the temples."[62] His successors followed this pattern. Theodosius, however, ordered the destruction of the "shrines of the idols" and "consigned [traditional rites] to oblivion."[63] Other Christians agreed with Theodoret. Prudentius, for example, saw the Theodosian-era temple destructions as a final step that would lead to a rush to the church.[64] John Chrysostom and Gregory Nazianzen claimed that the actions of Theodosius formed a sort of persuasion that would lead to superstition collapsing in on itself.[65] With the policies advocated by Eusebius finally in place by the later 380s, many thought that the extinction of paganism and a universal embrace of Christianity would soon follow.

They did not. By 391, a law issued in Milan during the consulship of the two pagan notables Symmachus and Tatianus suggests that Theodosius had learned that antipagan laws were difficult to enforce effectively. The law reiterated the earlier ban on sacrifice and divination before expanding upon what was meant by the prohibition of entry into temples. "No person," it states, "shall approach the shrines, shall wander through the temples, or revere the images formed by mortal labor, lest he become guilty by divine and human laws."[66] More interesting was the second part of the law, which not only fined judges and governors who were "devoted to profane rites and who should enter a temple" but also penalized their staffs a similar amount if they did not try to prevent the officials from doing this or did not immediately report these transgressions.[67] So significant was the enforcement problem that a different version of essentially this same law was sent to the prefect of Egypt four months later. Even this did not do the trick; the emperor and his advisors felt compelled to issue a longer elaboration of the same principles in November 392.[68] This last law expands the prohibition to include binding a tree with fillets, erecting altars of turf, and offering honors to gods within a household.[69] Far from "pretty nearly all mankind attaching themselves to the service of God," the Theodosian bans on sacrifice and closure of temples instead produced a practical nightmare in which people were moving their traditional religious activities to less publicly controllable locations and governors were personally disobeying laws that they were supposed to enforce.

Theodosius's failure to extinguish traditional religion was in large part due to the limitation of Christian imagination. Whereas those advising his sons Honorius and Arcadius pursued a legislative retrenchment in the later 390s that added penalties to existing Theodosian legislation, Christian thinkers had already begun sketching out an updated model of a depaganized empire that went farther than mid-fourth-century authors had thought necessary. At the turn of the fifth century, North African Christian leaders called attention to the need to eliminate idols, rural shrines, and traditional festivals. At a council in Carthage in 401, for example, canon 58 called upon the emperors to "command that the remaining idols throughout all Africa be utterly destroyed . . . as well as their temples, which have been set up in the countryside [*in agris*]."[70] Canon 60 of the same council called for the elimination of banquets in which Christians are forced to participate alongside pagans in activities "brought together by pagan error,"[71] a call that resembles a concern both expressed by Augustine and passed along to the court by African leaders as early as 399.[72]

As was the case in the mid-fourth century, early fifth-century imperial legislation initially lagged behind Christian thinking about depaganization. It did, however, soon catch up. The African call to abolish traditional festal banquets was brusquely denied in a law of 399 that decreed "according to ancient custom, amusements shall be furnished to the people, but without any sacrifice or accursed superstition, and they shall be allowed to attend festal banquets whenever public desires so demand.[73] By 408, however, the consistory and emperor had come around. They then prohibited "convivial banquets in honor of sacrilegious rites" and "granted to bishops of such places the right to use *ecclesiastica manus* to prohibit such practices."[74] Governors who chose not to enforce this law were to be fined twenty pounds of gold, as were their office staffs (who would be expected to inform against a reluctant governor).

Honorius acted with more speed against images of the gods. In 399, a law was sent to Africa ordering that "idols should be taken down under the direction of the office staff after an investigation has been held, since it is evident that even now the worship of a vain superstition is being paid to idols."[75] This law endorses the call to remove images and creates a formal administrative procedure for doing so that requires imperial officials to review any complaint about an image and then use their resources to take the image down. This not only prevented people from taking images down themselves but also intentionally crafted a procedure that could not be used in any large-scale fashion.[76] Its effect on the millions of images within the Roman world would have been negligible. Indeed, one suspects that this was the order's objective. Like Constantinian legislation against sacrifice, this directive endorsed the principle that images needed to be removed while creating an administrative process that made such a legal principle essentially unenforceable.

In the end, this second expansion of legal restrictions on traditional religion also failed to create an empire wholly devoted to the service of a Christian God. Restrictions on sacrifice did not have this effect. Even temple destructions could not be counted on to encourage devotees of the traditional gods to become Christians. Next to the site of the Serapeum, a massive Alexandrian temple destroyed by Christians after rioting in 392, Christians constructed not only a large shrine containing the remains of the prophet Elisha and John the Baptist but also a monastery filled with monks who could observe the site of the old Serapeum and discourage any furtive prayers.[77] A similar measure was effected in the Alexandrian suburb of Canopus, where a Pachomian monastery was erected on the site of another former temple to Serapis. In a third suburb, Menouthis, no monastic garrison was established after the destruction of an Isiac healing shrine. As a result, appeals to the Isis of Menouthis continued, apparently without significant interruption, until the end of the fifth century.[78] Even without the temples in place, these sites remained focal points of devotion for pagans who felt no inclination to attach themselves to the Christian God.

The reason for this is not difficult to understand. In the case of Alexandria, imperial policy, natural disaster, and architectural decay meant that the city must have had far fewer temples at the end of the fourth century than it had had at the century's beginning. It is hard to imagine any scenario under which the number would approach zero, however.[79] Some of the statuary publicly displayed in the city was pulled down and destroyed following the destruction of Serapeum and possibly more still after the legal procedure for its removal was established in 399, but again, most of it was not. In the 480s there remained enough pagan statuary in the city to keep a bonfire going for most of a day, and this included neither the statues in the Tychaion (which remained in place in the seventh century)[80] nor private collections of statuary.[81] Outside Alexandria, the situation would have been similar. Maximus of Turin wrote during the reign of Honorius that "apart from a few religious people, hardly anyone's field is unpolluted by idols; hardly any property is kept free from the cult of demons. Everywhere the Christian eye is offended; everywhere the devout mind, assailed: wherever you turn, you see either the altars of the devil or the profane auguries of the pagans."[82] Traditional festivals proved even more enduring. Prominent ones like the Lupercalia continued into the later fifth century in Rome and persisted until at least the tenth century in Constantinople.[83] The wide range of options for traditional religious expressions that survived the activities of the first century of Christian imperial power show how difficult it was to chart a path toward a Christian *oikoumenē*.

CONCLUSION

Romans conceiving of and creating a Christian *oikoumenē* failed to recognize the true nature of the problem that they wished to address. A Christian Roman Empire would result not from restricting practices but from aggressively regulating belief. This did not occur to fourth-century Christian thinkers, in large part because traditional Mediterranean religion was defined by actions, not beliefs. Pagans did not need to believe anything in particular; they merely needed to honor the gods appropriately. It was reasonable to assume that actions designed to limit these practices would fatally undermine traditional religion. This was especially true if, like Eusebius, one used the Israelite experience in Canaan as a model. Deuteronomy, however, offered a false parallel. Ancient Israelites, like Roman pagans, used practices, not beliefs, to define membership in their religious community. Christians defined their goals differently. Thinkers like Eusebius and Firmicus Maternus wanted a world in which nearly everyone embraced the Christian God, but the path they prescribed led only to the restriction of certain activities, not to a change in religious conviction. They failed to appreciate that a person who no longer performed traditional religious rites was not a Christian. Although his actions might have changed, his beliefs did not. The path that these fourth-century thinkers charted and the one that imperial law followed led not to a Christian *oikoumenē* but to a world in which traditional practice was increasingly marginalized. This undoubtedly had an effect on the sheer size of the pagan population, but this path alone would not bring a Christian empire.

Fourth-century laws addressing heresy pointed to a more promising approach. Unlike devotees of traditional religion, Christian heretics could be defined by what they believed. This was often a slippery concept, but a legal mechanism for defining a heretic existed as early as 380.[84] As one moves through the fifth century and into the sixth, one sees laws addressing pagans begin to look more and more like laws against heretics. The laws of the *Theodosian Code* all address traditional practices rather than beliefs. By the reign of Justinian, however, it was recognized that more needed to be done. *Codex Justinianus* 1.11.10, Justinian's monumental antipagan law of the early 530s,[85] penalizes not only those who "offer sacrifices to idols and celebrate wholly impious festivals" but even those who "have gone or will go to baptism disingenuously . . . as they obviously do not have pure faith in holy baptism."[86] These individuals "neither will have any part in our state, nor will our agents allow them to possess any movable or immovable property, but giving up all their goods, they will be left in poverty to suffer the suitable penalties."[87] This was, then, the first piece of legislation to actually penalize pagan belief. It was also the final recognition that a Christian empire did not simply result from the suppression of traditional religious practices. It was instead a world built on faith, and one in which the sincerity of Christian belief needed constant policing.

This transformation from the regulation of practice to the regulation of belief itself reveals to us the reciprocal and consequential relationships between beliefs and practices, between the world of ideas and the physical world. Beliefs about how a Christian world could be created were shaped by assumptions about how religion works, by biblical texts, by the physical landscapes of late ancient cities, by the memory of persecution, and by eschatological thought; and as they changed, these beliefs effected a transformation in imperial policies and legislation, guiding the actions of those who developed them. The dependence of actions on ideas, how greatly they are part of an intellectual effort, may be more visible to us when we do not share these ideas, when the intellectual outlook underlining action is, as in Eusebius's vision of Christianization, mistaken. But observing the different stages of the attempt to turn the Greco-Roman world into a new religious community allows us to see more completely the imagination that it required.

The antipagan campaigns of Justinian were better targeted and proved more effective than those of Constantius and Theodosius, but they too failed to create a true Christian *oikoumenē*. In the seventh century, Muslim armies conquering Syria and Mesopotamia found themselves negotiating surrender agreements not only with local Christian bishops but also with devotees of traditional cults.[88] Indeed, though this speculation is impossible to prove, the true eradication of traditional religion in the territory of the Roman Empire may have come only when such massive disruptions as those caused by Slavic and Avar attacks in Greece and the Mongol invasion of Mesopotamia uprooted whole populations accustomed to living in a particular way, deposited them in different surroundings, and forced them to adapt to new cultural practices. This was a particularly horrible method of conversion, one that seems to have been neither suggested by Christian thinkers nor implemented by imperial officials, but it does demonstrate the difficulty of the task that Eusebius and Constantine set for themselves. A Christian *oikoumenē* seemed always to lie just beyond the horizon, but its outlines forever remained too hazy to truly comprehend. And, however difficult a Christian *oikoumenē* was to imagine, it was much more difficult to actually create. Even if the Romans may have failed in remaking their *oikoumenē*, their centuries-long attempt to do so offers a unique moment in which imagination, imperial policy, and public response shaped the slow course of a religious revolution.

NOTES

1. The persecution begun in 303 had been officially suspended by Galerius in 311 (Lactantius, *De Mortibus Persecutorum* 33–34), though sporadic local persecutions continued to occur until the defeat of Maximinus Daia. For persecutions in the areas controlled by Maximinus Daia see Stephen Mitchell, "Maximinus and the Christians," *Journal of Roman Studies* 78 (1988): 105–24.

2. As the Eusebian description of Philip the Arab suggests (*Historia Ecclesiastica* 6.34), third-century events enabled Christians to imagine even a Christian emperor. For a critical discussion of this Eusebian portrait, see Hans Pohlsander, "Philip the Arab and Christianity" *Historia* 29 (1980): 463–73.

3. As Raymond Van Dam points out (*The Roman Revolution of Constantine* [Cambridge: Cambridge University Press, 2007], 10), Christians had always imagined that pagan Roman rule would be replaced by Christ's "heavenly and angelic empire," not a Christian Roman one. For this notion. see, for example, Eusebius, *Historia Ecclesiastica* 3.20.4.

4. On this see the excellent discussion of James B. Rives, "The Decree of Decius and the Religion of the Empire," *Journal of Roman Studies* 89 (1999): 145–47. Many people skipped the religious festivals and public sacrifices that crowded the calendar for a range of reasons (e.g., the pagan sophist Libanius, who required his students to skip a festival for Artemis because their declamations needed work [*Oration* 5.44–49]).

5. The edict itself does not survive, but its impact can be seen in documents ranging from forty-four different receipts given to those who sacrificed in accordance with it to letters and Christian historiography. For discussion of these sources, see Rives, "Decree" (above, n. 4), 135–39.

6. It has been argued, for example, that Decius did not issue this law in an attempt to target Christians but hoped instead to push lazy Romans to take a greater interest in the gods (Rives, "Decree" [above, n. 4], 147–51).

7. A similar dynamic may be imagined during the persecution of Valerian, though Valerian's persecution took a different form because it specifically targeted bishops, Christian senators, and church property (Cyprian, *Letter* 80). For nonelite Christians, though, the dynamic of remaining quiet and waiting things out probably did not change.

8. For the Tetrarchic persecution, see, most famously, Lactantius, *De Mortibus Persecutorum* 12–14. For a practical example of how Christian property was targeted, see *The Oxyrhynchus Papyri*, no. 2673.

9. The list reads: "At Alexandria one finds in Quarter A: 308 temples, 1,655 courts, 5,058 houses, 108 baths, 237 taverns, 112 porticoes. In Quarter B: 110 temples, 1,002 courts, 5,990 houses, I45 baths, 107 taverns. In Quarter Γ: 855 temples, 955 courts, 2,140 houses, . . . baths, 205 taverns, 78 porticoes. In Quarter Δ: 800 temples, 1,120 courts, 5,515 houses, 118 baths, 178 taverns, 98 (porticoes). In Quarter E: 405 temples, 1,420 courts, 5,593 houses, . . . baths, 118 taverns, 56 porticoes. Thus the total number of temples is 2,393 [in fact, 2,478]; of courts 8,102 [in fact, 6,152]; of houses, 47,790 [in fact, 24,296]; of baths, 1561; of taverns, 935 [in fact, 845]; of porticoes, 456" (P. M. Fraser, "A Syriac *Notitia Urbis Alexandrinae*," *Journal of Egyptian Archaeology* 37 [1951]: 103–8). The list has a somewhat odd provenance, but there is no reason to think that it has been corrupted or that its contents are inaccurate.

10. Pseudo-Libanius, *Alexandrian Tychaion*, chapters 4–6, in Craig Gibson, "Alexander in the Tychaion: Ps.-Libanius on the Statues," *Greek, Roman and Byzantine Studies* 47 (2007): 431–54.

11. On the *Codex Calendar of 354*, see the definitive study of Michelle Salzman, *On Roman Time: The Codex Calendar of 354 and the Rhythms of Urban Life in Late Antiquity* (Berkeley and Los Angeles: University of California Press, 1990).

12. Salzman, *On Roman Time* (above, n. 11), 117–20. Not all of these were given the same weight. Those that lasted for multiple days and involved circus races were the most important and mandated, among other things, a day of rest and the closure of the law courts. Less important were days whose festivals involved games or spectacles, and the least important were days devoted to cultic ritual that involved neither races nor spectacles.

13. For a list of these gods, see Salzman, *On Roman Time* (above, n. 11), 130–31. For imperial holidays, fully sixty-nine were devoted to members of the house of Constantine. An additional twenty-nine days honored earlier emperors or actions taken by them (ibid. 132).

14. Two were in March, one in April (a joint festival with the god Serapis), and one in August. October saw a four-day-long festival devoted to Isis that ran from the 28th to the 31st. The first three days of November too were devoted to festivals concerned with specific aspects of the cult. For the Isiac festivals, see the table found in Salzman, *On Roman Time* (above, n. 11), 170.

15. The best account of an Isiac procession remains that found in Apuleius, *Metamorphoses* book 11. It is worth noting here David Frankfurter's discussion of the downsizing of major religious festivals and the resiliency of minor ones in late antique Egypt (*Religion in Roman Egypt* [Princeton: Princeton University Press, 1998], 58–65).

16. Eusebius's *Vita Constantini* was composed after Constantine's death. As such, it is less a record of purely Constantinian ideas than a representation of ideas shaped both during and immediately after Constantine's reign.

17. Eusebius, *Vita Constantini* 2.44.

18. Ibid. 2.45.

19. Ibid.

20. Deuteronomy 12:2 (NRSV translation). I thank Jeremy Schott for calling my attention to this similarity to Deuteronomy.

21. Fergus Millar, *The Emperor in the Roman World, 31 BC–337AD* (Ithaca: Cornell University Press, 1992), 266, 271.

22. The ways in which a law could be made are described in *Codex Justinianus* 1.14.3, an address made to the Western senate by Valentinian III in 426, and *Codex Justinianus* 1.14.8, a law of 446 describing procedures. For discussion, see Jill Harries, "The Roman Imperial Quaestor from Constantine to Theodosius II," *Journal of Roman Studies* 78 (1988), 148–72, and John Matthews, *Laying Down the Law* (New Haven: Yale University Press, 2000), 171–72.

23. The consistory and its composition are discussed in detail in Jill Harries, *Law and Empire in Late Antiquity,* (Cambridge: Cambridge University Press, 1999), 38–42. Whereas its composition would have been slightly different in the time of Constantine, it had settled into this form by the reign of Constantius II. The counts of the consistory lacked any other defined office.

24. On this process see Edward Watts, "Justinian, Malalas, and the End of Athenian Philosophical Teaching in AD 529," *Journal of Roman Studies* 94 (2004): 174–75.

25. See, for example, the situations described in Ammianus Marcellinus 28.1 and Zosimus 4.3.

26. For a thorough discussion of the political aspects of the reign of Constantine, see Hal Drake, *Constantine and the Bishops: The Politics of Intolerance* (Baltimore: The Johns Hopkins University Press, 2000), 235–72.

27. Eusebius, *Vita Constantini* 4.23.

28. Ibid. 4.54.

29. Ibid.

30. Libanius, *Orations* 30.6.

31. Scott Bradbury, "Constantine and the Problem of Anti-Pagan Legislation in the Fourth Century," *Classical Philology* 89 (1994): 131–32.

32. For other assessments of this question see A. D. Lee, "Traditional Religions," in *The Cambridge Companion to the Age of Constantine,* ed. N. Lenski (Cambridge: Cambridge University Press, 2006), 172–74. Against the idea of a law banning sacrifice, see Robin Lane Fox, *Pagans and Christians* (New York: Knopf, 1987), 667; John Curran, *Pagan City and Christian Capital: Rome in the Fourth Century* (Oxford: Oxford University Press, 2000), 175–85.

33. Sarah Bassett, *The Urban Image of Late Antique Constantinople* (Cambridge: Cambridge University Press, 2004).

34. On the nature of the Serapeum site, see the excellent treatment of Judith S. McKenzie, Sheila Gibson, and Andres T. Reyes, "Reconstructing the Serapeum in Alexandria from the Archeological Evidence," *Journal of Roman Studies* 94 (2004): 73–121.

35. For the monody, see the summary offered in Libanius, *Epistles* F695 = B147. For other discussions, see Libanius, *Epistles* B146–48; N137.

36. "Emperor Constantius to Madalianus, Vice–Praetorian Prefect: Superstition shall cease; the madness of sacrifices shall be abolished. For if any man, in violation of the law of the

sainted emperor [Constantine], Our Father, and in violation of the command of Our Clem-
ency, should dare to perform sacrifices, he shall suffer the infliction of a suitable punishment
and the effect of an immediate sentence": *Codex Theodosianus* 16.10.2, this and all translations
of the Theodosian Code are based on those of Pharr, with occasional adaptations for clarity.

37. The manuscripts of the *Theodosian Code* date this law, *Codex Theodosianus* 16.10.4,
to 346, but its addressee, the praetorian prefect Taurus, held office from 355 until 361. The
dating of the addressee is more convincing based upon the evident contextual relationship
to *Codex Theodosianus* 16.10.6.

38. *Codex Theodosianus* 16.10.3, of November 1, 342.

39. On the Caesareum transfer, see Christopher Haas, *Alexandria in Late Antiquity*
(Baltimore: The Johns Hopkins University Press, 1997), 210. Constantius also transferred to
Christian ownership a basilica that once contained a subterranean Mithraeum (Rufinus,
Historia Ecclesiastica 11.22; Sozomen *Historia Ecclesiastica* 7.15).

40. E.g., Libanius, *Epistles* 724, 763, 1364.

41. All this occurs in Maternus's *De Errore Profanarum Religionum,* a work dated
between 343 and 350.

42. "Amputanda sunt haec sacratissimi imperatores, penitus atque delenda, et severis-
simis edictorum vestrorum legibus corrigenda, ne diutius Romanum orbem praesump-
tionis istius error funestus inmaculet": Maternus, *De Errore Profanarum Religionum* 16.4.

43. Ibid. 20.7.

44. Ibid..

45. Ibid. 16.4–5.

46. Libanius, *Orations* 1.119–21.

47. For a sense of the life span of emperors, see Walter Schiedel, "Emperors, Aristocrats,
and the Grim Reaper: Towards a Demographic Profile of the Roman Élite," *Classical Quarterly* 49 (1999): 254–81.

48. See, for example, Susanna Elm, "Gregory of Nazianzus's Life of Julian Revisited (Or.
4 and 5): The Art of Governance by Invective," in *From the Tetrarchs to the Theodosians*, ed.
S. McGill, C. Sogno, and E. Watts (Cambridge: Cambridge University Press, 2010), 171–84.

49. The reversal of the teaching law is *Codex Theodosianus* 13.3.6. Valentinian and
Valens are listed in the heading, but the date, January 364, suggests that Jovian issued the
law. On Jovian's moderation in religious matters, see Themistius, *Orations* 5. For a discussion of Jovian's religious policy and the reasons for its moderation, see Noel Lenski, *Failure
of Empire: Valens and the Roman State in the Fourth Century A.D.* (Berkeley and Los Angeles: University of California Press, 2002), 104–5.

50. Libanius, *Oration* 30.7.

51. Theodoret, *Historia Ecclesiastica* 4.21. Epiphanius (*Adversus Haereses* 51.22.9–11)
makes a similar claim, that nocturnal sacrifices continued at Alexandria and Petra under
Valens. Theodoret spends much of book 4 creating a narrative in which the heretical Valens
permits all religious activity but that of Nicene orthodox leaders. At 4.21 he also claims that
Jovian restricted sacrifices only to have Valens again remove that restriction. There is no
independent evidence supporting this final claim.

52. The law of Valentinian and Valens is *Codex Theodosianus* 9.16.7, a probable reiteration of the law of Constantius excerpted at *Codex Theodosianus* 16.10.5.

53. Zosimus 4.3 (trans. R. Ridley, *Zosimus, New History,* [Sydney: Australian Association for Byzantine Studies, 1982]).

54. Ibid.

55. For discussion of the policies of Valentinian and Valens, see Lenski, *Failure* (above, n. 49), 216–18.

56. This is made clear from a reference to a now-lost law of Gratian in *Codex Theodosianus* 16.10.20.1 and also from Symmachus's *Relationes* 3. For discussion, see Alan Cameron, *The Last Pagans of Rome* (Oxford: Oxford University Press, 2011), 39–51.

57. For the Altar of Victory, see Symmachus, *Relationes* 3, and Cameron, *Last Pagans* (above, n. 56), 33–28. On the Vestals, see Rita Lizzi Testa, "Christian Emperor, Vestal Virgins, and Priestly Colleges: Reconsidering the End of Roman Paganism," *Antiquité Tardive* 15 (2007): 251–62. For the uneven application of these laws see *Inscriptiones Graecae* II/III² 4841 and 4842, both *taurobolion* commemorations erected in Athens after the laws were issued.

58. *Codex Theodosianus* 16.10.8.

59. Ibid. 16.10.9.

60. Ibid.

61. These are the actions complained about at length by Libanius in *Oration* 30. Also note Theodoret's profile of Marcellus of Apamea, who, he claims, helped Cyngeius destroy a large temple to Zeus in that city (*Historia Ecclesiastica* 5.21). For discussion, see John Matthews, *Western Aristocracies and Imperial Court* (Oxford: Clarendon Press, 1975), 140–42; Garth Fowden, "Bishops and Temples in the Eastern Roman Empire, AD 320–435," *Journal of Theological Studies* 29 (1979): 53–78.

62. *Historia Ecclesiastica* 5.20.

63. Ibid.

64. Prudentius, *Peristephanon* 2.473–84.

65. For Theodosius's persuasion as working better than coercion, see Gregory Nazianzen, *Carmina* 2.11.1292–1304. For superstition just collapsing on itself, see John Chrysostom, *In Babylam* 13.

66. *Codex Theodosianus* 16.10.10.

67. Ibid.

68. Ibid. 16.10.11.

69. Ibid. 16.10.12.2.

70. Cameron, *Last Pagans* (above, n. 56), 784; D. Riggs, "Paganism between the Cities and Countryside of Late Roman Africa," in *Urban Centers and Rural Contexts in Late Antiquity,* ed. T. Burns and J. Eadie (East Lansing, 2001), 285–300, and "Christianizing the Rural Communities of Late Roman Africa," in *Violence in Late Antiquity,* ed. H. Drake (Ashgate, 2006), 297–308.

71. Cameron, *Last Pagans* (above, n. 56), 784.

72. Augustine, *Sermon* 62.9. As Cameron (*Last Pagans* [above, n. 56], 785) rightly notes, *Codex Theodosianus* 16.10.17 and 18, both sent to Apollodorus the proconsul of Africa, seem to address this issue directly.

73. Ibid. 16.10.17.

74. Ibid. 16.10.19.3.

75. Ibid. 16.10.18.

76. Shenoute's actions against Gesios show the danger of allowing for such actions to be taken by private individuals. On this incident, see David Brakke, *Demons and the Making of the Monk: Spiritual Combat in Early Christianity* (Cambridge, Mass.: Harvard University Press, 2006), 97–98.

77. Rufinus, *Historia Ecclesiastica* 11.27–28; T. Orlandi, *Storia della Chiesa di Alessandria* (Milan: Cisalpino, 1970), 2.14.10–16.2; Sozomen, *Historia Ecclesiastica* 7.15. On the martyrium and church, note the important discussion of the archaeological evidence by McKenzie, Gibson, and Reyes, "Reconstructing" (above, n. 34), 107–10. In his discussion of the aftermath of the Serapeum's destruction, Eunapius describes Theophilus as "importing so-called monks into the sacred places" (*Vitae Sophistarum* 472) and then later mentions that he did this too at Canopus. This seems to suggest that Theophilus created two monasteries, one at the Alexandrian Serapeum complex and the other in Canopus. For the monastery, see Edward Watts, *Riot in Alexandria* (Berkeley and Los Angeles: University of California Press, 2010), 196–98.

78. Watts, *Riot* (above, n. 77), 8.

79. The tsunami in 363 certainly would have done more damage to Alexandrian temples than any imperial policy was capable of doing. Even so, there is no indication in any source of the degree of damage this caused to structures in the city, including those, like the former Caesareum, that sat alongside the harbor. On the tsunami, see Gavin Kelly, "Ammianus and the Great Tsunami," *Journal of Roman Studies* 94 (2004): 141–67.

80. For the bonfire, see Zacharias, *Vita Severi* 33. For the Tychaion statuary, see Theophylact Simocatta 8.7–15.

81. The abbot Shenoute and the former governor Gesios argued over the significance of one such private collection in the later fourth century. On the conflict with Gesios, note the two Shenoutean works *Not because a Fox Barks* and *Let Our Eyes*, both written around the year 400. Important in understanding this conflict is Stephen Emmel, "From the Other Side of the Nile: Shenute and Panopolis," in *Perspectives on Panopolis: An Egyptian Town from Alexander the Great to the Arab Conquest*, ed. A. Egberts, B. Muhs, and J. van der Vilet (Leiden: Brill, 2002), 95–113.

82. *Sermon* 91.2 (trans. B. Ramsey, slightly modified).

83. Gelasius, *Epistle* 100 (*Adversus Andromachum*, Corpus Scriptorum Ecclesiasticorum Latinorum, vol. 35.1 [Leipzig, Freytag, 1895], 453–64).

84. *Codex Theodosianus* 16.1.2. This law requires adherence to the "religion that the divine Peter the Apostle transmitted to the Romans, . . . the religion that is followed by Pontiff Damasus and by Peter, bishop of Alexandria." Orthodoxy is thus defined by agreement with specified church leaders.

85. For an alternative dating of this law, see Simon Corcoran, "Anastasius, Justinian, and the Pagans: A Tale of Two Law Codes and a Papyrus," *Journal of Late Antiquity* 2 (2009): 183–208.

86. *Codex Justinianus* 1.11.10. preface; ibid. 1.11.10.6.

87. Ibid. 1.11.10.1.

88. J. Segal, *Edessa, "The Blessed City"* (Oxford: Clarendon Press, 1970), 108.

11

Cleric

Kristina Sessa

Studies tell us that the emergence of the cleric as a distinct late ancient figure of authority was an organic and uneven process, shaped by gradual institutional development and social change.[1] As these studies point out, some of the first texts produced by Christian writers and communities refer to bishops ("overseers"), presbyters ("elders"), and deacons ("ministers"), whose roles were undefined but whose positions within their churches were recognized as special offices or as entailing special duties, at least some of the time. By the third century, the monoepiscopate had definitively emerged, and with it both the rise of the bishop as a church leader (even if his domain and authority were still very much in the making) and the hierarchical delineation of ecclesiastical offices. The fourth century witnessed even more profound transformations to the figure of the cleric. The large-scale entrance of elites (from provincial *curiales* to senatorial aristocrats) into the ranks of the church meant that new expectations of status, wealth, and education, along with (in some cases) novel legal and fiscal privileges, came to define clerical identity. Additionally, the formation of powerful ascetic discourses in this period further influenced how late antique Christians recognized the cleric as a category of late antique person

This chapter seeks not to undermine the standard narrative of the early Christian cleric (sketched in brief above) but to complicate it by placing knowledge—rather than office, status, asceticism, or authority—at the center of analysis. It attempts to answer two questions: How did one know that a man was a present or potential cleric in late antiquity? And how did a cleric recognize himself as a church leader? Rather than studying the cleric as a holder of church offices or as a type of late ancient elite (two popular scholarly approaches), this essay examines late Roman discursive frameworks for knowing clergy that emerged in the post-Constantinian period.[2] More specifically, it highlights one particular knowledge system, which identified men as clerics through sets of absolute and objective metrics, such as age, marital status, and time in office.[3] Whereas other scholars have studied these metrics in exhaustive and encyclopedic fashion, this study examines the epistemological discourse that generated and authorized them.[4]

KNOWLEDGE SYSTEMS AND
THE MAKING UP OF CLERICS

"Social change," writes the philosopher of science Ian Hacking, "creates new categories of people, but the counting is no mere report of developments. It elaborately, often philanthropically, creates new ways for people to be."[5] In his essay, "Making Up People," Hacking examines the dynamic interplay between naming and categorization in the invention of new types of people such as the homosexual and the split personality, both of whom, he and others have argued, did not exist as distinct categories of people before the nineteenth century.[6] For Hacking, the nominal creation of new classes of people (the act of naming them as a class or category) operates in tandem with the application of scientific modes of classification and measurement (e.g., census taking) to generate novel forms of personhood and being. "The category and the people," he explains, "emerged hand in hand."[7] This essay will argue that Christian clerics in late antiquity were also made-up people, in the sense that they were the product of complex and ongoing epistemological processes involving naming, classification, and measurement.

In order to examine Christian clerics in this manner, we must adjust what we mean by scientific modes of classification and measurements in order to fit within a late antique context. Whereas demographic censuses and biometrics were unknown in the premodern world, other knowledge systems existed that could be used to evaluate and measure the cleric as a distinct type of late ancient person. Specifically, we shall examine a cluster of juridical ideas and practices drawn from a wide body of sources produced by ecclesiastical and civil authorities. These laws, strictures, and rule-making acts show how Christian authorities endeavored to devise sets of objective criteria and absolute measurements, which could determine a man's eligibility and suitability to enter and advance within the clergy. The rules and conditions were organized around four primary rubrics: age and other chronological parameters, marital status, the physical body, and sociolegal conditions. The requirements and metrics associated with these categories constituted dynamic elements of an emergent knowledge system, which shaped the category of the cleric on both the general level (as a person who was part of the clergy) and the specific (as a person who occupied a particular place within the clergy: bishop, presbyter, deacon, acolyte, exorcist, and so on). These criteria and rules, in other words, helped create the cultural conditions in which a cleric, bishop, presbyter, or deacon became known in an objective sense to ecclesiastical and secular officials, and perhaps to the general Christian population. However, this essay also underlines some of the limitations of this knowledge system in a period when multiple systems coexisted for recognizing Christian leaders and when clerical identity remained contingent.

The discourse examined in this study appears in a wide body of highly programmatic texts, which were created, edited, redacted, translated, or circulated (or all of these) in the fourth, fifth, and sixth centuries. The corpus includes several church order documents, such as the *Didascalia Apostolorum,* the *Apostolic Constitutions,* the *Apostolic Canons,* conciliar acts, and episcopal correspondence, especially the letters of Roman prelates from Siricius (384–99) to Gelasius I (492–96). All these sources were created by and for ecclesiastical leaders, especially bishops. Because emperors too were active in formulating the parameters of clerical identity and promotion, imperial legislation will also be studied. The dating of these juridical and disciplinary sources from the fourth century is significant.[8] It suggests that this knowledge system emerged in large part with the rise of an imperial Christianity and in response to competing systems of clerical knowing that became increasingly influential in the decades following Constantine's conversion.

MAKING UP CLERICS
Naming the Cleric

In order to know a cleric, a nomenclature was needed. In fact, Christians had developed terms to denote their leaders from an early period. Words designating individual leaders (e.g., *episkopos, presbyteros, diakonos,* etc.) appear in some of our first Christian texts.[9] In the course of the third century, a terminology emerged, when denominations such as *klēros* or *klērikos* (and in Latin *clerus* or *clericus*) were first used in a more limited and technical manner to refer to Christian leaders collectively as members of a distinct group within the church.[10] During this time, authorities like Origen and Tertullian also began to draw regularly on an inherited priestly vocabulary—for example, *hiereus, sacerdos,* and *antistes*—to indicate presbyters and, more typically, bishops.[11]

Yet, despite the existence of names for Christian leaders (of which there were many: Cornelius of Rome's letter to Fabianus of Antioch mentions seven different types of leaders), early Christians did not agree on which were essential to the church or on their associated functions.[12] Nor did they concur in how to rank the positions or even whether the church was best organized hierarchically according to church offices.[13] There was a growing consensus that a single bishop should lead the whole community of Christians within a city, and that the church leadership was ideally ordered according to higher and lower offices.[14] However, what criteria made one recognizable as a particular type of cleric and under what terms and conditions a lower cleric might rise through the ranks to become a bishop had not been established universally.[15] There were undoubtedly local traditions that governed the leadership structures in specific communities. But these traditions were often opaque to outsiders. For example, in 313 Constantine's legal advisors saw the need to define the term *clericus* in one of the earliest imperial laws governing Christian leadership. Tellingly, their definition was vague and not especially Christian: "Those persons who devote the services of religion to divine worship—that is, those who are called clerics ["qui divino cultui ministeria religionis impendunt, id est hi, qui clerici appellantur"]."[16] The ambiguity was probably strategic. When Constantine personally adopted Christianity in the first decades of the fourth century, Christians had not collectively determined exactly who the *klērikoi* (or *clerici*) were; nor did they agree on how to objectively distinguish clerics from other Christian (and non-Christian) religious authorities. Naming, in other words, did not make the cleric a person.

Absolute Knowledge: Labeling the Cleric from Above

Emperors were not alone in their concern that Christian leadership required interpretation and definition. Church leaders too generated documents that endeavored to delineate the parameters of clerical identity. Like the imperial laws, these church orders, conciliar acts, and episcopal letters claimed to legislate the cleric into existence through the imposition of criteria and conditions said to emanate from high authorities. The church order documents purport to be the writings of the apostles and thus to preserve apostolic teachings on the correct conditions for clerical entrance and advancement.[17] The conciliar canons circulated as the collective utterances of bishops and clergy, and claimed to contain orthodox teachings of authoritative individual communities or the ecumenical church writ large.[18] Additionally, episcopal letters could be written as institutional pronouncements. Many of the Roman epistles examined here were encyclical letters sent to multiple sees or composed using language and rhetorical forms meant to mimic the authoritative utterances of the emperors in imperial rescripts.[19] In short, these sources rhetorically perform what Hacking called "labeling from above."[20] In late ancient Christian terms, this process of ordering and labeling could be imagined as a legislative effort initiated by God and enacted by his holiest disciples. Consider the following passage from the *Apostolic Constitutions*:[21]

> If there was no legislation [*thesmos*], no distinction of orders, it would have sufficed to group all under a single name; but being taught by the Lord the series of things, we distributed the function of the high priests to bishops, of the priests to the presbyters, and the ministration under them both to the deacons, . . . because God is not a god of disorder. . . . Moses, whom God loved, instituted the grand priests, priests, and

Levites [Exodus]; then our Savior instituted us, the thirteen apostles; then the apostles instituted us, me, Clement, and me, James, and others with us; . . . finally all those
together we instituted, the presbyters, the deacons, the subdeacons, and readers.

The *Apostolic Constitutions* presents (one particular) differentiated sequence of
clerics as constitutive of the cosmic order. The establishment of clerical identity
and status was thus understood as a divine mandate executed by human agents—
including the first generation of Christian bishops—whose rules governing clerics
mirrored and maintained sympathies between heaven and earth.

Objective Criteria and the Formation of the Clerical Cursus

Alongside pretensions to absolutism and universality, the knowledge system made
claims to objectivity. In 384, Siricius of Rome wrote a letter to Himerius of Tarra-
gona that presented his views on the conditions of eligibility and advancement "for
the most sacred orders of clerics" ("sacratissimi ordines clericorum"). In it, Siricius
delineated a streamlined path to the episcopate that was organized around life-
cycle stages, precise chronological criteria, and domestic conditions. For men
dedicated to ecclesiastical duties in their youth, Siricius prescribed the following
course: following baptism (to be performed "before the years of puberty") the candidate became a reader, and remained in this post "from the beginning of adolescence" (probably around fourteen years old) to the age of thirty. At thirty, he
became an acolyte and a subdeacon. Thereafter, "if he lives properly, content with
only one wife whom he received as a virgin with public benedictions from a priest
[*sacerdos*]," he advanced to the grade of deacon. After five years as a deacon, the
cleric was eligible for the presbyterate, an office that he must undertake for ten
years. Thereafter, the cleric was "able to reach the episcopal office, provided that
during these times the integrity of his life and faith was demonstrated."[22]

Scholars of ecclesiastical history call attention to Siricius's letter in light of its
clear presentation of what is frequently called the clerical *cursus*.[23] They borrow the
term *cursus* from Roman political history, wherein the *cursus honorum* denotes
the successive offices and age requirements structuring the civic careers of Roman
statesmen.[24] Like the Roman magisterial course, Siricius's path to the episcopate
includes age and other temporal conditions, and it presents advancement as a
sequential progression (from lector to acolyte or subdeacon to deacon to presbyter
to bishop). However, it also demands specific marital conditions for advancement,
which were not part of the Roman civic system, and its chronology is far more
detailed. Thus, although it is not entirely inappropriate to view Siricius's version of
clerical advancement as a Christianized *cursus honorum,* we do better to compare
it with other late ancient Christian discourses of clerical identity.

Traditionally, early Christian thinkers defined their leaders in ethical terms,
through the observed performance of behaviors that were understood to reflect

and inflect moral values.[25] Within this knowledge system, the perceived conduct of a man was the key variable in assessing his suitability for specific church posts. Consider the earliest ethical profile of a bishop, from 1 Timothy 3:1–7:

> Now a bishop must be beyond reproach, the husband of one wife, temperate, sensible, dignified, hospitable, an apt teacher, no drunkard, not violent but gentle, no lover of money. He must manage his own household well, keeping his children submissive and respectful in every way . . . He must not be a recent convert, . . . [and] he must be well thought-of by outsiders, or he may fall into reproach and into the snare of the devil.

Apart from the requirement for a single marriage to a virgin and the prohibition against neophytes, all the conditions listed in 1 Timothy are subjective, in the sense that they cannot be measured in any absolute or definitive sense. They can be assessed only through another person's reading of the man's conduct—a facet of this particular discourse that is explicitly acknowledged in the final sentence regarding the opinions of those outside the community (which evidently mattered too). An ethical mode of evaluation was both ancient and commonplace. Greeks, Romans, and Jews had long used moral standards to assess the strengths and weaknesses of men in power and their ability to govern. Late ancient Christian writers too drew on ethical discourses for identifying and evaluating clerics, especially in treatises on the priesthood and pastoral care, which present philosophically inflected programs on the ideal personality, conduct, and attitude of a church official.[26] They emphasize criteria such as speech, comportment, and education, and they recommend diagnostic tools such as physiognomy for determining who was the right man for the job.[27] Ambrose, for example, rejected a man vying for the episcopate despite his proven record of good acts because his gestures were too unseemly.[28]

Alternatively, Siricius's path to the episcopate rests primarily on concrete metrics, specific ages, and periods of time served in office, and precise marital conditions (including the blessing of the union by a priest or bishop), which were not, on one level at least, dependent upon another person's point of view. A cleric was either thirty years old or he was not; a deacon had either married once or he had not; his wife was either a virgin at the time of marrying or she was not; a bishop had either spent a minimum of ten years as a presbyter or he had not, and so on. In other words, claims to seemingly incontrovertible forms of knowledge—what we may call "facts"—are what made this particular discourse of clerical identity objective and hence different from the more subjective ethical discourse. To be sure, Christian authorities debated some of these facts in late antiquity and argued passionately for alternative interpretations of seemingly straightforward conditions, like the meaning of one wife for a cleric.[29] Nevertheless, Siricius and other bishops intended their facts to function as objective measurements, independent of subjective ethical analysis, which could differentiate a cleric from a noncleric, a lector from a bishop.

Classifying, Enumerating, and Replicating the Cleric

In addition to assertions of absolutism and objectivity, the system organized knowledge about clergy in a manner that was evocative of late Roman legal writing. To be clear, few documents fully systematized the conditions and criteria for clerical entry and advancement to the same extent as the Theodosian or Justinianic codes. However, they share with these collections three rhetorical features: classification, enumeration, and replication. Siricius, for example, laid out not one but three paths to the episcopate: one for children vowed to the church from their youth, another for former monks, and a third for lay adults who entered the church at midlife. Each path was tailored to reflect the original status of the candidate. Siricius, in other words, classified clerical advancement according to the cleric's individual status at entry to the church. Many of his Roman successors adopted similar classification systems for episcopal candidates, as did Justinian in his extensive law on religious personnel.[30]

Moreover, the discourse typically enumerated and replicated the conditions and criteria that defined them. The *Apostolic Constitutions* and *Apostolic Canons,* and the *Statuta Ecclesiae Antiqua,* a late fifth-century Gallic church order, combine discussions of ecclesiastical conditions (some of which are ethical) with numbered lists of canons that delineate objective rules. Some Roman episcopal letters read like veritable checklists for clerical entry and advancement, which repeated criteria laid out in the earlier writings of Roman bishops, including their own previous correspondence.[31] "May no one accede to the sacred orders who is married twice," proclaimed Gelasius, "who married a wife who is not a virgin, who is illiterate, or vitiated in any part of the body, or a former penitent, or designated for the curia or for any bonded condition [*obnoxium*] whatsoever."[32] A similar dynamic of replication can be seen in the *Statuta Ecclesiae Antiqua,* which reproduces criteria delineated in earlier Greek church orders and Western synodal decisions.[33] The rhetorical tenor of the knowledge system thus reveals a strong interest among certain Christian authorities to define clerical identity in terms that were both highly precise and resoundingly legal, even if they were open to interpretation—a point to which we shall return.

Age and Other Chronological Classifications

Beginning in the fourth century, Christian authorities began to create fixed chronological requirements for the clerical orders. Although considerable variation existed between churches (and even among bishops within a particular see), there was a developing consensus that time should be a metric in the making up of clerics.[34] Two types of temporal conditions emerged. First, Christian authorities defined minimum age requirements for advancement to a particular office or for general entrance into the ecclesiastical order. The *Didascalia Apostolorum* stated that a man must be at least fifty years old before entering the episcopate, and the councils of Neocaesarea (314) and Seleucia (410) ruled that thirty was the appropriate minimum age for a presbyter.[35] The African clergy at the Council of Hippo, in 393, held that the minimum age for becoming a cleric (position unspecified) was twenty-five, and just four years later bishops at Carthage pronounced this to be the minimum age for deacons.[36] According to Siricius's rubrics, a man dedicated to the church from birth could not reach the presbyterate before thirty-five and the episcopate before forty-five.[37] Alternatively, Caesarius of Arles (ca. 468–542) claimed that southern Gallic churches customarily forbade men to advance to the deaconate and presbyterate before thirty years.[38] Emperors too decreed minimal ages for clerics. An imperial law issued in 390 stipulated that a woman must be sixty years old to become a deaconess, whereas another from 528 stated that a bishop and presbyter could be no younger than thirty-five, a deacon and subdeacon twenty-five, a reader eighteen, and a deaconess forty.[39]

Second, clerics were often required to spend an established period of time in an office before advancing to the next level. Siricius demanded that men remain readers from "the age of adolescence" to the age of thirty, thus for approximately fifteen years, and to be deacons for five and presbyters for another ten years before becoming bishops. Zosimus presented a somewhat different time frame (demanding only five years as a reader, four as a subdeacon or acolyte, and five as a deacon), whereas Gelasius recommended an especially compressed path, requiring only a few months in lower offices and a few years in the deaconate and presbyterate.[40] In a few cases, lay adults aspiring to the episcopate were required to endure a waiting period before they could enter the lowest level of church orders.[41]

Marital Conditions

Requirements governing the marriages and sexual practices of clerics and clerical candidates are arguably the oldest criteria for clerical identity.[42] The first and most fundamental was a single marriage. The author of 1 Timothy commanded that all bishops and deacons must be the "husband of one wife" (thereby restricting the general Pauline injunction to these particular church leaders).[43] Siricius, we recall, made a single marriage a criterion for all acolytes and subdeacons, whereas Innocent I required it for all clergy.[44] Linked to the single-marriage requirement was the condition of a virgin wife: men who wished to advance up the clerical ranks would have to have married virgins. These two rules are repeated passim in numerous church order documents, in multiple ecclesiastical conciliar *acta,* and in an array of episcopal correspondence, much of which emanated from Rome.[45] Additional marital strictures emerged in late antiquity. For instance, while lower clerics were permitted to marry in some communities (so long as it was their first marriage and they wed virgins), higher clerics (from the deaconate) were often prohibited from forging unions after ordination.[46] Moreover, some patristic writers and church councils demanded that married clerics who aspired to higher orders (i.e., the episcopate, the presbyterate, the deaconate, and, from the fifth century in Italy and Gaul, the subdeaconate) renounce all sexual relations with their wives on a permanent basis.[47] For the most part, the celibacy requirement was limited to Western churches, although in 528 it was indirectly extended to Eastern clerics when Justinian ruled that no man with a family or children could become a bishop.[48]

Physical State

Clerics were supposed to have a particular type of body. Specifically, their bodies had to be physically whole: that is, visibly free from disfiguring blemishes, cuts, or mutilations.[49] Several ecclesiastical councils, including the Council of Nicaea, expressly forbade self-castrated men from entering the clerical orders.[50] Other forms of self-mutilation or willful cutting were also prohibited.[51] Innocent pronounced that men who deliberately severed a finger could not be admitted *ad clerum,* and the *Statuta Ecclesiae Antiqua* commanded that a *clericus* could neither shave his beard nor comb his hair.[52] Exceptions, however, were legislated. At Nicaea, for example, the bishops forbade autocastrati from entering the clergy, but they welcomed men unwillingly maimed by their masters.[53] Alternatively, two of the *Apostolic Constitutions* proscribed the blind, deaf-mute, and those possessed by demons from the episcopal office, but another permitted those with poor eyesight or who were crippled.[54]

Legal, Fiscal, and Social Criteria

Christians in late antiquity developed legal and social criteria to govern access to and advancement within the clergy. These criteria were for the most part negative: they consisted of prohibitions against men who had certain legal, fiscal, and professional statuses from joining the clergy and rising through its ranks. They were, in other words, rules about the sort of man a cleric could not be. For example, many sources preclude soldiers or men who had committed grave crimes from joining the clergy. More consistently, ecclesiastical and imperial authorities banned slaves and other obligated laborers (i.e., *coloni* or *originarii*) from becoming clerics at any level of the church order without their master or landowner's permission.[55] As Leo I lamented in a letter to Italian bishops in 443, "men are commonly admitted to the sacred order who are not qualified by any dignity of birth or character; even those who have failed to obtain freedom from their masters are raised to the rank of the priesthood, as if slavish worthlessness might take this honor."[56] To be clear, Leo's issue was not with slaves per se as episcopal candidates but with slaves and laborers who joined the clergy in order to escape their masters.[57] What he and other authorities protested was a process of making up clerics that came at the financial expense of an unwilling landowner.[58]

In addition to prohibitions against the ordination of slaves and tenant laborers who joined the clergy to evade their condition, the sources increasingly limited access for decurions. The regulation of curial participation in the clergy is a complex matter, for it relates directly to the distribution of lucrative and honor-generating fiscal privileges by emperors to Christian clerics. Beginning with Constantine, Roman emperors exempted clerics from many compulsory public duties, which had traditionally been undertaken by the *curiales*. These fiscal exemptions for clerics of curial status had important social resonance, since such exemptions were typically bestowed upon former palatine administrators or military officials and hence constituted a distinct type of honor.[59] In this respect, the imperial rules governing the fiscal obligations of clerics had a direct impact on their formation as a type of late antique person. A cleric was, by imperial definition, a man exempt from onerous civic duties, and by the nature of this exemption, he shared a position of status with other, more traditional elites.

However, the exemptions generated problems for the state, since the movement of decurions into the church orders led to some loss of civic support.[60] Emperors, including Constantine, consequently scaled back the generous exemptions and erected new boundaries between the curia and the clergy. These laws constituted additional criteria for becoming a cleric, involving wealth limits and oversight. According to fourth-century legislation, *curiales* seeking clerical positions were mandated either to transmit their wealth to family members still legally bound to support the state or to provide a substitute to undertake their duties.[61] In 452, Valentinian III pressed such regulation further by prohibiting any *curialis* from joining the clergy who owned property that was worth more than three hundred *solidi*.[62] In short, imperial legislation governing the *curiales* directly contributed to clerical definition: a cleric may have had a curial background and shared an elite fiscal status with senators, but he also had to meet (maximum) property limits and be no longer financially obligated to the civic community.[63]

RECOGNIZING AND MISRECOGNIZING THE CLERIC

The process of making up the cleric was discursive. It involved the delineation and replication of a distinct knowledge system. This knowledge system differed from other contemporary systems in that it was predicated upon sets of conditions and requirements that could be evaluated—theoretically, at least—without recourse to an individual's subjective perceptions or particular point of view. Epistemologically, therefore, the discourse was objective, in the most basic sense of the term. Rhetorically speaking, it was produced and disseminated through juridical sources, texts that were conceived and created as rule books, whose content was succinctly enumerated and itemized rather than expansively discussed or dialectically debated. Ideologically, the discourse presented itself as a consummately elite knowledge system, designed by apostles, emperors, and bishops to harmonize ecclesiastical leadership with the hierarchical ordering of state, society, and cosmos.

But to what extent did this knowledge system enable Christians to recognize a man as a cleric or a particular type of church leader? And to what degree did they shape how men recognized themselves as clerics? Unsurprisingly perhaps, we possess limited evidence for how it operated in actual circumstances, especially on the level of individual subjectivities. On the one hand, epitaphic evidence strongly suggests that late antique clerics increasingly self-identified with their church offices. A recent study of epitaphs from Asia Minor catalogues numerous cases in which men chose to highlight their ecclesiastical posts rather than a *gentilicium*, suggesting that church office increasingly came to connote social standing.[64] In a few cases, clerics sequentially listed past offices on their tombstones, ostensibly to underline their proper advancement through the grades of the church.[65] And in Italy at least, the vast majority of bishops had previously served as either presbyters or deacons, suggesting that the clerical *cursus* oriented promotion to some extent.[66] On the other hand, there is no record of a man's being proclaimed bishop simply because he met all the conditions and criteria outlined above. Nor do we have testimony from clerics who defined their status exclusively in terms of these criteria. Rather, the sources suggest a far less systematic reality, where an objective knowledge system coexisted with other ways of knowing a cleric.

Consider the case of Valerius Pinianus, would-be presbyter and husband of Melania the Younger. When the citizens of Hippo attempted to co-opt Pinianus into the priesthood around 411, they did not choose the wealthy senator in light of his sequential advancement through the lower orders of the clergy, since Pinianus was a layman. His property and connections, Augustine sheepishly admitted, were significant factors in the public press for his ordination.[67] However, Pinianus did meet other criteria that may also have recommended him. He easily surpassed the minimum age set by the Council of Hippo in 393 for entrance to the clergy.[68] Moreover, he possessed the right social and marital conditions: not only was he not a *curialis* (nor a slave or *colonus*, for that matter), but he was also a once-married man, who reputedly had already adopted a celibate marriage.[69] And although our sources do not positively attest to the integrity of his physical state, they make no mention of disqualifying disfigurements. Thus, although Pinianus failed to meet all the requirements delineated in sources, he nevertheless fulfilled several key conditions associated with the presbyterate. It is possible, therefore, that for these reasons (among others) Pinianus was especially recognizable to the general public as a good choice for the priesthood. Yet from his own perspective, Pinianus was misrecognized as a priest: despite his qualifications, he did not self-identify as a cleric, and he successfully resisted ordination.

More commonly, late ancient authorities used the rules and requirements described above in a disciplinary capacity, as a means to disqualify or remove (or both) an inappropriate candidate from the clerical order. Here we see labeling from above in action. Roman bishops, for instance, rejected men who failed to comply with their church's emergent rules governing marriage and celibacy. Some even used local informants to keep tabs on the sexual activities of suffragan clerics in Italy, and when news came of a blatant breach, they demanded hearings and appropriate action (which ranged from demotion to deposition) against the offending priest.[70] Local bishops also used objective criteria to determine the fitness of already ordained clerics to fulfill their offices. For example, around 494 Gelasius received a petition from a Tuscan presbyter named Stephanus who had suffered a disfiguring mutilation and was consequently deposed by his bishop.[71] Stephanus had evidently protested his deposition and asked the Roman bishop to intervene. In this case, a prelate rejected a priest as a cleric because of his failure to fulfill an objective condition. However, the case also testifies to the possible disjuncture between an objective knowledge system and internalized self-understanding: Stephanus, who formally protested his removal, obviously still considered himself to be a legitimate presbyter despite his bodily disfigurement. Objective conditions thus presented a means for bishops to control access to and advancement within the church orders, but they did not fully shape how clerics viewed themselves or how others viewed them.

A DISCOURSE IN COMPETITION AND FLUX

In a letter to the bishops of Mauretania, Leo of Rome responded to a request from unnamed parties for guidance in recognizing clerics. Apparently a great deal of misrecognition had ensued in Africa, and Leo was vexed at the rapid ordination of adult laymen, especially those with inappropriate marriages. In the letter, Leo highlighted objective conditions as the most certain means to know a true cleric. Ordination to the priesthood (*sacerdotium*), he insisted, should commence only after men had reached the proper age, and had been tested during a lengthy service in lower offices, when proofs of uprightness could be witnessed.[72] Here temporal requirements served both as a means of ensuring that the right men reached the highest levels of the church and as a mechanism for blocking laymen who sought to leapfrog into the episcopate. Although Leo hinted at the possibilities for the training and education of clerics in the lower offices, he was more concerned to establish a lengthier and more certain process for character assessment. Ethics, in other words, were not absent from Leo's program for knowing clerics, but he and other Christian authorities reasoned that they were best evaluated within an objective framework (i.e., time served and offices held).[73] However, Leo also registered some discomfort with subjective knowledge. Elsewhere in the letter he privileged the fulfillment of concrete rules over the possession of ethical qualities. "Though a man may be endowed with good character and furnished with holy works," he explained, "he may nevertheless in no way ascend either to the grade of deacon or the dignity of the presbytery, or to the highest rank of the bishop if it has been spread abroad either that he himself is not the husband of one wife, or that his wife is not the wife of one husband."[74] For Leo, a deeply legalistic thinker, the recommended marital conditions were biblical injunctions, legislated in the Hebrew Bible and by Paul. (He cites both Leviticus and 1 Timothy.)[75] They were also more certain indexes of morality and thus took precedence over imprecise personal characteristics, which could be assessed only subjectively by fellow clerics. After all, one could misread character, as Augustine had famously done when he promoted a young monk named Antoninus to the see of Fussala.[76] Objective rules—especially those undersigned by biblical or apostolic authorities—were a far more definite path to recognizing a true priest.

Of course, Leo's reactions to the Africans were political as much as they were epistemological. His subordination of moral display to the fulfillment of concrete conditions must also be read as an apology aimed at other clerics, who insisted that a man's conduct and character ought to determine his fitness to lead the church. Writing at a great distance from the Mauritanian churches, Leo wished to avoid a muddled debate with the North Africans over the morality and behavior of men whom he would never know personally. Insisting on a set of objective, juridical criteria avoided the hermeneutic challenges of ethical evaluation and thus allowed Leo to assert his authority from afar. In fact, Roman bishops were arguably the most dedicated architects of this developing juridical knowledge system. Scholars have often misread Rome's involvement in clerical definition as evidence of an already powerful position, arguing that their letters constitute early canon law and had monolithic impact on the trajectory of the clerical order in the West. However, Leo's deliberate disaggregation of the objective from the subjective was a defensive gesture, made at a moment when many Christians, including many bishops, believed that the process of making up clerics ought to be grounded in ethical truth claims. Although it was a rhetorical effect (as we have seen, no single knowledge system could determine definitively who was or was not a cleric), an objective process for identifying legitimate clerics nevertheless offered certain political advantages because of its strong resonances with both imperial administrative dynamics and a conception of God as the ultimate legislator of the ecclesiastical order.

A PLIANT SYSTEM: WAR AND ITS AFFECT ON THE MAKING UP OF CLERICS

Yet as Leo himself undoubtedly recognized, even the most seemingly concrete facts for determining clerical status could be subject to interpretation (or reinterpretation). In this respect, the discourse cohered with the dynamics of late Roman law. Like late ancient imperial legislation, ecclesiastical decisions and episcopal disciplinary measures were reactive and responsive formulations.[77] They were also impossible to enforce on anything like a universal level. Consequently, perhaps, the specific criteria governing clerical entrance and advancement varied enormously on the level of detail across time and space. Moreover, authorities could and did introduce changes when circumstances required. The letters of the late fifth-century Roman bishop Gelasius speak to these precise dynamics. Gelasius, as we have already seen, replicated an inherited system for knowing clerics that depended upon concrete conditions and criteria. He clearly believed that objectively ascertained facts were preferable to subjectively assessed ethics when it came to governing clerical entrance and advancement within the hundreds of Italian churches that he oversaw. However, when faced with a shortage of clerics to serve Italy's churches following a war between Odoacer and Theoderic over control of the peninsula (489–93), Gelasius amended the received system.[78] While maintaining the general epistemological framework, Gelasius radically shortened the time-served and age conditions for clerical advancement. Instead of requiring thirty years in various clerical offices, Gelasius allowed a monk or adult layman to sequentially advance to the episcopate after only a few years.[79]

More striking was Gelasius's response to Stephanus, the mutilated Italian presbyter discussed above. Stephanus was also a casualty of the war, his injuries inflicted by an unidentified group of barbarian soldiers. His bishop's decision to depose him was entirely in accordance with the knowledge system: a man with physical disfigurements was theoretically unrecognizable as a cleric. Stephanus, we recall, had appealed his bishop's decision and petitioned Gelasius (who stood in the place of his metropolitan) to reverse the decision.[80] In Gelasius's response, he acknowledged the importance of physical integrity in the process of selecting and ordaining men to the priesthood. But he nevertheless sided with Stephanus. The injuries, Gelasius reasoned, were sustained after Stephanus became a presbyter and thus could not disqualify him from the post. Gelasius's response was certainly compassionate, not to mention pragmatic (it prevented the loss of yet another high cleric). But it speaks to the inherent fluidity of the knowledge system. Its malleability was perhaps its most important feature, for it meant that authorities could recalibrate the system without dismantling it altogether.

CONCLUSIONS

Instead of approaching the late ancient Christian cleric as a new type of elite, an officeholder, or an ascetic, this essay has explored a system of knowledge that made the cleric legible in late Roman society, both to others and perhaps to himself. As emphasized, there was no single dominant discourse for knowing clerics in late antiquity. Rather, (at least) two coexisted and were sometimes in tension: a subjective system grounded in ethical judgments and an objective system based on ostensibly universalizing facts of identity. Whereas considerable scholarly attention has been paid to the first system, the second has remained largely unexplored. By placing the question of knowledge at the center of its analysis, this chapter has made a case for seeing the formation of clerical identity in late antiquity in a new way.

An objective knowledge system helped form the cleric as a particular type of late antique person. It delineated a set of qualifying conditions and criteria, organized into classes, listed in canons, laws, and letters, and reproducible across time and space, which presented Christians with a means for recognizing a true cleric and distinguishing him from other religious leaders. Although Jews and pagans recognized requirements for priestly status that might be deemed objective, neither defined the priesthood through the same (or even a similar) matrix of chronological, marital, physical, and sociolegal conditions.[81] More important, the discourse's finite claims, its presentation of clerical identity in terms of enumerated facts and concrete metrics, were powerful tools in the contest for spiritual and ecclesiastical authority among Christians. They constituted a system for recognizing legitimate (and for rejecting illegitimate) church officials, a system that differed in form and substance from other prevailing late ancient systems, notably those based on ethics and subjective techniques of moral diagnosis. Whereas monks might be known for their exemplary behavior and feats of renunciation, Christian clerics were theoretically identifiable by their age, time in office, marital status, physical state, and sociolegal condition. Ethics (and asceticism, for that matter) remained components of the objective system, but they were subsumed within an epistemological framework that privileged empirical knowledge over perceptions of excellence.

This new and alternative system thus presented a means for seeing the clergy as a distinct and unique body of religious authorities. Such a system had obvious advantages for an already established state. (To what extent early imperial legislation on clerics or laws governing entrance to military service or the civil administration, or both, served as models for the knowledge system developed by ecclesiastical authorities demands further attention than has been given here.)[82] It was also potentially advantageous for a religion that was not yet a hegemonic institution but, rather, was a network of hierarchically ordered communities that only circumstantially viewed themselves as members of a single church. In this respect, the epistemological process of making up clerics went hand in hand with the institutional vicissitudes of making up the church.

Nevertheless, Stephanus's tumultuous experiences as a presbyter remind us that the cleric remained a contingent person in late antiquity and that many aspects of clerical identity were in flux. In short, the facts of clerical status did not dictate in any absolute ontological sense who was or was not a minister of the church. The people of Hippo collectively recognized Valerius Pinianus as a potential presbyter, but Pinianus rejected their assessment and successfully resisted ordination. And although the mutilated Stephanus recognized himself as a presbyter (going so far as to appeal his deposition), his local bishop disagreed. For him, the head of an unremarkable see in suburbicarian Italy, who was undoubtedly eager to demonstrate his adherence to Rome's earlier pronouncements, the objective system proved deterministic in his approach to recognizing clerics. Alternatively, for Gelasius, who faced the challenge of filling vacant churches, it was possible to amend received knowledge without dismantling the entire system. By allowing Stephanus to remain a priest, Gelasius tacitly acknowledged that objective requirements were helpful guides but not always definitive markers of clerical identity. Moreover, his willingness to permit even adult laymen to reach the episcopate with only a few years of experience suggests an understanding that clerical offices amounted to part-time positions, performed alongside more traditional (and more consuming) practices of everyday life. In late antiquity, clerics were also husbands, fathers, brothers, and sons, as well as landowners, merchants, small farmers, doctors, and artisans.[83] Clerics, in other words, were persons with multiple social allegiances, roles, and financial obligations, for whom serving the church was perhaps a calling but not yet a day job.[84] The objective knowledge system described in this essay, therefore, represents an attempt by Christian authorities to produce a distinct clerical person precisely at a moment when ecclesiastical identity was contested and in flux.

NOTES

1. The literature on early Christian ministries and ecclesiastical orders is vast, but see Gregory Dix, "The Ministry in the Early Church," in *The Apostolic Ministry,* ed. K. Kirk (London: Hodder and Stoughton, 1946), 185–303; Hans von Campenhausen, *Ecclesiastical Authority and Spiritual Power in the First Three Centuries,* trans. J. A. Baker (Stanford: Stanford University Press, 1969); Alexandre Faivre, *Naissance d'une hiérarchie: Les premières étapes du cursus clérical* (Paris: Beauchesne, 1977); Allen Brent, *Hippolytus and the Roman Church in the Third Century: Communities in Tension before the Emergence of a Monarch-Bishop,* Supplements to Vigiliae Christianae, vol. 31 (Leiden: Brill, 1995); Paul Bradshaw, *The Search for the Origins of Christian Worship* (Oxford: Oxford University Press, 2002); and Claudia Rapp, *Holy Bishops in Late Antiquity: The Nature of Christian Leadership in an Age of Transition* (Berkeley and Los Angeles: University of California Press, 2005).

2. On the Christian cleric as a new type of elite, see generally Peter Brown, "The Study of Elites in Late Antiquity," *Arethusa* 33 (2000): 321–46; and on bishops, see Claudia Rapp, "The Elite Status of Bishops in Late Antiquity in Ecclesiastical, Spiritual, and Social Contexts," *Arethusa* 33 (2000): 379–99; and Rita Lizzi Testa, "Privilegi economici e definizione di status: Il caso del vescovo tardoantico," *Rendiconti dell'Accademia Nazionale dei Lincei, Classe di Scienze Morali, Storiche, e Filologiche,* ser. 9, 11 (2000): 55–103, and "The Bishop as *Vir Venerabilis*: Fiscal Privileges and Status Definition in Late Antiquity," *Studia Patristica* 34 (2001): 125–44.

3. By "knowledge system" I mean a set of interacting prescriptive components that made a man recognizable to others as a Christian cleric. These components comprised both positive assertions (a cleric must be *X*) and negative preclusions (a cleric must not be *Y*). They collectively constituted an epistemological framework for determining whether an individual was a true Christian cleric.

4. See, for example, Jean Gaudemet, *L'église dans l'empire romain* (Paris: Sirey, 1958), 99–185; Paul-Henri Lafontaine, *Les conditions positives de l'accession aux ordres dans la première legislation ecclésiastique (300–492)* (Ottawa: Éditions de l'Université d'Ottawa, 1963); and Faivre, *Naissance* (above, n. 1). In this essay, I shall focus on a handful of metrics in order to illustrate my argument about the wider discourse.

5. Ian Hacking, "Making Up People," in *Historical Ontology* (Cambridge, Mass.: Harvard University Press, 2002), 100.

6. Cf. Michel Foucault, *The History of Sexuality*, trans. M. Hurley, vol. 1 (New York: Pantheon Books, 1978).

7. Hacking, *Historical Ontology* (above, n. 5), 107.

8. In dating the *Didascalia Apostolorum* to the fourth century, I follow Alistair Stewart-Sykes, *The Didascalia Apostolorum: An English Version with Introduction and Annotation* (Turnhout: Brepols 2009), 5–55. The *Apostolic Constitutions* and *Apostolic Canons* were produced in the late fourth century (ca. 380 C.E.).

9. Cf. Philippians 1:1 and 1 Corinthians 12; 1 Clement 40–44; 1 Timothy 3:5, 4:4, 5:1; Titus 2:21–27; and Didache 15:2.

10. Clement of Alexandria, *Quis Dives Salvetur* 42; Origen, *In Jeremiam* 11.3; Cyprian, *Epistles* 29, 49, and 50 (ed. G. Diercks, Corpus Christianorum, Series Latina, vol. 3B [Turnhout: Brepols, 1994], 137–38, 231–37, and 238–39). The *Apostolic Tradition* uses *klēros* or *klērikos* in precisely this manner. (Cf. 3.4–5, 7.) The Greek *klēros* originally meant "lot" or "apportioned share." Etymologies of the Christian meaning of *klēros* (or Latin *clerus*) varied widely in late antiquity: cf. Jerome, *Epistles* 52 (ed. I. Hilberg, Corpus Scriptorum Ecclesiasticorum Latinorum, vol. 54.1 [Vienna: Tempsky, 1910], 413–41), and Augustine, *Ennarrationes in Psalmos* 67.19.

11. *Hiereus* or *sacerdos:* Tertullian, *De Baptismo* 17; Cyprian, *Epistles* (above, n. 10) 1.1.1 and 61.3; Origen, *Homiliae in Leviticum* 6 and *Homiliae in Ezechielem* 9.2. Further examples and discussion in Christine Mohrmann, "L'étude du grec et du latin de l'antiquité chrétienne," in *Études sur le latin des chrétiens*, vol. 4 (Rome, 1977), 9–10, and "*Episkopos-Speculator*," ibid. 251–52.

12. Eusebius, *Historia Ecclesiastica* 6.43.11.

13. Some Gnostic communities, for example, were organized according to teacher-student relationships. These were obviously also hierarchical, but in a different manner from the emergent ecclesiastical model.

14. Brent, *Hippolytus* (above, n. 1), and Paul Bradshaw, *Early Christian Worship: A Basic Introduction to Ideas and Practice* (Minneapolis: Liturgical Press, 2010).

15. Multiple versions of the clerical hierarchy circulated in late antiquity. For example, whereas *Apostolic Traditions* 1–9 presented a church led by the bishop, presbyters, deacons, confessors, widows, virgins, and subdeacons, the *Didascalia Apostolorum* recognized only the bishop, presbyters, deacons, widows, and deaconesses. See Sabine Hübner, *Der Klerus in*

der Gesellschaft des spätantiken Kleinasiens (Stuttgart: Steiner, 2005), 27–30, and Faivre, *Naissance* (above, n. 1).

16. *Codex Theodosianus* 16.2.2 (313). The law exempted all *clerici* from compulsory public service, a development discussed below.

17. Joseph G. Mueller, "The Ancient Church Order Literature: Genre or Tradition?" *Journal of Early Christian Studies* 15 (2007): 337–80, and Stewart-Sykes, *Didascalia Apostolorum* (above, n. 8), 3.

18. On the institutional pretensions of church councils and conciliar acts, see Richard Lim, *Public Disputation, Power, and Social Order in Late Antiquity* (Berkeley and Los Angeles: University of California Press, 1995).

19. Philip McShane, *La romanitas et le pape Léon le Grand: L'apport culturel des institutions impérials à la formation des structures ecclésiastiques* (Montreal: Bellarmin, 1979).

20. Hacking, "Making Up People" (above, n. 5), 111.

21. *Constitutiones Apostolorum* 8.46.10–13. *Constitutiones Apostolorum* 8,46.10-13 (ed. M. Metzger, *Les Constitutions Apostoliques*, 3 vols., Sources Chrétiennes 320, 329, 336 [Paris: Les Éditions du Cerf, 1985–87]). Translation adopted from Metzger, *Les Constitutions Apostoliques*, vol. 3, 269–71.

22. Siricius, *Epistles* 1.13 (ed. J.-P. Migne, *Patrologia Cursus Completus, Series Latina* [hereafter *PL*], vol. 20 [Paris, 1862], 1142–43).

23. Lafontaine, *Conditions positives* (above, n. 4), 150–53; Faivre, *Naissance* (above, n. 1); and John H. St. Gibaut, *The Cursus Honorum: A Study of the Origins and Evolution of Sequential Ordination* (New York: Lang, 2000).

24. See Andrew Lintott, *The Constitution of the Roman Republic* (Oxford: Clarendon Press, 1999), 144–46.

25. As emphasized by Rapp, *Holy Bishops* (above, n. 1).

26. See Chrysostom, *On the Priesthood,* and Ambrose, *De Officiis.*

27. On physiognomy, ethics, and power, see Maud Gleason, *Making Men: Sophists and Self-Presentation in Ancient Rome* (Princeton: Princeton University Press, 1994).

28. Ambrose, *De Officiis* 1.18.72.

29. On the debate among Christian clerics over the meaning of "one wife," see Kristina Sessa, *The Formation of Papal Authority in Late Antique Italy: Roman Bishops and the Domestic Sphere* (Cambridge: Cambridge University Press, 2012), 183–84; and Geoffrey Dunn, "Clerical Marriage in the Letters of Late Antique Roman Bishops," in *Men and Women in Early Christian Centuries,* ed. W. Mayer and I. Elmer, Early Christian Studies, vol. 18 (St. Strathfield: Saint Paul's Publications, 2014), 297–317.

30. Cf. Innocent, *Epistles* 3.6 (*PL* 20.492–93), Zosimus, *Epistles* 9.1 (*PL* 20.671), and Gelasius, *Epistles* 14.2–3 (Andreas Thiel, *Epistolae Romanorum Pontificum Genuinae et Quae ad Eos Scriptae Sunt a Sancto Hilaro usque ad Pelagium II* [Braunsberg: Peter, 1868], 362–64), who all recognized two rather than three classes of episcopal candidates. In Justinian, *Novellae* 123.1 (546), the emperor recognized four categories: those who were already clerics, laymen, monks, and former *curiales* who had subsequently become monks.

31. *Epistles* 15 and 16 of Gelasius (abovè, n. 30) present compressed versions of *Epistles* 14, an encyclical letter addressed to the prelates of Bruttium, Lucania, and Sicily. See also Innocent, *Epistles* 2 and 3 (above, n. 30), which largely reproduce Siricius, *Epistles* 1.13

(above, n. 22). The Roman ecclesiastical archives enabled bishops to consult and reproduce their predecessors' decisions.

32. Gelasius, *Epistles* 15 (Thiel, *Epistolae* [above, n. 30], 379–80). See also Siricius, *Epistles* 5 (above, n. 22), which lists rulings from the Roman synod of 386 and was preserved among the proceedings of the Council of Telepte (ed. C. Munier, Corpus Christianorum, Series Latina [hereafter "CCL"], vol. 149 [Turnhout: Brepols, 1974], 58–63) and Hilarus, *Epistles* 16.4.5 (Thiel, *Epistolae* [above, n. 30], 167–68), a letter to Spanish bishops from 465 that discusses the decisions of a Roman council in the same year.

33. Charles Munier, *Les "Statuta ecclesiae antiqua": Édition, études critiques*, Bibliothèque de l'Institut de Droit Canonique de l'Université de Strasbourg, vol. 5 (Paris: Presses Universitaires de France, 1960), reprinted in CCL, vol. 148. Dionysius Exiguus's Latin translation of the first fifty *Apostolic Canons* ca. 490 for a Roman readership is another example of the replication of clerical knowledge across time and space.

34. Gaudemet, *Église* (above, n. 4), 124–27, and Lafontaine, *Conditions positives* (above, n. 4), 121–53, 235–68.

35. *Didascalia Apostolorum* 4.2.1; Council of Neocaesarea, canon 11 (ed. P.-P. Joannou, *Fonti, Fascicolo IX: Discipline générale antique (IIe–IXe s.)*, vol. 1.2 [Rome: Pontificia Commisione per la Redazione del Codice di Diritto Canonico Orientale, 1962–63], 74–82).

36. *Breviarium Hipponense*, canon 1 (CCL, vol. 149 [above, n. 32], 33).

37. Siricius, *Epistles* 1.13 (above, n. 22). Compare Zosimus, *Epistles* 9 (above, n. 30), who requires ages slightly different from those prescribed by his predecessor.

38. Caesarius, *Sermones* 1.1. See also Council of Agde (506), canons 16 and 17 (ed. C. de Clercq, CCL, vol. 148 [Turnhout: Brepols, 1963], 201), which pronounced a minimum age of twenty-five for deacons and thirty for presbyters; and *Statuta Ecclesiae Antiqua*, canon 13 (CCL, vol. 148, 168).

39. *Codex Theodosianus* 16.2.27 (Valentinian, Theodosius, and Arcadius; 390); Justinian, *Novellae* 123.1.

40. Zosimus, *Epistles* 9 (above, n. 30), and Gelasius, *Epistles* 14.2 (above, n. 30).

41. Gelasius, *Epistles* 14.3 (above, n. 30), and Council of Arles (524), canon 2 (ed. C. de Clercq, CCL, vol. 148A [Turnhout: Brepols, 1963], 43–44).

42. Lafontaine, *Conditions positives* (above, n. 4), 155–216, and Gaudemet, *Église* (above, n. 4). For a broader overview, see David Hunter, *Marriage, Celibacy, and Heresy in Ancient Christianity: The Jovinianist Controversy* (Oxford: Oxford University Press, 2007).

43. 1 Timothy 3:2 and 3:12.

44. Cf. Siricius, *Epistles* 1.13 (above, n. 22); Innocent, *Epistles* 2, 3.6, and 37.2 (*PL* 20.473–75, 492–93, and 604). Dunn, "Clerical Marriage" (above, n. 29), offers a detailed analysis of Innocent's position on this precise issue.

45. Cf. Tertullian, *De Exhortatione Castitatis* 7; *Didascalia Apostolorum* 4.3.2; *Constitutiones Apostolorum* 6.17.1–4; *Canones Apostolorum* 18, 19; Council of Valence (376), canon 1 (CCL, vol. 148 [above n. 38], 38–39); Siricius, *Epistles* 1 and 5 (above, n. 32; = Council of Telepsis, canon 5); Innocent, *Epistles* 2.4–7, 3.6, 17.1–2, 37.2 (above, n. 30); Zosimus, *Epistles* 9.3 (*PL* 20.673); Celestine, *Epistles* 4.6 (ed. E. Schwartz, *Acta Conciliorum Oecumenicorum*, vol. 1.2 [Berlin: de Gruyter, 1914], 24); Leo, *Epistles* 4.2, 5.3, 6.3, 12.5 (*PL* 54.612–13, 615–16, 618, 651–53); Council of Orange (441), canon 25 (CCL, vol. 148 [above, n. 38], 84–85); Coun-

cil of Arles II (442–506), canon 45 (CCL, vol. 148 [above n. 38], 123); Council of Rome (465), canon 2 (= Hilarus, *Epistles* 15 [Thiel, *Epistolae* (above, n. 30), 161]; Hilarus, *Epistles* 16.4 (above, n. 32); Gelasius, *Epistles* 14.2–3, 15, and 16 (above, n. 30). Gaudemet, *Église* (above, n. 4), 116, and Lafontaine, *Conditions positives* (above, n. 4), 185–91, offer additional references.

46. *Canones Apostolorum* 6.17.1–4.

47. Sessa, *Formation* (above, n. 29), 177–82, with bibliography.

48. *Codex Justinianus* 1.3.41(42).3–4. *Codex Justinianus* 1.3.47 (531) states that bishops must not have a living wife, and *Novellae* 123.1 (546) adds concubines and illegitimate children to the list of *proscripta*. For discussions of Justinian's laws and their impact on the clerical household, see Sessa, *Formation* (above, n. 29), 103, 183.

49. Gaudemet, *Église* (above, n. 4), 127–28, and R. Godding, *Prêtres en Gaule mérovingienne* (Brussels: Société des Bollandistes, 2001): 81–84. This particular criterion had roots in Levitical statements governing the bodies of Jewish priests: Leviticus 21:5, 18–22.

50. Nicaea (325), canon 1 (ed. Joannou, *Fonti,* vol. 1.1 [above, n. 35], 23-41).

51. Cf. Arles II (442–506), canon 7 (CCL, vol. 148 [above n. 38], 115); and Orléans (538), canon 6 (CCL, vol. 148A [above, n. 41], 116–17).

52. Innocent, *Epistles* 37.2–3 (*PL* 20.604–5). *Statuta Ecclesiae Antiqua,* canon 25 (CCL, vol. 148 [above n. 38], 171). The beard-shaving rule has strong Levitical resonances. See also *Constitutiones Apostolorum* 4.3.2.3; Hilarus, *Epistles* 15.2.2 (= Roman Synod of 465; Thiel, *Epistolae* [above, n. 30], 161) and 16.4.5 (above, n. 32); and Gelasius, *Epistles* 14.2–3, 16, 17; fr. 9 (Thiel, *Epistolae* [above, n. 30], 488). A prohibition against physical deformation also appears in Jerome, *Epistles* 52.10.

53. Nicaea (325), canon 1 (above, n. 50).

54. *Constitutiones Apostolorum* 8.47.77–79. Translation adapted from C. L. Feltoe, *Nicene and Post-Nicene Fathers,* Second Series, vol. 12, ed. P. Schaff and H. Wace (Buffalo, NY: Christian Literature Publishing Co, 1895), 3.

55. Cf. Council of Toledo (400), canon 2; (which excepts porters and lectors from needing permission from their landowners); Leo, *Epistles* 4 (*PL* 54.610–14); Gelasius, *Epistles* 14.2–3, 22 (above, n. 30). For a survey of the imperial legislation, see Marco Melluso, *La schiavitù nell'età giustiniano: Disciplina giuridica e rilevanza sociale* (Paris: Presses Universitaires de Franche-Comté, 2000).

56. Leo, *Epistles* 4.1 (*PL* 54.611).

57. Cf. *Constitutiones Apostolorum* 8.47.82 and Rapp, *Holy Bishops* (above, n. 1), 174–75. As Rapp notes, slaves could and sometimes did accede to the episcopate, but the master's permission was essential.

58. Emperors too desired to protect the interests of landowners whose slaves and peasant laborers joined the clergy without permission. Cf. *Novellae* 35.1.6, issued by Valentinian III in 452 and reissued by Justinian, *Novellae* 123.4 (546).

59. Lizzi Testa, "Privilegi" and "Bishop" (both above in n. 2). Gaudemet, *Église* (above, n. 4), remains a solid study of this phenomenon.

60. Cf. Rapp, *Holy Bishops* (above, n. 1), 283, who sees *curiales* joining the clergy as clever tax dodgers.

61. *Codex Theodosianus* 12.1.49.1 (Constantius, 361) and 12.1.163 (Arcadius, 399).

62. Valentinian III, *Novellae* 3.4.

63. Lizzi Testa, "Privilegi" (above, n. 2), 135.

64. Hübner, *Klerus* (above, n. 15), 66–70.

65. Cf. E. Diehl, ed., *Inscriptiones Latinae Christianae Veteres*, nos. 967 and 972, vol. 1 (Berlin: Weidmann, 1961), 179-81; and Damasus, *Epigrammata* 57 (ed. A. Ferrua, *Epigrammata Damasiana* [Rome: Pontificio Istituto di Archeologia Cristiana, 1942], 210–12).

66. Claire Sotinel, "Le recruitment des évêques en Italie auz IVe et Ve siècles: Essai d'enquête prosopographique," in *Vescovi e pastori in epoca teodosiana: XXV Incontro di studiosi dell'antichità cristiana, Roma, 8–11 maggio 1996* (Rome: Institutum Patristicum Augustinianum, 1997), 201.

67. Augustine, *Epistles* 125, 126 (ed. A. Goldbacher, Corpus Scriptorum Ecclesiasticorum Latinorum [hereafter "CSEL"], vol. 34 [Vienna: Tempsky, 1904], 3–18).

68. According to Gerontius in his *Life of Melania the Younger* 1, she and Pinianus married in 396, when Pinianus was seventeen, making him thirty-two in 411—a full eight years older than the minimum of twenty-five set at the Council of Hippo. (See above, n. 36.)

69. Ibid. 5–6.

70. Sessa, *Formation* (above, n. 29), 182–90.

71. Gelasius, fr. 9 (above, n. 52).

72. Leo, *Epistles* 12.2, 4 (*PL* 54.648–51). Fast-tracking candidates was generally frowned upon (cf. Innocent, *Epistles* 37 [above, n. 30]), but it was commonplace.

73. Cf. *Didascalia Apostolorum* 4.2.1; Council of Serdica (343), canon 10 (above, n. 35: 737–823); Siricius, *Epistles* 1.13 (above, n. 22); Innocent, *Epistles* 37 (above, n. 30); Celestine, *Epistles* (above, n. 45) 4.3.4.

74. Leo, *Epistles* 12.3 (*PL* 54.648–49). Translation adapted from Feltoe, *Nicene and Post-Nicene Fathers*, vol. 12, 13.

75. Leviticus 21:13, 1 Timothy 3:5, Ephesians 5:23.

76. Augustine, *Epistles* (above, n. 67) 209 (ed. A. Goldbacher, CSEL, vol. 57 [Vienna: Tempsky, 1911], 347–53) and 20 (ed. J. Divjak, CSEL, vol. 88 [Vienna: Hoelder, Pichler, Tempsky, 1981], 94–112).

77. Jill Harries, *Law and Empire in Late Antiquity* (Cambridge: Cambridge University Press, 1999); Peter Van Nuffelen, "The Rhetoric of Rules and the Rule of Consensus," in *Episcopal Elections in Late Antiquity*, ed. J. Leemans, P. Van Nuffelen, S. W. J. Keough, and C. Nicolaye, Arbeiten zur Kirchengeschichte, vol. 119 (Berlin: de Gruyter, 2011), 243–58.

78. The war lasted from 489 until 493 and largely affected northern Italy, but Gelasius's letters demonstrate that it also impacted Rome and the Suburbicarian churches. See John B. Bury, *History of the Later Roman Empire*, vol. 1 (New York: Dover 1958), 422–28.

79. Gelasius, *Epistles* 14.2–3 (above, n. 30).

80. Technically, Italy did not have metropolitans, but the bishop of Rome had direct jurisdiction over all sees in Italia Suburbicaria, which included Tuscany, where Stephanus served.

81. Martha Himmelfarb, *A Kingdom of Priests: Ancestry and Merit in Ancient Judaism* (Philadelphia: University of Pennsylvania Press, 2006); Jörg Rüpke, "Controllers and Professionals: Analyzing Religious Specialists," *Numen* 43 (1996): 254; and Albert Henrichs, "What is a Greek Priest?" in *Practitioners of the Divine: Greek Priests and Religious Officials*

from Homer to Heliodorus, ed. B. Dignas and K. Trampedach, Hellenic Studies, vol. 30 (Washington, D.C.: Center for Hellenic Studies, 2008), 1–14.

82. Another potentially fruitful line of inquiry is to assess the impact of Jewish modes of argumentation, such as in the Mishnah, on the Christian juridical system for identifying clerics, especially since scholars have already identified parallels between Jewish legal discourse and the church orders. See Charlotte Fontrobert, "The *Didascalia Apostolorum:* A Mishnah for the Disciples of Jesus," *Journal of Early Christian Studies* 9 (2001): 483–511.

83. Sessa, *Formation* (above, n. 29), 174–207; Hübner, *Klerus* (above, n. 15), 91–98, 103–5. Moreover, while clerics received some payment for their services to the church (a *stipendium*), the amount varied from church to church, since it depended upon a see's gross revenues. It also varied from office to office: Italian bishops received a full quarter of ecclesiastical income, but all other clerics shared another 25 percent as a group. In most cases, additional sources of income were likely necessary.

84. For the juggling of multiple allegiances by clerics in late antique Italy, see Sessa, *Formation* (above, n. 29). On the development of the presbyterate as something like a career, see Godding, *Prêtres* (above, n. 49), whose evidence dates largely from the sixth century.

12
———

Countryside

Cam Grey

THE *EPISTULA DE REBUS RUSTICIS HOPKINSENSIS:* INTRODUCTION, ENGLISH TEXT, COMMENTARY, AND AFTERWORD

Among the papers found in the estate of the late Keith Hopkins is a curious text that bears many of the hallmarks of late antique literature. It reveals both classicizing tendencies and a self-conscious awareness of present Christian concerns. It defies easy categorization into one genre, sitting instead amid the epistolary, technical, hagiographical, and panegyrical forms. It demonstrates also a robust sense of the literary and cultural merit of its present, while at the same time seeking to consciously reconstruct and remodel its past.[1] Unfortunately, the names of both the addressee and the author are lost, and nothing further is known of the provenance or manuscript tradition of the text. Nevertheless, its stated intention, at least, is to further its addressee's knowledge of the countryside of Gaul, and it therefore seems appropriate to publish an English version and historical commentary of the text here, with the further aim of using it as a vehicle for exploring the various ways in which authors of late antiquity understood the countrysides of their world and communicated that understanding through their texts.

TEXT AND GENRE

The text, which on the advice of Professor Hopkins's literary executor, has been given the title *Epistula de Rebus Rusticis Hopkinsensis,* may be placed at the intersection of a number of genres well represented in late Latin literature. It appears to take the form of a letter, although no felicitation or signature has been preserved in the manuscript, and so we are left to speculate about the identity of both the work's intended addressee and its author. Equally, the text both explicitly quotes and implicitly references the technical treatises of Vegetius and Palladius, and there is more than a hint of panegyric in the language employed both to praise the ruler in question and to celebrate the land, heroes, and people of Gaul. The author is familiar with hagiographical literature of the fourth and fifth centuries as well as the poetic and panegyrical works of Sidonius Apollinaris and other Gallo-Roman authors of the period. In particular, he demonstrates a quite intimate knowledge of the many and varied literary works of Ausonius of Bordeaux, and it is tempting to view that author's project of explicitly challenging genre boundaries, literary expectations, and textual forms as something of a model for our author.

Certainly, geographical writings in the late Roman and post-Roman period encompassed a broad range of genres and entailed a multiplicity of modalities for knowing and engaging with the countrysides that they purported to describe.[2] A text such as the anonymously authored *Expositio Totius Mundi,* for example, which was written in Greek during the reign of Constantius II and survives in a fifth- or sixth-century Latin translation,[3] may with some degree of plausibility be related to other encyclopedic or codificatory projects of the period, such as the codifications of law undertaken under Theodosius II and Justinian, the *Medical Compilations* of the fourth-century physician Oribasius, and the Babylonian and Palestinian Talmuds. These collections of texts may be viewed as attempts to fix or constrain information in time and space, both in response to perceived perturbations of the social and political order and as exercises in encompassing or expressing the totality of knowledge on a topic. A comparable impulse may be found in Christian historiography of the period, where the geographical excursus was a bold expression of control and understanding, encompassing the extent and limits of the Christian world.[4] Meanwhile, in the literary tour de force of Sidonius Apollinaris's letter to his friend Heronius, which contains an account of his journey to Rome to take up the post of urban prefect (*Ep.* 1.5), or Rutilius Namatianus's melancholic *De Reditu Suo,* we see authors lingering on particular geographical locations in order to situate their works—and themselves—within a cultural milieu of literary production in which they explicitly claimed membership. Underpinning all these projects was a deep appreciation among members of the lettered aristocracy of the importance of place and a collection of educational processes and literary practices whereby they acquired and expressed that appreciation—principally by means of attaching stories to particular physical locations.[5] It is certainly tempting to see in documents such as the one under discussion here a clever and artful combination of elements of each of these techniques for both knowing and expressing knowledge, and it is for this reason that this text seems to be especially apt in the present collection.

However, alongside such considerations of generic complexity and authorial ambition must be placed the somewhat rough and unfinished feel of the text, which also contains some rather mechanical and awkward passages. These elements encourage comparison with schoolboy exercises of the type discussed by A.C. Dionisotti.[6] At this point questions about the purpose, genre, and intended audience of the work remain open to debate, although the more detailed consideration of the authorship and date of the text that follows may shed further light upon the problem.

AUTHOR AND DATING

Some clues in the text itself encourage a date in the very late fifth or early sixth century and suggest that the author was a member of the Gallo-Roman church, perhaps even a bishop. The final lines of the text contain a plea to the addressee that he allow his own baptism to serve as an inspiration for the baptism of his realm. This individual is addressed throughout as "Your Majesty" or "my Lord," and together these clues encourage an identification with the Frankish king Clovis, who was baptized sometime between 496 and 508 C.E.[7] It is further tempting to suggest that this text was written in the immediate aftermath of that event. Certainly there is a hint of opportunism in the language and stated purpose of the text, and it betrays signs of hasty composition that might be attributable to the somewhat unexpected nature of Clovis's baptism.

It is also worth considering a possible relationship between this work and the battle of Vouillé, of 507, where Clovis defeated the Visigothic kingdom based in Toulouse and established a consolidated Frankish kingdom in Gaul. It is possible that the peregrination mentioned in this text was envisaged by the victorious king shortly after his victory at Vouillé. That peregrination is otherwise unattested—and given the king's ongoing campaigning it may never have actually happened—but it does not seem altogether unreasonable to ascribe this text to the period immediately after this victory, when such an event was a real possibility. If so, this ascription may also shed light upon the contested date of the king's baptism and encourage the adoption of the later date on the grounds of this author's close association of baptism and the hoped-for peace and prosperity of Gaul.

We may surmise from the focus upon the Gallic countryside that the author resided somewhere in Gaul, perhaps in Aquitania.[8] This supposition is further supported by his privileging of Gallo-Roman authors and saints in his text. Indeed, Italian and other Western Latin authors seem entirely absent from the work, as too are Greek sources. We may perhaps take this as evidence for the abbreviated range of texts available to our author. On the other hand, it is interesting to note the breadth in the genres of the sources that he does make use of, which will be signaled in the commentary that accompanies the text. It is also worth emphasizing that our author clearly does not appear to have considered the fourth and fifth centuries to be a period of decline in terms of literary production, technical knowledge, or culture. On the contrary, given the choice between an author of these centuries and one from an earlier period, he appears characteristically to choose the former.

However, some caution is necessary. The somewhat artificial and forced tone of the text and the self-conscious embrace of Ausonius as a model raise the possibility that this document should perhaps be regarded as an artful confection. It betrays at least some of the sly humor of that most artful of late antique confections, the so-called *Scriptores Historiae Augustae*, and displays an almost too-neat knowledge of those texts that we might expect to have been canonical in the period. It is therefore difficult to determine whether the author is sincerely invested in the project of presenting himself as an expert in matters rural and championing the countryside to a real (if unknown) ruler; whether he is simply responding to a prompt from an unusually broad-minded teacher; or whether he is perhaps even poking fun at the dry, earnest tone in which information of this sort is usually presented. That question must at this stage be left as a matter of conjecture.

. . .

THE *EPISTULA DE REBUS RUSTICIS HOPKINSENSIS*

. . . it is your desire to acquire a deeper knowledge of your realm.[a] You intend, therefore, to imitate the Hellene-loving emperor and make a journey from town to town, bringing the blessing of your presence to urban and rural communities alike.[b] Since

a. It is difficult to determine how much is missing from the beginning of the manuscript, although the introductory nature of the remaining portion of this sentence allows for the possibility that it may be as little as the name of the addressee and the beginning of the sentence.

b. This is probably a reference to the travels of the emperor Hadrian, the most extensive account of which may be found in the late fourth-century *Vita Hadriani*, contained in the *Scriptores Historiae Augustae*. For the *iter principis* as an exercise in the expression of an emperor's power, and the connection between travel and power that it represents, cf. F. Millar, *The Emperor in the Roman World (31 BC–AD 337)* (Ithaca: Cornell University Press, 1984); J. Halfmann, *Itinera Principum: Geschichte und Typologie der Kaiserreisen im römischen Reich* (Stuttgart: Steiner, 1986). For travel as an exercise in experiencing, knowing, and remembering a landscape, see the phenomenological approaches of C. Y. Tilley, *A Phenomenology of Landscape: Places, Paths and Monuments* (Providence: Berg, 1994); T. Ingold, *The Perception of the Environment: Essays on Livelihood, Dwelling and Skill* (London and New York: Routledge, 2000; reprint with new preface 2011). Responses, critiques, and alternative perspectives in M. Fitzjohn, "Viewing Places: GIS Applications for Examining the Perception of Space in the Mountains of Sicily," *World Archaeology* 39 (2007): 36–50; H. A. Forbes, *Meaning and Identity in a Greek Landscape: An Archaeological Ethnography* (Cambridge and New York: Cambridge University Press, 2007).

you have also embraced the example of that most illustrious of emperors—I mean the emperor Augustus—and like that prince and so many of his successors you have willingly extended your beneficence to poets and literary practitioners, I have thought it useful on this occasion to provide you with some short remarks, in the form of a letter, on the country that you rule, the character of its people and their customs, and the aspect and nature of its fields, rivers, and mountains.

The consideration of Your Majesty's superior indulgence for attempts of this sort has induced me to follow this example and makes me at the same time almost forget my own inability when compared with previous writers. One advantage, however, I claim for this work: I seek no elegance of expression or extraordinary share of genius, but only great care and fidelity in collecting and explaining for your use the instructions and observations of those writers who have already written expressly concerning these matters.[c]

Nor would I wish to associate Your Majesty with the rustics whom my learned predecessor sought to teach with his treatise.[d] Nevertheless, who could deny that knowledge of these matters is not only of the greatest importance for the happiness of the state but also useful and necessary in the present times? Therefore, my design in this letter is to share with you, my Lord, the love that certain men of our own time have shown for their fatherland, the fruits and perils that it offers, and the particular characteristics that make it truly most bountiful and blessed.

Where else to start but with the bounties of the country itself? Rightly did the saint speak of his native land as comparable even to the riches of Campania.[e] Well

---

c. This passage is modeled very closely upon the preface to Vegetius's *De Re Militari*.

d. Cf. Palladius, *Opus Agriculturae* 1.1.1, who claims explicitly to be writing for *rustici*. Certainly, Palladius is aware of the immense diversity of environmental, topographical, and agricultural niches throughout the Mediterranean world, offering advice on different strategies for opening and situating fields as well as different sowing times according to the climatic conditions (e.g., *Opus Agriculturae* 1.7; 2.3; 4.2, 4.10.16, 4.10.24). For more extensive discussion of the diversity of ancient climates and conditions, with further references, see C. Grey, "Concerning Rural Matters," in *The Oxford Handbook of Late Antiquity*, ed. S. F. Johnson (Oxford and New York: Oxford University Press, 2012), 625–66, at 627–28. The basis of Palladius's knowledge is difficult to determine, for he offers no explicit statements in his work, and little is known about his life and career (F. Morgenstern, "Die Auswertung des opus agriculturae des Palladius zu einigen Fragen der spätantiken Wirtschaftsgeschichte," *Klio* 71 [1989]: 179–92, at 180; D. Vera, "I silenzi di Palladio e l'Italia: Osservazioni sull'ultimo agronomo Romano," *Antiquité Tardive* 7 [1999]: 283–97, at 284; C. Grey, "Revisiting the 'Problem' of *Agri Deserti* in the Late Roman Empire," *Journal of Roman Archaeology* 20 [2007]: 362–76, at 364). It seems unlikely that Palladius was in fact writing specifically for *rustici,* but it is possible that aspects of his treatise draw upon knowledge that he gained directly or indirectly from peasants themselves. (E. Frézouls, "La vie rurale au Bas-Empire d'après l'œuvre de Palladius," *Ktèma* 5 [1980]: 193–210, at 196, provides specific references, although these are by no means unproblematic or entirely self-evident.) For Palladius's engagement with previous agronomists, see Morgenstern, "Auswertung des opus agriculturae," 180–81.

e. Sidonius Apollinaris, *Carmina* 18, *On the Baths of His Country House*. Campania continued to enjoy a reputation for fertility in the period, as evidenced by the comments of the anonymous author of the indeed do we know the advantages of his own villa of Avitacum—"a name," he says, "of sweeter sound in my ears than my own patrimony," and sweeter also than any praised in Lucilian verse.[f] Truly we should heed the poet, for what he said of the

---

Expositio Totius Mundi (J. Rougé, ed., trans., and comm., *Expositio Totius Mundi et Gentium*, Sources Chrétiennes, vol. 126 (Paris: Éditions du Cerf, 1966), para. 55). Equally, though, it could be presented as stricken by shortage and in need of relief if the circumstances required it. A law of Honorius seems to acknowledge the truth of claims that at least some fields of Campania are barren and deserted when it agrees, in response to a petition from Campanian *curiales,* to remit taxes due on those lands. However, it is possible that Honorius's actions were politically expedient and motivated in part by his desire to secure the support of these *curiales* at a time when the Province of Africa under Gildo was in a state of considerable unrest (*Codex Theodosianus* 11.28.2 [395, Campania], with Grey, "*Agri Deserti*" [above, n. *d*], 372–73. Cf. Symmachus, *Epistles* 1.5.2 [375]: "Namque hic usus in nostram venit aetatem, ut rus, quod solebat alere, nunc alatur").

The fertility and richness of Gaul is less easy to determine. The topos of depredation of the land by barbarians or the tax collector, or both, was well established in the literature of the period (e.g., *Panegyrici Latini* 3[11].1.4 [364]; Rutilius Namatianus, *De Reditu Suo* 1.21–30; Salvian, *De Gubernatione Dei* 5 passim), and there exists also evidence of petitions from the communities of Gaul to the emperor to request relief from taxation, which had been hampering the natives' enjoyment of their riches (e.g., Constantius, *Vita Germani* 19–24). On the other hand, celebrations of the richness and fertility of the land continue to be relatively common in the period: for an example of the novel uses to which the trope could be put, see Salvian's argument that the Aquitani should have been particularly pious be-cause they were particularly blessed with riches, and hence their lack of piety was especially grievous (Salvian, *De Gubernatione Dei*, 7.2.8–9). In both cases, one gains the suspicion that the realities of the countrysides in question are less important than the ideological purposes to which consideration of those countrysides is being put.

In our late Roman sources, claims of desertion and rural poverty coexist alongside celebrations of prosperity and rustic ease, and neither should be uncritically embraced. It is possible that some aristo-cratic authors of the period embraced more intimately and personally their rural estates and the inhabit-ants of them. But this proposition is impossible to quantify, and any further implications of this trend are likely to have been rather diffuse and heterogeneous. At the very least, however, it seems reasonable to suggest that we should not expect either complete ignorance or total understanding of the countryside on the part of our ancient authors. Therefore, to frame our approach to their texts in terms of this dichot-omy is a somewhat limited and limiting strategy. Rather, in seeking to access what our ancient authors actually knew about the countryside, we must take account of the dialectical relationships between the literary strategies that they employed in presenting that countryside in their texts, the particular inter-pretation of the countryside that they wished to embrace, and their own experience of that countryside.

f. Sidonius Apollinaris, *Epistles* 2.2. Cf. Ausonius, *Carmina* 3.1, *De Heredolio*. Sidonius's letter falls within a long tradition of villa owners' offering elaborate letters of praise of their estates. In Sidonius's case, as with his predecessors, it is difficult to disentangle elements of reality from the demands of the genre. (Cf. J. Percival, "Desperately Seeking Sidonius: The Realities of Life in Fifth-Century Gaul," *Latomus* 56 [1997]: 279–92; D. Frye, "Aristocratic Responses to Late Roman Urban Change: The Examples of Ausonius and Sidonius in Gaul," *Classical World* 96 [2003]: 185–96; D. Amherdt, "*Rusticus Politicus:* Esprit de caste? L'agriculture et la politique chez Sidoine Apollinaire: Réalité et lieux communs," *Hermes* 132 [2004]: 373–87; K. Dark, "The Archaeological Implications of Fourth- and Fifth-Century Descriptions of Villas in the Northwest Provinces of the Roman Empire," *Historia: Zeitschrift für Alte Geschichte* 54 [2005]: 331–42; C. Grey, "Two Young Lovers: An Abduction Marriage and Its Conse-quences in Fifth-Century Gaul," *Classical Quarterly* 58 [2008]: 286–302.)

land he loved can now be true again. It was a land where husbandman, boatman, and traveler conversed freely, as each went about his separate business, free from care and toil. Shepherds, swineherds, and other rustics also could be found.[g] Now,

It may, perhaps, be useful to view praise of rural estates and praise of the countryside as two complementary but not necessarily coterminous phenomena. In particular, the two present subtly different landscapes. The villa landscape is managed and ordered, for it revolves at least in part around the *dominus* and expresses or reflects his control over his *familia* and dependents and the places in which they live (Cf., for example, Sidonius Apollinaris's elaborate praise of the *burgus* of Pontius Leontius: *Carmina* 22). The rural landscape has more scope for diversity or heterogeneity, for it was not on the whole quite so closely connected to the author's personal identity. Rather, it was informed by a sense of shared or collective identity, which was manifested through common linkage to or even descent from the land. A particularly apt example of this may be found in Ausonius's *Mosella*, which the present text appears to reference or respond to quite explicitly at several points.

g. We should be cautious about assuming that our author's representation of the countryside of Gaul is anything other than an idyllic topos. Although it is probable that the countrysides of the late Roman world were populated by individuals who fulfilled an immense diversity of economic roles and occupied a multiplicity of social niches (cf. C. Grey, *Constructing Communities in the Late Roman Countryside* (Cambridge and New York: Cambridge University Press, 2011), 26–33; also, for swineherds, *Vita Genovefae* 17), it is not entirely clear whether aristocratic authors of the period knew this—or, perhaps better, whether they cared or deemed it necessary to acknowledge this in their texts. It is therefore interesting that our author does offer at least some broad distinctions between different types of *rustici*. In this he is somewhat unusual, for in general authors of the period tended, like their predecessors, to treat rural inhabitants as an undifferentiated mass.

There are some instances of individual *rustici* receiving attention as individuals. Preserved in the letter collection of Sidonius Apollinaris, for example, are several letters that appear to have been written on behalf of *rustici* who have petitioned him for intercession in a dispute or sought a letter of introduction to another aristocratic landowner. (Cf. in particular *Epistles* 4.7 with Grey, *Constructing Communities*, 157–58, and, more generally for travel by *rustici*, C. Grey, "Letters of Recommendation and the Circulation of Rural Laborers in the Late Roman West," in *Travel, Communication and Geography in Late Antiquity*, ed. L. Ellis and F. L. Kidner [Aldershot and Burlington: Ashgate, 2004], 25–40.) The purpose of these journeys by *rustici* is only occasionally spelled out, but the fact of those journeys accords well with our author's picture of travelers participating regularly in conversations with those working on the land. We gain the impression of a landscape where the traveler is far from an unusual sight.

We may connect these texts, in turn, with legislation from fourth-century Gaul that seems to suggest regular movement between city and country (e.g., *Codex Theodosianus* 12.19.2 [400, Gaul], with further remarks in C. Grey, "Contextualizing *Colonatus:* The *Origo* of the Late Roman Empire," *Journal of Roman Studies* 97 [2007]: 155–75, at 163; Grey, *Constructing Communities*, 48) and evidence from an anonymous fifth-century comedy that offers hints that movement around the countryside was so unremarkable as to have been undertaken by household slaves independently of their masters (*Querolus* 68–69, with C. Grey, "Slavery in the Late Roman World," in *The Cambridge World History of Slavery: The Ancient Mediterranean World*, ed. K. R. Bradley and P. Catledge [Cambridge and New York: Cambridge University Press, 2011], 482–509, at 502). It is worth noting also the necessary existence of regular travelers to carry the correspondence back and forth between our various late Roman letter writers. There has been some work done on these epistolary networks, although less attention has been paid to the carriers themselves. (See now, for example, the detailed treatment of the Lérins circle in R. W. Mathisen, *Ecclesiastical Factionalism and Religious Controversy in Fifth-Century Gaul* [Washington, D.C.: Catholic University of America Press, 1989]).

again, with your great victory, we can look forward to a time when we no longer fear the threat of bandits on the road. No guide need worry that his charge will fail to reach his destination or that he himself will be negligent in his duty to his patron.[h]

For the land itself can justly claim to now be blessed or at least to hope that it be so. Our celebrated rivers cry out to you with joy. The Loire, once home to brigands,

---

h. Our author is perhaps thinking of situations such as we observe in Possidius's account of Augustine's deliverance from a violent ambush by the Circumcelliones because his guide got lost along the way: Possidius, *Vita Augustini* 12. Guides are not often mentioned in our extant sources, but we must assume that they were commonly employed in the period as bishops, imperial officials, and other dignitaries moved across the landscape. Although the circumstances are clearly somewhat different, we may glean some idea of the potential for a guide's knowledge of the landscape to impact significantly upon the experience of his charge from Egeria's account of her travels through the Holy Land (the *Itinerarium Egeriae*) and the description by an anonymous fourth-century monk of his journey around the Egyptian desert (the so-called *Historia Monachorum in Aegypto*). In both cases, guides appear not only to have controlled the route taken but also to have provided information, contacts, places to stay, and so on.

We may imagine that such individuals would mitigate at least some of the many dangers of travel: the threat of bandits and wild animals; losing one's way, particularly in the event of unseasonable weather or the destruction of a known bridge or river crossing; discomfort thanks to an ill-planned or unlucky day's travel.

Such events are occasionally mentioned in our ancient sources. The fourth-century Italian senator Symmachus (*Epistles* 7.7), for example, complains of unseasonable rains washing out a river crossing, as well as mentioning an experience of robbery on the roads (*Epistles* 2.22).For more extensive discussion, see M. Salzman, "Travel and Communication in *The Letters of Symmachus*," in *Travel, Communication and Geography in Late Antiquity* (above, n. g), 81–94, at 86). Sidonius Apollinaris, meanwhile, mentions an encounter with grave robbers seeking to despoil the tomb of one of his ancestors (*Epistles* 3.12). Encounters with bandits are a common theme of the hagiographical literature, at least. In his account of the life of Martin of Tours, for example, Sulpicius Severus relates both Martin's capture by and subsequent conversion of a bandit (*Vita Martini* 5) and his demolition of an altar raised to a supposed saint who turned out to have been a bandit (ibid. 11). This second anecdote is echoed by Constantius's account of an encounter between Germanus of Auxerre and a pair of ghosts at a chance stopping point, which turns out to hinge on the fact that these ghosts are bandits wrongly buried there (*Vita Germani* 10).

Given these concerns about safety on the one hand and the apparent increase in the incidence of travel around the late antique countryside on the other (cf. J. F. Drinkwater, "Introduction: And Up and Down the People Go," in *Travel, Communication and Geography in Late Antiquity* [above, n. g], xv–xix, for the need to nuance and test this proposition further), it is worth considering briefly to what extent we should expect the countryside of the fifth and sixth centuries to have been in reality more violent and unsafe than previously. There is a certain amount of scholarly debate on the topic, the contours of which can be observed in the following: W. Pohl, "Perceptions of Barbarian Violence," in *Violence in Late Antiquity: Perceptions and Practices*, ed. H. A. Drake (Aldershot and Burlington: Ashgate, 2006), 15–26; R. W. Mathisen, "Violent Behavior and the Construction of Barbarian Identity in Late Antiquity," in *Violence in Late Antiquity*, 27–36; J. H. W. G. Liebeschuetz, "Violence in the Barbarian Successor Kingdoms," in *Violence in Late Antiquity*, 37–46; together with the synthetic remarks of H. A. Drake, "Gauging Violence in Late Antiquity," in *Violence in Late Antiquity*, 1–11. Whichever side of the argument one comes down on, it is difficult to quantify the phenomenon, for above all the safety or danger of the countryside continued to carry cultural and ideological resonances into this period and beyond, regardless of the realities. See further the discussion at note q below.

can now take its rightful place alongside the Moselle, so amply praised by the emperor's teacher, while the noble Seine and the Garonne clamor also for attention.[i] Not only fish but fruits of the fields too can now be enjoyed. Our wool has long been the envy of our neighbors, and our woods provide materials for the celebration of the works of both men and God.[j]

i. Our author also explicitly references here lines 461-83 of Ausonius's *Mosella,* where that river is compared to the Loire and other rivers and judged to exceed them. The poem was apparently quite popular in late antiquity: Symmachus *Epistles* 1.14.

It seems useful to connect our author's mention of brigands here to the literature on the Bagaudae. Scholars have long debated the realities that lie behind the vague and allusive references to these shadowy figures, for they may be viewed equally as representing a utopian or a dystopian vision of a society beyond the political reach of the Roman state (summarized nicely by C. R. Wickham, *Framing the Early Middle Ages: Europe and the Mediterranean 400–800* (Oxford and New York: Oxford University Press, 2005), 530–34. Brief comments in Grey, *Constructing Communities* (above, n. g), 187–88. Also, for further alternatives, D. De Decker, "À quelles langues, contrées, religions, rattacher le mouvement social des Bagaudes," *Acta Antiqua Academiae Scientiarum Hungaricae* 45 [2005]: 423–66). The details of this debate need not concern us here, for regardless of whether these individuals had a social program, religious expectations, or cultural aims, they emerge from our sources, at least, as a locus for the expression and exploration of Otherness. That Otherness is located in the woods: that is, outside the usual urban-agricultural-pastoral nexus that tends to dominate both ancient representations and modern interpretations of identity and belonging in the Roman world.

It is perhaps worth exploring further the sylvan elements of this representation. It is possible, for example, to interpret this focus upon forests as an attempt to create a new, even more marginal space for the exploration of identity in a world where the urban-rural divide has collapsed somewhat and the pastoral Other has been to a certain extent integrated within the Roman world by detaching the truly "barbarian" practices of the Huns, for example, from the somewhat less extreme but nonetheless problematic behavior of shepherds. Note, for example, the contrast between Ammianus Marcellinus's ethnography of the Huns and other barbarians in Book 31 of his *Res Gestae* and the relatively standard fears about lack of control over the mobility of Campanian shepherds in *Codex Theodosianus* 9.30.2 (364, Campania). (For attitudes toward nomadic pastoralists, see B. D. Shaw, "'Eaters of Flesh, Drinkers of Milk': The Ancient Mediterranean Ideology of the Pastoral Nomad," *Ancient Society* 13–14 [1982–83]: 5–31. More extensive discussion of shepherds in V. Neri, *I marginali nell'occidente tardo antico: Poveri, "infames" e criminali nella nascente società cristiana* [Bari: Edipuglia, 1998], 143–51.)

Further, it might be suggested that the river and forest that form the backdrop and refuge for the Bagaudae function for our late Roman authors as a tacit acknowledgment of their perception that Roman culture, law, and administration continued to be ubiquitous in the period. In this construction, the escape from the demands of the Roman tax system—and, by extension, from everything deemed morally, culturally, or politically suspect about the Roman state in the period (cf. in particular book 5 of Salvian of Marseilles's *De Gubernatione Dei*)—is no longer possible simply by retreat to the countryside, or by seeking the guise, anonymity, and mobility of a shepherd, but must be effected by an almost total abandonment of anything even marginally or tangentially touched by *Romanitas.* Again, it surely does not need to be stressed that whatever reality might lie behind these representations of the Bagaudae is of little importance or value to our authors.

j. The *Edictum de Maximis Pretiis* of Diocletian (19.73) suggests that the Ambianenses in Gallia Belgica and the Bituriges in Aquitania were particularly well known for the quality of their wool. There has been little work done on the socioeconomic importance of woods and forests in late antiquity,

But what of the people? What is their lot? What are their hopes? Well may you ask. Once we were celebrated as a land of warriors,[k] but let me speak now of the deeds of the men and women who have made this land famous by their victories in the spiritual struggle. By their actions the very land itself was made a celebration and witness to their virtues; for demons who had once been numerous were driven beyond our bounds.[l] Pride of place was held by the blessed Martin, who caused the

---

although there are some references to their exploitation, and to those who worked and perhaps dwelled in them: e.g., Sidonius Apollinaris, *Carmina* 7.325–26; *Codex Justinianus* 12.33.3 (Arcadius and Honorius to Pulcher, *magister militum*); Gregory of Tours, *Liber in Gloria Confessorum* 30. For the medieval period in France, see now R. Larrère and O. Nougarède, *L'homme et la forêt* (Paris: Gallimard, 1993); A. Corvol-Dessert, ed., *Les forêts d'Occident du moyen âge à nos jours: Actes des XXIVes Journées Internationales d'Histoire de l'Abbaye de Flaran 6, 7, 8 septembre 2002* (Toulouse: Presses Universitaires Mirail-Toulouse, 2004). For Italy, M. Montanari, "La foresta come spazio economico e culturale," in *Uomo e spazio nell'Alto Medioevo* (Spoleto: Presso la Sede del Centro, 2003), 301–45. Certainly it seems that wood was more employed as a medium for building in the period: see *Vita Genovefae* 19 for an explicit description of carpenters cutting wood in order to build a church; also, more generally, É. Faure-Boucharlat, "Les constructions rurales: L'âge du bois?" in É. Faure-Boucharlat, ed., *Vivre à la campagne au Moyen Âge: L'habitat rural de Ve au XIIe siècle (Bresse, Lyonnais, Dauphiné) d'après les données archéologiques* (Lyon: Association Lyonnaise pour la Promotion de l'Archéologie en Rhônes-Alpes, 2001), 77–92.

k. The topos of Gaul as a land of warriors was well established in antiquity: for a quite late expression, cf. the fifth-century *Expositio Totius Mundi* (above, n. e) 58. In his treatise on military matters, Vegetius explicitly states that country folk make the best soldiers (*De Re Militari* 3), and this too is a well-established trope. However, when authors of the period speak with more direct personal knowledge of the inhabitants of the countryside, they tend to portray them as either cowardly (or at the very least fearful) or distasteful: cf. Sidonius Apollinaris, *Epistles* 4.7, 7.4; Paulinus of Nola, *Epistles* 12.12; Ruricius of Limoges, *Epistles* 2.20; Ausonius, *Epistles* 26.

Clearly, these two topoi are somewhat at odds with each other, and the tension between the two is instructive. On the one hand, the land (both Gaul in general and the countryside of Gaul more specifically) is perceived to shape or determine a particular set of shared characteristics, which are recognized and celebrated in the abstract. On the other hand, individual *rustici* are of necessity alien to, alienated from, and dominated by the authors of our texts.

l. We may perhaps connect this with Constantius, *Vita Germani* 32, who describes demoniacs screaming out in the church at Milan to ask the saint why he continues to pursue them even into Italy. Demons were considered a fundamental element in the late ancient landscape. Salvian of Marseilles, for example, compares them to an enemy army that has prepared a series of ambushes and hazards for the wary and the unwary alike (*De Gubernatione Dei* 6.3.14, with further discussion in C. Grey, "Demoniacs, Dissent and Disempowerment in the Late Roman West: Some Case Studies from the Hagiographical Literature," *Journal of Early Christian Studies* 13 [2005]: 39–69, at 52–53. Cf. also the more general account of V. Flint, *The Rise of Magic in Early Medieval Europe* [Princeton: Princeton University Press, 1991], 20). Further, the natural and supernatural worlds were understood to be inextricably linked together (more extensive references in Grey, "Demoniacs," 54–56; cf. *Vita Genovefae* 34, where a tree held responsible for shipwrecks is chopped down and found to contain a pair of fearsome supernatural monsters).

In the present context, two implications follow. First, it is worth reflecting briefly upon the geography of demonic possession. In a detailed discussion of the roles assigned or available to demons in the eastern Mediterranean, Horden has argued that in fact they filled a limited number of ecological very trees, rocks, and stones of Gaul to bend to his will.[m] Rightly also do we recall the sainted Germanus, that most excellent of bishops and envoys, who gave his body to Gaul that it could be truly blessed by his perpetual presence. Truly did each city embrace the saint as he made his own *iter* to Auxerre.[n]

Let your own *iter* now return us to those days. Your lands themselves come to you as supplicants.[o] Feed us, they say; nourish and protect us. Let your own thirst for knowledge inspire a quest in others. But let that quest not simply be to count the fields and farms.[p] Let it be not merely to pass from town to town by road or

---

niches: P. Horden, "Responses to Possession and Insanity in the Earlier Byzantine World," *Social History of Medicine* 6 [1993]: 177–94, at 182–84). At least some of those niches could be clearly identified, and foremost among these were locales that bore the traces or the continuing presence of pagan religious practices. Certainly, Constantius's account reveals a clear (if to the modern reader unexpected) awareness among demons of geographical boundaries. Salvian's observations, too, assume that demons both possess a particular (and particularly human or natural) kind of spatial awareness and are subject to certain limitations upon their ability to move across the landscape.

Second, if the supernatural and natural worlds are inextricably connected with each other, then natural and supernatural landscapes are inseparable. As a consequence, scholars may have to approach descriptions of landscapes that stress the divine influence of gods or emphasize the intervention of other supernatural beings as not merely topoi of the genres in which those descriptions appear but also a reflection of a widely disseminated intellectual and cultural understanding of the nature and components of the world in which those authors lived. If our ancient authors are simultaneously imagining both a tree and the spirit associated with or inhabiting that tree every time they describe the tree, then the choices they make in representing the landscape as more or less influenced by the supernatural are as much the product of a prevailing set of cultural expectations or constraints as they are determined by genre conventions. Furthermore, Christian attempts both to detach the physical landscape from its metaphysical associations and to overwrite that landscape with a Christian geography take on an even more urgent aspect in the period.

m. Cf. Sulpicius Severus, *Vita Martini* 13, a story of a tree changing direction in mid-fall rather than crush the holy man. For a more extensive discussion of this story, see Grey, *Constructing Communities* (above, n. g), 154–55.

n. One of our better accounts of an imperial-style progress is to be found in Constantius's account of the return of Germanus's body from Ravenna (*Vita Germani* 44–46). Indeed, the whole of Constantius's text is an extended travel narrative, recounting the multitudinous journeys that the holy man took and connecting those journeys with his embrace of the duty of care for his flock, both within Gaul and outside it. For the connectivity between *adventus* and pilgrimage in the homiletic texts of Augustine, see P. P. Liverani, "Victors and Pilgrims in Late Antiquity and the Early Middle Ages," *Fragmenta* 1 (2007): 83–102.

o. Cf. the extended metaphor of the city of Rome as a supplicant in Symmachus, *Relationes* 3.

p. This appears to be a reference to the imperial census. The most striking description of the process of taking the census may be found in the early fourth-century Christian polemicist Lactantius (*De Mortibus Persecutorum* 23.1–2), who depicts imperial officials swarming the landscape like a conquering army. The details of the tax system in late fifth- or early sixth-century Gaul are more difficult to determine, although there is some evidence for the continuation of Roman tax practices in Visigothic Aquitaine and Spain, at least (L. A. García Moreno, "Estudios sobre la organización administrativa del reino visigodo de Toledo," *Anuario de Historia del Derecho Español* 44 [1974]: 5–155, at 21–65; M. Rouche, *L'Aquitaine, des Wisigoths aux Arabes, 418–781: Naissance d'une région* [Paris:

river.[q] Let it rather be to bring the love and fear of God to rivers and woods, to mountains and valleys. Let your baptism presage our own. Let demons be banished, monsters slain, and ghosts excised from the country. Let rustics be safe and happy once more. Let them embrace their hearths, free from the ills of the cities. Let them enjoy a peaceful tranquillity day by day, season by season.[r] Let them, finally, speak your name with love and reverence as the bringer once again of . . .[s]

AFTERWORD

The reader will have already divined that the text under discussion here is in reality an artificial construction. As such, it is at least in part an explicit response to the work of Keith Hopkins, whose name was invoked in both the title and the introduction to this fictional work. But the somewhat playful form adopted here is underpinned by sincere analytical, methodological, and theoretical concerns.[9] In

---

Éditions de l'École des Hautes Études en Sciences Sociales, Éditions Touzot, 1979], 338–42; Grey, "Two Young Lovers" [above, n. *f*], 296–97). However, in the present context, it is important to note that any process of quantifying the landed and human assets of a state amounts to an exercise in abstraction and simplification. That is, states legislate in an attempt to impose a certain limiting logic upon a reality that is immensely complex and impossible to comprehend fully (J. C. Scott, *Seeing Like a State: How Certain Schemes to Improve the Human Condition Have Failed* [New Haven: Yale University Press, 1998], 11–12, 22–23, 24–29; for this problem and its implications in a specifically late Roman context, see Grey, *Constructing Communities* [above, n. *g*], 8–9).

q. It is difficult to quantify the relative incidence of road- and river-based travel even in the case of imperial or royal figures and their agents. It is certainly not difficult to find in our ancient sources the fear of barbarians being used as an excuse not to travel or an explanation for why particular routes or modes are taken (e.g., Symmachus, *Epistles* 7.13 14; Rutilius Namatianus, *De Reditu Suo* 1.37–42).

However, too much analytical weight has probably been placed upon perceived changes in the relative incidence of the two in the period, and upon the specific circumstances motivating our authors to select a particular mode or modes. Sidonius Apollinaris's account of his travels on the *cursus publicus* from Gaul to Rome, for example, mentions both road and river transportation (*Epistles* 1.5). For a broad synthetic approach to human movement around the Mediterranean world in our period, see P. Horden and N. Purcell, *The Corrupting Sea: A Study of Mediterranean History* (Oxford and New York: Oxford University Press, 2000), 123–72, although there is little discussion of travel at the scale and on the terms noted here.

r. Our author's explicit gloss on the rustic existence as "day by day, season by season," reminds us that our ancient authors were aware of seasonal variation in the tasks and rhythms of life in the countryside. Note, for example, Palladius's attention to documenting the different hours of sunlight from month to month as well as his organization of his text by month, which highlights different aspects of the work calendar even with reference to tasks that are essential over the whole year. Such a strategy not only provides a useful structuring device for the work; it also echoes previous authors' use of the temporal rhythms of the day or week to explore the relationship between time, activity, and morality: cf., for example, the slightly subversive version of this textual form taken by Ausonius's *Ephemeris*.

s. The manuscript breaks off here. But given the perorative aspects of this sentence, it seems reasonable to assume that there is little further missing beyond a final felicitation and perhaps the author's name.

inventing this text, my intention has been to ask a series of interconnected questions about ancient ways of knowing and knowledge construction, and about our own processes of engagement with those ways: What would the perfect plausible text on the countryside of late antiquity look like, and under what textual and informational constraints would it operate? How would I, as a scholar of *ruralia* in the period, engage with such a text? What expectations would I have of it, and how would I construct my responses? I wished also to explore the limits and opportunities presented by the commentary as a textual form that is, arguably, particularly suited to the fragmentary and disarticulated state of our information about the countrysides of late antiquity. The following reflections upon these questions will serve, I hope, to clarify the role of this (admittedly rather unusual) project as a response to the analytical challenge laid down by the editors of the present volume and to emphasize the intellectual bind in which a strategy of reading against the grain of our texts places us. Although the intention of these reflections is not explicitly self-exculpatory, I hope that they will at least make explicit a collection of implicit assumptions that I have long taken into my own work and expose those assumptions to a useful and necessary scrutiny.

It goes without saying that the perfect source is an impossibility, even if we were able adequately to define what we mean by the term. Perfect for whom? To what purpose? In the present context, the problem is more intractable still, for we tend to work on the assumption that our predominantly urban, aristocratic male authors knew little about the *realia* of rural life. We view the countrysides that they wrote as essentially collections of literary and cultural tropes with occasional fleeting glimpses of realities upon which we want—indeed, are forced—to place a heavy interpretive burden. Characteristically, therefore, we mine our sources, extracting nuggets of information that we deem to be relevant to our own questions. In the process, we implicitly or (rarely) explicitly acknowledge that the information that we seek is often wholly ancillary or incidental to the purposes of the authors of the texts from which it has been extracted.[10]

This approach (and it is one of which I am undeniably guilty in my own work) has the tendency to pass too quickly over the aims and objectives of the authors of these texts in favor of our own concerns. Consequently it runs the risk of missing or ignoring our authors' role in the construction and presentation of both their knowledge and our own. Most particularly, in the present context, it tends to privilege the demographic or socioeconomic elements of the countrysides under discussion and to ignore or undervalue the physical places that are being described. As already noted in the introductory remarks, ancient authors did not separate these two elements quite so readily as we might wish them to have, or wish to ourselves. Rather, their knowledge of the countrysides that they described was intimately tied up with—indeed, iteratively reinforced by—the stories that they told about them. These stories served in some sense as mnemonics of the physical places to which they were attached. Detaching the places from the stories or the people from the places is therefore a rather difficult task, and certainly one that runs counter to the objectives of the authors of these texts. Ultimately, then, in attempting to construct the perfect plausible source (and I do not think that I have by any means succeeded in the attempt), I wished to acknowledge the essential importance of engaging with our texts as texts written by authors in specific contexts and with particular aims, objectives, and information.

The quintessential form that this engagement takes in contemporary classical scholarship is the commentary. Much has been written about the philosophical and analytical frameworks within which this textual form exists. Often it is perceived or described as objective, scientific, or useful and contrasted explicitly with the more subjective, transient monographic work.[11] By explicitly anchoring his or her textual production to the structure of another, already existent text, the commentator consciously or unconsciously fosters the impression that he or she is an explicator and interpreter rather than an author of a text. This is, of course, a useful fiction. But it is a fiction nevertheless. In selecting, among other things, how to organize the text and the accompanying notes, and what to comment upon, the commentator sets the interpretive agenda for his or her reader, thereby constraining and directing that reader's engagement with and analysis of the text. Clearly, in creating a fictional text upon which to comment, I have taken this process to a rather ridiculous and illogical conclusion. However, the exercise has highlighted (for me at least) the potential fertility of the commentary as a historiographical form. By militating against the construction of a sustained, coherent argument and in favor of a series of loosely connected interpretive vignettes, the commentary is infinitely adaptable and malleable. In many ways, then, it is just as subjective and individual as the more traditional monograph, with its (implicitly or explicitly recognized) narrative structures and novelistic form. Indeed, it is tempting to suggest that the commentary is in fact particularly well suited to the sensibilities and objectives of contemporary historiography.[12]

This is not to embrace the postmodernist historiographical project, which adds a somewhat nihilistic element to the thought-provoking observations of Hayden White concerning narrative strategies and emplotment devices in the modern writing of history.[13] Far from it. It is, simply, to place the current project more explicitly within the context of contemporary debates over how we write history and for what purpose. In that context, it is worth emphasizing both the explicitly self-serving nature of the process of constructing a text and then commenting upon it, and the necessity of explicitly adopting a stance of sincere struggle with that text. In writing my commentary, I continued instinctively to read against the grain of the text that I had created. That is, my interpretational starting point continued to be the assumption that our authors knew next to nothing about the things that they described. My role and responsibility as commentator and interpreter of the text continued to be to extract the *realia* that lay, as I imaginatively suspected, behind it. In the process, I continued to ask questions of the text that its supposed author had not intended it to answer—even though I was, myself, the author and had explicitly constructed the text so that I could ask precisely those questions. This tension between satisfying one's own needs for the text and struggling sincerely with it is a key element in any scholar's engagement with his or her material. Further, in the present context—namely an attempt to recapture or recreate late ancient knowledge of the countryside—this tension is fundamental to a reading strategy that runs, of necessity, against the grain or into the silences of the text. But that strategy is heavily freighted with the scholar's own wishes, desires, and objectives for the text.

This observation is particularly apposite in the context of modern scholarly approaches to the countrysides of the late Roman world, for rural contexts and the fates of their inhabitants have tended to be employed as encapsulations of our preferred visions of late Roman society. In some constructions, therefore, the late Roman countryside is a rather brutal world, its structures of power and dependence determined and shaped by a state that was principally and fundamentally interested in extracting revenues.[14] In others, it is a world shocked to its core by the irruption of barbarians, bringing entirely new cultural norms and destabilizing already fragile socioeconomic, fiscal, and political structures.[15] The late Roman countryside of this particular text is rather different, for two interconnected reasons. The first is the constraints of the putative genre (or genres) in which I was attempting to write the text—a panegyrical work is more likely to emphasize the idyllic rather than the unsavory aspects of the countryside. But my choice of genre reflects, in part at least, my own vision of the countrysides of the late Roman world, which I regard as experiencing opportunity as much as oppression and socioeconomic dynamism as much as political and fiscal devolution.[16] The disparity between catastrophist and transformationist points of view that this (deliberately overstated) contrast reveals is in part a product of differences in focus, for the former is principally located in the thought world of (at least some of) our late Roman authors, whereas the latter purports or seeks to recapture the *realia* of the lived experience of the population more generally. Most important, however, it should be somewhat self-evident in the present context that neither tells the full story, and neither is sufficient in and of itself, if our aim is to reveal or recapture what late antique people knew about their world. What they knew interacted with the literary conventions within which they wrote to produce the texts that confront us now. It is therefore dangerous in the extreme to approach a text such as Rutilius Namatianus's *De Reditu Suo* or Sidonius Apollinaris's letter to his friend Heronius (*Ep.* 1.5) without first considering both the constraints within which these texts were written and the ways in which the authors acknowledged, modified, or manipulated those constraints.[17]

It is important to note, too, that the textual sources that survive from the period can be employed to support all these interpretations.[18] As scholars, we mold that evidence in accordance with the analytical or interpretational axes that we wish to grind. To emphasize this point further, I sought throughout the commentary to direct and shape the reader's interpretation of the text by focusing to different degrees upon different topics: the extreme Othering of the Bagaudae received a short paragraph of (somewhat florid) speculation; the place of demons in conceptual geographies was slightly more extensively explored but sparsely referenced; ideas about the inscription of memory and identity into a landscape by means of travel across it were mentioned only fleetingly. This illustrates the ways in which the particular form of the commentary can present an opportunity to raise issues without necessarily crafting an internally consistent, cohesive argument about them. But this very phenomenon and the impulse toward brevity that the form encourages also have the potential to frustrate both commentator and reader, since no single, coherent argument will emerge from the text and the commentator's decision making about what to comment upon will be intensely and necessarily subjective. The explicit juxtaposition of claims to objectivity with subjective focuses and practices make the commentary simultaneously a somewhat troubling medium and an immensely useful tool—both for explicating a text and for exploring our own processes of explication, whatever form that explication may take.

I do not pretend to have identified or even articulated answers to any of the questions raised here. But they are, I think, implicit in all that we do, not only as scholars of the marginal or voiceless in antiquity but also more generally as students of the ancient world. I have found the exercise of making them explicit, if only for a moment, to have been a useful one. In particular, I find myself reflecting in new ways upon certain assumptions that I have long made about the engagement of our ancient authors with the countrysides around them. I am no longer so certain about the boundary between knowledge and construction of the countryside in these texts, for I have a keener appreciation of the dialectical relationship between the two. I am no longer so convinced that the silences and gaps into which I habitually seek to read are simply or merely gaps of knowledge on the part of our ancient authors. I would now argue that, in more cases than I was previously prepared to admit, the omission is the result of a conscious decision-making process on the part of the author. Although I remain convinced that there was a great deal that our ancient authors did not know about the countrysides of their world and the inhabitants of those countrysides, I am more keenly aware of the fact that the gap between their knowledge and ours is greater still.

Our ancient authors constructed countrysides in their texts. Those countrysides resemble the real countrysides that social historians might wish to access, but they are at the same time much more complex, nuanced, and sophisticated phenomena. We must be conscious of the particular contexts within which those countrysides were created and acknowledge the effects that those contexts might have had upon the texts before us. Equally, we must be careful lest, in our haste to extract from our authors' writings the nuggets of information that we need to construct our countrysides, we lose sight completely of the knowledge and experiences encoded in their countrysides.

NOTES

I wish to thank my co-contributors and the editors of the current volume for their many thoughtful and challenging critiques and comments upon earlier versions of this text. I also thank Keith Hopkins's literary executor, Christopher Kelly, with whose full knowledge and blessing this project was undertaken, for his indulgence and enthusiasm.

1. Cf. the discussion of late antique literary production in A. Cameron, "Remaking the Past," in *Late Antiquity: A Guide to the Postclassical World*, ed. G. W. Bowersock, P. Brown, and O. Grabar (Cambridge, Mass.: Belknap Press of Harvard University Press, 1999), 1–16. Also, for the particular aesthetic characteristics of late Roman literature, M. Roberts, *The Jeweled Style: Poetry and Poetics in Late Antiquity* (Ithaca: Cornell University Press, 1989); A. Cameron, *The Last Pagans of Rome* (Oxford and New York: Oxford University Press, 2011), particularly 743–82. Insights from art-historical approaches to the period are also instructive: D. Kinney, "Spolia, Damnatio and Renovatio Memoriae," *Memoirs of the American Academy in Rome* 42 (1997): 117–48; J. Elsner, "From the Culture of *Spolia* to the Cult of Relics: The Arch of Constantine and the Genesis of Late Antique Forms," *Papers of the British School at Rome* 68 (2000): 149–84.

2. Cf. the excellent studies of N. Lozovsky, *"The earth is our book": Geographical Knowledge in the Latin West ca. 400–1000* (Ann Arbor: University of Michigan Press, 2010); idem, "Geography and Ethnography in Medieval Europe: Classical Traditions and Contemporary Concerns," in *Geography and Ethnography: Perceptions of the World in Pre-Modern Societies,* ed. K. A. Raaflaub and R. J. A. Talbert (Malden, Mass., and Chichester: Wiley-Blackwell, 2010), 311–29.

3. For dating, see Jean Rougé in his edition of the text: J. Rougé, ed., trans., and comm., *Expositio Totius Mundi et Gentium,* Sources Chrétiennes, vol. 126 (Paris: Éditions du Cerf, 1966).

4. For the specific function of the geographical preface to late antique and early medieval Christian historiography, see A. H. Merrills, *History and Geography in Late Antiquity* (Cambridge: Cambridge University Press, 2005), 1–4.

5. For a sustained argument to this effect, see F. Racine, "Literary Geography in Late Antiquity," unpublished PhD dissertation, Yale University (2008).

6. A. C. Dionisotti, "From Ausonius' Schooldays? A Schoolbook and Its Relatives," *Journal of Roman Studies* 72 (1982): 83–125. Further on writing exercises and the fluidity of supposedly canonical forms and texts with particular reference to rewriting the *Aeneid* in the period, see S. McGill, "Other *Aeneids*: Rewriting Three Virgilian Passages in the Codex Salmasianus," *Vergilius* 49 (2003): 84–113.

7. Avitus of Vienne, *Epistle* 46; Gregory of Tours, *Decem Libri Historiarum* 2.30. For full discussion of the debate over dating and other issues related to the conversion of Clovis, see

D. Shanzer, "Dating the Baptism of Clovis: The Bishop of Vienne vs the Bishop of Tours," *Early Medieval Europe* 7 (1998): 29–57, who rejects 496, 498, and 505 in favor of 508 C.E.

8. For the existence of a particularly strong and vibrant literary culture among the so-called Lérins circle of Gallo-Roman bishops, see R. W. Mathisen, *Ecclesiastical Factionalism and Religious Controversy in Fifth-Century Gaul* (Washington, D.C.: Catholic University of America Press, 1989).

9. Cf. Keith Hopkins's own forays into the realm of invention, most notably *A World Full of Gods: The Strange Triumph of Christianity* (London and New York: Weidenfeld and Nicolson, 1999), with its account of time travel, film script, constructed primary sources, and letters from colleagues. Also M. K. Hopkins, "How to Be a Roman Emperor: An Auto-biography," in *History and Fiction: Six Essays Celebrating the Centenary of Sir Ronald Syme (1903–89)*, ed. R. Tomlin (London: Grime and Selwood, 2005), 72–85. For a somewhat more erudite exercise in forgery than that presented here, cf. R. Syme, "*Titus et Berenice*: A Tac-itean Fragment (text and commentary)," in his *Roman Papers*, vol. 7, ed. A. R. Birley (Oxford: Clarendon Press, 1991), 647–62.

10. For more extensive discussion of the problems attendant upon reconstructing rural life from our sources, see C. Grey, *Constructing Communities in the Late Roman Countryside* (Cambridge and New York: Cambridge University Press, 2011), 4–15.

11. Further discussion and full references in C. S. Kraus, "Introduction: Reading Com-mentaries/Commentaries as Reading," in *The Classical Commentary: Histories, Practices, Theory*, ed. R. K. Gibson and C. S. Kraus (Leiden and New York: Brill, 2002), 1–27, at 2–3.

12. See the classic account of H. White, "The Structure of Historical Narrative," *Clio* 1.3 (1972): 5–20. Also idem, *Metahistory: The Historical Imagination in Nineteenth-Century Europe* (Baltimore: The Johns Hopkins University Press, 1973), for the particular nine-teenth-century context in which the disciplinary and generic structures of historiography developed. For more extensive critical treatment of White, his interlocutors, and his critics, see W. Kansteiner, "Hayden White's Critique of the Writing of History," *History and Theory* 32 (1993): 273–95.

13. For a set of recent, stimulating responses to the postmodern impulse in contempo-rary historiography, see now A. L. Macfie, "On the Defence of (My) History," *Rethinking History: The Journal of Theory and Practice* 14 (2010): 209–27; idem, "The Present State of (My) History," *Rethinking History: The Journal of Theory and Practice* 15 (2011): 539–50.

14. Cf. especially Wickham's synthetic account of the period, particularly his argument that Salvian of Marseilles's account of the ills of late Roman society rests upon the argument that rural socioeconomic relations are framed and defined by the oppressiveness of the tax system: C. R. Wickham, *Framing the Early Middle Ages: Europe and the Mediterranean 400–800* (Oxford and New York: Oxford University Press, 2005), especially 62–64. See also, for critical responses to Wickham that nevertheless preserve the focus upon the role and influ-ence of the state and an assumption that socioeconomic relations were fundamentally oppressive, J. Banaji, "Aristocracies, Peasantries and the Framing of the Early Middle Ages," *Journal of Agrarian Change* 9 (2009): 59–91; P. Sarris, "Introduction: Aristocrats, Peasants and the Transformation of Rural Society, c.400–800," *Journal of Agrarian Change* 9 (2009): 3–22. For a sustained, intensely stimulating review of Wickham's picture, see now B. D. Shaw, "After Rome: Transformations of the Early Medieval World," *New Left Review* 51

(May–June 2008): 89–114; and cf. Grey, *Constructing Communities* (above, n. 10), particularly chapters 5 and 7, 148–77 and 198–225.

15. Cf. P. Heather, *The Fall of the Roman Empire. A New History of Rome and the Barbarians* (Oxford and New York: Oxford University Press, 2005); B. Ward-Perkins, *The Fall of Rome and the End of Civilization* (Oxford and New York: Oxford University Press, 2005).

16. A much more detailed exposition of this argument is to be found in Grey, *Constructing Communities* (above, n. 10).

17. Cf. Racine, "Literary Geography" (above, n. 5), 203–4.

18. Note also the dearth of archaeological evidence in the purported commentary to this text. For a contrasting approach to the balance between archaeological and textual evidence, cf. C. Grey, "Concerning Rural Matters," in *The Oxford Handbook of Late Antiquity*, ed. S. F. Johnson (Oxford and New York: Oxford University Press, 2012), 625–66.

13

Demon

Dayna S. Kalleres

For this essay I was asked to examine and imagine (or reimagine) the word and the category "demon" in late antiquity. In the spirit of this book's mission, I began asking questions intended to place the word in an experiential (and thus knowledge-producing) context. What meanings did "demon" express in late antiquity? What rituals, behaviors, beliefs, and discourses did "demon" indicate? What systems of knowledge were generated through the rituals, behaviors, beliefs, and discourses tied to the word "demon"? In what ways did "demon" contribute to the construction and management of a late antique person's identity, community, or environment? How did the construct "demon" participate in a person's self-fashioning when interacting with others and his or her environment? And finally, then, how might the various meanings of and knowledges surrounding "demon" feed our endeavor to reimagine and reconfigure the history representing the third to the eighth century? Or inversely, during this process of our historiographic reformation, what might we uncover regarding the place and purpose of "demon" not only in that past era but in both current and less recent historiographies of the period? What may surprise us as we shift the word "demon" to the center from the peripheral edges of history where it has loitered for so long and where so many pieces of the ancient world have existed—discarded, rejected, and collecting dust for generations?

As answers began to assemble tentatively in my mind, a certain realization emerged. Undoubtedly the prospect of discussing, even disinterring, the dismissed and buried depths of the word and the category "demon" would quickly energize and sustain my consideration—especially my investigation into the related production of demonic knowledge in that past period. Still, I increasingly sensed the need for caution when I turned to consider various historiographies for the third through to the eighth century—predominantly the two competing historical narratives of decline and transformation in late antiquity, most clearly seen in the work of Edward Gibbon and Peter Brown.[1] A close and patient look at the word and category "demon" within the two histories began to unravel, disassemble and, finally, destroy many of the fragile and fraudulent elements within the two historiographies. Indeed, it exposed the problematic nature of leading this examination with the modern word "demon."

In its earlier incarnations in the ancient world, the construct *daimōn* dwelt in a wider and richer ritual and religious pluralism and polytheism. I propose that by consciously and conscientiously searching for and imagining *daimōn* and related ritual constructs (rather than "demon"), we may uncover the original category and its much more complicated character; *daimōn* encompassed positive, negative, and neutral moralities, ethical meanings, and ontologies. Thus, rather than appraising the later medieval and early modern, Christianized incarnation "demon," which issued forth from a constraining post-Reformation crucible of duality, malevolence, and moral intransigence, I turn to the word *daimōn* in its fourth- to fifth-century context—a word that sheds deliberate and determined light upon antiquity's religious pluralism, ritual improvisation and innovation, and any attendant moral ambiguities.

. . .

Before we approach these earlier meanings and assemblages of knowledge though, we must divest ourselves of the stubborn anachronisms by which we have transformed a late antique *daimōn* into a narrowly construed and misplaced "demon." This involves briefly visiting "demon" in the two historiographic projects mentioned above: Gibbon's history of decline and fall and Brown's history of transformation and continuity. In the production of these historical narratives, then, "demon" has often been relegated to the periphery—and thus been made seemingly harmless. In that area, however, hidden in the margins of recorded history, I contend that "demon" has managed to express a hardly innocuous, Christian, Protestantized meaning, semantic range, dualizing efficacy, and symbolic effect. The firmly Christianized construct "demon" is much more than a haphazard semantic category of a medieval and early modern Western world.[2] It is a word that, although it may not do so by design, nonetheless imposes deliberate and dangerous falsehoods and misdirections into the earlier history of the third through the eighth century.

Gibbon is quite clear: in earliest Christianity within the late imperial period, people had tried to cling to the higher moral, ethical, and intellectual principles of an earlier era. By the third century, though, economic crises wore down many different aspects of Roman civilization to allow the increasing seepage of a degrading Christianity into society; eventually, by the fourth century monks and their aco-

lytes covered the ground. And Gibbon placed the blame for the erosion of civilization on an increasing belief in demons followed by ritual practice engaging the
demonic: a growing superstition was soon to follow and overtake and darken any
light of intelligence left in the empire. The influx of demons had a direct effect on
the caliber of rational thinking: increasing belief in demons and superstition in
general had worn away the human ability to think clearly. In fact, according to
Gibbon, demonological belief and rational or philosophical thought could not
inhabit the same mind:[3]

> The fame of the apostles and martyrs was gradually eclipsed by these recent and
> popular Anachorets; ... a believing age was easily persuaded, that the slightest
> caprice of an Egyptian or a Syrian monk had been sufficient to interrupt the eternal
> laws of the universe. The favorites of Heaven were accustomed to cure inveterate
> diseases with a touch ... and to expel the most obstinate demons from the souls or
> bodies which they possessed. . . . . These extravagant tales, which display the fiction,
> without the genius, of poetry, have seriously affected the reason, the faith, and the
> morals, of the Christians. Their credulity debased and vitiated the faculties of the
> mind: they corrupted the evidence of history; and superstition gradually extin-
> guished the hostile light of philosophy and science.

Gibbon bemoans the influx of a host of demons bringing irrationality, magic, and
superstition and thus sinking the civilization that had existed in a pre-Christian
Roman Empire. He fails to emphasize the new ritual tools that expel the rationality
(e.g., exorcism). In the Gibbonian reading, "demon" carries within it the opposite
of the civilized; "demon" is the chaotic Other to rational thinking, Greco-Roman
moral philosophy, and order. It is by this measure an extreme model of human
degradation and mental decay. Although this reflects elements of late antique
demonology, it is only a minute fragment. This "demon" has been reduced through
Cartesian, Christianizing, Protestantizing, and Enlightenment lenses of modernity.
"Demon" reflects and contains what a human being claims to have shed through
his or her progress through time. This narrative of decline and its related fatalistic
outlook of inevitable bouts of civic decadence left its mark on most scholarship on
the later Roman Empire in the nineteenth and the early twentieth century.[4]

The historiography of late antiquity began as and continues to be an interpretive
practice with an agenda of intervention, a deliberately directed hermeneutical and
critical approach to and restoration of history collected and contorted first by the
Gibbonian narrative of the decline and fall of empire.[5] Since Peter Brown's 1971 article "The Rise and Function of the Holy Man in Late Antiquity," then, the term
"demon" has served a more subtle ideological purpose in this project; it still functions as a dualizing marker and Othering tool in both late antique history and historiography, but it does so in precisely circumscribed socioreligious and political conditions.[6] In this more recent discourse, "demon" severs the magical, superstitious,

and decadent from what Brown and late antique historians define as late antiquity's rationality and civilized populations. Contemporary interpreters have clarified how the category "demon" functioned (Othering, dualizing, diabolizing) in specific and set discursive and ritual contexts in late antiquity as well socioreligious and political frameworks.[7] Exorcism is valued and lauded as a ritual tool that rids the world of the irrational and the uncivilized.[8]

These interpreters have made important corrections in the historiographical practices involving the third through the eighth century. Still, they have over-looked certain anachronistic systems of knowledge that the term "demon" has pro-duced and deposited into their own interpretive writing. Although the term "demon" and the ritual tool of exorcism are correctly valued in this more liberal consideration of the era, both are still markers that manage inadvertently to instill anachronistic divisions, divides, boundaries, and borders.

The historiographic "demon" still imposes a bifurcated field in late antique his-toriography, and so the construct "demon"—when it on occasion emerges into the narrative—marks a division between the space of rationality, of civilization, of Christianizing, of imperializing progress or continuity, and the darker picture of irrationality, primitivity, and decline. In this manner, a constrained ritual field of "the demonic" mirrors—only briefly and in the moment of the ritual—Gibbon-ian claims of the Roman Empire's decline into an age of magical thinking, supersti-tion, irrationality, and general decadence. The late antique "demon" does echo Gibbon's claims of decline, but then that demon is quickly expelled through exor-cism. Gibbon focuses on the irretrievable loss of rationality in the rise of the demonically possessed. By contrast, in his recognition of the rise of the charis-matic holy man, Brown places value upon a ritualist's ability to exorcize—whether he is a holy man, a priest, or merely a baptized congregant. All such Christian rit-ual figures can expel Gibbon's demons and their irrationality. Most especially, Brown's holy man possesses the ability to remove the threat of what Gibbon claimed would take over and degrade civilization.[9]

In short, the late antique "demon" captures and contains, and then—in the rit-ual of exorcism—distances Gibbon's age of decadence (i.e., magical thinking, irra-tionality, superstitious belief and practice). In this way, late antique historiography creates space to construct and consider new types of figures—rational and civi-lized within a Christianizing late antique framework: the holy man, Christian asceticism, the orthodox Christian priest, the baptizand, the church versus the heretic and the Jew—and all exist within the ritual and discursive processes of Christianization under the Roman Empire.

· · ·

In what follows, I shall endeavor to avoid such historiographical designs upon the material reality and texts of the third through the eighth century by uncovering the wider and deeper sense of the word *daimōn* through a two-part analysis. First I present a brief taste of the Greco-Roman *daimōn* in order that we may begin to grasp the consequences of the religiously pluralistic context in which *daimones* were embedded; second, this essay shall take us to a particular time and place, attempting to follow *daimones* in situ; I shall trace the daily ritual engagement that a person has with *daimones* in one city (Antioch) and during a certain time (the late fourth and early fifth century). Complete avoidance of anachronisms is impossible, of course; however, armed with an understanding of the malleability of "demon" in other historiographies, I move forward cautiously with *daimōn* in the center and taking the lead.

ENTERING THE WORLD OF *DAIMONES*

In *Cratylus* 398a-b, Plato describes *daimones* as wise (*phronimoi*), "noble . . . , averters of evil, guardians of mortal men." Upon death, a good man who has a greater portion of honor among the dead becomes a *daimōn*, which is tantamount to becoming an incarnation of wisdom. Plato goes further in *Cratylus* 398c, describing the good man (*agathos anēr*) as possessing a spiritual nature (*orthos daimōn*) in both life and death. Plato's *daimōn* diametrically opposes our modern Western view of "demon." In *Symposium* 202e–203a, Plato firmly anchors the intermediary cosmological location of *daimones* and defines their ritual interaction with humanity and divinity. This presents a demonological model in which humans exert agency and power over *daimones* rather than *daimones* holding power over people. In the *Symposium*, Diotima aggrandizes "a very powerful *daimōn*," Erōs, granting it tremendous cosmological territory—"The whole of *to daimonion* is between divine and mortal":[10]

> [*Erōs* is] halfway between mortal and immortal, . . . a very powerful *daimōn*, and the whole of *to daimonion* is between divine and mortal. [*Daimones* have the power (*dynamin*)] as the envoys and interpreters that ply between heaven and earth to interpret and carry over human ["things"] concerns to gods and divine ["things"] concerns to human beings; . . . . They form the medium of all divination and priestly craft concerning sacrifice and initiations and incantations, and all prophecy [*manteia*] and magic [*goēteia*]. For indeed [God] divinity does not mingle with a human being, but *to daimonion* has enabled [or "facilitated"] all discourse and conversation between the gods and men either awake or asleep. And the man who is versed in such matters is said to be *daimonion*. . . . There are many *daimones* and many kinds of *daimones*, and Erōs is one of them.

In facilitating human-divine communication, *daimones* maintain an essential unmixed state of the immortal (divine) and mortal (human) while ensuring the two opposites' continual interaction. *Daimones*' primary purpose is to sustain unity in a dynamic cosmos. Thus, they must maintain moral neutrality in the actions they carry out: *daimones* are the same whenever recruited, whether to perform a prayer to divinity or a curse against another human being.

In Plutarch's *De Defectu Oraculorum,* by contrast, daimonic intermediaries have fallen from the lofty heights that Diotima claims for them.[11] *Daimones,* and not gods, are the guardians of the oracles and mystery cults; *daimones* have also fundamentally changed from the earlier, calm, removed variety we find in Plato's *Symposium.* Here their mixed nature produces an unhealthy imbalance of mortal passions; too many *daimones* assigned to oracles are driven by unleashed passions.[12] They are holding the land ransom until they receive satisfaction for the cravings that they are now suffering; in short, a cosmos once perfectly balanced has fallen. *Daimones,* Diotima's sure measure of the cosmological median and thus universal balance, fall much lower in Plutarch's estimation, becoming an infamous symbol of earth's madness: *daimones* are driven insane by an insatiable lust for human souls; they cause "pestilences and barrenness of the earth and stir up wars and seditions until they get and obtain what they lust after."[13] Before *daimones* departed the oracles altogether, their behavior at the shrines was deplorable.

The *daimones* fell into a rapacious desire for the human soul. In effect, Plutarch draws together what Plato is so cautious to keep apart: *daimones* are part divine and part mortal passion. *Daimones* that draw closer to the emotional side bring human beings into greater harm. As Plutarch explains, countless rapes, a plague of sexual depravity and other abuses, described in numerous legends, testify to the dangerous lusts of "powerful and impetuous *daimones.*"[14] Plutarch dwells on *daimones'* base, uncontrollable drives: the metaphorically carnal part of *daimones,* which they share with human beings. And, according to Plutarch, *daimones* are all-too-attracted to this part of humanity. He sexualizes the daimonic lust for the human soul, transforming a *daimōn* into an aggressive, relentless predator: a cultic oracular *daimōn* has "insane and imperious passions" for—a "human soul, which is incarnate within a mortal body."[15] The embodied state of the soul only enrages *daimones* further. Daimonic lust and attraction necessarily lead to a kind of violence that is brutal and sadistic. The *daimones* are driven by a lust for a soul separated from its body: *daimones* "either could not, or would not, enjoy souls with their bodies, or by their bodies." Only human sacrifice would quell the daimonic attack—the rite surrenders a soul to a *daimōn*'s lascivious embrace. As protection from *daimones,* according to Plutarch, people engage in "abusive language at the sacrifices and other mad doings attended with tumult and head-tossing," all of which served to "turn away evil *daimones.*"[16]

These two competing models of the demonic, from Plato and Plutarch, both informed late antique human experiences with *daimones.* I turn now to one particular case of human-*daimōn* interaction in order to explore how these models put knowledge of *daimones* in order in the lives of late ancient people.

CREATING A LITTLE BIT OF LATE ANTIQUITY

The Princeton and French excavations in Antakya in the 1930s produced rich archaeological materials for both Antioch and Daphne.[17] In the 1933–35 season, twelve curse tablets were found, several relating to the marketplace. Two of the curse tablets identify the same person as victim, a greengrocer named Babylas. These two curse tablets attack Babylas's business and thus provide us with reliable historical proof of his personage. Babylas will be our ritual anchor for understanding the embodied knowledge of *daimones* in the city of Antioch. Antioch features an abundant textual and archaeological archive. We have enough information to imagine other family members in Babylas's life: a wife and a daughter of marriageable age, all of them living a nominally Christian life in which they enjoy martyr festivals. Through Babylas and his family, we catch a glimpse of a city of *daimones*, which ran the spectrum from malevolent to beneficent, ritually interwoven into the lives of all the citizenry. We can also begin to apprehend the mechanisms by which people gained an embodied knowledge of diverse *daimones* and the means whereby they contributed to an ever-evolving knowledge production as well.

BABYLAS AND ANTIOCH

The two curse tablets that name the greengrocer Babylas were discovered in a well beneath a villa situated at the base of Mount Staurin, on the northeast side of the city. The inscriptions upon the tablets invoke Iao and Seth as well as several *daimones* to bind Babylas. The invocations on the first tablet command lower deities and *daimones* to "to lay him low, to sink him like lead, to destroy his animals and his house in general." The second features similar imprecations. Florent Heintz has studied these two tablets alongside other curse texts. He observes that the *daimōn* is provided with precise detail to find his prey expeditiously.[18] In addition to providing the *daimōn* with the exact location of Babylas's vegetable stall, he is equipped with three aliases of Babylas's mother to aid in his hunt. Thus, Babylas's enemies must have known him well. The inscribed invocation features the names of multiple deities to ensure daimonic compliance. In light of the marketplace's competitive atmosphere, Heintz suggests that rival greengrocers commissioned the tablets and were intent on accomplishing their desired goal of destroying the competition.[19]

As John Gager has shown, curse tablets are ubiquitous throughout the ancient Mediterranean world; they provided an accessible ritual means of seeking justice and revenge.[20] The curse tablet generally consisted of a sheet of lead upon which were inscribed magical formulas and symbols. Certain rituals were performed over the tablet—including incantation utterances as well as sacrificial practices. After this, the tablet was often buried in a body of water or placed in the grave of one who had died young. Most important: *defixiones* feature the binding (*katadesmoi*) of *dai-mones* as well as other cosmological forces for the purpose of inflicting material harm upon a victim. To that end they provide important insight into ritual knowl-edge of *daimones* that was accessible for a price to the general population; here we have a means of controlling human-*daimōn* interaction at the lay level; in other words, these texts do not describe the actions of a holy man, a monk, or a priest. Rather they are marketable objects that convey knowledge of daimonic powers to anyone for a price. Furthermore, *defixiones* speak to the belief that people can be controlled by *daimones,* that human beings are not autonomous agents but extremely vulnerable to the influence of invisible forces that in turn are easily manipulated by human ritual agents. The two curse texts demonstrate that the general population understood a wider and deeper ritual integration between human and suprahuman (i.e., the spiritual realm, including *daimones*) populations that attended to as well as influenced the socioeconomic and political spheres. Instead of humans and supra-humans on the opposite sides of an impassible ontological divide—as we might pre-sume in reading the material purely from a Christian (demonizing) standpoint—the two populations interacted constantly through the ritual languages of curses, bind-ing formulas, oaths (*exorkizein*), and so forth; these activities were the means of maintaining social cohesion in the many disparate spheres of urban life.

So too, then, I propose, someone of Babylas's socioeconomic status would have had a vested interest in maintaining his own material success. He would have a variety of means of protecting his interests. Among them, he would seek out pro-tection against curses. We have multiple examples of antidaimonic *apotropaia* found throughout the region of Antioch and Daphne. John Chrysostom describes a variety of practices to keep *daimones* away: copper coins of Alexander of Mace-don encircling a person's head or feet offered powerful amuletic protection;[21] salt, soot, and ash could be used as repellents of evil.[22] Both of these are remedia that an old wisewoman could provide.[23] A person might turn to Bible verses hung as liga-tures, recalling an amulet he or she had seen in a synagogue.[24] Or people might pick up tricks they had learned from their nurses as children, such as tying ribbons with the names of rivers on their wrists or dabbing mud markings on their fore-heads so that the evil eye would cause no harm.[25] The irony here, of course, is that though these are all apotropaic activities, the practice of any and all of these ritu-als—particularly in their display—performatively constructs the chilling fear that substantiates and sustains the reality of *daimones,* the forces of jealousy, anger, and the evil eye within the overall late antique worldview. Through the mere sight of a woman, man, or small boy draped in *apotropaia,* the fear of *daimones* as well as the defense against *daimones* is communicated to others, and thus *daimones* them-selves (though invisible) certainly continue to exist.

Babylas might also have sought protection for his business through the ritual contours of his religious identity. After all, Christian priests were hardly tone-deaf to the propaganda value in advertising the apotropaic power of the baptismal seal or the Eucharist. We should ascribe a similar power to the Torah, though evidence for this stands on John Chrysostom's testimony alone.[26] We may imagine Babylas practicing protective rituals within formal Christianity as well as visiting the synagogue—a location that held the holy books.[27] He may have also visited the Matrona, a Jewish holy site where he could receive divination through incubation.[28] Babylas would have also sought protective aid at one of the many martyr shrines. In Antioch three were noted for their antidaimonic power:[29] the Babylas shrine, the Julian shrine outside the city, and the Drosis cult in the cemetery. Finally, of course, Babylas could choose from among a number of holy men who lived just outside Antioch; many of them were noted for their ability to release people from such binding curses—Macedonius, especially, was noted for making house calls in some cases.[30]

Undoubtedly, Babylas would cast his own curse in response to those of his enemies. He might even turn to the subterranean deity Hecate, whose temple stood in Daphne. Diocletian built her shrine among his other improvements to Daphne at the beginning of the fourth century. Its inner-sanctum shrine was reached by descending three hundred and sixty-five steps and therefore projected its underworld magical or mystical ritual emphasis.[31] Hecate, who had long been associated with *daimones,* was increasingly associated with her status as a subterranean deity. It is intriguing to imagine Babylas constructing a curse in the name of Hecate against his enemies, all the while having the actual location of the temple in Daphne in mind—a physical location for the *daimones* from which they would emerge and carry out their deed.

Depending upon his cultural leanings, Babylas might also try to gain the aid of a *daimōn* to protect his business. In view of his humble background as a greengrocer, though, Babylas would have had to lean quite far to gain an education that would take him in the direction of Iamblichan theurgy or the higher initiation circles in the magical arts.[32] Nonetheless, this kind of ritual—gaining a *daimōn* as an aid known as a *paredros*—leads to a much different human-*daimōn* relation.[33] Rather than considering a human being invoking a *daimōn* to bind and bring harm to another human being, this kind of initiation spell brings power to the ritualist. In effect, the *daimōn* becomes a lifelong aid to the ritualist, amplifying the power and status of the human being in a variety of ways. The *daimōn* can engage in divination or produce wealth or good fortune for the agent. The *daimōn* can simply dress a dinner table. Such ritual activities had a rich connection to Antioch and Apamea, especially Daphne, in light of the cities' connection with Iamblichan theurgy.[34]

Thus, knowledge production for *daimones*—indeed, production of *daimones* themselves—began and ended in social conflict. The modus of production was ritual. Furthermore, competition and diversity fueled knowledge production; rituals were accessible from a variety of competing sources in a city of Antioch's size, especially in light of its religious pluralism—magicians, old women (*graes*), a variety of religious experts: all such ritual sources creating their own strands of demonological (or daimonological) knowledge in the process of each competing with the rest.

To that end, material and textual evidence offer a persuasive picture of a late antique Antioch that was fully immersed in an enchanted worldview.[35] The city was thickly bound in an atmosphere inundated with invisible forces. *Daimones* alongside other named entities ran the spectrum from good to neutral to malevolent. Human populations—at all socioeconomic, educational, and cultural levels—maintained continual ritual interaction and communication with otherworldly forces through a variety of ritual experts (as mentioned above, everything from magicians to priests and monks, etc.) or through their own ingenuity and charismatic power through baptism or other initiation rituals (theurgic, Mithraic, Manichaean). Modern discovery of ritual material indicates the belief that a person was actively engaged in his own protection as well as the subjugation of daimonic powers for other means; a person was not hopelessly at the will of daimonic forces. Rather a sophisticated ritual system was in place—one rooted in fundamental principles of power and reciprocity.

We see most especially in a city that daimonic knowledge (and the rituals attached) involved economics as well as sociology; by purchasing and choosing to wear daimonic (or antidaimonic) ritual objects, late ancient people were visibly engaging with *daimones* in some manner. To all who could read the objects, they announced how their bodies and their identities had been vulnerable; and in the same moment, they also announced how their bodies had been transformed into invulnerable or at least fortified objects now that they were draped in *apotropaia* or had engaged in ritual protections of another kind. Thus, we should not view late ancient people as having fallen irretrievably into the realm of superstitious, irrational, magical thinking. Rather, we should consider them sophisticated, intuitive ritual agents, brokering for positions of power wherein the concept of power simply translated to the ritual task of maintaining a personal status quo, of surviving in the late ancient world.

When we include the evidence of archaeology (ritual papyri and objects), we must acknowledge that the ability to interact intentionally with the daimonic and other spiritual forces was not an exclusive possession of only a few members of society. Authority and power (*exousia, dynamis*) over *daimones* was not the contested prerogative of holy men, priests, and magicians, for example: the power could be purchased, as in the case of those persecuting Babylas and, indeed, of Babylas in response. Similarly, one could inherit power in the amuletic objects passed down in families. One could inherit the knowledge of apotropaic gestures in families or tightly knit communities—and to that end, knowledge of *daimones* passed down in families in the form of amuletic objects, carefully passed-down histories, mythologies, gestures. Finally, one could come to possess a brand of such power through baptism or another religious initiation (e.g., theurgy, Gnosticism, Mithraism). Consequently, the holy man's authority and ecclesiastical power in sacraments represent competing discourses of antidaimonic authority amid a much wider collection of modes of ritual power over *daimones;* in making this adjustment in our perspective of ritual agency, we open up different possibilities when reading the texts.

Returning briefly to the curse spells, then, to speak toward the ecumenical nature of daimonic knowledge, Heintz argues that the marketing and selling of such curses were common strategies in "enhancing the economic position and social status of the magician's client."[36] Heintz has surmised, I believe correctly, that such artifacts attest to the presence of magic workshops in Antioch throughout late antiquity. The practitioners of magical arts advertised both their ability to protect their clients' businesses and stymie the competition. We should not be shortsighted in thinking that such workshops would have purveyed their products only to those working in the marketplace. Spells for horse races, erotic spells, protection against erotic spells, healing spells, and divination spells are among the many kinds of ritual products available in Antioch. All include reference to daimonic powers—as the central mechanism of agency. Once again, the ubiquity of these spells supports the ecumenical nature of daimonic knowledge—dissemination of daimonic knowledge through ritual texts and ritual practices as practical situations arise.[37]

With these thoughts in mind, let's return to Babylas and meet his family.

THE DAIMONOLOGY OF BABYLAS

In a city of Antioch's size, complexity, and unpredictability, we should consider how frequently a person like Babylas, as well as members of his family (or Babylas on behalf of members of his family), turned to ritual aids in a variety of locations not only to enhance economic position and social status but also to maintain what he already had, especially if he had a family—a wife, a daughter of marriageable age, young children vulnerable to illness, or all these. In other words, how great would his demand for ritual power have been in light of the vulnerabilities of his family? While they were pushed to invoke the aid of *daimones* by their vulnerable situation, they were at the same time also driven to seek the aid of *daimones* by their desire for socioeconomic improvement.

In the whirl of protective spells, divination, or even erotic spells, what sort of daimonic knowledge might Babylas and his family not only acquire but create? Each of these family members had vulnerabilities that gave shape to their ritual demands: vulnerabilities particular to their place in the family and larger society, vulnerabilities reflecting their gender, age, and power struggles with other members of the family, and vulnerabilities in the larger public social arena that outsiders could exploit through rituals invoking *daimones*. Space here allows only two examples: a nubile daughter and a wife well past nubile age.

Antioch was a city that hosted a multitude of diverse and temporary populations. Libanius boasts of different races and ethnicities traveling through.[38] Although Libanius boasts proudly, one cannot help wondering what predators also swept through Antioch on its famous roads. J. H. W. G. Liebeschuetz, for example, observed the negative fallout from the exploitation of the craftsmen by the military, who were also brought in upon those roads along with the imperial court:[39]

> Ordinary shopkeepers and craftsmen had to submit to numerous abuses. The tavern-keepers suffered from the officials of the three high dignitaries who had their head-quarters in Antioch, and from other persons of power such as *agentes in rebus*. All exploited their rank to obtain goods, particularly drinks, without paying for them. Even local or semi-local officials, the *curator* and *defensor* abused their very limited power to the loss of the shopkeepers. The garrison . . . joined in the exploitation. These soldiers carried off everything there was in the shops, and if there was no meat, nor anything else that appealed to them, they took money. This suggests that the soldiers were exploiting an obligation on the part of the shops to supply the soldiers' rations.

The constant presence of the military in the city would only augment fears a father such as Babylas might already harbor for his daughter's chastity. A father and mother would fear for their child's safety and reputation, which inevitably extended to their own family's reputation and standing.

This was a culture familiar with the danger of men preying upon women. Outside the city of Antioch, for example, there were several martyr cults of young women who chose death rather than submitting to soldiers' desires. Men preyed upon women in other ways in Antioch as well. In *Historia Religiósa* 12, Theodoret of Cyrrhus described the fate of a young girl who unfortunately caught the eye of a young man. In his account, the Christian parents find her one morning completely manic and pulling out her hair. Her transformation from an obedient, calm child to an insane hysteric was abrupt and frightening. The girl's sudden extreme mood swing from sweet temperament to angry hysteria could be explained by an erotic spell gone awry. It was imperative that her father should take her to a holy man as soon as possible to find a cure: the Christian holy ascetic Macedonius was well known for his power over *daimones*. And, indeed, upon examination Macedonius reveals the demonic binding.[40] After a series of questions, the demon, recalcitrant at first, finally confesses that he was forced to enter her "under the compulsion of magical spells" and that it was a young man's lust that "motivated the use of *goēteia*." The demon caused the young girl to go insane. An event such as this, through its oral transmission and eventual narration, generated daimonic knowledge. Not only did this story offer ideas regarding daimonic possession (such possession as would eventually cause insanity in a young woman); it also defined a mode of proper ecclesiastical practice for the young woman: Macedonius complained that the girl was vulnerable to possession only because she had neglected her ritual practice in church.

Theodoret's young possessed girl was victim of an erotic or *agōgē* ritual. Such a spell contains *katadesmoi* that produce a daimonic-human relation in which violent domination of the human will and physical body takes place—much more so than in general *katadesmoi*. This is particularly the case in texts involving female victims. The rituals are generally staged at night, usually when a woman is asleep and thus vulnerable, her soul and mind unprotected. The *agōgē* ritual literally functions to lead (*agō*) the victim involuntarily from her bed to a ritual practitioner's house and bed. The daimonic *katadesmoi* secure sexual compliance and amplify the lust of the female victim. Most important: the texts of the spells as well as their literary descriptions demonstrate the acute vulnerability of the human body to both a *daimōn* and another human agent.

The following example, from *Supplementum Magicum,* is dated to the late antique period. It shares many similarities with the earlier examples, evincing a certain degree of consistency in Greco-Roman erotic magic in late antiquity. Archaeologists discovered this text in a clay pot buried in a cemetery, the papyrus wrapped around two wax figurines in an erotic embrace. Below are the first eight lines of the fifty-three-line spell:[41]

> I bind you with the indissoluble bonds of chthonic Fate and mighty necessity, for I adjure you, *daimones,* you who lie here and who are nourished here and who pass your time here, and the untimely dead youths here. I adjure you, by the unconquerable god *Iaô Barbathiaô brimiaô chermari:* rouse yourselves, *daimones,* you who lie here, and seek Euphemia, whom Dorothea bore, for Theon, whom Proechia bore. Through the entire night let her not be able to get sleep, but drive her until she comes to his feet, loving with mad love and affection and intercourse. For I have bound her brain and hands and abdominal organs and genitals and heart to love me, Theon.

How could a father of little means such as Babylas protect his daughter against such powerful magic? Should he drape her in amulets? Should he send a curse to any who might desire her? Should he scold her for slacking in her sacramental responsibilities? In searching for an answer and reaching out for daimonic aid, Babylas either confirms or creates daimonic knowledge.

Another example comes to us from an archaeological find close to Antioch. In a grave near Beirut a silver amulet was discovered that provides insight into other forms of ritual protection. The thin band, engraved with 121 short lines of text, was rolled up and placed a bronze cylinder worn around the neck as a protective amulet. This third- or fourth-century amulet served to protect its owner, Alexandra, from a variety of evils; included among them seems to be the possibility of an erotic binding spell, curses, and pernicious *daimones.* The spell invokes the aid of a large collection of familiar angels and divine powers, including the first through to the seventh heavens, the deities over rain, snow, forests, and so forth. Then, intriguingly, it invokes protection from those entities who overlook roads, cities, and the level ground; the spell asks that each of those invoked: "Protect Alexandra, to whom Zoê gave birth, from *daimonia* and spells and dizziness and from all suffering and insanity. I invoke you, the living god in *ZAARABEMôn zamadôn.*" Finally, in the midst of all these requests, we encounter the specific request for protection:[42]

> Flee from Alexandra, to whom Zoê gave birth,* * * under springs and the abyss of m* * * so that you may not bring any stain on her—not by a kiss, a greeting, a meeting; not by drink or food, or through intercourse[or "conversation"] or by a look or through a piece of clothing; nor while she is praying or on the road or away from home, either in a river or in the baths. Holy, powerful, and mighty names, protect Alexandra from every *daimonion,* whether male or female, and from every disturbance by *daimonia,* whether those of night or those of the day. Remove them from Alexandra, whether those of night or of the day. Remove them from Alexandra, to whom Zoê gave birth. Now, now. Quickly, quickly. One God and his Christ, help Alexandra, help Alexandra.

The spell would have projected a palpable sense of the constant fear of victimization—and the anxious belief in the many dangers that can befall the ritually unprotected in a city such as Antioch. *Daimones* filled the environment and were available for any call to attack. But they were also compelled to react to proper ritual formulas ordering their retreat and exile. Although people were always in danger of being victims—and perhaps someone young, female, marriageable was in even more danger—they also had the ability to defend themselves and fight back through ritual.

What this spell text and amulet communicate to us is that people in late antiquity could not afford to ignore an invisible reality of *daimones* and other spiritual entities. And in light of this worldview, they could not afford to shut their eyes to a visible reality of enemies with the ritual wherewithal and financial means to overpower them. As people engaged in rituals of binding and loosening, expelling and casting *daimones* and invisible spirits they could not see in an effort to manipulate human beings—simply in an effort to survive life in an urban environment—they generated a worldview in which supernal populations grew and deepened and specialized in complexity. Through continuous ritual action and reaction, *daimones* came to press hard against the skin and minds of the collective and individualized urban identities. Very few social relations existed untouched by daimonic ritual, especially if the relationship was complicated or constrained. With that in mind, next, let us turn to what would seem to be counterintuitive: daimonic rituals igniting marital passions.

In his *Homily 24 on Romans,* John Chrysostom warned of prostitutes (*pornai*) who "use incantations, libations, philters, potions, and innumerable other things [to retain lovers]"; they also invoke the devil and use incantations to the dead (*nekyomanteia*) against their clients' wives.[43] This is one of a cluster of warnings in which Chrysostom transformed the word *pornē* and its derivatives into a *daimōn* incarnate. He insisted on a counterstrategy of chastity to rid the city of the rising epidemic of *epithymia* and emphasized the practice of moderation (*sōphrosynē*), as a means of quelling the rising plague of desire (*epithymia*) overtaking and over-turning families. Some wives found other ways to fight back and win over their husbands. Theodoret offers a picture of a similar scenario from a different per-spective in *Historia Religiosa* 13. A woman of noble birth visited the monk Aphra-hat. She was troubled by her "debauched husband." She was convinced that a con-cubine had "bewitched" him by "some magical enchantment"; his personality altered, and he became hostile. In this case, Aphrahat took pity, and "he quenched the power of the magic by prayer, and blessing by divine invocation a flask of oil that she had brought he told her to anoint herself with it."

We have several curse tablets (separation curses, *Trennungszauber*) from late Republican Rome onwards that also suggest a picture in which wives target female slaves who have attracted the attention of their husbands—a situation that left their own positions in their families endangered. One such tablet dating to the second century has rather harsh words for a female slave by the name of Tyche: "Infernal gods, I hand over to you . . . Tyche, the slave of Carisius, that everything she does should turn out against her. Gods below, I commit to you her limbs, com-plexion, figure, head, hair, shadow, brain, forehead, eyebrows."[44] A terracotta tablet from Pannonia dating to the fourth or fifth century expressed analogous hope that Zimia should fall prey to "gorgon-killing Athena" for her sexual licentiousness—presumably with the husband of the person who authored the curse.[45] Paula Ripat has written with remarkable insight about these texts, noting the socioeconomics motivating some of the brutal language in these rituals.[46]

Admittedly these curse tablets do not mention *daimones;* nonetheless, they offer interesting precursors as we turn to consider our Babylas's wife. To that end, David Frankfurter has argued that we indeed need to be more flexible in under-standing wives' agency when it comes to the female ritualist managing erotic or romantic marital relationships.[47] He argues that we need to recognize the wife as dealing with the same struggles as every other woman in antiquity—desperate to negotiate with her sexual power to gain financial security.[48] Any woman, regard-less of her socioeconomic or marital status, could easily be pushed to engage in more aggressive rituals to attain as well as maintain social standing if she felt threatened. We see such a scenario in a spell text in Carthage in which a woman by the name of Domitiana seeks the hand of Urbanus:

I invoke you, *daimonion* spirit who lies here, by the holy name *Aôth ABAÔTH*, the god of Abraham, and *IAÔ*, the god of Jacob, . . . hear the honored, dreadful, and great name, go away to Urbanus, to whom Urbana gave birth, and bring him to Domitiana, to whom Candida gave birth, [so that] loving, frantic, and sleepless with love and desire for her, he may beg her to return to his house and become his wife.

Domitiana asks that her beloved Urbanus be tormented and sleepless with desire and love for her so that he may take her into his house as his wife. The *daimones* are to be "awakened, startled, terrified, and bring Urbanus" to her so that they may marry.[49] It is not difficult to imagine the threatened wife in the situation John Chrysostom illustrates above turning to an erotic spell or curse spell to regain the financial security of a philandering husband. We could very easily add these characteristics the wife in our scenario. Was Babylas wealthy enough to take up with a regular prostitute and, thus, cause his own wife concern about her social security? It would not take much to find an old woman or a magic worker offering magical curse for the prostitute or a female servant causing difficulty. Or perhaps Babylas's wife was sentimental, wishing to rekindle the marriage bed, and sought out an erotic spell. In either case, *daimones* would be involved and drawn intimately into their lives.

CHRISTIAN RITUAL AND DEMONIC PRODUCTION

In the cemeteries, martyr cult was a place of worship, veneration, healing, and exorcism. It was also a place of intentional spirit possession as well as charismatic power for the worshipper. In other words, the martyr cult was a ritual site very much in the making, but it was also located in a place, the cemetery, that was already ritually overdetermined, most especially regarding the purpose and meaning of *daimones*. This would lead to confusion and debate regarding the ambiguous power of the holy dead.

As the martyr cult grew in and around Antioch and monks on Mount Silpius developed a reputation as healers and exorcists, people such as Babylas had more opportunities to see those possessed or afflicted by *daimones*. For the most part, in a person's daily activities the daimonic and supernatural world remained invisible and silent. To that end, a martyr cult's *daimones* differed distinctively for its public and performative nature. As David Frankfurter has recently made quite clear, a martyr's or saint's shrine was a confined location at which the chaos and turmoil of the spirit realm would punch through the relative tranquillity elsewhere. Here, in the spectacles of possession and exorcism, a person would encounter, with a frightening and inescapable immediacy, what Frankfurter has described as the "broader supernatural pantheon."[50] Such an experience was fundamentally transformative in a variety of ways: first and foremost demoniacs "served as authenticating spectacles of shrines."[51] They validated or confirmed the *praesentia* and *potentia* of the holy ones. Encountering the torturous screams of the demon-possessed at saints' shrines, according to Peter Brown, onlookers "witnessed more clearly and with greater precision the manner in which God through his lords the saints could stretch forth into their midst the right hand of his healing power."[52] In the words of Gregory of Tours: "In this way [demoniacs] bring home the presence of the saints of God to human minds, that there should be no doubt that the saints are present at their tombs."[53] The more disruptive the spectacle of demonic possession, the more imposing the saint and his or her shrine. And as we can see in Paula's reaction to the tombs in Jerusalem, such phenomena could take on a carnivalesque air, utterly overwhelming the spectator:[54]

> She shuddered at the sight of so many marvelous happenings. For there she was met by the noise of demons roaring in various torments, and, before the tombs of the saints, she saw men howling like wolves, barking like dogs, roaring like lions, hissing like snakes, bellowing like bulls; some twisted their heads to touch the earth by arching their bodies backwards; women hung upside down in midair, yet their skirts did not fall down over their heads.

I wish to add that these spectacles—and most crucially, the texts circulating that feature these spectacles—also deeply familiarized a late ancient person with a raw, embodied experience of the daimonic and how *daimones* could manifest dramatically and disruptively in the human body and the mind controlling that body. Whereas ritual texts presented people with ritual means of binding and controlling *daimones* and other spiritual entities, the literature featuring these spectacles provided sensory insight into how easily and grotesquely one could lose control to these cosmological beings. The ritual texts that described how *daimones* entered, possessed, and controlled the human body may have been unclear. That said, the bombast of the performance offered an irrefutable sensory encounter with the physical effects of possession as well as of the dramatic effects of exorcism.

The martyr Julian's *dies natalis* offers the perfect example of how lay Christians could have learned the art of demonic possession and expulsion. The two-day procession and festival would have given celebrants ample opportunity to witness other daimoniacs' behavior prior to and after their healing.[55] In his sermon honoring the martyr, John Chrysostom described in vivid detail the exorcistic power adhering in the martyr's bones:[56]

> If you grab someone who's demon-possessed and exhibiting manic behavior and take them into that holy tomb wherein the martyr's remains lie, without a doubt you'll see them jumping back and fleeing. For they instantly leap right out of the front doors as if about to set foot on hot coals, and they don't dare to look directly at the coffin itself. . . . After so long a time they don't dare to look directly at the memorial nor at the bare bones of the saint.

He speaks in similar manner at the site of Drosis, where he describes an immediate and therapeutic antidemonic power inhering in the remains of Drosis. As the sound of her sizzling flesh banished *daimones* in her life's final moments, her remains now compelled the departure of any inhabiting those who approached her grave.[57] Christians had most likely witnessed such performances here as well. Such sites were central locations in the production of a particular kind of daimonic knowledge in Antioch—one in which audience participation and collaboration were valued.

In his discussion of a Christian exorcism cult in the middle of Buddhist Sri Lanka, R. L. Stirrat describes a collaborative relationship between exorcists and the exorcized. Almost as important as the spectacle of demonic possession and the ritual of exorcism were the conversations that took place at the site among the participants and spectators:[58]

> Regular attenders at shrines such as Kudagama were and are fascinated by the demonic. At Kudagama, demons have a very real existence, as real an existence as people or animals or objects. The nature of the demonic is a continual topic of conversation at the shrine. Newcomers . . . who arrive knowing little or nothing about the demons quickly learn their names and habits. *Furthermore, during the fits and trances of the possessed, more knowledge is generated.* The world of demons is continually being reshaped and reformed in its details. New demons are discovered; new aspects of their being are made plain. Yet at an overall level certain contours of the cosmos remain constant, in particular the essentially dualistic framework of the Catholic tradition which is made manifest in the continual cosmic battle between the forces of good and evil.

People like Babylas, his daughter, and his wife appropriated the general cosmological and demonological outline to generate and express their own understanding of demonic possession and expulsion. Through the process, they reconfirmed the overarching cosmology and demonology while at the same time working through the problematic details of their own personal lives: jealousies, rivalries, sicknesses, and anxieties.

As we have imagined Babylas and his family in the city throughout this paper, it is fitting that we visit them once more during Julian's *dies natalis*: a festival that would have taken them beyond the city walls to somewhere three kilometers outside the city. In the festival for Julian, Babylas may have found a festival wherein he could find release from the anxiety of any curses he naturally assumed to have been cast upon him. In the midst of others who might express daimonic shivering in front of the relic, perhaps Babylas would have done the same, a sign that he or his business had been cursed? Would he use the name of Julian in casting a new curse upon a competitor? How might this holy day for a martyr suddenly find a connection with shifting the socioeconomic balance in the marketplace?

Let us turn our attention to Babylas's daughter, nubile but not married. She has long been aware of sexual feelings that she has for a young man, or perhaps for many, but she is confused by and ashamed of those feelings. On the long walk to the shrine, she is fed on the stories of Macedonius's, Julian's, and Drosis's exorcisms, but she herself has been fasting for two days. Suddenly, she catches sight of one demoniac, and then another, and then another. Can we imagine Babylas's daughter suddenly breaking out in howling cries as she too approaches the relic? Would the latest demoniac reveal itself before the shrine? How would such behavior be read by others? Could a young girl's nervousness be mistaken for an erotic curse gone awry? Undoubtedly there would be more than one overexcited celebrant keen to diagnose the demonic.

Finally, what of Babylas's wife, who attempted to ensnare her own husband with an erotic spell? How would she feel traveling in company with the saint's relic? Would she fear the saint would undo the binding? Perhaps she would hope to pray to the saint for help to aid and reinforce the erotic spell. Power is power, after all.

CONCLUSION

In late antiquity, how did one know the concept *daimōn?* To know *daimōn* was to produce the knowledge in ritual activity. It was to attempt to set in order the relationships between oneself, one's social and physical surroundings, and the supernal figures living throughout one's environment. *Daimōn* was not merely textual, literary, or written definition; it was embodied; experienced, sensory, in action. We can come to know the late antique *daimōn* only through Babylas and his family or other proxies from late antiquity.

The particular place of *daimōn* in some intellectual traditions as well as in modern historiography makes exploring this ritual construction of knowledge particularly productive with *daimōn;* it is also this kind of inquiry that exposes the apologetic underbelly of "the demonic" as an analytical category of modern interpretation. But the implication of ritual and practice in the production of knowledge are hardly unique to *daimōn,* and the kind of investigation undertaken here can be pursued fruitfully with elements of the late ancient world that had better reception than the demonic. Admittedly, the knowledge products of late antique practice may be slippery and elusive to grasp; reconstructing their production, as we have seen, relies more on imagination than on theory. Still, this imagination allows us to consider how people lived their worlds and in doing so created certain ideas; and it allows us to understand how these ideas about *daimones* are as dynamic and multiform as were the daily contexts in which they were produced or became known. It allows us to consider how details of daily life were understood in terms of cosmic forces and how the invisible became tangible—something felt on one's body or a fact to consider in everyday family life.

NOTES

I am especially grateful to Catherine Chin and Moulie Vidas for the survival of this article from its unsure, fetal state to full life. These two formidable scholars generously took on the task of clarifying my meaning—not only for readers but for the author as well. I thank you both. In addition I thank many of the other authors who attended a workshop for this volume and offered valuable comments: in particular, I owe thanks to Heidi Marx-Wolf, Tina Sessa, Ellen Muehlberger, and Mira Balberg for their comments. All mistakes in this article are completely my own.

1. Edward Gibbon, The History of the Decline and Fall of the Roman Empire, ed. David Wormersley, 3 vols. (London: Penguin, 1997). In light of the importance of Gibbon to later historiography—both late antique scholarship and the recent return to decline-and-fall interpretation—Gibbon and his historiographical legacy have become the object of study in and of themselves: Glen Bowersock, John Clive, and Stephen Graubard, eds., *Edward Gibbon and the Decline and Fall of the Roman Empire, Daedalus* 105 (1976), special issue, which was also published separately as a volume of essays (Cambridge, Mass.: Harvard University Press, 1977); see especially the contributions of Peter Brown, Henry Chadwick, Peter Burke, and Arnaldo Momigliano; also Glen Bowersock, *From Gibbon to Auden: Essays on the Classical Tradition* (Oxford: Oxford University Press, 2009), which includes "Gibbon's Historical Imagination," reprinted from *American Scholar* 57 (1988): 33–47. For the fundamentals of Peter Brown's position that the period of late antiquity represents a transformation rather than a decline of the Roman world, see his *The World of Late Antiquity: A.D. 150–750* (London: Thames and Hudson, 1971), and *The Making of Late Antiquity* (Cambridge, Mass.: Harvard University Press, 1978). The debate continues regarding which model is more attuned to describing this period. Brief bibliography on the debate over the historiographic use of decline and fall versus continuity and transformation: a remarkably insightful and incisive overview can be found in Andrew Gillett, "Rome's Fall and Europe's Rise: A View from Late Antiquity," *Medieval Review* 7.10.12: https://scholarworks.iu.edu/dspace/bitstream/handle/2022/6332/07.10.12.html?sequence=1, accessed 11 November 2014. See also Clifford Ando, "Narrating Decline and Fall," in *A Companion to Late Antiquity,* ed. Philip Rousseau (Oxford: Blackwell, 2008), 59–76; idem, "Decline, Fall, and Transformation," *Journal of Late Antiquity* 1 (2008): 30–60; J. H. W. G. Liebeschuetz, "Late Antiquity and the Concept of Decline," *Nottingham Medieval Studies* 45 (2001): 1–11; idem, "The Birth of Late Antiquity," *Antiquité Tardive* 12 (2004): 253–61; C. Straw and R. Lim, eds., *The Past before Us: The Challenge of Historiographies of Late Antiquity* (Turnhout: Brepols, 2004); Polymnia Athanassiadi, "Antiquité tardive: Construction et déconstruction d'un modèle historiographique," *Antiquité Tardive* 14 (2006): 311–24; *The World of Late Antiquity Revisited, Symbolae Osloenses* 72 (1997), special issue; Philip Rousseau and Manolis Papoutsakis, eds., *Transformations of Late Antiquity: Essays for Peter Brown* (Burlington: Ashgate, 2009).

2. Especially if we consider the word's strictly dualizing and Othering meaning. I do not suggest here that the dualizing and Othering aspects of this word were absent in the ancient and late antique periods. (Consider, of course, J. Z. Smith, "Towards Interpreting Demonic Powers in Hellenistic and Roman Antiquity," in *Aufstieg und Niedergang der römischen Welt,* ed. H. Temporini and W. Haase, vol. 2.16.1 (Berlin: de Gruyter, 1978), 425–39.); I propose only that these aspects increased to overtake the semantic meaning and effect of "demon" irrevocably in these later, fully Christianized, eventually Protestantized, even secularized periods in Western history. In the inexcusably brief genealogy of "demon" that I provide here, I keep to the side analogous categories found in non-Western environments—e.g., most especially *jinn* in the Middle Eastern contexts that geographically overlap our own in late antiquity.

3. Gibbon, *History* (above, n. 1), 2.428.

4. J. B. Bury, *The Later Roman Empire from the Death of Theodosius I to the Death of Justinian, 395–565*, 2nd ed., 2 vols. (London, 1923); Ernst Stein, *Histoire du Bas-Empire*, vol. 1, *De l'état romain à l'état byzantine (284–476)* (Paris, 1959); vol. 2, *De la disparition de l'empire de l'Occident à la mort de Justinien (476–565)* (Paris, 1949); A. H. M. Jones, *The Later Roman Empire (284–602): A Social, Economic and Administrative Survey*, 2 vols. (Oxford, 1964); Alexander Demandt, *Die Spätantike: Römische Geschichte von Diocletian bis Justinian, 284–565 n. Chr.*, Handbuch der Altertumswissenschaft, Abteilung 3, Teil 6 (Munich: Beck, 2007). There has been a recent spate of publications that have revisited Gibbon's use of decline and fall—what James O'Donnell has described (in his *BMCR* 2005.07.69 reviews of Heather and of Ward-Perkins: http://bmcr.brynmawr.edu/2005/2005-07-69.html, accessed 11 November 2014) as a "Counter-Reformation in late antique studies": P. Heather, *The Fall of the Roman Empire: A New History* (Oxford: Oxford University Press, 2005); B. Ward-Perkins, *The Fall of Rome and the End of Civilization* (Oxford: Oxford University Press, 2005); A. Cameron, B. Ward-Perkins, and M. Whitby, eds., *The Cambridge Ancient History*, vol. 14, *Late Antiquity: Empire and Successors, AD 425–600* (Cambridge: Cambridge University Press, 2001); Stephen Mitchell, *A History of the Later Roman Empire, AD 284–641: The Transformation of the Ancient World*, Blackwell History of the Ancient World (Malden, Mass.: Blackwell Publishing, 2007).

5. See above, note 1, especially, e.g., the discussions in Peter Brown, "The World of Late Antiquity Revisited," *Symbolae Osloenses* 72 (1997), special issue: 5–30.

6. Peter Brown, "The Rise and Function of the Holy Man in Late Antiquity," *Journal of Roman Studies* 61 (1971), 80–101, reprinted in idem, *Society and the Holy* (Berkeley and Los Angeles: University of California Press, 1982), 103–52. His own reflections on the impact of this article: idem, "The Rise and Function of the Holy Man in Late Antiquity, 1971–1997." *Journal of Early Christian Studies* 6 (1998): 353–76; see in this issue several other scholars influenced by Brown's model of the holy man (e.g., Rapp, McLynn). See also the series of scholarly responses to Brown's work in "World of Late Antiquity" (above, n. 5), 31–69, especially Bowersock's reflections on Brown and his own work in the conception of late antiquity. Also, P. Brown, *Authority and the Sacred: Aspects of the Christianization of the Roman World* (Cambridge: Cambridge University Press, 1997), in which he revisits the model of the holy man once again. Several scholars have begun their own studies of charismatic figures by reading Brown's works; indeed his article's footprints are virtually everywhere in late antique scholarship: below I offer more specific examples. More intriguing: in Brown we have an example of a late antique scholar who has influenced those in other fields; see the anthropologist R. L. Stirrat, "Sacred Models," *Man* 19 (1984): 199–215, 211–14, also his ethnographic study *Power and Religiosity in a Post-Colonial Setting: Sinhala Catholics in Contemporary Sri Lanka* (Cambridge: Cambridge University Press, 1992), for which Brown's article was formative.

7. But also in precisely understood socioreligious and political circumstances: exemplary are Peter Brown, "Rise and Function" (1971: above, n. 6); idem, "Sorcery, Demons and the Rise of Christianity from Late Antiquity into the Middle Ages," in *Religion and Society in the Age of Saint Augustine* (London: Faber and Faber, 1972), 119–46; David Brakke, *Demons and the Making of the Monk* (Cambridge, Mass.: Harvard University Press, 2006).

See also Richard Valantasis, "Daemons and the Perfecting of the Monk's Body: Monastic Anthropology, Daemonology, and Asceticism," *Semeia* 58 (1992): 47–79; D. Frankfurter, "Holy Man and Syncretism," *Journal of Early Christian Studies* 11 (2003): 339–85.

8. Of course there are exceptions to the general historiographical portrayal of exorcism as a rationalizing and civilizing ritual, and these exceptions tend to reflect earlier Gibbonian tendencies: e.g., A. A. Barb, "The Survival of Magic Arts," in *The Conflict between Paganism and Christianity in the Fourth Century,* ed. A. Momigliano (Oxford: Oxford University Press, 1963), 100–118.

9. In addition to Brown's "Rise and Function" (1971: above, n. 6), we can recognize a rationalization of the demonic in his "Sorcery, Demons and the Rise of Christianity" (above, n. 7).

10. Plato, *Symposium* 202e–203a: my translation, with reference to the translation of Michael Joyce in Edith Hamilton and Huntington Cairns, eds., *The Collected Dialogues of Plato, Including the Letters,* 17th printing (Princeton: Princeton University Press, 1999), 554.

11. In Plutarch's *De Defectu Oraculorum,* sections 14–17 are the key passages. It is important to remember Plutarch's overriding concern in writing *De Defectu Oraculorum:* the slow decline of the oracles required an explanation that salvaged polytheistic cosmology and divinity. *Daimones* became the sacrifice to salvage the *Symposium*'s cosmology as the gods were transforming via Middle Platonism into hypostatic entities.

12. Plutarch, *De Defectu Oraculorum* 13–14.

13. Ibid. Plutarch develops the argument meticulously and deliberately but hesitatingly, beginning by explaining that there are also *daimones* capable of good works.

14. Ibid.14.

15. Ibid.

16. Ibid.

17. Richard Stillwell, ed., *Antioch-on-the-Orontes* (Princeton: Published for the Committee by the Department of Art and Archeology, 1934). For sample images of the curse texts, Florent Heintz, "Magic Tablets and the Games at Antioch," in *Antioch: The Lost Ancient City,* ed. Christine Kondoleon (Princeton: Princeton University Press in association with the Worcester Art Museum, 2000), 164–65.

18. Florent Heintz, "Magic Tablets" (above, n. 17), 163–67.

19. Ibid. See also the discussion in Silke Trzcionka, *Magic and the Supernatural in Fourth Century Syria* (London: Routledge, 2006), 54–56, 59–62.

20. John Gager, *Curse Tablets and Binding Spells from the Ancient World* (Oxford: Oxford University Press, 1992), chapter 5, 175–99.

21. John Chrysostom, *Ad Illuminandos Catecheses* 12.57 (*Ancient Christian Writers* [hereafter *ACW*], vol. 31, ed. Paul Harkins [Westminster, Md.: Newman Press, 1963], 190; ed. J.-P. Migne, *Patrologiae Cursus Completus, Series Graeca* [hereafter *PG*], vol. 49 [Paris, 1862], 250).

22. John Chrysostom, *Homily 8 on Colossians* (*A Select Library of the Nicene and Post-Nicene Fathers of the Christian Church* [hereafter *NPNF*], series 1, vol. 13, ed. Philip Schaaf [Grand Rapids: Eerdmans, 1956], 298; *PG* 62.238).

23. For an old woman (*graus*) involved in magical practice, see Dayna S. Kalleres, "Drunken Hags with Amulets and Prostitutes with Erotic Spells: The *Re-*Feminization of

Magic in Late Antique Christian Homily," in *Daughters of Hecate: Women and Magic in the Ancient World,* ed. Kimberly Stratton and Dayna S. Kalleres (Oxford: Oxford University Press, 2014), 219–51.

24. For an in-depth discussion of the place and purpose of such amulets, see the essay by AnneMarie Luijendijk, "A Gospel Amulet for Joannia (P.Oxy. VIII 1151)," in *Daughters* (above, n. 23), 418–44.

25. John Chrysostom, *Ad Illuminandos Catecheses* 11.24, 25 (*PG* 49.240).

26. For discussion, see Gideon Bohak, *Ancient Jewish Magic: A History* (Cambridge: Cambridge University Press, 2008), 320–22.

27. Amulets in synagogues: John Chrysostom, *Adversus Iudaeos* 1.7.5–11, 8.4–8.7 (*PG* 48.854–55, 935–38, 936); John also described Jewish sorcerers who took healing potions to the homes of sick Christians: *Adversus Iudaeos* 8.7 (*PG* 48.937). This passage had traditionally been dismissed until the discoveries of Babylonian magic bowls and magical texts such as the *Sepher Ha-Razim* (see Mordecai Margalioth, *Sepher Ha-Razim* [Jerusalem: Yediot Achronot, 1966]; English translation: Michael A. Morgan, *Sepher Ha-Razim: The Book of Mysteries* [Chico, Calif.: Scholars Press, 1983]; also Joseph Naveh and Shaul Shaked, *Amulets and Magic Bowls: Aramaic Incantations of Late Antiquity,* 2nd ed. [Jerusalem: The Hebrew University and Magnes Press, 1987]; also Joseph Naveh and Shaul Shaked, *Magical Spells and Formulae: Aramaic Incantations of Late Antiquity* [Jerusalem: The Hebrew University and Magnes Press, 1993]). Since that point, the synagogue has appeared in direct competitive relationship to other religious institutions (e.g., the temple, the church, and the martyr shrine) as a place of "numinous power": Robert Wilken, *John Chrysostom and the Jews* (Berkeley and Los Angeles: University of California Press, 1983), 83–84. See also Lee L. Levine, *The Ancient Synagogue: The First Thousand Years* (New Haven: Yale University Press, 2000). Bohak, *Ancient Jewish Magic* (above, n. 26), 315–18, supports Chrysostom's statement of "outsider evidence" of synagogue magic with "insider support." Bohak introduces nineteen metal lamellae discovered in the apse of one late ancient synagogue, quite close to the location of the ark of the Torah. They were rolled or folded, with some of the original fabric in which they were wrapped still remaining.

28. For the Matrona, see John Chrysostom, *Adversus Iudaeos* 1.6.2–3 (*PG* 48.852), 1.8.1 (*PG* 48.855). For a discussion of Matrona incubation in the wider context of synagogue-related magical practice, see Gideon Bohak, *Ancient Jewish Magic* (above, n. 26), 320–22; see also Lee L. Levine, *Ancient Synagogue* (above, n. 27), 294, who places the Matrona in the context of the synagogue's general reputation in late antiquity as a locus of holiness and therefore healing. The Daphne synagogue, Levine argues, would have drawn itself into competitive parallel with the Asclepian cult: during a night's sleep, a person would receive a healing visit from the God of Israel. Divination was an extremely popular and important practice in the late antique world. Thus, a brief survey of recent relevant scholarship is in order: Leda Ciraolo and Jonathan Seidel, eds., *Magic and Divination in the Ancient World,* Ancient Magic and Divination, vol. 2 (Leiden: Brill, 2002), especially the articles by Peter Struck (pp. 119–32) and Anitra Bingham Kolenkow (pp. 133–44). Also: Sarah Iles Johnston and Peter T. Struck, eds., *Mantikê: Studies in Ancient Divination,* Religions in the Graeco-Roman World, vol. 155 (Leiden: Brill, 2005); Sarah Iles Johnston's "Introduction" is essential reading for understanding divination as an ideologically shifting object of analysis in the history of religion and in

ancient religions in particular (pp. 1–28); also significant in this volume are the articles by William E. Klingshirn (pp. 52–129) and David Frankfurter (pp. 233–55). For a general overview of divination practice in antiquity, see Sarah Iles Johnston, *Ancient Greek Divination* (Oxford : Wiley-Blackwell, 2008), 1–32, 109–82; also Valerie Flint, *The Rise of Magic in Early Medieval Europe* (Princeton: Princeton University Press, 1991), 88–91. David Potter has introduced a central question in the study of divination, namely the relationship between power and politics: David Potter, *Prophets and Emperors: Human and Divine Authority from Augustus to Theodosius* (Cambridge, Mass.: Harvard University Press, 1994); also idem, *Prophecy and History in the Crisis of the Roman Empire: A Historical Commentary on the Thirteenth Sibylline Oracle* (New York: Oxford University Press, 1990). On the relation between imperial power's claims to complete and sole control over divinatory practice and the expanded category of *ars magica* or *maleficia* to include a larger range of divination practice (in imperial legislation), see Marie Theres Fögen, *Die Enteignung der Wahrsager: Studien zum kaiserlichen Wissensmonopol in der Spätantike* (Frankfurt am Main: Suhrkamp, 1993), 160–62.

29. For the shrines of Babylas and Drosis, see Julian, *De Sancto Babyla* (*PG* 50.571–78; J. Leemans et al., "*Let Us Die That We May Live*": *Greek Homilies on Christian Martyrs from Asia Minor, Palestine, and Syria (c. AD 350–AD 450)* [London: Routledge, 2003], 140–47); *De Sancta Droside Martyre* (*PG* 50.683–694; trans. W. Mayer, *St John Chrysostom, The Cult of the Saints: Select Homilies and Letters* [Crestwood, N.Y.: St. Vladimir's Seminary Press, 2006], 193); *In Julianum Martyrem* (*PG* 50.665–76; Leemans et al., "*Let Us Die That We May Live*," 126–40). Also *In Sanctum Ignatium Martyrem* (*PG* 50.587–96; trans. Mayer, *St John Chrysostom*, 101–18). Jerome, *De Viris Illustribus* 16, located Ignatius's relics in the cemetery; Evagrius, *Historia Ecclesiastica* 1.16, declared that during the reign of Theodosius II the relics had been translated to Antioch and placed in a Tychaeum temple, which was then converted into a church dedicated to the saint.

30. See in general Theodoret of Cyrrhus, *Historia Religiosa*, Sources Chrétiennes, vols. 234, 257 (Paris: Éditions du Cerf, 1977–79), trans. R. M. Price, *A History of the Monks of Syria* (Kalamazoo: Cistercian Press, 1985), passim.

31. Glanville Downey, *A History of Antioch in Syria: From Seleucus to the Arab Conquest* (Princeton: Princeton University Press, 1961), 327; Malalas 307.16–20. E. Soler, "Le sacré et la salut à Antioche au IVe siècle après J.-C.: Pratiques festives et comportements religieux dans le processus de christianisation de la cité," unpublished PhD dissertation (Rouen, 1999), 86, theorizes that Iamblichus must have taught in Daphne at some point and ties the Hecate shrine as well as the temple of Apollo and the Nymphaeum to Neoplatonic theurgic activity.

32. On Iamblichus and the practice of theurgy in a sociopolitical context specific to Antioch, see the important article "An Oracle of Apollo at Daphne and the Great Persecution," *Classical Philology* 99 (2004): 57–77; Also, of course, on theurgy in Antioch, Soler, "Le sacré et la salut" (above, n. 31).

33. For *paredros*, see Leda Jean Ciraolo, "Supernatural Assistants in the Greek Magical Papyri," in *Ancient Magic and Ritual Power*, ed. Marvin Meyer and Paul Mirecki (Leiden: Brill, 2001), 279–96. Also *paredroi* are especially important in the arts of divination; on this topic see Richard Gordon, "Reporting the Marvellous: Private Divination in the Greek Magical Papyri," in *Envisioning Magic: A Princeton Seminar and Symposium*, ed. Peter Schäfer and Hans G. Kippenburg (Leiden: Brill, 1997), 65–93, especially 71–74.

34. On the fascinating art of divination, see Johnston, *Ancient Greek Divination* (above, n. 28), especially the first chapter, pp. 1–32.

35. In general scholars do not consider the enchanted worldview of late antiquity during their investigations, presuming instead (quite naturally) a disenchanted view, which thus excludes or dismisses the active participation of the suprahuman in the socioeconomic and political arenas: see the relevant discussion in Dayna S. Kalleres, *City of Demons: Violence, Ritual, and Christian Power in Late Antiquity* (Berkeley and Los Angeles: University of California Press, forthcoming), "Introduction."

36. Heintz, "Magic Tablets" (above, n. 17), 166.

37. Much of this would have ended with the edicts against magic in the mid-fourth century. Increased legislation against magic from 358–89 C.E. (e.g., *Codex Theodosianus* 9.16.9; 9.17.5, 6, 7) extending from Constantius II, Valens, and Valentinian, combined with the rash of lawsuits against magical practices in 356/7 C.E.; witch-hunt trials of 371/2 C.E. involving THEOD divination conspiracies at Antioch support the view of a rise in superstitious views in late antiquity (Ammianus Marcellinus, *Res Gestae* 29.1.37–44); likewise Ammianus Marcellinus's colorful descriptions of the zealotry of the accusations of the supposed practices of the accused do not help to alter this bleak view (e.g., Ammianus Marcellinus, *Res Gestae* 16.8.2). Still relevant regarding the rising wave of lawsuits, J. Maurice, "Le terreur de la magie au IVe siècle," *Revue Historique de Droit Français et Étranger*, sér. 4, 6 (1927): 108–20. For an important corrective to this view, see Fögen, *Enteignung* (above, n. 28), 151–70. Though the laws in the *Theodosian Code* are aimed at elite political issues, especially those tied to Constantius II and Valens and Valentinian in 371 C.E., it is interesting to consider what kind of fallout they would have had on the itinerant or established magical practitioners in Antioch. Cf. Peter Brown, "Sorcery, Demons and the Rise of Christianity" (above, n. 7), 121, whose excellent article draws our attention to the sociopolitical issues at stake in the *Theodosian Code;* note especially Brown's astute critique of previous scholarship, which follows the model of decline, treating the fourth century as an era marking the beginning of the age of magical thinking and superstition.

38. Libanius, *Oration* 11.166–73 (ed. R. Foerster, *Libanii Opera,* vol. 1.2 [Leipzig: Teubner, 1903], 492–95). English translation available in Glanville Downey, "Libanius' *Oration in Praise of Antioch* (Oration XI)," *Proceedings of the American Philosophical Society* 103 (1959): 652–86; the relevant passage is on pp. 670–71.

39. J. H. W. G. Liebeschuetz, *Antioch: City and Imperial Administration in the Later Roman Empire* (Oxford: Clarendon Press, 1972), 58–59.

40. Theodoret of Cyrrhus, *Historia Religiosa* (above, n. 30), 13.10–12, trans. Price, *History* (above, n. 30), 104–5.

41. *Papyri Graecae Magicae* no. 101, 1–53; the text can also be found with commentary in *Supplementum Magicum,* ed. R. W. Daniel and F. Maltomini, vol. 1 (Opladen: Westdeutscher Verlag, 1990), no. 45, 162–73. Similar examples with the same adjuration: *Papyri Graecae Magicae,* no. 4, 296–466; no. 15, 1–21; no. 16, 1–75; *Supplementum Magicum,* vol. 2 (Opladen: Westdeutscher Verlag, 1992), nos. 52, 71. For text and translation of these examples, consult *The Greek Magical Papyri in Translation,* ed. H. D. Betz, 2nd ed. (Chicago: University of Chicago Press, 1996), and *Papyri Graecae Magicae: Die griechischen Zauberpapyri,* ed. K. Preisendanz, 2 vols., 2nd ed. (Stuttgart: Teubner, 1972).

42. Gager, *Curse Tablets* (above, n. 20), 233–34.

43. John Chrysostom, *Homily 24 on Romans* (*NPNF*, series 1, 11.520; *PG* 60.627).

44. I thank Pauline Ripat, "Cheating Women: Curse Tablets and Roman Wives," in *Daughters* (above, n. 23), who provided a smart discussion of this and the following passage referenced in note 43: *Archaiologikē Ephēmeris*, 1950, 41 no. 112; Rudolf Egger, "Liebeszauber," *Jahreshefte des Österreichischen Archäologischen Institutes in Wien*, 1948, 112–20; Cf. A. M.-H. Audollent, ed., *Defixionum Tabellae* (Frankfurt am Main: Minerva, 1967), no. 100.

45. Franjo Barišić, "Une *defixionis tabella* grecque de Progar en Srem," *Archaeologia Iugoslavica* 11 (1970): 23–28.

46. Pauline Ripat, "Cheating Women: Curse Tablets and Roman Wives," in *Daughters* (above, n. 23), 340–59.

47. David Frankfurter, "The Social Context of Women's Erotic Magic in Antiquity," in *Daughters* (above, n. 23), 319–39, argues quite convincingly *contra* Christopher Faraone, *Ancient Greek Love Magic* (Cambridge, Mass.: Harvard University Press, 1999), and Matthew Dickie, *Magic and Magicians in the Greco-Roman World* (London: Routledge, 2001), that we should not divide the female population into wives who use *philia* spells only with their husbands and prostitutes resorting to the aggressive *agōgē* spells.

48. Frankfurter, "Social Context" (above, n. 47), 328, 332–33.

49. Gager, *Curse Tablets* (above, n. 20), 113–14.

50. David Frankfurter, "Where the Spirits Dwell: Possession, Christianization, and Saints' Shrines in Late Antiquity," *Harvard Theological Review* 103 (2010): 46.

51. Ibid. 40.

52. Peter Brown, *The Cult of the Saints: Its Rise and Function in Latin Christianity*, The Haskell Lectures on History of Religions, n.s., 2 (Chicago: University of Chicago Press, 1982), 107.

53. Gregory of Tours, *Vita Iuliani: Liber De Passione et Virtutibus Sancti Iuliani Martyris* 30, 127, p. 109.

54. Jerome, *Epistle* 103.3; cf. 108.13 (ed. J.-P. Migne, *Patrologiae Cursus Completus, Series Latina*, vol. 22 [Paris, 1845], 889); Brown, *Cult* (above, n. 52), 106.

55. John Chrysostom, *In Julianum Martyrem* (*PG* 50.665–76) (Leemans et al., "Let Us Die" [above, n. 29], 126–40).

56. Ibid. 2 (*PG* 50.669–70).

57. John Chrysostom, *De Sanctae Droside Martyre* (*PG* 50.683–94; trans. Mayer, *St John Chrysostom* [above, n. 29], 201).

58. Stirrat, *Power* (above, n. 6), 87; emphasis added.

Afterword

Maud W. Gleason

The chapters of this book are true essays, in the original sense of the term: attempts, explorations, provocations. They range widely over what is now known as late antiquity, from Augustine ("God") to the rabbis of the Mishnah ("Artifact"), from the court of Justinian to the court of his Sassanian contemporary ("Emperor"), from dueling interpreters of oracles in fourth century Antioch ("Language") to the rioting of Peter Valvomeres in Rome ("*Ordo*"). Picture them as soundings, probing for the configuration of the ocean floor, or as core samples from which we may hope to construct a three-dimensional picture of geological deposits. How did the layers of supernatural beings in the ancient world shift, expand, or subside over time? What were the fault lines created and the tectonic plates that moved during the long, slow upthrust of Christianity? The finished map would require soundings conducted over a systematic grid to discover to what extent particular conceptual frameworks were shared by specific groups in particular regions over more precisely defined periods of time.

. . .

But before mapping comes exploration. These essays explore how daily, embodied activity might create characteristic ways of seeing and knowing the late ancient world. Interest in embodied cognition has not been dominant in Western philosophy but can be found here and there, as in Husserl's critique of Descartes's objective body, or in Sara Ruddick's difference feminism, which sought to derive characteristic ways of knowing from the quotidian activities of protection, nurturance, and training.[1] The amazing progress of cognitive science over the last generation may at last be spurring humanists to consider the embodied dimensions of cognition. Another stimulus has been the work of George Lakoff and Mark Johnson on metaphor.[2] They see conceptual systems as inherently metaphorical: people develop abstract concepts by analogy with their concrete experiences of the physical world. If we grant that physical experience is not a transhistorical constant but is mediated and informed by different understandings of how the world works, then it makes sense to investigate how people in other times and places built their conceptual systems on different sets of metaphors.

Such investigations invite us to wonder: do people of another time and place, engaging in their quotidian activities, using their culturally conditioned bodies, thinking in their particular sets of metaphors—do they simply have different worldviews than we do, or do they in some sense inhabit different worlds? These questions force us up against a massive epistemological problem, discussed in Daryn Lehoux's recent book on Roman science: realism versus relativism.[3] The worldview position is realist: it assumes that there really is but one world out there, which various cultures variously misperceive. Realism promotes cultural condescension, since it is easier to assume that we have a more accurate conceptual machinery for grasping what really is than to admit that our worldview seems superior merely because it is ours.

The different-worlds position is relativist. It goes back to Thomas Kuhn's analysis of what happens when conceptual paradigms about the physical world suddenly shift. "We may want to say that after a revolution scientists are responding to a different world."[4] On its face, this is a provocative claim. Despite the lapse of centuries, are not Plutarch's *lithos Magnētis* and my magnet the same thing? If we decide that they are not, because they belong to two incompatible conceptual systems, then it would seem that a relativist position requires us to give up on any sort of correspondence theory of truth. Should we decide instead to use a coherence model of truth, then there are multiple truths. Not everyone wants to go there. But despite its problems, relativism appeals to historians because talking about the past in terms of different worlds permits us to explore defunct ideas in a level playing field, as it were, unburdened by assumptions of cultural superiority.

So, to take up the relativist approach: What needs to change before we can say that people living in the same space as preceding generations are now living in an essentially different world? Ian Hacking took Kuhn's claim about living in different worlds to mean that what changes is classification—the world of kinds.[5] Thus Plutarch's way of knowing magnets was based on the powers of sympathy and antipathy, a set of classificatory metaphors that permeated his world but is officially defunct in ours. How people classify things in their world usually remains opaque to them: their categories simply are what is. Yet these obvious, seemingly natural, and uninterrogated categories determine to a large extent what can exist and what can happen in their world. Without the category of impurity, for example, impure objects cannot exist. Introduce the category of impurity, and space opens up for an elaborate knowledge system about which objects can or cannot contract impurity and how they may or may not be cleansed ("Artifact").

I suggest that classification is integral to ways of knowing and constitutes a major theme of this collection. Classification is a matter not just of boundaries but also of connections. What ontological categories are there, and which can communicate with which? How do these categories change over time? "Angel" describes classification in terms of ontological circles: what are the boundaries and possible interactions between human beings, angels, and demons? "Animal" addresses similar issues. In late antiquity, at least, minds are connected to what they know. We can come to know the cosmos because the cosmos itself is a rational organism ("Language," "Cosmos"). Rabbinic purification lore extends human subjectivity not upwards but laterally, into the artifacts of daily use. Human beings are connected to things, and this connection is a way of knowing.

The chapter titles of this collection are themselves acts of classification: all forms of *ordo* presuppose component parts. "Cleric" presupposes nonclerics, defective clerics, future clerics. "Countryside" contrasts with urban space and sylvan otherness. The list could be expanded; it is to be hoped that these essays will inspire a series of further studies. I can imagine essays on flesh and *pharmaka* showing how bodies and plants alike were conceived of as force fields of powers and antipathies. "Cosmos" touches on magic and music, but each could easily be the subject of a separate study. An essay on stars could expand on ways of knowing human destiny and the heavenly bodies, already alluded to in several of the essays in this volume. One on compendia could tackle systemization and encyclopedic ways of knowing, from Oribasius's medical collection to Hermes Trismegistus. Another on *caput* might start with Diocletian's reforms to open up a discussion of the Roman economy and the ways of knowing fostered by a tax system founded on the systematic fungibility of persons and things. Similarly, one on *militia* could explore how late Roman civilian and military administration shared practices and metaphors. Along the lines of Ambrose's octagonal baptistery, mentioned in "Cosmos," an entire essay on building might explore the ways of knowing fostered by late Roman architecture. In fact, many times while reading this collection I have found myself going back to H. P. L'Orange and his architectural illustrations. His *Art Forms and Civic Life in the Late Roman Empire* persuasively articulated a shift, starting with Diocletian, toward more static, simplified, symmetrical structures in architecture, art, and government, a change in which the controlling principle of a universal order dominates increasingly standardized individual components.[6] To appreciate this contrast, scholars juxtapose the naturalistic Hadrianic tondos with the stylized crowd scenes on the Arch of Constantine.[7] Sabine MacCormack took L'Orange a step further, incorporating ritual behavior and ceremonial rhetoric into her study of how these forms of late imperial representation also became increasingly stylized and static over time.[8]

Juxtaposing polarities may help us locate historical changes, but polarities have a hard time staying neutral. Within each pair invoked by L'Orange—free versus subordinated, natural versus stylized, autarchic versus autocratic, organic growth from below versus artificial order imposed from above—the second term always seems to signal decadence. (Today it is less acceptable to scant the aesthetics of late antique art, though it is still acceptable to critique late Roman government from the perspective of what currently passes for democracy.) A further problem with using polarities as markers of change is that the polarities themselves take on a static and reified aspect, as if they sprang into being without human agency. Indeed, finding nonreductive ways to account for connections between human consciousness and social structures is still a huge challenge for the social sciences. Does consciousness reflect social structures, or does it determine them? And how can we determine in which direction the lines of influence run?

The notion of ways of knowing offers a more process-oriented approach to this problem. It leaves plenty of room for human agency in establishing the limits of what can be known, thought, or felt in a particular historical context. But in defining that context, we cannot dispense with the material and political indicators that L'Orange and MacCormack employed as signs of cultural change. These have the virtue of being tangible. If ways of knowing are to be more than the mentalities so beloved at one time by French ethnographers and so zestfully indicted by Geoffrey Lloyd as mere means for redescription—in order for ways of knowing to be specific characteristics of a historical period, they must be pegged to other things that visibly change over time.[9]

One of the changes characteristic of late antiquity, as "Cosmos" points out, is the increasing visibility of the invisible. "Demon" makes this spectacularly clear. It's not that there were more demons, or that people ceased to deal with them by traditional, private, means, but that Christian shrines gave them a public venue unavailable before. Thus it became possible to know them, and their saintly antagonists, in new ways. Because in a Christian empire salvation becomes, in effect, mandatory, belief becomes more visible as it enters the purview of institutional coercion, which had not hitherto extended itself beyond taxes and public order to the soul. "Christianization" makes the interesting case that this change came late, through a failure of imagination. Initial attempts by Christian emperors to repress pagan worship, like the militant pagan piety of Decius, demanded visible, universal conformity of praxis. It was only gradually, inspired by intra-Christian efforts to control heresy, that imperial efforts to control paganism began to focus on belief, rendering it more visible too.

As the editors' introduction suggests, monotheistic rhetoric (not to mention the rhetoric of absolutist monarchy) may have sharpened preexisting tendencies to assert the unity of the cosmos and the knowledge structures necessary for knowing it. So, to reformulate L'Orange's question, along with the political centralization of the Dominate and the religious centralization of catholic Christianity, what changed in people's ways of knowing? We may consider this under three headings: symmetry, hierarchy, and sympathy.

Symmetry is a striking feature of late Roman art. Imagine the four porphyry Tetrarchs, each of whom grasps his colleague with one hand and the globe with the other, their double-outlined eyes mirroring the medallions on their belts. Similarly, a Tetrarchic panegyrist emphasizes the fourfold cosmic symmetry of the four emperors, the four seasons, the four quarters of the globe and the four-horse chariot of the Sun.[10] Art honoring a single emperor, not surprisingly, focuses symmetry around a central point, as in the crowd reliefs reused on the Arch of Constantine. In administrative life, the encyclical letters of Christian bishops form themselves in mimesis of imperial rescripts. As the ancient world becomes late ancient, the microcosm anchors itself more firmly in the macrocosm. "All teems with symbol. . . . All things must be enchained, and the sympathy and correspondence in any one closely knit organism must exist, first and most intensely, in the All." And Plotinus continues, "the parts are not merely members, *but themselves alls.*"[11] Thus microcosm and macrocosm are enchained in the symmetry of fractals.

Fractal symmetry informs the idea that God's relationship to the cosmos resembles the sun's relationship to the planets and the soul's relationship to the body. This symmetry is not new; it pervades Cicero's *Dream of Scipio,* which itself harks back to Plato and to Pythagorean wisdom traditions. But in the late ancient world it matters more, or matters more widely, as political and religious systems become all-encompassing. The empire forms itself into a set of nesting power relationships in which the governing *ordo* of the cities, firmly seated within the governing *ordo* of ever smaller and more uniform provinces, imagines itself as a mimesis of the senatorial *ordo* in the capital.

Just as unity entails order, so order entails hierarchy. "God is not a god of disorder," sniffs the *Apostolic Constitutions,* laying out its preferred vision of clerical hierarchy, "as if it were constitutive of the cosmic order" ("Cleric"). While Christians organized angels into hierarchies, Platonists were equally concerned to organize the realm of *daimones* into orderly ontological ranks that spanned the gulf between man and the divine Mind ("Medicine"). Pagan philosophers and Jewish rabbis debated the extent of animal volition, but none of them doubted the cosmic necessity that animals should be subject to man ("Animal"). Perhaps some of these debates about animal consciousness and culpability were proxies for submerged paradoxes generated by slavery, but no debates about that form of intraspecies hierarchy ever come to the surface. And no one in either the Roman or the Sassanian Empire questioned the need for autocracy. Order simply could not be imagined without it.

The principle of sympathy predates bureaucratic order and autocracy, as we can tell from the vast magico-medicinal world of herbal lore and agricultural know-how that predated philosophical medicine and finally tripped up poor Priscillian. Of course things have powers; that's just the way the world works. And who could doubt that powers act in opposition to each other? How else to explain change? Thinking in terms of sympathies and antipathies allows human beings to know material substance as quasi-intentional. It explains the operations of food, magic, music, and medicine on the human body and connects the serene pathways of the heavenly bodies with the uneven trajectories of human lives.

As we observe how symmetry, hierarchy, and sympathy thread through these essays, it becomes clear that these three principles constitute not merely an aggregate, bound by rough continuity in time and space, but a system, in which the constituent parts affect each other. For example, as God becomes more remote, and the ontological hierarchy more steeply pitched, the role of angels expands to fill the gap because of the power of sympathy that connects the angelic with the human mind ("Angel").

Among the controlling principles of this system, sympathy is the one that persists today, particularly among those who cannot access scientific modes of explanation or who find them unsatisfying. Sympathy persists because it responds to the deep-seated human need to inhabit an interconnected and responsive cosmos, a need felt more strongly in social contexts wherein hierarchies have been discredited and symmetries hang askew. In the United States, both New Age movements and evangelical Christianity are committed to cultivating sympathic connections with invisible beings and reframing individual experience in terms of cosmic significance. Tales of angelic intervention flutter round the Internet. Should we find this embarrassing? Well, how many of us supposedly educated folk understand Newtonian physics anyway, much less Einstein? This brings me back to magnets.

Plutarch and Ptolemy knew for certain that a magnet loses its power when rubbed with garlic, a fact they embed in discussions of sympathy and antipathy.[12] Late antique alchemists knew this too. A tenth-century miscellany adds the detail that goat's blood will restore the magnet's power. Lehoux finds the explanation for this in Pliny: only goat's blood can break adamant, and adamant, like garlic, can vitiate the power of a magnet. See?

Utterly delighted by this discovery, (which inspired Lehoux to write an entire book on Roman epistemology), I had to tell someone. So I telephoned my daughter, a geologist in Colorado. "Guess what the Romans thought: Garlic cancels magnets!" She was driving her pickup at eight thousand feet and warned me that she was about to turn a corner where the cell signal fails. "Stay tuned, then," I said. "You'll never guess what restores the magnet's power." "Goat's blood?" she ventured –and the line went dead.

I was dumbfounded. How was her response to be explained? Nineteenth-century telepathy? Jungian synchronicity? New Age mystification of the mother-daughter bond? We were both in the mountains, 1,022 miles apart. Did the rarefaction of the *aithēr* facilitate the meeting of our minds? I floated these hypotheses to some young computer scientists; they resolutely asserted that the utterance "Goat's blood?" was a random event in a universe wherein events that lack the appearance of coincidence are vastly more numerous and quickly forgotten. Plutarch would have been equally though differently unimpressed. To him her answer was obvious.

I find myself unable to digest or dismiss the alleged coincidence. My own ways of knowing are still too ancient, perhaps. But modernity may be catching up. In fact, as of autumn 2013, intuition, imagination, faith, and memory have been added to the official ways of knowing on the International Baccalaureate epistemology exam.[13] As Peter Brown has been known to say, late antiquity is always later than you think.

NOTES

1. Sara Ruddick, *Maternal Thinking: Toward a Politics of Peace* (Boston: Beacon, 1989). This book characterizes the ways of knowing informed by maternal work as applicable to the expanding symmetry of home, neighborhood, and nation, extending perhaps to the planet—but not, as a late antique person would see it, to the stars.

2. Mark Johnson and George Lakoff, *Metaphors We Live By* (Chicago: University of Chicago Press, 1980); idem, *Philosophy in the Flesh: The Embodied Mind and Its Challenge to Western Thought* (New York: Basic Books, 1999).

3. Daryn Lehoux, *What Did the Romans Know?* (Chicago: University of Chicago Press, 2012). Lehoux's work has been fundamental to my understanding of these issues.

4. Thomas Kuhn, *The Structure of Scientific Revolutions,* 2nd ed. (Chicago: University of Chicago Press, 1970), 11, cited in Lehoux, *What Did the Romans Know?* (above, n. 3), 226.

5. Ian Hacking, "Working in a New World: The Taxonomic Solution," in Paul Horwich, ed., *World Changes: Thomas Kuhn and the Nature of Science* (Cambridge, Mass.: MIT Press, 1993), 275–310.

6. Hans Peter L'Orange, *Art Forms and Civic Life in the Late Roman Empire,* trans. Dr. and Mrs. Knut Berg (Princeton: Princeton University Press, 1972).

7. Images in L'Orange, *Art Forms* (above, n. 6), 85–91; Ernst Kitzinger, *Byzantine Art in the Making: Main Lines of Stylistic Development in Mediterranean Art, 3rd–7th Century* (Cambridge, Mass.: Harvard University Press, 1977), 7–19.

8. Sabine MacCormack, *Art and Ceremony in Late Antiquity* (Berkeley and Los Angeles: University of California Press, 1981).

9. G. E. R. Lloyd, *Demystifying Mentalities* (Cambridge: Cambridge University Press, 1990).

10. *Panegyrici Latini* 8(4), discussed by L'Orange, *Art Forms* (above, n. 6), 47–52; and R. Rees, *Layers of Loyalty in Latin Panegyric, AD 289–307* (Oxford: Oxford University Press, 2002), 110–13. On panegyric as "a trained method of perception," see MacCormack, *Art and Ceremony* (above, n. 8), 26.

11. Plotinus *Enneads* 2.3.7, trans. MacKenna; cited above in "Cosmos," p. 99.

12. Plutarch, *Table Talk* 641C5; Ptolemy, *Tetrabiblos* 1.3.13. Discussed by Lehoux, *What Did the Romans Know?* (above, n. 3), 136–51.

13. The original four were sense perception, reason, emotion, and language: http://en.wikipedia.org/wiki/Theory_of_knowledge_%28IB_course%29.

ACKNOWLEDGMENTS

We would like to thank our contributors for their generosity, creativity, and patience in taking on the ideas that they describe in this volume and for agreeing to multiple iterations in the conversational and editing process that brought those ideas into their current form.

This book is not a conference volume, but when we were planning it, we decided that the best way to have a conversation among its contributors was to convene a workshop. The event took place at the University of California, Davis, in November 2011. We are grateful to the Loeb Classical Library Foundation and the Davis Humanities Institute for the financial support that made it possible, as well as to the UC Davis staff who made sure rooms were booked and food was served. Ra'anan Boustan, Charlotte Fonrobert, and Megan Williams presented papers in the workshop and contributed enormously to its success, and we note them here since their papers are not included in the book. Both the workshop and the book benefited greatly from the collegiality, encouragement, and intellectual generosity of members of the UC Davis faculty.

We thank Eric Schmidt of UC Press for accompanying the project from its beginning with great enthusiasm, as well as Maeve Cornell-Taylor and Cindy Fulton for shepherding the book through publication. Paul Psoinos has done a truly remarkable job as a copy editor, and PJ Heims prepared the index.

Catherine M. Chin
Moulie Vidas

CONTRIBUTORS

LEWIS AYRES is Professor of Catholic and Historical Theology in the Department of Theology and Religion at Durham University. He is the author of *Nicaea and Its Legacy: An Approach to Fourth Century Trinitarian Theology* (Oxford: Oxford University Press, 2004) and *Augustine and the Trinity* (Cambridge: Cambridge University Press, 2010).

MIRA BALBERG is Assistant Professor in the Department of Religious Studies at Northwestern University. She is the author of *Purity, Body, and Self in Early Rabbinic Literature* (Oakland: University of California Press, 2014) and *Gateway to Rabbinic Literature* (Raanana: The Open University of Israel, 2013 [in Hebrew]).

BETH BERKOWITZ is Ingeborg Rennert Associate Professor of Jewish Studies in the Department of Religion at Barnard College. She is the author of *Execution and Invention: Death Penalty Discourse in Early Rabbinic and Christian Cultures* (Oxford: Oxford University Press, 2006) and *Defining Jewish Difference: From Antiquity to the Present* (Cambridge: Cambridge University Press, 2012).

MATTHEW CANEPA is Associate Professor in the departments of Art History and Classical and Near Eastern Studies at the University of Minnesota. His publications include *The Two Eyes of the Earth: Art and Ritual of Kingship between Rome and Sasanian Iran* (Berkeley and Los Angeles: University of California Press, 2009) and *Theorizing Cross-Cultural Interaction* (Washington, D.C.: Smithsonian Institution Press, 2010).

CATHERINE M. CHIN is Associate Professor in the Department of Religious Studies at the University of California, Davis. She is the author of *Grammar and Christianity in the Late Roman World* (Philadelphia: University of Pennsylvania Press, 2008) and is currently writing a book on the textual transmission and cosmology of the work of Rufinus of Aquileia.

MAUD W. GLEASON teaches in the Department of Classics at Stanford University. She is the author of *Making Men: Sophists and Self-Presentation in Ancient Rome* (Princeton: Princeton University Press, 1995) and other studies of the culture of the Greek-speaking Roman Empire in the second and third centuries C.E.

CAM GREY is Associate Professor in the Department of Classical Studies at the University of Pennsylvania. He is the author of *Constructing Communities in the Late Roman Countryside* (Cambridge: Cambridge University Press, 2011) and papers on late ancient social history.

DAYNA S. KALLERES is Associate Professor in the Program for the Study of Religion at the University of California, San Diego. She is the author of *City of Demons: Violence, Ritual, and Christian Power in Late Antiquity* (Oakland: University of California Press, 2015) and coeditor, with Kimberly Stratton, of *Daughters of Hecate: Women and Magic in the Ancient World* (Oxford: Oxford University Press, 2014).

MICHAEL KULIKOWSKI is Professor in the departments of History and Classics at the Pennsylvania State University. He is the author of *Late Roman Spain and Its Cities* (Baltimore: The Johns Hopkins University Press, 2004), *Rome's Gothic Wars from the Third Century to Alaric* (Cambridge: Cambridge University Press, 2007), and, with Richard Burgess, *Mosaics of Time: The Latin Chronicle Traditions from the First Century BC to the Sixth Century AD*, volume 1, *A Historical Introduction to the Chronicle Genre from its Origins to the High Middle Ages* (Turnhout: Brepols, 2013).

HEIDI MARX-WOLF is Assistant Professor in the Department of Religion at the University of Manitoba. She is currently at work on her book *Late Platonists and High Priests: Spiritual Taxonomy and Religious Identity in the Third Century* C.E. and has published a number of articles on philosophy and religion in late antiquity.

ELLEN MUEHLBERGER is Assistant Professor of Christianity in Late Antiquity in the departments of History and Near Eastern Studies at the University of Michigan. She is the author of *Angels in Late Ancient Christianity* (Oxford: Oxford University Press, 2013), and her current project studies death as it was imagined by late ancient Christians.

JEREMY SCHOTT is Associate Professor in the Department of Religious Studies at Indiana University. His publications include *Christianity, Empire, and the Making of Religion in Late Antiquity* (Philadelphia: University of Pennsylvania Press, 2008) and, as coeditor with Aaron Johnson, *Eusebius of Caesarea: Tradition and Innovations* (Cambridge, Mass., and Washington, D.C.: Harvard University Press and The Center for Hellenic Studies, 2013).

KRISTINA SESSA is Associate Professor in the Department of History at the Ohio State University. She is the author of *The Formation of Papal Authority in Late Antique Italy: Roman Bishops and the Domestic Sphere* (Cambridge: Cambridge University Press, 2012) and the editor of a special issue of *The Journal of Early Christian Studies* (15.2 [2007]) titled *Holy Households: Space, Property, and Power.*

MOULIE VIDAS is Assistant Professor in the Department of Religion and the Program in Judaic Studies at Princeton University. His first monograph is *Tradition and the Formation of the Talmud* (Princeton: Princeton University Press, 2014), and his publications include

Revelation, Literature and Community in Late Antiquity, co-edited with Philippa Townsend (Tübingen: Mohr Siebeck, 2011).

EDWARD WATTS is Alkiviadis Vassiliadis Chair and Professor of History at the University of California, San Diego. His books include *Riot in Alexandria: Historical Debate in Pagan and Christian Communities* (Berkeley and Los Angeles: University of California Press, 2010) and *The Final Pagan Generation* (Oakland: University of California Press, 2015).

INDEX

abstract concepts from concrete experience, 286

accensi, 192n12

Aelian, 39, 44, 60

Africa, 180, 181, 193n24, 208–9, 216n72, 225, 229–30

agōgē ritual, 271, 284n47

agricultural magic, 11, 101–4

aisthēsis (perception), 38

alchemists, late ancient, 290

Alexander the Great, 199, 266

Alexandria, 199, 204, 209–10, 213n9, 215n51, 217n79

Alexandrian Serapeum, 202–3, 209, 210, 217n77

aloga (creatures without reason), 38

Altar of Victory, 207

Ambrose of Milan, 111, 115n54, 116n60; and Augustine, 138, 150–51n36; basilica crisis, Milanese, 108–10; *De Isaac vel Anima,* 150–51n36; and episcopate, 190, 223; octagonal baptistery, 110, 287; and Priscillian, 108; *Sermo contra Auxentium,* 109

Amidah, the (Eighteen Benedictions), 73

Ammianus Marcellinus, 66, 105–7, 178, 184, 187–90, 283n37; *Res Gestae* (Ammianus), 105–7, 187–90

Ammonius Saccas, 91

Amoun of Nitria, 117

Anatolius, 101–2, 104

ancient Israelite model, 68

Ando, Clifford, 2

angels, 117–33; dual nature of, 10; Gabriel, 121–22, 128, 131; information from, 131n2; in late ancient texts, 117–19; ontological circle, 120–25; textual sources on knowing, 117–19; transformative nature of interactions, 125–31

animal consciousness/culpability, 289

animal reason: Aristotle's theory of locomotion and animal soul, 85; classical debates about, 38–40; *Digest,* 52n20; knowledge boundaries, 36–38; late ancient debate on, 10; lessons from learning about, 49–50; in the Mishnah, 40–43; in the Talmud, 44–46

anthropological concept of culture, 82

anthropomorphic extrapolation, 50

Antioch, 157, 163; Christians' expulsion, request for, 79n45; oracle at, 65–71, 75. *See also* Babylas (greengrocer)

antipathies, 290

Antoninus, 230

Aphrahat, 273

Apollo, 9–10, 65–71, 78n40

Apostolic Canons, 220, 224, 234n8

Apostolic Constitutions, 220, 221–22, 224, 234n8, 289

apparitores, 192n12

Arcadius, 198, 208

Arch of Constantine, 289

Ardaxshir I, 156

narrative genre, late ancient, 117–19
natural history genre, 39–40, 44, 56n60
Neoplatonism, 4, 39, 86, 112n7
Neusner, Jacob, 35n36
New Age movements and evangelical Christianity, 290
Nicene theology, 11, 134–48
Nicomachus of Gerasa, 4
Noam, Vered, 34n24
Numbers, book of, 21, 33n6, 33n10
Numidia, 175
Nutton, Vivian, 82, 92

Odoacer, 231
oikoumenē, Christian, 210–12
ona'ah (verbal wrong), 72–73, 79n61
Oppian, 39
opus mundi, 104, 114n33
oracle at Daphne, 9–10, 65–71, 78n40
oracle at Delphi, 64–65, 66
oracle collection genre, 65
oracle of Zeus Philios, 65, 68–69, 79n45
ordo equester, 179–80, 192n19
ordo salutationis, 175
ordo senatorius, 179–80, 181, 186, 192n19, 194n42
Oribasius, 83, 91–92, 98n56, 287
Origen, 52n23, 100, 220; *Against Celsus*, 39; *On First Principles*, 90
Orosius, 103
Orsi, Robert, 113n14

Pachomius, 129, 130, 132n25
Palestine, 29, 34n26, 34n34, 36
Palestinian Talmud. *See* Talmud, Palestinian
Palladius, 101–2, 104
Pasztory, Esther, 99
Paulinus of Nola, 182
Paulus, 183
Peisistratus, 10
Perpetua, 184, 191
Philo, 38, 39
Philostorgius, 70–71
Photius, 101
Physiologus, 40
Pisistratus, 67, 68, 70, 78n40
Plato, 42, 289; animal reason, 39; *Cratylus*, 263; on *daimones*, 263; on music, 108; Myth of Er, 90; *Phaedrus*, 95n5; *Symposium*, 95n5, 263–64; *Timaeus*, 85, 92, 96n18, 108; tripartite structure of the soul, 85–86

Platonists: debates concerning linguistics, 58–59; on language, 71–72; realm of *daimones*, 289
Plautus, 177
Pliny, 39, 44, 113n21, 290
Pliny the Elder's Natural History (Murphy), 2
Plotinus, 59; Augustine, 150nn20,36; enchainment of ideas of the cosmos, 99, 100, 289; *Enneads*, 150n20, 151n36; *Against the Gnostics*, 131n4; image for order of being, 59; on music, 108; mystical dimension, 91; Porphyry, 80; sympathy doctrine, 99; as vegetarian, 76n11
Plutarch, 38–39, 44, 64–65, 264, 280nn11,13, 286, 290–91; *Beasts Are Rational*, 39; *De Defectu Oraculorum*, 264, 280nn11,13; *lithos Magnētis*, 290; *Whether Land or Sea Animals Are Cleverer*, 38–39, 53n34; *On Why the Oracles Are No Longer Given in Verse*, 64–65
Polemius Silvius, 23
pontifices, 176, 180
Porphyry, 6, 39, 44, 59, 60–64, 65, 76n11, 77nn18,20, 80–82; *On Abstinence from Killing Animals*, 39, 60–61; on afterlife, 90; on astrology, 89–90; and Augustine, 150–51n36; *On the Cave of the Nymphs*, 90; commentaries on Aristotle, 61; embryo as plant, 87–88; embryological theory, 85–95, 95n5, 96n16, 97n41; on ensoulment, 95n5; and Galen, 98n56; on language, 61–62; *Launching Points to the Intelligible*, 60; *Philosophy from Oracles*, 65; on reincarnation, 90; *On the River Styx*, 90; on the soul, 89; on Stoics, 88–89; use of ancient Chaldean sources, 90; *On What Is in Our Power*, 90
praefectus urbi, 188–90
Praetextatus, 206
Priscillian, 7, 9, 101–4, 108, 114n33, 183–84, 189, 191, 289
Proclus, 71–72, 120–21, 131n5
Prudentius, 208
Pseudo-Dionysius, 129, 131nn5–6
Pseudo-Macarius, 127
publicani, 192n12
punishment, 183–85, 194n32
Pythagoras and Pythagoreans, 4, 38, 39, 91, 108, 150–51n36, 176n12, 176n12, 289

quadrivium, 4
Qur'an, 75n3, 130; Surah, 6, 130; *umm al-kitab* (Mother of the Book), 58, 75n3

Rabbenu Hananel, 56n57
Rabbi Abahu, 46